Rugby League in Twentieth Century Britain

Called 'the greatest game of all' by its supporters but often overlooked by the cultural mainstream, no sport is more identified with England's northern working class than rugby league. This book traces the story of the sport from the Northern Union of the 1900s to the formation of the Super League in the 1990s, through war, depression, boom and deindustrialisation, into a new economic and social age.

Rugby League in Twentieth Century Britain uses a range of previously unexplored archival sources to investigate the lives of those who played, watched and ran the sport. It considers the impact of two world wars, the significance of the game's expansion to Australasia and the momentous decision to take rugby league to Wembley. It investigates for the first time the history of rugby union's long-running war against league, and the sport's troubled relationship with the national media.

Most importantly, the book sheds new light on broader issues of social class, gender and working-class masculinity, regional identity and the profound impact of the decline of Britain's traditional industries. For those interested in the history of sport and working-class culture, this is essential reading.

Tony Collins is Senior Research Fellow at the International Centre for Sports History and Culture at De Montfort University, Leicester, UK and editor of the journal *Sport in History*. His publications include the award-winning *Rugby's Great Split*.

The principal rugby league towns in Britain.

Rugby League in Twentieth Century Britain

A social and cultural history

Tony Collins

Routledge
Taylor & Francis Group

LONDON AND NEW YORK

First published 2006
by Routledge
2 Park Square, Milton Park,
Abingdon, Oxon, OX14 4RN

Simultaneously published in the USA and Canada
by Routledge
270 Madison Ave, New York, NY 10016

Reprinted 2007

Routledge is an imprint of the Taylor & Francis Group, an informa business

Typeset in Bembo by
Keyword Group Ltd

British Library Cataloguing in Publication Data
A catalogue record for this book is available from the British Library

Library of Congress Cataloging-in-Publication Data

Collins, Tony, 1961
  Rugby League in twentieth century Britain : a social and cultural
history / Tony Collins.
     p. cm.
  Includes bibliographical references and index.
  ISBN 0-415-39614-X (hardback) — ISBN 0-415-39615-8 (pbk.)
  1. Rugby League football—Social aspects—Great Britain—History.
  I. Title.
  GV946.C65 2006
  796.3330941—dc22   2005029759

ISBN10: 0-415-39614-X (hbk)
ISBN10: 0-415-39615-8 (pbk)
ISBN10: 0-203-08835-2 (ebk)

ISBN13: 978-0-415-39614-1 (hbk)
ISBN13: 978-0-415-39615-8 (pbk)
ISBN13: 0-978-0-203-08835-7 (ebk)

Contents

Plates

The following plates appear between pp. 114 and 115.

1   The 1916 Grove Park Army Service Corps rugby union team, featuring Harold Wagstaff (front row, second from right), Ben Gronow (middle row, third from right) and Douglas Clark (back row, far right).
2   A 1924 RFU poster for display in rugby union club houses warning players of the dangers of 'professionalism' and contamination by the Northern Union.
3   Wigan's triumphant team parade the Challenge Cup through the streets of the town in 1929 after their victory in the first Wembley cup final.
4   The 1929–30 Australian tourists in the garden of 10 Downing Street as tour manager Harry Sunderland shakes hands with Prime Minister Ramsey MacDonald.
5   Gracie Fields in the kit of her home-town team Rochdale Hornets shakes hands with Hornets' Victor Armbruster and St Helens Recreation's Billy Greenall in the early 1930s.
6   Handbill produced for the first-ever rugby league versus rugby union match at Headingley in January 1943. Playing under union rules, the league side won 18–11.
7   Mrs Minnie Cotton is escorted from the pitch at the 1966 Challenge Cup semi-final after rushing on to defend her lodger, St Helens' forward John Warlow.
8   League meets the swinging sixties. Star of the *Avengers* TV series and 1960s icon Diana Rigg is interviewed at Headingley in 1965 while Leeds play Oldham.

Preface

In February 1936 George Orwell visited Wigan as part of his research for *The Road to Wigan Pier*. Shocked by the poverty and unemployment in the town, he nonetheless found that his journey confirmed most of his prejudices: the lower classes smelled, 'no genuine working man' was ever truly a socialist, and the English working class did not 'show much capacity for leadership'. On the basis of his two months' trip around Lancashire and Yorkshire he declared that the working man 'does not act, he is acted upon'. Indeed, Orwell made little attempt to engage with the working-class people and families he met or to understand the culture of their daily lives.[1]

This book is about one aspect of working-class life in Wigan and the north of England that Orwell chose to ignore completely. Less than half a mile from his lodgings in Wigan stood Central Park rugby league ground. On Orwell's first Saturday in the town over 15,000 working-class Wiganers assembled to watch their team take on Liverpool Stanley. If he had joined them, he would have discovered a vibrant, thrilling spectacle played and watched almost exclusively by working-class men and women.[2]

Wigan's team featured athletes from around the world at the peak of their powers. Among them were full-back Jim Sullivan, one of rugby league's greatest-ever players; George Bennett, the first black player ever to appear in a league international; Hector Gee, an Australian who had travelled halfway around the world to play for Wigan; and Charlie Seeling, a New Zealander whose father had played for the 1905 All Black tourists but who had made his home in the town. Not only did these players share the working-class origins of those who watched them, but they also shared the same nagging sense of collective injustice. Rugby union's strict amateurism had forced Sullivan to leave Wales as a teenager. Bennett had switched to league to reach sporting heights previously unavailable to him because of the colour of his skin. Players and spectators alike believed that their game was unfairly relegated to the status of a minor sport by the class snobbery and regional bias of a southern-based establishment. In this, it was a metaphor for the position of the industrial working classes in the north of England.

This book aims to tell the story of rugby league in twentieth century Britain, ending with the 'Super League' upheavals of 1995. Like its predecessor, *Rugby's*

Great Split, which took the story up to 1910, its goal is to explore and explain the links between the sport and the society into which it was born, and from which it drew its support and strength. To a large extent, the circumstances of rugby league's birth and life in the industrial north of England mean that this is also a study of the leisure activity of a section of the 'old industrial' working class, which was rooted in the mines, the docks and the mills of the industrial conurbations of Lancashire and Yorkshire. Although that powerhouse of industrial capitalism has been dismantled and destroyed, much of the culture of that class remains, some of which is embodied in rugby league.

It takes the story from the élan of the years before the First World War, through the Depression and the Second World War, to the self-confidence of the immediate post-war period. Then the story changes, as the profound economic and social shifts of the latter half of the twentieth century cause a deep sense of self-doubt and pessimism in the game, which was only relieved in the 1980s. It ends with the acceptance of £87 million from Rupert Murdoch's British Sky Broadcasting, one hundred years after the split from rugby union and the founding of the sport.

Writing about his own family, Richard Hoggart noted that 'working-class people have virtually no sense of their own history, except the oral and that is usually scrappy, confused and soon lost as they reach back to those unrecorded years'.[3] To some extent this also applies to rugby league. In the sixty-three years of its history before 1958, only one book on the sport, Gus Risman's short *How to Play Rugby League Football* (1938), was published. Even today, the majority of books produced about the game are self-published by their authors. This book aims to tilt the balance back slightly. As well as the normal sources and archives used by the historian, I have also sought to use neglected sources, such as match-day programmes, brochures written to raise money for players' benefits, supporters' club handbooks and other similar ephemera, to understand the culture of the sport. These were more often than not produced by supporters for supporters, and speak the language and address the concerns of those for whom the sport played a significant role in their lives.

In its approach, the book carries with it an implied criticism of those who seek to understand the working classes by using the predominantly literary criteria of middle- and upper-class society, of which perhaps the most notable recent example is Jonathan Rose's 2001 *The Intellectual Life of the British Working Classes.* Although this can offer important insights into the culture of certain sections of the working classes, it ignores the fact that intellectual life in working-class communities was not based primarily on the written word. Discussions about life, society, politics and many other 'abstract' concepts often took place in the context of sport, leisure and even hobbies (as Ross McKibbin has noted). Understandings of class and masculinity, concepts of fairness and reward, and ideas about the workings of society were expressed in the everyday discourse about football, rugby, cricket and many other sports. Sport not only became 'a sort of lingua franca' between working-class men, in Eric Hobsbawm's words, but by the end of the nineteenth century it had also become a language that was used to understand society. In some cases, as Brian

Jackson and Dennis Marsden discovered, 'sport was a critical point of conflict' for working-class boys entering grammar school in the north of England. This is not to claim a privileged position for sport in working-class life above other forms of cultural experience, merely to acknowledge that it was, and remains, an important part of its fabric.[4]

However, this is not only the story of working-class culture. Especially at the professional level, rugby league was also dependent to a large extent on the patronage of the local small businessman. These men occupied the leading committees of clubs and the Rugby Football League, and often devoted considerable amounts of money and time to the sport. Their motivations, perceptions and ideas are also a recurrent theme throughout this book; hopefully it will contribute to our understanding of those at the lower levels of the provincial middle-classes, some of whom had risen from the working-classes yet still retained cultural ties to their origins. Overall the book seeks to examine the ways in which all those involved in the sport have sought to influence and impose their will on the game in the social and economic conditions of industrial and post-industrial capitalism.

There is also an element of 'auto-ethnography', to use currently fashionable jargon. I was first taken to watch Hull Kingston Rovers in 1969 at the age of seven by my father, who had himself been taken by his father at a young age, who likewise was taken by his father. I too took my two daughters to watch rugby league. Much of what I learned about the adult world as a child was gleaned from the folklore and culture of rugby league; what it meant to be a man, the importance of intelligence, why to distrust authority, and many other attitudes that survive primarily as oral, rather than written, traditions. Like countless others, members of my family have thus played a role, albeit peripheral, in some of the events with which this book deals.

When rugby union broke with its century-old customs and traditions in 1995 and abandoned the amateur ethos for professionalism, it became fashionable to say that rugby league now had no reason to exist. The implication – which this book seeks to demonstrate is wholly erroneous – was that there was nothing to the sport but professionalism and the cash nexus. From some rugby union writers this was simply mischievous. Yet for others it represented a genuine failure to understand that there could be a sport with its own structures, culture and traditions that was outside of those 'national' sports, which were controlled by the socially powerful. In this, these commentators echoed something of Orwell, whose failure to comprehend the cultural aspects of working-class life was also typical of almost all middle-class observers of his era. And even if he had attended the match at Central Park in 1936, his mix of pity and condescension would have probably blinded him to its broader significance. He would, however, have witnessed a small piece of history being made. For the first and only time at Central Park, little Liverpool Stanley defeated the mighty Wigan.

Acknowledgements

The act of writing a book is a singular task, yet this one would not have been possible without the help, assistance and support of a legion of people. I would particularly like to thank Richard Holt for reading the manuscript and making many valuable suggestions, Robert Gate for also reading it and for responding to my many queries about the history of the game, my editor Samantha Grant for her exemplary professionalism and support for the book, Ron Bailey, Mary Bushby, Tony Capstick, Andy Carr, Trevor Delaney, Harry Edgar, Sean Fagan, Robert Fassolette, Dave Fox, Mike Gardner, Trevor Gibbons, David Hinchliffe, Phil Hodgson, Tony Hughes, John Jenkins, Martin Johnes, Terry Kelly, Rob Light, Charles Little, Peter Lush, Greg Mallory, Kate Manson, Phil Melling, Andrew Moore, Graham Morris, Lisa O'Keeffe, Richard Pitchfork, Huw Richards, Dave Russell, Greg Ryan, Alex Service, Adrian Smith, Cliff Spracklen, Karl Spracklen, Matt Taylor, Wray Vamplew, Brian Walker, Gareth Williams, Terry Williams, Neil Young, and Emma Rosewarne, Geoff Keith, John Huxley and Richard Lewis at the Rugby Football League, Jed Smith, Rex King, Ross Hamilton, Laura Stedman, Lindsay Simmons and Phil Mead at the Rugby Football Union, the anonymous staff at numerous libraries and archives around Britain, and my colleagues Neil Carter, Mike Cronin, Margaret Groenveld, Jeff Hill, Pierre Lanfranchi, Kevin Marston, Tony Mason, Dil Porter and Eliza Reidi at the International Centre for Sports History and Culture at De Montfort University. Finally my utmost gratitude goes to Cathy, Rachel and Jodie, without whose support and forbearance this project would not have been completed.

Introduction: the origins of rugby league

Almost alone among all other sports, the birth of rugby league has a precise date: Thursday, 29 August 1895. Rich in symbolism and potent in its apparent demonstration of northern distinctiveness and self-assertion, it was on this day that twenty-one of the leading rugby clubs in the north of England met at the George Hotel in Huddersfield to found the Northern Rugby Football Union, better known as the Northern Union (NU).[1]

The NU's heartlands were regions that had been built on the industrial power-houses of the Victorian era: coal and textiles in Lancashire and West Yorkshire, ship-building in Barrow, docks in Hull, chemicals in Widnes and glass manufacture in St Helens and the Wakefield area. Its players, spectators and officials were drawn from these industries and the communities that had grown up around them. But, ironically, the NU was born just at the moment when many of those industries were beginning to be eclipsed by foreign competition or had reached the zenith of their success and were soon to begin their long structural decline. In fact, most of the accepted ideas about the north belonged to an age that was disappearing as the NU was being born. The dominant stereotypes of the north – pounds, shillings and pence businessmen like Elizabeth Gaskell's John Thornton in *North and South*, or the dark satanic mills portrayed by Blake – belong to the early and middle decades of the century. Writing just a year after the formation of the NU, Talbot Baines noted that the differences between 'the upper ranks of society in North and South have not survived in any appreciable form the fusing of public school and university education'.[2] Although members of the northern industrial bourgeoisie and merchant classes had played a central role in founding the first rugby clubs in the region in the 1860s, the number of factory-owners who went on to support the NU could be numbered in single figures. The northernness of rugby league was inextricably bound up with the industrial working class.

From the late 1870s, when rugby had become a mass spectator sport in the industrial towns and villages of Yorkshire, Lancashire and Cumberland, it had begun to fracture along class lines. The influx of working-class players and spectators had been viewed ambiguously by the middle classes who had founded the Rugby Football Union (RFU) in 1871. They had no objections to working men playing what they viewed as their game, provided it was on their terms. But the working classes who flocked to the game brought with them markedly different cultural traditions to those who had been educated in the public and grammar schools. Traditional working-class sports of the time, such as knur and spell, foot-racing, hare-coursing and pigeon-shooting, were all played for cash or other valuable prizes. To the industrial working classes, it was unthinkable that excellence in sport should go unrewarded.

As early as 1879, in response to rumours of men being paid to play rugby, the Yorkshire Rugby Union had attempted to outlaw payments to players. This soon proved to be ineffectual. As great crowds flocked to matches, especially in the Yorkshire Cup competition that had begun in 1877, it became an open secret that leading players received, at the very least, payments in kind for playing: legs of mutton, suits, watches, bottles of port and offers of employment were regular forms of remuneration. 'Poaching', or offering players inducements to change clubs, became commonplace. In order to build a winning team, the leaders of many northern clubs simply accepted these practices in order to attract the best players.

But others were not so phlegmatic. Some clubs withdrew from the Yorkshire Cup because they felt it to be detrimental to the interests of sport, but the competition's huge popularity meant that a club could not retain credibility as a serious force without taking part. Clubs that did attempt to maintain their middle-class exclusivity, such as the Leeds-based Yorkshire Wanderers and the original Hull, York and St Helens clubs, often found themselves forced into collapse or merger with less socially prestigious clubs. By the mid-1880s, there was a widespread fear that working-class participation was driving out the middle classes, causing the *Yorkshire Post* to ask:

> why are so few public schoolmen and clergymen found in our leading fifteens? It is because the associations of the game are now becoming so distasteful to any gentleman of sportsmanlike feeling. They do not care to be hooted and yelled at as part and parcel of a sixpenny show or to meet and associate with men who care nothing for the game other than as a means to an end.[3]

Such opinions were widespread among those who had learnt the game as part of their public school education. At its October 1886 general meeting, the RFU officially banned all forms of payment and inducement, monetary or otherwise. The aim was explicitly to curtail the influence of the working-class player. Arthur Budd, a future president of the RFU, argued that professionalism would inevitably mean that the middle-class amateur would become subordinated to the working-class professional, as had happened in soccer, and called for 'no mercy but iron rigour' in order to 'throttle the hydra'. Harry Garnett, a leader of the Bradford club, declared that: 'if working men desired to play football, they should pay for it themselves'. Only four clubs voted against the new policy, the Dewsbury representative arguing that many clubs 'were composed of working men and they could not afford to lose time when engaged away from home'.[4] The reported reaction of one

Yorkshire rugby player to the new laws probably summed up the attitude of many of his fellow players: 'Noa mutton, noa laaking' (no mutton, no playing).[5]

Within months it became clear that the new rules were not going to stem the tide of professionalism. In Lancashire identical problems had emerged. As the decade drew to a close, virtual civil war had broken out in northern rugby. Between October 1888 and January 1890 six of the leading clubs were suspended for periods of up to fourteen weeks for offering money or jobs to players. In the same period, ten players were put on trial by the Yorkshire committee for violating the amateur code, six of whom were suspended from the game for receiving cash, testimonial gifts and, in one case, an unauthorised wedding present from his club. The RFU's fear of working-class domination of the game was heightened by the growing success of northern teams on the pitch. 'The majority of Yorkshire fifteens are composed of working men who have only adopted football in recent years, and have received no school education in the art,' wrote a London commentator in 1892. 'The majority of members of London clubs have played it all their lives, yet when the two meet there is only one in it – the Yorkshiremen'.[6] In the first seven years of rugby's county championship, it was won six times by Yorkshire and once by Lancashire. As Arthur Budd and others feared, if the supporters of the RFU could not hold their own against working-class players on the field of play, their control of the game would inevitably come into question – and the greater the success of working-class players, the less likelihood there was of the middle classes continuing to play the game.

Unlike most rugby-playing areas in the south of England, where attendances at matches were low and players came from a narrow social strata, the game in the north had become one where working-class players and crowds dominated. It was now one of the most important forms of mass entertainment in the north, far outstripping soccer in Yorkshire and parts of Lancashire. To purge all forms of payment from the game, as desired by the RFU leadership, would mean alienating a large part of its working-class support in the face of the growing threat of professional soccer. For the game to lose its mass appeal in the north would mean a corresponding loss of standing in the community for the clubs and their officials. The constant witch-hunts of 'veiled professionals' by the RFU's supporters meant that clubs could find their best players, their most attractive opponents or even themselves suspended from the game for long periods. Clubs that relied on regular matches and high attendances for income could not survive on such an unstable basis. Yet increasingly, professionalised soccer had demonstrated that, far from being an unmitigated disaster as had been predicted, professional football could be successful.

It was at this point, forced into opposition to the RFU's drive for pristine amateurism, that the leaders of some of the major Yorkshire clubs began to argue for 'broken-time' payments, the reimbursement of wages lost because of time taken off work to play rugby. The demand for equality for all players, regardless of class, took centre stage in the debate on rugby's future.[7] *The Yorkshireman* magazine summed up the cause as a 'fight for the creation of a system which shall in the playing of Rugby football place the working men in the North on more equal terms with those in better circumstances in the South'.[8] In the volatile industrial climate of the early 1890s such demands could seem inflammatory. The first few years of the decade had seen the areas of Yorkshire, Lancashire and Cheshire record the highest incidence of strike activity throughout the UK.[9] In the Yorkshire region, Bradford millworkers, Leeds gasmen, Hull dockers and Wakefield miners all engaged in mass strike action in the 1890–93 period, troops being called out in the latter three disputes, leaving two dead and twelve wounded in Featherstone. To many of the middle classes, here was a glimpse into the abyss – and to talk of working-class rights in a sport that the middle classes cherished as their own was beyond the pale.

The response of the RFU to the broken-time proposal was unambiguous. Arthur Budd stated that if 'blind enthusiasts of working men's clubs insist on introducing professionalism, there can be but one result – disunion ... it will be the duty of the Rugby Union to see that the division of classes dates from the dawn of professionalism'.[10] The 1893 annual general meeting of the RFU – which took place on the same day that the government announced the setting up of a Royal Commission to investigate the shooting of the Featherstone miners – proved to be the decisive battleground in the war over broken time. James Miller of the Leeds club and president of the Yorkshire Rugby Union moved the motion, 'That players be allowed compensation for bona-fide loss of time.'[11] He argued that the pre-eminence of working-class players was due to the RFU's success in popularising the sport. But:

> having introduced the new type of player, the RFU at once did him an injustice. These men were constantly called upon to lose their wages in order to play for their county or their club and at the same time they were debarred from recompense for the loss of time involved. Why should not the working man be able to play the game on level terms with the gentleman?[12]

The debate, however, had no bearing on the outcome of the largely pre-arranged vote, which went against broken-time payments by an unexpectedly large 282 to 136. Now that it held the initiative, the RFU was determined to press home its advantage and the endgame began. In September 1894 the Lancashire Rugby Union charged Leigh with making illegal payments to players. The club was suspended for ten weeks. Three weeks later, Salford were also charged with professionalism and promptly escalated the dispute by counter-charging six other clubs with the same offence. There were now only three Lancashire First Division clubs not involved in the dispute. The contradiction between the RFU anti-professional laws and the day-to-day commercial interests of the clubs was now at breaking point.

Determined to drive out its opponents, the RFU issued a draft 'manifesto' on amateurism, which announced that any club or player charged with professionalism should be assumed to be guilty unless they could prove their innocence. In a special general meeting in December 1894, former RFU president William Cail announced that the amateur regulations would be redrafted on the lines of the manifesto for introduction in September 1895. The future was clear to all, as the *Yorkshire Post* pointed out: 'if the obnoxious "class" feeling introduced at last Friday's meeting by men who should know better is allowed to have its full sway, the inevitable result is a split in the Union'.[13]

On 29 January 1895 the Lancashire committee announced that Leigh and Wigan, who had both been placed at the bottom of Lancashire's Division One after being found guilty of professionalism, would be automatically relegated to the Second Division. This had an immediate impact in Yorkshire, and the following day the twenty-two leading teams in Lancashire and Yorkshire formed an alliance. Needless to say, the RFU outlawed it. Finally, having extinguished all possibilities of a compromise with the RFU, representatives of Brighouse Rangers, Halifax, Leeds, Bradford, Hull, Huddersfield, Hunslet, Wakefield Trinity, Manningham, Liversedge, Dewsbury, Batley, Oldham, Broughton Rangers, Leigh, Warrington, Tyldesley, Wigan, St Helens and Widnes met on 29 August and unanimously adopted the resolution 'That the clubs here represented decide to form a Northern Rugby Football Union (NU), and pledge themselves to push forward, without delay, its establishment on the principle of payment for *bona-fide* broken-time only.'

Broken-time payments were set at six shillings per day. As a group, the clubs announced their intention to resign from the RFU, with the exception of Dewsbury, who had suddenly baulked and were shortly to make their peace with the RFU. Stockport were also invited to join, which they did immediately, and Runcorn were drafted in to replace Dewsbury. The following month the rebels were joined by the amateur clubs of the Hull and District Rugby Union. In September the RFU introduced its new anti-professionalism laws. Players and clubs were ordered to break all contact with the new body. Anyone who was in anyway connected with the NU was banned for life by the RFU, regardless of whether they were a professional player, a policy that was to be enforced with 'iron rigour' over the next one hundred years.

Initially, the NU was careful to insist on its fidelity to amateur principles. William Hirst of Huddersfield claimed that the NU was 'as strongly opposed as ever to professionalism' but that 'payment of working men players for loss of wages through playing a match was not professionalism'.[14] But the rule that players could receive only broken-time payments soon became more honoured in the breach than in the observance. In 1898 the NU legalised professionalism, albeit tightly restrained by the fact that all players had to be in 'bona-fide employment' and that any change in employment had to be approved. Based on the paternalism of the northern factory system, the 'work clauses' explicitly excluded 'billiard markers, waiters in licensed houses, or any employment in connection with a club' as acceptable occupations.[15] To control wages, players were not allowed to be paid outside of the season, unlike professional soccer players. Despite the NU's rhetoric about the rights of working-class players, the regulations governing employment were as strict as the amateur regulations of the RFU. But the complex organisational burden involved in administering the work clauses and the leading clubs' increasing opposition to them, eventually led to their abolition in 1905. Fears that unrestricted professionalism would lead to the bankruptcy of clubs proved unfounded.

Another reason for the abolition of the work clauses was the threat of soccer. In 1903 the Football League had established a beachhead in the rugby heartland of West Yorkshire when Manningham, the inaugural NU champions, had switched to soccer and reinvented themselves as Bradford City. In 1904 the leadership of Holbeck NU side, which played at Elland Road, wound up the club and founded Leeds City, the forerunner of Leeds United. In many previous strongholds of rugby across the north, professional soccer clubs began to challenge the oval ball's dominance. Wherever it was played, soccer attracted huge crowds, which dwarfed those of rugby, and the simplicity of the game made it easier both to watch and play. More than that, it was a truly national sport, giving it an attraction beyond the regional appeal of the NU or the social exclusivity of rugby union.

The very real prospect of being buried under the landslide of soccer's popularity focused the minds of the NU leadership on the long-running debate over the rules of the game. Over the previous decade the game had gradually moved away from rugby union rules. In 1897 the value of all goals was reduced to two points and the line-out was abolished. Various other minor changes were made to move the game away from the rucking and mauling of rugby union and to place a greater emphasis on the scoring of tries. Even before the split, there had been a discussion within rugby union about reducing the number of players to thirteen, and this had been raised again in 1895 but rejected as too radical. But the desire to make rugby a more open and spectacular game was given extra impetus by the events of the 1900s. Eventually, in 1906 the number of players in a team was reduced to thirteen and an orderly play-the-ball, whereby a tackled player had to get to his feet and roll the ball behind him with his foot, was introduced. These two changes completed the break from the playing rules of rugby union and marked the birth of rugby league as a distinct sport with its own unique rules.

Less than a year after these fundamental rule changes, the NU made its most important breakthrough when the game was established in New Zealand and Australia. Led by A. H. Baskerville, a New Zealand touring team dubbed 'the professional All Blacks' came to Britain in September 1907, to be followed the next year by Australia. The success of these tours was crucial in giving the NU a sense of national, and imperial, importance and the subsequent importation of Antipodean star players gave the game a unique cosmopolitan cachet. In 1910 the first British touring team visited Australia and New Zealand, helping to consolidate the sport in those countries and establish a cycle of reciprocal tours that set a template for the sport for the rest of the century.

By 1910 the NU had not only evolved into a separate and distinct sport but it had also developed a culture based on the perceived virtues of the industrial north of England. Its values had originally been drawn from those of Gladstonian

Liberalism, with its supposed preference for the 'masses' against the 'classes', and had merged in the early 1900s with a non-political social democratic worldview, in much the same way as Labourism was derived from the earlier liberalism. The NU was overtly egalitarian, based on its birth in opposition to the exclusivity of the RFU. It was intensely parochial, a significant factor in its failed attempts at expansion in Wales, the South West, the Midlands and the North East. And it staked out its territory in the nation's life by laying claim to be a representative of the democratic 'true' England of the overlooked and ignored ordinary people. This was demonstrated in the common northern saying of the time, 't' best in t' Northern Union', a phrase that carried with it the implication that the best in the Northern Union was the best that existed anywhere, regardless of what those in the Southern establishment thought. Although the root cause of its split with rugby union had been class, the NU's restricted geography meant that it would always be seen as 'the northern game' and inevitably identified with the mines, mills and manufacturing industries of the region, by both the majority of its own supporters and the world at large.

As the First World War approached, the gulf between the two forms of rugby had never been wider. Played and watched overwhelmingly by members of different classes, rugby had become a microcosm of the social divisions between the classes in British society. Rugby union's purity as a middle-class amateur game was symbolised in 1909 by the opening of its new headquarters at Twickenham, situated in the leafy professional suburbs of southwest London where its very inaccessibility seemed to underline its exclusivity. In contrast, and no less emblematically, it seemed appropriate that the NU's greatest team of the age belonged to the town that had given birth to the game. Led by Harold Wagstaff, Huddersfield assembled a side that combined native northern talent, Welsh imports and Antipodean stars. Hailed as 'the Empire Team of All Talents', in the four years up to 1915 Huddersfield finished top of the Championship table every season, won the Challenge Cup twice and the Yorkshire Cup three times. They played the game in a fast, open style that made the fullest use of the opportunities provided by the NU's rules, developing new tactics – such as 'scientific obstruction', whereby the passer of the ball continued his run after releasing the ball in order to attract defenders, and a reliance on the power of the pass rather than the kick – which moved the game far beyond the static set-pieces of its origins. It was no accident that the metaphors and adjectives most commonly used to describe the team were those of science and industry, as exemplified by a 1924 description of the side:

> There was an absolute understanding between all parts of a perfectly working machine which resulted in the most audacious and unexpected movements being carried out with a precision that left the opposing defence aghast. Fast and clever three-quarters were served by halves whose brains were ever working at high pressure behind forwards who, as occasion demanded, could play the traditional scrummaging game or convert themselves into temporary three-quarters and handle the ball.[16]

For spectators whose day-to-day lives were based on synchronised, collective labour of the town's textile mills, the Huddersfield side was the embodiment of working-class industrial collectivity at play.

There was also something almost totemic about Wagstaff himself, in his achievements, his reputation, and the respect in which he was universally held. Even his name was quintessentially northern, seemingly designed to emphasise the flat vowel sounds of Yorkshire and Lancashire. And of course the aitch was rarely sounded – he was 'Arold, not Harold. 'I am a Northern Union man all the way through', he declared in the opening sentence of a series of autobiographical articles published in 1934, 'and I was suckled in the Northern Union game.' Born in 1891 in Holmfirth, he made his debut for the local amateur side, Underbank Rangers, aged fourteen and the following season scored their first try under the new thirteen-a-side rules in September 1906. Two months later he signed as a professional for Huddersfield, aged fifteen years and 175 days, then the youngest ever. Two years later he made his debut in representative football for Yorkshire. A few weeks after, he made his England debut against the 1908 Kangaroos. Eighteen months later, at the age of just nineteen, he was appointed captain of Huddersfield, a post he was to hold for the next fifteen years. Aged twenty-two, he was made captain of the national side.

These leadership qualities were nowhere more apparent than on the 1914 England tour to Australia and New Zealand. The tour repeated the huge promotional and financial success of the 1910 tour but it also acquired a mythic status in rugby league because of one game: the third and deciding test match at Sydney on 4 July 1914. It had originally been scheduled for Melbourne in August but the New South Wales Rugby League had unilaterally changed the date and venue to maximise its profits. The English management protested that it would be their third test match in seven days and that five first-team players were injured, but to no avail. From home, the NU's Emergency Committee simply instructed the tourists to play. 'More honour if you win', read the telegram.[17] As the kick-off approached, tour manager John Clifford addressed the players:

> You are playing in a game of football this afternoon, but more than that, you are playing for Right versus Wrong. You will win because you have to win. Don't forget that message from home: England expects every one of you to do his duty.

Leading 9–3 at half-time, the English were reduced to just ten men within minutes of the re-start. Amazingly, in a second half that lasted fifty-four minutes owing to stoppages for injuries, they scored a further try and held on to win 14–6.[18]

Dutifully aware of imperial precedent, the Australian sporting press dubbed the match the 'Rorke's Drift Test', in favourable comparison to the rearguard action fought by a hundred British troops in South Africa against King Cetshwayo's Zulu armies in January 1879.[19] From Sydney, *The Referee's* football correspondent J. C. Davis wrote that 'Wagstaff, always a great player, that day became *the ubiquitous*, and the King of the game ... . Here, there and everywhere, all the time he was doing the work of half-a-dozen men. Wagstaff the Great.' Wagstaff's Huddersfield and England team-mate Douglas Clark, who was forced to leave the field through injury, noted simply that 'Harold was the man'.[20]

But by the time the team arrived back in England on 26 September its feats had all but been forgotten. On 4 August Britain had declared war on Germany. Warfare was no longer a metaphor for sporting endeavour but a bloody reality. As the tourists disembarked from their ship at Plymouth, three players who were Army reservists rushed off to join their regiments. As they left, Leeds full-back Billy Jarman spoke for all three when he told the press, 'I am hoping to gain as good honours [on the battlefield] as we have done in Australia and my prayer is that I may come safely back to my wife and children and to take part again in a sport I dearly love.'[21]

Like those of millions of other young men whose lives were swept away in the ensuing slaughter, Billy Jarman's prayer was ignored.

Chapter 1

Rugby league and the First World War

Like the authorities of all sports, it took the NU General Committee some time to respond to the outbreak of war. When it met on 11 August it provisionally decided to continue with the season. This initial response to continue with the season was taken before militarist hysteria had fully gripped the country. But by September, professional football of whatever code was under severe pressure to suspend its activities while the nation was at war. The Football Association became a favourite target of the anti-football campaigners, despite the fact that the War Office had declared itself 'favourable to the continuation of football'.[1] In London, the *Evening News* stopped the publication of its football edition and newspapers were full of letters condemning those who continued to play. 'A Soldier's Mother' writing to the *Yorkshire Post* captured the spirit of those who called for an end to football: 'If a Zeppelin were to hover over football grounds in England and drop a few bombs amongst the idle loafers gathered there, then perhaps, and I feel not until then, would those shirkers wake up to a sense of their duty to their King and their country.'[2] Regardless of the propaganda of the national and local newspapers, there were many who thought the continuation of football would be good for morale: an editorial in *Athletic News* argued that sport

> will assist to keep the body fit and the mind calm until such time as right is vindicated. Courage, determination and patience are demanded of non-combatants, and sport tends to the development of these virtues. Let us not hastily give up that which has served a free people so well.[3]

Such arguments did not stop those who clamoured for an end to football from claiming the moral high ground, with RFU spokesmen occupying its most elevated reaches. RFU secretary Rowland Hill claimed that the FA Council 'had allowed one of the greatest sports in the world to be solely and entirely governed by commercial principles.'[4] Yorkshire Rugby Union official James Miller felt that 'playing fields were being desecrated at the present time' and that 'it was necessary to compel those who idled around the streets – those shirkers and bullet-funkers – to join the ranks.'[5] The references to shirkers indicated the underlying class prejudice at the heart of much of this criticism and Miller had little hesitation in pointing an accusing finger, regretting that members of other football bodies had not responded in a like manner. It seems to me that a hot blush of crimson must come into the faces of those footballers who remained at play when others went abroad to fight their battles for them.[6]

In fact, the NU was no less patriotic than the RFU. Joseph Platt, the NU secretary, had declared that it was 'the bounden duty of every player as well as every football enthusiast of suitable age and capacity to give his best service to the nation' but its decision-making machinery lagged behind events. It was not until 8 September that its governing General Committee met in Manchester to discuss the clamour for the football codes to suspend operations. Taking a lead from the FA, the meeting unanimously passed a resolution stating that

> matches be played as usual, as it is impossible for all men to take up active war service, and it is thought unwise to have no relaxation from the more serious objects of life. ...
> all clubs be asked to encourage their players to join the army for active service, unless their employment is such that by not doing so they equally serve the country's welfare.

The committee also recommended that clubs provide facilities for enlistment at matches and that they should not sign new players from outside of their immediate districts.[7] In fact, the decision to continue playing did nothing to deter its players from enlisting in droves.[8] The Manchester district league was decimated after only three weeks of the war owing to a huge loss of players. In early September the St Helens league suspended activity for the duration after losing virtually all of its players to the forces; over 70 per cent of eligible men had joined up following Lord Derby's personal recruitment drive in the town. In Bradford, the local league was reduced to just four sides and numerous other amateur NU sides simply stopped playing. At a professional level, every club lost men to the army. Runcorn shed almost all of its playing staff as twenty-three players volunteered. At Oldham, the club doctor re-enlisted as a colonel in the 10th Manchester Regiment and was allowed to address the players on their patriotic duty; nearly all enlisted, including the club secretary A. J. Swann. Swinton and Broughton Rangers both offered their grounds to the military and Wigan reserved one stand for free admission to men who had signed up. The NU appears to have escaped the criticism directed at soccer clubs that they were insufficiently supportive of attempts to recruit at matches, although there are few records of any recruitment actually taking place at NU grounds. By April 1915, Joe Platt could announce that 1,418 amateur and professional NU players had enlisted.[9]

Nevertheless, the pattern of volunteering did differ markedly between the NU and the RFU. In general, men in white-collar occupations and the professions enlisted earlier and more enthusiastically than the working classes. Recruitment of workers in textiles areas, which were severely affected by the sudden interruption to international trade, was particularly low, although miners, the NU's other major industrial constituency, had a higher percentage of volunteers than most working-class occupations. The low levels of family allowances paid to soldiers and the well-known delays in making the payments were also a disincentive to working men enlisting. As *Athletic News* pointed out, unlike the usually single and often financially independent young men of rugby union, many working-class footballers could 'not afford to throw their wives and families on the fickle charities of the public by enlisting.'[10]

But even if the NU had wanted to follow rugby union and abandon the season there were other factors to take into consideration. As Hunslet president Joe Lewthwaite explained, 'It must be borne in mind too that football is a business concern in many cases. What would be said if works were closed down? Football is run largely on commercial lines. If the grounds are closed, will the landlord forego rent, and the authorities their rates?'[11] Although the builder of Hunslet's new stand publicly offered to forego his £2,500 payment until the end of the war in response to Lewthwaite's rhetorical question, the reality was that the fortunes of the game at the professional level were almost entirely tied to its commercial success.

This became clear almost as soon as the season started. By the first week of October there was already concern that attendances at matches had fallen to half those of 1913. Similarly dramatic decreases at soccer matches had already led to the Football League proposing a cut in players' wages for the duration. On 8 October NU official John Houghton wrote to clubs noting that 'the past five weeks shows a marked falling off in gate receipts and members' subscriptions, the average income being reduced by as much as 50 per cent', and recommending that each club discuss with its players the need to reduce wages and costs. Houghton feared that the game's poorer sides could not survive the fall in gate receipts and that 'the loss of four or five clubs would so materially cripple the League that it is felt that the continued existence of the League would be in serious jeopardy.'[12]

Although there were some positive responses to what was a non-binding request – Keighley players agreed to a 50 per cent pay cut 'until better days arrive' – commercial reality dictated that the bigger clubs simply continued to pay their players at pre-war levels while the weaker clubs continued to struggle. Faced with an impending financial crisis and a desire to demonstrate that professional NU players were making sacrifices for the war effort, a special meeting of clubs was called for 20 October. The attendees heard that only one club, Halifax, had not seen a decline in gate receipts. Crowds at both Leeds and Hunslet had fallen by a half, Wigan season-ticket holders had fallen by two-thirds, Hull's turnover had fallen by almost £700 compared to the previous season and St Helens season-ticket sales had collapsed from £420 in 1913 to just £19. By sixteen votes to five, the meeting imposed a wage cut of 25 per cent, made similar cuts to referees' fees and ordered all clubs to report players' wages levels and the savings made from the cuts.[13]

The decision was met with uproar from players with the leading clubs. Within days Wigan, Halifax and Huddersfield players declared themselves 'keenly opposed' to the wage cut and in response the Wigan committee appealed for a delay in its introduction. But the General Committee was unbending: 'it is, though with the utmost regret, thought better that unwilling players should be sacrificed' rather than concessions be made. In response, players at Wigan, Halifax, Huddersfield, Rochdale and Oldham went on strike on Saturday 7 November, while those at Bradford and York turned out under protest. The following Friday players' representatives from thirteen clubs met in Manchester to discuss the situation. They decided to play that Saturday's matches under protest and elected a four-man deputation to meet with League officials the following week.[14]

The four men elected represented the very cream of the Northern Union. As well as Harold Wagstaff there was Gwyn Thomas, who chaired the players' meeting; Thomas was a twenty-one-year-old full-back from Treherbert who had joined Wigan after captaining London Welsh while barely out of his teens. Charlie Seeling was a veteran Wigan forward from New Zealand who had toured Britain with both the 1905 union and the 1907 league All Blacks, while Leeds' Australian centre-threequarter Dinny Campbell was to prove one of his club's greatest players. On 17 November they met officials to outline their case. In fact, the clubs' resolve was already crumbling by the time the meeting took place. Earlier that week referees from Lancashire and Yorkshire had met and resolved to strike if the cuts to their fees were implemented, while fourteen clubs had called for an end to the arbitrary imposition of wage cuts on the grounds that it represented interference in their own business affairs.[15] Some, such as York, were even supporting the players' demands. The following week yet another special general meeting of the clubs voted to rescind the wage cuts both for players and referees, deciding that 'any deduction in a player's wages shall be by mutual arrangement only between individual clubs and players'. It was also resolved to set up a relief fund for clubs in financial difficulty which would be funded by a levy on gate money and donations from clubs and players. Although the threat of a complete strike by players was now averted, the next fortnight saw strikes by Salford and Wakefield players against their clubs' attempts to cut wages.[16]

The season continued but enthusiasm drained away as war casualties mounted and it became clear that the conflict would not be over quickly. Increasing numbers of spectators and players joined up – Gwyn Thomas enlisted just before Christmas 1914 and, along with Wigan's Lance Todd, became one of a handful of NU players to receive a commission – while the longer working hours caused by the needs of war production in industrial areas meant that the opportunities to watch sport were drastically reduced. The season also became increasingly uncompetitive as Huddersfield simply destroyed the rest of the league, winning every competition open to them, scoring 103 points against 5 in the three finals they contested and losing only two games during the entire season. There was a palpable sense of relief when the season finally came to an end with Huddersfield's anticipated demolition of St Helens in the Challenge Cup final. The following month the NU voted to suspend operations for the duration, except for schoolboy and under-eighteen competitions. Widnes's John Smith proposed the suspension, asking if there was 'a single person who can honestly say that he got any satisfaction at all out of football last season?' while Wakefield's J. B. Cooke admitted that one of the reasons they had voted to continue in September was that 'there was hardly a man among them who thought that the war would continue very long'. He had now changed his mind however: 'After 10 months of hard fighting, with dreadful losses to the country and lives, they realised what the great game that was going on in France really meant.'[17]

★

However, within the 'great game' rugby union was undergoing a resurgence with matches being organised for new recruits almost as soon as the first volunteers arrived in training camps in September 1914. In contrast, matches played under NU rules by services teams were virtually non-existent. The only recorded example in the first months of the war was in January 1915 when a Miners' Battalion team of the King's Own Yorkshire Light Infantry played Featherstone Rovers at Otley's rugby union ground to raise money for the widow of a Corporal Dixon of Featherstone. Even army matches played on NU grounds at this time were rugby union games.[18] Nor does it appear that NU football was played much in army units on active service, although Rochdale winger and 1914 tourist Jack Robinson, who was badly wounded at Neuve Chappelle in March 1915, reported that they had played 'rugby' during the battle while bombs were dropping, saying that

> our boys out yonder will have their game of football under all sorts of conditions. It comes as a tonic and a relaxation from trench duty and I cannot understand anybody in England ever questioning the advisability of the game.[19]

But in fact, rugby of whatever code occupied a distant second place when compared to the popularity of soccer with troops in the field. Douglas Clark's war diary for 1917 describes a number of soccer matches of varying degrees of formality in which he played while in France but only one game of 'rugby'. Harold Wagstaff was reduced to playing soccer while stationed in Egypt owing to a complete absence of any form of rugby. The danger of injury and the difficulty of playing on an improvised pitch naturally gave soccer a natural advantage. A 1915 letter from an unidentified officer in a Lancashire regiment that played both rugby and soccer encapsulated the problem:

> The slush on our football 'pitch' is awful. Shall recommend that in the future all football matches be postponed until the mud is knee-deep. We were called the mudlarkers at home and truly we've sustained the reputation since coming to France. Our last football will be in use on Monday, and I dread to think of it bursting in this dreary hole. I suppose I shall have to improvise a ball or two from pigs' bladders – anything to keep the game and the boys going.[20]

The simplicity of soccer's rules and the ease with which a game could be organised gave it an additional advantage over the handling codes. But its popularity was also based on more than technical simplicity. As J. G. Fuller has noted, army soccer was a 'practical exercise in class collaboration', a sport which men of all ranks could play and which helped to cement *esprit de corps* among the troops.[21] Outside of regiments from NU areas or South Wales, rugby was generally viewed as a game almost exclusively for officers. Soccer was the sport of the masses and therefore the ranks.

Despite this, the beginning of 1916 marked a rise in rugby union's fortunes, ironically owing in large part to the back-door introduction of conscription in early 1916 by Lord Derby (who was also the official patron of the Northern Union). This brought in to the army many NU players who had not already volunteered and helped to expand greatly the pool of players available to military rugby union sides. The first major union match to be played in the north took place at Headingley in April 1916 between a 'North of England Military Team' and an Australasian representative side. When selected, all of the North's players had been officers and rugby union men, but when the final teams were announced two weeks before the match was due to take place, the North had been augmented by four non-commissioned men: Harold Wagstaff, Ben Gronow and Douglas Clark of Huddersfield plus Willie Davies, captain of Leeds, all of whom had recently been called up. For the Antipodean side, Oldham's Viv Farnsworth, Huddersfield's Tommy Gleeson and Hull's Syd Deane and Jimmy Devereux were selected. Although this was not the first time a NU player had played rugby union during the war – Gwyn Thomas had turned out for the Barbarians against South Africa in November 1915, his fellow Wigan player Percy Coldrick had played for Newport in January 1916 and three NU players, including Huddersfield forward Fred Longstaff, had appeared in a union match at Leicester that February – the prominence of the game and the players involved raised obvious questions about the validity of the RFU's long-standing ban on NU players. 'The teams will play under Rugby Union rules, but they will do so as soldiers of the King; questions of amateur or professional principles do not come into view at all,' explained the *Yorkshire Post*. Perhaps inevitably, the NU players dominated, scoring fourteen of the points in the match as the North won 13–11, with Wagstaff, who had only ever seen one rugby union match before that day, much less played in one, beating several opponents and running half the field to score a memorable try.[22] Three weeks later the team beat the Tees and Hartlepool Garrison in front of 7,000 spectators and on 20 May, now boasting seven NU players, they defeated a Welsh side chosen by the Welsh rugby union secretary Walter Rees before a crowd of over 15,000 at Liverpool's Anfield soccer ground.

The success of the side opened a debate over the RFU's ban on NU players. Ever since the 1895 split, the RFU had banned for life any rugby union player found guilty of playing NU football or playing with someone who had played NU football, regardless of whether any payments had changed hands. Now it seemed that the war could bring about a breach in that intransigence. Sir William Forster-Todd, the Lord Mayor of York, argued that 'the fact of the professional footballer and the university student rubbing shoulders and shedding their blood together in the trenches' would lead to the distinctions between the NU and the RFU disappearing after the war. C. C. Lempriere, who captained Hull before and after the 1895 split, believed that rugby

> under whatever rules … is far better preparation for the fighting and combative spirit of mankind if, as now, there is call for their display. Why then should a different standard, as between amateurs and professionals, be any more obtained in Rugby football to that obtaining in cricket and Association?

But these arguments carried little weight with the hardline supporters of amateurism in the RFU. 'War-time recognises no rules,' pointed out W. L. Sinclair sagely in the *Athletic News*.

> But in times of peace the cherished canons of Rugby football will once more be observed. Rugby Union men will be tolerant of the Northern Union player, but there can be no intermingling of the two organisations in common system of play.[23]

But the fact that many rugby union officials had voted with their feet and included NU men in their sides regardless of the rules meant that the RFU had to act to maintain control of the situation. On 4 October 1916 the RFU therefore issued a statement to clarify its position:

> Northern Union players can only play with Rugby Union players in bonafide naval and military teams. Rugby Union teams can play against naval and military teams in which there are Northern Union players. Munitions workers cannot be regarded as naval and military players. These rulings only obtain during the war.[24]

This was not so much a concession as a recognition of the new status quo. It allowed the RFU to embrace national unity while also signalling its intention to remain an exclusive organisation as soon as the war ended. Nevertheless, the temporary lifting of the ban was seized upon by the more active recruiters for military sides. In particular, Major R. V. Stanley, the Oxford University representative on the RFU Committee, had been working since at least December 1915 to recruit NU players to his Army Service Corps (Motor Transport) team at Grove Park in south London.[25] When the new season began the week after the RFU announcement, his diligent work was clear to all – the ASC team included Huddersfield's Wagstaff, Clark, Gronow and Rosenfeld, Rochdale's Joe Corsi and international Ernest Jones, together with Oldham's Frank Holbrooke. They then proceeded to tear apart almost every other team in the south of England, including Australian and New Zealand services sides, winning twenty-five out of twenty-six games and scoring 1110 points while conceding just 41. In the process they broke the senior club record for points in a season. Their only defeat was a 6–3 loss to a United Services side that included eight rugby union internationals, plus Wigan's Billy Seddon and Leeds' Willie Davies. Even in the heat of the match, the team was expected to observe the etiquette of social and military rank: Wagstaff called his winger, the Harlequins' player Lieutenant Nixon, 'Sir' and Nixon reciprocated by calling the centre 'Wagstaff'. The attention which Grove Park's success brought was not all complementary. Echoing the criticisms of football in 1914 the team was accused of being 'a dumping ground of professional slackers', a characterisation probably not unconnected with the fact that the ASC was unfairly seen as an easy option for soldiers and was known by its detractors as 'Ally Sloper's Cavalry', after the work-shy cartoon character of the era.[26]

A similar side was assembled at the Devonport Royal Navy depot and this eventually comprised nine NU players, captained by Willie Davies and featuring at various times his team-mate and future international Joe Brittain, future England captain Jonty Parkin and Harold Buck, who became rugby league's first £1,000 transfer in 1921. Unlike the ASC side which broke up when its members were posted to France in April 1917, the Devonport side played together for the rest of the war, making three tours of the north of England. By playing against NU club sides and under NU rules, the Devonport tours were contrary to both the letter and the spirit of the RFU's laws but the prevailing atmosphere of national unity meant that there was little that could be done to stop them. In May 1917 a Yorkshire NU representative side had even played against and defeated a New Zealand army team, including three All Blacks, under union rules at Headingley.

Despite this intermingling of players, it is noticeable that regardless of the public debate, no NU player or official called for unity of the two games – other than lifting the ban on players, the most radical proposal was former NU chairman J. B. Cooke's call for an annual charity match between them.[27] No NU player with a services rugby union side expressed a desire to carry on playing union after the war and even W. L. Sinclair admitted that most rugby union converts to NU preferred the thirteen-a-side game.[28] The same appears to be true of spectators in the north – with the exception of the 1916 match at Anfield, none of the rugby union games in the north in which NU players participated attracted larger crowds than the major NU games during the war. Few attracted more than 4,000 spectators and even the showpiece North versus Australasia match at Headingley in April 1916 attracted only somewhere between 10,000 and 12,000 spectators. Two weeks later 13,000 saw the Leeds versus Dewsbury NU match on the same ground.[29]

★

Crowds of such sizes underlined the continuing strength of the NU in its heartlands. Despite the formal suspension of competitions in June 1915, the professional game had continued on a regional basis, organised by the Lancashire and Yorkshire county committees. And despite difficulties due to the enlistment of players and spectators, the majority of clubs continued to play. Only four did not compete in the 1915–16 season, but to bolster the ranks Brighouse Rangers, Featherstone Rovers and St Helens Recreation were promoted from district leagues to join the senior clubs for the duration, although Featherstone only lasted one season. The announcement of conscription in 1916 also helped clubs to justify playing because they could no longer be accused of keeping men from volunteering. Wakefield, Warrington and Widnes, all of which had closed for the 1915–16 season, recommenced playing in 1916 following its introduction. Some experienced a surge in their fortunes owing to the munitions factories in their areas. Barrow, despite being forced to close by the town's military authorities at the start of the war, soon re-established themselves and, boosted by an influx of players and spectators into the local shipyards for war production, became one of the dominant teams of the war, winning the unofficial championship title in 1917–18. Dewsbury were even more successful, finishing champions in the 1915–16 and 1916–17 seasons, and attracting players and crowds owing to the town's prominence as a manufacturer of woollen cloth for uniforms.[30]

In recognition of the economic fragility of professional sport in wartime, the NU's 1915 annual general meeting banned payments to players and relaxed registration rules to allow players to play for clubs based near their work or military base.[31] Naturally the ban on payments was widely ignored and the freeing of players from their pre-war club registrations also created difficulties; none more so than in October 1917 when Billy Batten was selected to play by both Dewsbury and Hull in the same match. He plumped for Dewsbury and helped them to a 32–0 victory.[32] Despite the supposed wartime camaraderie, there is no evidence that the war led to a more chivalrous mode of play. As the *Yorkshire Post* pointed out after six players had been sent off in two Leeds matches in March 1917, games were 'fought in a much rougher and keener spirit than was the case in the normal competition days'.[33] Nor were crowds any better behaved. The Runcorn and Keighley grounds were shut after crowd trouble in March 1915. Six months later the Brighouse versus Rochdale match was abandoned by the referee because of crowd trouble and the November 1917 derby between Broughton Rangers and Salford ended ten minutes early after spectators joined in a fight between players.[34] The occurrence of these incidents was no greater than in pre-war times – in the four years up to 1910, eight instances of crowd disturbances were reported to the NU – but the fact that they continued in wartime suggests that the social pressure to behave differently during a national crisis was neither as strong nor as prevalent as supporters of the war would have hoped.[35]

The same reluctance to change pre-war behaviour was also true for the RFU leadership. Within a month of the war ending, RFU secretary C. J. B. Marriott had written to a Royal Artillery team based at Ripon in North Yorkshire forbidding them from playing planned matches against NU sides. On 14 January 1919, at its first committee meeting since war broke out, the RFU's first act was to pass a resolution stating that NU players could play rugby union in the services only if they did not play NU football or sign for an NU team while in the services.[36] It tightened its restrictions further in April when it announced that 'civilian clubs are not permitted to play against Service teams containing Northern Union players'.[37] Such shenanigans indicated that the core leadership of the RFU was determined to re-establish the status quo ante bellum, despite coming under pressure internally towards the end of the war to moderate its stance. Those leading the RFU saw the war as a complete vindication of their pre-1914 policies, not a cause for change. The authority that it had gained during the war and its close identification with the military allowed the RFU to brush aside easily the reformers in its ranks: 'moderation is impossible' was how one supporter summed up its position.[38]

Much of this authority came from the huge and tragic toll of death that had cut a swathe through the RFU's ranks during the war. Rugby union's supporters were proud of their mortal sacrifice and pointed to the hundreds of dead players, twenty-seven of them England internationals, as a justification for its assumed moral superiority over other sports. The NU too lost numerous players at all levels: Billy Jarman, Fred Longstaff and Walter Roman of the 1914 touring side were killed, St Helens' 1907 New Zealand tourist Jum Turthill lost his life and Hull's Jack Harrison was posthumously awarded the Victoria Cross in 1917 for his bravery at Oppy Wood in France. At a club level, Leeds lost fifteen of fifty-one players who served, Widnes lost thirteen, Hull twelve and Swinton nine. But no figures for the total number of NU players killed, either at professional or amateur level, were ever compiled. The only information available for the sport as a whole is that relating to fifteen of the professional clubs published by *Athletic News'* correspondent in 1919. Of 760 players of these clubs who served in the armed forces, 103 lost their lives.[39]

Unlike the RFU and its clubs, which sought to create what George Mosse has described as a 'cult of the fallen soldier' and celebrate the deaths of players and supporters, the NU never produced a roll of honour or lists of players' war records, and the memorials which were so common at rugby union clubs were either short-lived, such as one erected to Jack Harrison at Hull, or non-existent.[40] The sport's annual handbook, the *Official Guide*, for the first season after the war did not even mention it. Wakefield Trinity's annual report for 1918–19 not only makes no reference to the war but does not refer to the death of its captain, W. L. Beattie, in action in France in 1917. The minute books of the Yorkshire Society of Referees contain not a single reference to the war at all between 1914 and 1918. Indeed, the only remembrance ritual that the game as a whole undertook was the laying of wreaths at the Cenotaph before the Challenge Cup final at Wembley. Even this seems to have petered out by the mid-1930s – and this symbolism could also be interpreted, in the absence of any militarist rhetoric accompanying the ceremony, as part of rugby league's attempt to establish its legitimacy in national sporting traditions.

This contrast with rugby union's elaborate rituals of remembrance can partly be explained by the differing social purpose of the club in the two sports. Rugby union clubs were essentially social institutions organised for the purpose of playing the game, composed chiefly of current and former players, and equipped with a full bureaucratic structure like any other form of middle-class association. Senior

NU clubs were professional organisations designed for the purpose of providing entertainment. Amateur NU clubs generally had no wider purpose other than to organise matches and training. Almost none had any level of permanent organisation other than that needed to rent a pitch and arrange fixtures. There is no way of knowing how many members of amateur clubs were killed – only forty-two clubs were listed in the 1919–20 *Official Guide*, down from 210 in the 1914–15 edition, but this decline was probably in large part due to the economic and organisational difficulties facing clubs. Nor is there any way of knowing how many thousands of supporters of NU clubs never returned from the war to take their places back on the terraces.[41]

There are also deeper reasons that explain the contrasting remembrance of the war by the NU and the RFU. Perhaps most strikingly, the everyday experience of death and injury was profoundly different for the working class and the middle class. For members of the working class, especially those in heavy industry, death in the course of daily work was not an unusual occurrence. For example, in 1913 there were 1,149 fatal accidents in the British coal industry, a shocking figure which itself was overshadowed by a record 1,818 deaths in 1910, and 178,962 non-fatal injuries. In December 1910, 344 men lost their lives in an explosion at the Pretoria pit in Westhoughton, near Wigan. Although even this could not compare with the 20,000 men slaughtered on the first day of the Battle of the Somme in 1916, it highlights the daily familiarity of working-class people with death and serious injury. And, as Joanna Bourke points out, 'even without the war, physical disabilities were not rare in many communities. It was also a common part of urban life and employment'. As late as the 1960s, sociologist Dennis Marsden noted that in Huddersfield textile factories 'disablement was an everyday fact of working at the mill'. But for professional and white-collar workers, who provided the backbone of rugby union, this familiarity with mortality and serious disablement was largely unknown. Thus faced with the awful loss of sons, brothers and friends, they reached to create a 'cult of the fallen soldier' in order to justify the sudden and devastating appearance of everyday death in their midst. For rugby union and other sections of the middle classes, this highlighting of their sacrifice had the broader political purpose of reasserting Edwardian middle-class values and leadership during a period of great social dislocation.[42]

One must also consider the extent to which patriotic militarism was popular within the working class. Clearly in certain areas and in particular sections of industrial workers the war was indeed popular. For example, around 25 per cent of miners had enlisted by mid-1915, although even here it can be argued that the prospect of escaping from pit life was a greater push to enlistment than the pull of patriotism; the truth was perhaps a shifting amalgam of reasons. Certainly the initial 'rush to the colours' in the early months of the war was far more apparent among middle-class and white-collar workers than it was among the majority of the working classes.[43] And in certain areas of the country there was a positive resistance by sections of the working class to wartime jingoism. The large-scale industrial conflicts in South Wales, Glasgow and Sheffield have been well-documented by historians but it is also noticeable for our purposes that Huddersfield was also a centre of anti-war feeling. The town had a long tradition of radicalism and in 1914 demonstrated no great enthusiasm for the declaration of war. Peace meetings were staged regularly without interference and by 1917 the town had become, in the words of historian Cyril Pearce, 'a virtual citadel for the anti-war cause'.[44] This would suggest that, at the very least, pro-war enthusiasm was not as widespread or as uniform as has previously been believed, and that this was reflected to some extent by the attitudes shown towards remembrance by the Northern Union, and perhaps also the Football League.

So whereas rugby union had pledged itself not to forget the war, the NU showed little desire to look back on it – indeed, references to the war by NU administrators and players are comparatively rare. To some extent this also reflected a degree of irritation that developed during wartime about the way the game had been treated. The Army had shown a marked reluctance to organise matches under NU rules, even in the north, and it was felt that there was a distinct lack of publicity given to its war dead in comparison to those of rugby union. When the war was mentioned after 1918 it was generally at international matches, when the links between the competing nations during the war were referred to as a sign of international friendship. For example, when Warrington hosted a visit by the pioneering French club Villeneuve in 1934, an article in the match programme pointed out that:

> There was no question of amateurism or professionalism in the Great War. English and French men fought and fell side by side on the battlefields of Flanders, irrespective of their standard in life, and now in times of peace it is most gratifying to know that Frenchmen and Englishmen can join together on the playing fields of our two great countries.[45]

The implication that rugby union's attitude to the NU ran counter to the experience of the war was made most pointedly by S. G. Ball, the manager of the 1920–21 Australian tourists who, after the French rugby union authorities had forced the cancellation of an exhibition match in Paris, told his players that 'Northern Union players of England and Australia had helped France in the Great War, but had they been Germans the French Rugby Federation could not have treated them worse'.[46] This use of the war and the common sufferings of soldiers of Britain and other nations to argue for 'democratic' reform of sport was made explicit by a NU supporter writing during 1916 to *Athletic News*: 'as the war in this country is being fought on democratic lines, so will the future government of this land be on more democratic lines. There will be far less class distinction than we have been accustomed to. Merit will be recognised. Is it not possible that this may obtain in our sports?'[47]

The idea that the war should serve as a catalyst for social change was in direct contrast to the views of the RFU and more in line with mainstream liberal and social democratic thinking, perhaps best expressed in the call to build a post-war 'land fit for heroes'. Even in the necessarily limited context of sporting culture, it adds weight to the idea that disillusionment with the war at this time was more prevalent among the working classes than the middle classes. Indeed, the months immediately following the war were marked by soldiers striking to demand demobilisation and major strikes in the mines, cotton industry and the railways, among others, emphasising the sense that the working classes felt they were owed something for their sacrifices during the war. Similar disenchantment with the war and militarism could be detected in soccer too. John Osborne's study of *Athletic News*, in many respects the house organ of the Football League, has shown how its attitudes changed at the end of the war. 'There was no more talk of training players in drill and marksmanship and, in a more impressionistic light, the language of even the match reporting signified war weariness', he noted, pointing to a substantial decline in the use of military metaphors to describe the action on the pitch.[48] This is not to say that the NU or the Football League were articulating a political programme, merely that they reflected to some extent the prevailing feelings of their working-class supporters. And even conservative working-class patriotism differed from that of rugby union and its followers. Despite the tremendous weight of official patriotism on the national psyche, working-class men also proved stubbornly resistant to embracing its structures; the British Legion, even with its national network of social clubs, never had more than 500,000 members, less than 10 per cent of the total number of men who served.[49]

If Britain was still divided at the end of the war, rugby was no less so.

Chapter 2

League on the dole?
The game in the
depression years

The first two full seasons following the end of the First World War saw rugby league on the crest of an economic wave. Crowds flocked to matches. By 1922 the finals of all four major tournaments had recorded their highest-ever attendances and Dewsbury, Hull Kingston Rovers and Rochdale Hornets had established crowd records which still stand today. Even St Helens Recreation, admitted to the league permanently after being deemed a success in the wartime competition, returned a profit for the only two seasons in their professional history. Wigan's conversion to a limited liability company in early 1921 saw the initial share offer oversubscribed by 55 per cent. And, as if to trumpet the game's new found wealth, in 1921 Leeds purchased Hunslet's star three-quarter Harold Buck for £1,000, the first time that any player had been valued in four figures. Buoyed with self-confidence, many clubs invested heavily in their stadia. Hull spent almost £2,000 improving and increasing the capacity of their Boulevard ground, Halifax bought their Thrum Hall ground for £8,000 and Hull KR opened a brand new ground in 1922, which cost over £18,000. To some extent these improvements were necessary to address problems that had arisen before the war, such as the provision of adequate dressing rooms and expanded seating facilities for higher-paying spectators, but the growth in attendances and the success of the 1920 tour to Australia, which had brought home a handsome profit, revivified the self-assuredness that had animated the sport in the years before 1914.[1]

But the economic boom that fuelled this affluence was short-lived. From late 1921 worsening trade conditions and rapidly increasing unemployment sent the game, as with British industry in general, into a depression. Both coal and textiles, the twin industrial pillars upon which the Northern Union had been built in the 1890s, were sent spiralling into a slump. Cotton, the staple of East Lancashire towns such as Oldham, Rochdale and, to a lesser extent, Wigan, saw its exports collapse to half their 1913 levels by 1922. Wool, its equivalent in the towns of the West Riding, also saw its exports fall precipitously. Coal, whose relationship with rugby league ran like a black seam through the heart of the game – in 1922 many clubs had opposed a proposal to bring forward kick-off times because it would mean matches starting before miners' shifts had ended – witnessed a calamitous fall in exports to just one-third of their 1913 level. Unemployment surged past the two million mark in June 1922 and between 1920 and 1923 wages fell by nearly 40 percent to real levels lower than in 1914.[2] Addressing the first annual conference of the Rugby Football League in 1922, the chairman, John Counsell of Wigan, highlighted the financial difficulties that the economic depression had brought to the game. Only three clubs had made a profit in the previous season and his own club had made a loss for the first time in twenty years. Bradford had effectively been taken into receivership by the RFL; a new board of directors had been appointed under the direction of the League, which had also ensured the club's survival with a grant of £500.

Throughout the rest of the 1920s and 1930s almost every rugby league club found itself with little more than a tenuous hold on financial health. For many, that grip was almost impossible to maintain. Bradford, York and Rochdale were placed under the financial control of the RFL between 1927 and 1930. Barrow, Swinton and Featherstone Rovers relied on four-figure loans from the RFL to keep them afloat.[3] Many of these problems were related to the slumps in the industries that dominated those towns. Bradford was hit by the long-term decline in the wool trade, Barrow by the halving of the national shipbuilding workforce between 1920 and 1929, Rochdale by the collapse of the cotton trade, Leigh, Swinton and Featherstone by that of coal.[4] But while industrial decline played a major role, it was not the only reason for the difficulties faced by clubs; these were often exacerbated by the policies of the clubs themselves. Counsell had argued in 1922 that 'the time had arrived for a substantial reduction in playing terms, in view of such losses [by clubs], the industrial depression and the reduced earning capacity of followers of the games.[5] But in contrast to soccer, the RFL had historically resisted calls for the introduction of a maximum wage, on the grounds that it 'tended to become a minimum and would not be in the interests of the poorer clubs'. There was also a recognition that the underlying problem was the low turnover of most clubs, with many unable to generate enough income to cover the costs of wages. In the 1928–29 season Featherstone's wages bill exceeded its takings from spectators by £79. By 1937 the gap between income and wage costs had risen to £307, which meant that wages were 143 per cent higher than money taken at the gate.[6] Although Featherstone was somewhat atypical, with the small town's population being just under 15,000 in 1936, other clubs in larger towns were not immune from the same problem.[7] At its most extreme end stood Hull KR, who in the 1934–35 season saw wages dwarf gate money by £959. In general, it was rare for a club to keep its wages/gate money ratio below 50 per cent, particularly when it is taken into account that, especially in the 1920s, many clubs employed players to work on their ground staffs, a sinecure which usually added significantly to the wages bill but little to the amount of work actually carried out.

Wage levels were not the only problem. Transfer fees paid to other clubs and signing-on fees paid to players also accounted for substantial proportions of clubs' incomes. Although transfer fees did not rise substantially during this period – by 1939 the record fee had risen to just £1,350 – most transfers during this period cost at least £200–£300, meaning that the signing of even three or four quality players could make a substantial difference to a club's bottom line. Signing-on fees paid to rugby union players would also start in a similar range. Wigan paid the seventeen-year-old Jim Sullivan £750 to move from Cardiff in 1921 while Scottish centre Roy Kinnear reputedly got £1,000 to move to the club in 1926. Although Wigan were one of the few examples of a club which could afford to spend its way out of a financial crisis by buying players, such a strategy was highly risky, even for them. In the 1926–27 season the club had made a loss of £2,000, largely because they were knocked out of the Lancashire Cup in the first round. The previous season's run to the final brought in over £2,000 in additional gate money. Indeed, for many clubs a good cup run could make the difference between financial success and failure: Hunslet's Challenge Cup of 1934 saw gate takings rise by more than £4,000 over the previous season but their failure to repeat the achievement in 1935 saw gates slump by more than 50 per cent.

★

The importance of cup games to a club's finances had long been appreciated – indeed, the Lancashire and Yorkshire Cups had been initiated in 1905 to provide an early season cash boost for clubs – and the increasing profile of the Challenge Cup competition following the 1929 move to Wembley for the final in 1929, helped increase its importance to club coffers. An example of the greater appeal of cup games over 'bread and butter' league games was illustrated in 1927 when over 5,000 people saw Featherstone play Barrow in the Challenge Cup but the following week only 2,000 turned out to see a league game between the two sides. But such was the decline in the working-classes' disposable income in the north that clubs often found that their crowds fell regardless of on-field success. Hull's average attendance halved from 12,692 to 6,212 between 1921 and 1926, despite finishing in the league's top four in both seasons. Lower down the scale, Featherstone averaged 3,470 spectators in their first season in the league in 1920–21 but never reached that figure again in the next two decades. In March 1930 just 200 supporters paid to watch their match against Bradford and by the 1933–34 season the crowds averaged less than 1,000.[8]

Any attempt to draw a complete picture of the sizes of rugby league crowds during this period is hampered by the fact that accurate figures were given only sporadically in press reports or club records. Unlike the Football League, which began compiling crowd figures in 1925, the RFL did not do likewise until the late 1940s. In a tradition going back to the 1880s, clubs generally only announced the amount of admission money taken at matches. Although this was originally intended to highlight the financial success of a particular match, it rapidly became a device to manipulate club finances, for example by using cash from admission money to pay players before the total receipts were announced, a form of reverse money-laundering. The introduction of Entertainment Tax in 1916 gave clubs an additional reason to hide the true size of their crowds, as any tax official with an adequate knowledge of admission charges and rudimentary mathematical skills could use the information to calculate the tax liability. The only accurate figures available are those for Challenge Cup and Australian tourists' matches, both occasions when the admission money was divided between the two teams and as a matter of course was counted and checked by representatives of both sides. By using Challenge Cup crowd figures we can get a reasonable insight into the size of crowds going to rugby league matches during the inter-war years, although this is somewhat distorted by the extra publicity and local interest that was generated by cup games. As Appendix 1 demonstrates, the crowd levels of the immediate post-war years were only approached again at the end of the 1930s, after dipping through the 1920s and reaching rock bottom at the height of the depression in 1931.

From the limited data that is available, it seems that by the second half of the 1930s both cup and league crowds began to increase. The 1938–39 season saw both Leeds and Bradford average over 12,000 spectators per league match. Barrow's average gate rose from 6,720 in 1931–32 to 9,092 in the last full season before the war, as they became one of the top six clubs in the league.[9] Record attendances were established for the Challenge Cup and Yorkshire Cup finals and new records of over 60,000 were also set both for a Challenge Cup semi-final and the Championship final, partly owing to the availability of grounds with exceptionally high capacities, such as Odsal and Manchester City's Maine Road. Castleford, Hull and Salford all set new ground attendance records in the second half of the decade. Average Challenge Cup attendances also increased from 1934, from 11,583 to 15,296 in 1939, excluding the Wembley final.[10]

Attendances for the matches of the touring Australian sides also dropped throughout the depression, but showed no sign of rising in the late 1930s. They had hit a peak in the 1921–22 season when almost 385,000 had seen the Australians play, recording an average attendance for non-test matches of 9,408. Although this dropped in subsequent tours to 9,370 in 1929–30, 8,636 in 1933–34 and 7,771 in 1937–38 (a tour that coincided with an economic downturn and which was adversely affected by a weak Australian side that had lost key players to English clubs), the average test match crowd remained constant around the 25,000 mark. Although international matches were crucial to the credibility and the self-confidence of the game, the largest crowds for test matches were almost always eclipsed by those for major club finals, perhaps highlighting the importance of community and locality, rather than nation, to the culture of rugby league.

When we compare these attendances with those of rugby league's major sporting rival in the north of England, soccer, it is no exaggeration to say that the round ball game's popularity dwarfed that of league and every other sport. When Manchester City won the FA Cup in 1934 they attracted over 493,000 people to their cup matches, some 58,000 more than the total number at all of that year's Challenge Cup matches. Soccer was the undisputed victor in the war between the football codes that had begun with Manningham's 1903 defection and transformation into Bradford City. Throughout the early 1920s, the Football League continued its attempts to colonise rugby league areas. In August 1917 the Football League had asked Leeds City (the forerunner of Leeds United) to continue to play in the

League's Midland Section because of the boost that would be given to rugby if there was no top-class soccer being played in the city.[11] The success of wartime soccer leagues in Wigan and St Helens, not to mention the rise of women's soccer in Lancashire, had also given rise to hopes that soccer would be able to extend its dominance in peacetime.[12] Both Wigan Borough and Halifax Town had been admitted to the Football League in 1921. Castleford Town and Wakefield City had also applied but did not win enough votes. Halifax Town continued to limp along as the sickly child of West Riding soccer, while Wigan Borough dragged themselves from crisis to crisis before resigning from the Football League in October 1931 with debts approaching £30,000.[13] These failures perhaps demonstrated that it was harder for soccer to dislodge rugby in the smaller northern towns than it was in larger ones such as Bradford and Manchester. Despite soccer's national profile, its weaker clubs in the north tended to suffer more than their rugby league counterparts during the inter-war years, not least because the costs of paying full-time professional players were so much higher.

Nevertheless, where it was strong, soccer still represented a threat to rugby league, not simply in terms of attendances but also in the numbers of schoolboys playing the game and the support it could draw from local businesses. In 1932 Salford manager Lance Todd, backed by fellow Mancunians, Broughton Rangers, had called for rugby league to be played in the summer, partly in order to avoid bad weather – which had caused over one hundred games to be cancelled in the 1931–32 season – but also to avoid direct competition with Manchester's City and United soccer sides.[14] Huddersfield was a partial exception to this in that both league and soccer clubs co-existed relatively harmoniously, although it is noticeable that, with the exception of the 1922–23 and 1931–32 seasons when they both finished in the top four of the Rugby League and Football League Division One respectively, a high league place for one usually meant a disappointing season for the other. However, league's resilience was such that even Huddersfield Town's astonishing success in the 1920s – winning a hat-trick of First Division titles and finishing second in the two subsequent seasons between 1923–24 and 1927–28 – did not threaten Huddersfield rugby league club. As Dave Russell has noted, 'patterns of sporting preference were effectively established by 1920' and Huddersfield, perhaps to the disappointment of the partisans of the older game, continued to be a town with dual and overlapping loyalty to both codes of football.[15]

The decline in rugby league attendances meant that clubs that had invested heavily in grounds in the 1920s found themselves facing almost intractable problems. Despite having initially been proclaimed a huge success, Hull KR's Craven Park ground became an increasingly heavy millstone around the neck of the club. A decline in the playing fortunes of the club and a slump in attendances meant that it was unable to meet a scheduled repayment in 1927. New debenture stock was issued but the club's financial position continued to deteriorate until in 1938 it was forced to sell the ground to a greyhound company for a loss of more than £6,500.[16] Swinton also faced similar problems following the purchase of their new Station Road ground in 1929. Falling gates and failure to reach its previous heights meant that a greater proportion of revenue had to go on debt repayments and less on players – and a weak team did nothing to attract new spectators. The vicious circle in which the club found itself was not appreciated by its supporters: 'What's the point of having a good shop if there's nothing to show in window?' complained a shareholder at the club's 1934 annual general meeting. When the chairman replied that he was hunting for new players, a voice retorted 'Aye, yer might 'ave done some 'untin but tha's not taken tha gun and tha's shot nowt!'[17]

Nor were clubs helped in the 1920s by the RFL's intransigent attitude to reducing the cost of admission for the unemployed. Between 1921 and 1939 nationwide unemployment averaged 14 per cent but was much higher in league's heartlands. In December 1921 the Council had responded to a request to allow the unemployed into matches for free by sending out a circular to all its clubs stating that 'no such admission of unemployed to matches be granted or allowed by any of its clubs'. Despite this, in September 1922 Barrow unilaterally reduced the minimum admission to ninepence from the League's official minimum of one shilling in order to boost their falling attendances, much to the chagrin of the local soccer club, which begged the Football League to allow them to do the same. The year before Warrington had donated 350 season tickets to their local Unemployed Committee.[18] Throughout the decade there were repeated calls for the RFL to change its stance, especially during the miners' lock-out of 1926, which lasted from April to November. In August the St Helens' Newspaper & Advertiser called on the RFL to think of the thousands 'who will have to stand outside gates and listen to the cheers of the favoured ones within. They have not the money to pay even the modest admission fee charged.' The issue was highlighted again in September when unemployed Leigh supporters, many of them miners, forced their way into the club's Mather Lane ground to see the match against the New Zealand tourists, in defiance of the RFL's insistence that the minimum admission for tour games should be no less than one shilling and sixpence. In fact, during the lock-out many clubs ignored the RFL and allowed miners in for sixpence.[19] Even this was still beyond the means of most, but what the pocket lacked was made up for by the ingenuity of supporters, as a reporter described at a match at Featherstone:

> Yard walls and bedroom windows were used as grandstands, or rather grand sit-downs, for I noticed over a hundred lads perched rather precariously on one wall. They simply didn't get excited or they would have clattered down into the passage. Some of the old colliery houses had trap-doors on the roof and from each tiny trap-door there peeped forth a pair of eyes intently watching the game. It was for all the world like one of Heath Robinson's sketches.[20]

Many clubs also allowed the unemployed in at reduced prices after half-time. In the early 1930s Keighley went so far as to allow the unemployed in for five pence ten minutes after kick-off. Alf Ellaby, the great St Helens winger of the inter-war years, remembered years later how the roar of the home crowd grew considerably louder in the second half of St Helens' matches after unemployed spectators had been allowed in.[21]

Despite the severity of the economic difficulties facing the majority of the sport's supporters, crowds appear to have been largely orderly during the 1920s and 1930s. There were nineteen incidents of crowd misbehaviour reported to the RFL, compared to thirty in the first fifteen years of the sport's existence. Apart from two instances where stones were thrown at visiting players and a fracas at Bradford between home supporters and Dewsbury players as they left the pitch in April 1926, all disturbances were directed against match officials. The most serious of these occurred in 1937 when a touch judge was knocked out by a stone thrown from the crowd. Hull KR officials, desperate to avoid their ground being closed, claimed that the official had merely fainted in the course of his duties. It was to no avail and the ground was closed for two weeks. There seems to be a significant correlation between on-field failure and crowd disturbances; with the exception of incidents at Wigan in 1932 and Hull in 1934, none of the clubs where disturbances took place finished in the top ten of the league. Eleven incidents took place in the seven seasons leading up to 1926, perhaps suggesting that the social dislocation of the years preceding the General Strike gave rise to a greater questioning of authority as represented in the person of the referee. Possibly reflecting a similar attitude, at the 1922 Cup Final held at Headingley a thousand Rochdale fans arrived late and were let in for free by officials after they threatened to storm the gates. In contrast, those incidents that took place after 1926 are notable largely for their scarcity in a time when political violence was on the increase. There are no reports of any incidents of violence or disturbance by supporters travelling to Wembley or any other away matches.[22]

The issue of admission charges came to a head in 1932 when, claiming that clubs were undermining their own economic well-being, the RFL officially forbade clubs from allowing anyone into a match for less than the official admission price of one shilling before half-time. This provoked widespread protests from the clubs, who argued that the decision would only reduce attendances. Faced with a backlash, in December 1932 the game's leaders relented and voted to allow the unemployed into league, but not cup, matches for sixpence, a privilege that was also extended to 'ladies'.[23] For some of those clubs in towns hard hit by unemployment, the concession was initially very successful: in 1934 Leigh recorded its first profit for ten years, owing to gate takings increasing by £1,220, 'despite the fact that there had been severe unemployment in the town and the unemployed had been allowed admission for 6d'. The fact that the RFL allowed concessionary admission to the unemployed, in contrast to the Football League, was also viewed by the consortium that set up the Newcastle club in 1936 as a means of attracting unemployed soccer supporters to the sport. The limited evidence available suggests that the proportion of unemployed attending matches was not insignificant. For example, at the 1936 Cumberland versus Yorkshire game at Workington it was estimated that half of the 10,600 crowd were unemployed. Featherstone's league derby with Castleford in

April 1933 saw 1,800 of the record 9,334 fans let in at the sixpenny unemployed rate. Faced with yet another financial crisis in 1938, Leigh secretary Harry Prescott noted that 416 out of an attendance of 1706 at one match paid the unemployed rate to get in but complained that many were not really jobless.[24]

★

Given the severity of the economic climate in northern industrial towns, it is perhaps remarkable that only one club in this heartland was forced to close during this period: St Helens Recreation. The club was effectively the works side of glass-makers Pilkingtons and was closed down at the end of the 1938–39 season by the firm, who were forced to underwrite eighteen consecutive loss-making seasons and whose owners were never fully comfortable with rugby league – indeed, the club switched to soccer in the 1890s to avoid joining the Northern Union. Despite a respectable playing record, they had to compete for spectators with St Helens in a town that was hit particularly hard by the depression in the coal industry. Unlike Wigan Highfield, who had been admitted to the League in 1922, moved to London in 1933 and then to Liverpool in 1934, Recreation's link to Pilkingtons meant that they could not attempt to solve their financial problems by changing location.[25]

Moving was also not an option open to other clubs, who sought to deal with their financial difficulties in a number of complementary ways. As we have already seen, many approached the RFL for assistance in the form of loans and, in extreme cases, direct management. A common method of raising additional capital was to convert the club into a limited company and raise cash through a share issue. However, success was not guaranteed or even common during the period. Bramley converted in 1927 but could only sell 700 of their 2,000 shares. Ten years later St Helens found themselves in the same position when less than 6,000 of their 8,000 issued shares were bought. Keighley and Rochdale also faced similar prob-lems. Only Halifax's conversion in 1936 was considered successful.[26] Indeed, the end of the 1930s saw Leigh and Rochdale converting back to become members' clubs once again in order to clear their debts.

Clubs also sought the support of wealthy benefactors from among local busi-nessmen. In 1931 G. A. Close made a donation of £1,000 to Rochdale, for which he was made an honorary president. In the same year Keighley were saved from closure by loans from two local businessmen. Abraham Bullock, the owner of a local bus company and Featherstone Rovers' president, financed a new stand and terraces from his own pocket. Until the late 1920s York were heavily reliant on the largesse of Sir William Forster-Todd. At a corporate level, it was local brewers Greenall Whitley who financed St Helens' purchase of their Knowsley Road ground in 1925. In 1931 Barrow named their newly opened ground Craven Park in honour of C. W. Craven, the managing director of the local Armstrong-Vickers naval shipyard, in recognition of the support they had received from the company. In some way this was a reassertion of the industrial paternalism that had helped establish rugby in the north in the nineteenth century. Other forms of support from civic leaders were available to high profile clubs. When Wigan met with Welsh international rugby union winger and policeman Arthur Bassett in the late 1930s, they took the Chief Constable of Wigan with them to offer him a job if he joined the club.[27]

The relationship of these local businessmen sheds substantial light on the question of who controlled rugby league clubs. Even those clubs that were membership clubs, and therefore ostensibly under the democratic control of their members, often abrogated the ultimate decision-making power to their wealthiest supporters. Featherstone Rovers' constitution gave the club committee power to elect 'guarantors', those who were prepared to put substantial sums of money into the club. As a reward for their largesse, they were uniquely exempt from either election or recall by the club's annual general meeting. The formation of a limited liability company was also a means of securing the control of a club in the hands of the wealthy. The minutes of Liverpool Stanley committee's discussion about the conversion of the club in 1950 suggest that it was their eagerness to avoid personal liability for the club's debts that animated their desire for limited liability status. And ultimately each club was subject to the caprices of market forces, regardless of how democratic its constitution was: at the first sign of financial difficulties, every club was at the mercy of its benefactors or the banks.[28]

From the early 1930s – when unemployment among coalminers reached a height of over 41 per cent and that of cotton workers over 31 per cent – a number of clubs sought to increase their revenue by diversifying, either by promoting or by renting out their grounds to speedway or greyhound racing, the two new 'boom' sports of the late 1920s.[29] Barrow, Rochdale and the two Hull clubs had already experimented with these by 1932. The survival of Hull KR in the 1930s seems to have been due in large measure to the money it made from greyhound racing. The club also staged baseball during the summer months, as did a number of other clubs in the late 1930s. Even the amounts brought in by this seemingly alien sport were not negligible. In 1936 Bradford raised over £500 by renting out Odsal for baseball matches. Not all clubs were successful, however. Rochdale were forced to close down their speedway operation after just two years because it failed to attract crowds. Diversification, albeit of a different type, was also one of the reasons for the financial success in the inter-war years of Leeds rugby league club. As the owner of the Headingley sports ground, the club drew significant income from the fact it was both the home of Yorkshire County Cricket Club during the height of its success and a regular venue for Test match cricket. In 1927, a time when many other clubs were viewing the future with great apprehension, Leeds announced the payment of its first-ever dividend to shareholders, a distribution that was to be repeated regularly over the next decade. The huge difference which cricket made to Leeds can be gauged by their profit margin of £4,093 in the 1930–31 season, which was more than the aggregate profits of every other league club and contrasted sharply with the loss of £76 made by their conquerors in that season's Championship final, Swinton.[30]

But Headingley was almost unique in British sport by being the home of leading teams in two sports. For most rugby league clubs, however, probably the most important factor in ensuring their economic survival during the inter-war period was the organisational and financial contribution of their supporters and the local communities in which they were based. From the 1920s supporters' clubs began to play an increasingly important role in the financing of the professional clubs. Supporters' clubs emerged immediately after the First World War and by 1923 were sufficiently numerous in Yorkshire for the creation of a county federation. In its first season of operation it was reported that Featherstone supporters had raised £100 to help fund the purchase of the club's ground and that Huddersfield supporters had raised £114 to pay the club's heating bills. Bramley, Castleford, Hunslet, Keighley and Wakefield supporters also reported raising money for ground improvements. Supporters' clubs played a key role in the organisation of player's testimonial funds too. Huddersfield collected almost £200 for Ben Gronow's benefit and Bramley's Lou Marshall received £104 from fans. In 1929 Bradford's supporters even took over the running of the club's 'A', or reserve, team. In the mid-1920s Leigh supporters augmented their sides funds by organising an annual brass band contest. In 1938 the transfer of Liverpool Stanley forward George Davies to St Helens was made possible by the supporters' club raising £250 of the £275 transfer fee.[31] Looking back in 1946, Huddersfield supporters' club calculated that they had raised around £4,800 since being formed in 1921. Liverpool Stanley supporters were even more directly responsible for the survival of their side. When the club's owners, the Electric Greyhound Racing Company, tried to shut it down in 1937 they took it over and formed a limited liability company to ensure it carried on playing, although its subsequent history continued to be a tightrope walk over the abyss of financial ruin.[32]

As well as financial aid, many supporters' clubs provided a great deal of organisational support too, all of it unpaid. At Bramley, Keighley and Wakefield the supporters clubs edited and published the match-day programmes. Most, if not all, organised trips to away matches and to Wembley for the Challenge Cup final. Many also provided refreshment facilities for spectators on match days. Batley, Bradford, Hunslet and York also ran their sides' end of season workshops competitions, tournaments in which local factory sides would compete at the local professional club's ground, bringing both gate receipts and potential new players to the club. Just as importantly for the future of the sport, in 1925 the Yorkshire Federation set up and ran the county's inter-town rugby league for boys aged between fourteen and sixteen years old.[33] The work, commitment and collective spirit which animated supporters' involvement with their clubs was captured by journalist Stanley Chadwick, himself a staunch Huddersfield fan:

> Members of Northern League clubs are not only content to attend home matches but organise motor coach trips to away matches; run whist drives and concerts to augment club funds; scrub the pavilion floor, serve in the dry canteen, assist with programme selling, encourage the junior leagues, and indulge

in many other activities. There is no loss of prestige in doing the most menial job, and men and women everywhere in the North are proud to help *their* club in this way. [emphasis in original][34]

Even so, this work did not always receive the recognition it deserved: at various times the directors of Keighley, Swinton and York refused to recognise their supporters' clubs following criticisms of their teams. But these tended to be isolated reactions by clubs in crisis. Provided that they did not criticise their club's management or the RFL publicly, their work was highly valued. RFL secretary John Wilson met regularly with the Yorkshire Federation and in 1928 the RFL insisted on the inclusion of two supporters' representatives on the reconstituted York club committee. Both Halifax and Huddersfield supporters' clubs also had delegates on their sides' management committees.[35]

If supporters' clubs represented a financial and organisational cadre of volunteer workers and fund-raisers, clubs also relied on broader sections of the community for monetary support, especially but not exclusively during times of crisis. In the early 1930s Keighley raised money through a successful 'Shilling Fund', which asked local people to give a shilling to the club's funds, and also by publishing a recipe book in which local 'ladies' could have their own recipes included for a payment of sixpence. It also launched a scheme to borrow £10 at 3.5 per cent interest from sixty of its wealthier supporters, who were repaid one at a time at each of the club's next sixty home games – although none of the sixty requested the interest payments to which they were entitled.[36] In the mid-1930s both Bramley and Dewsbury launched similar 'shilling funds'. To help them equip their new Odsal stadium in 1934, Bradford launched a financial appeal in the town by offering ownership of a strip of the turf on the pitch for sixpence. With 49,500 such strips covering the playing surface, the club hoped to raise over £1,230 but were more than pleased with the £900 the scheme eventually brought in.[37]

Nowhere was this reliance on supporters and the wider community more apparent than in Featherstone. The club's dominance of local junior rugby league and its success during the First World War, when it had played alongside the professional clubs, saw it elected to the Northern Rugby Football League in 1921. Confidently expecting to attract average crowds of 5,000, the economic downturn of 1922 meant that it never got anywhere near that amount, yet the club survived owing to the extensive and ongoing support of local miners. In 1926 the local Miners' Welfare bought the club's Post Office Road ground from its owners and rented it back to the club, and in June 1934 over 1,000 miners at the town's two pits voted for a weekly deduction of threepence to be taken from their wages and given to the club.[38]

Ultimately, it was on this foundation of volunteer and community support that rugby league was built and which ensured its survival through the depression. Professional sport of all kinds was, and is, based largely on a system that at the top relies on the patronage of the rich but which underneath is reliant for its survival on the voluntary activities of tens of thousands of enthusiasts. When patronage was not available or it needed to be complemented, it was supporters with varying degrees of commitment – from the die-hard to the fair-weather – whose time and money ensured the survival of their clubs.

★

If the depression hit professional rugby league hard, its impact was even greater on that sector of the game entirely dependent on voluntary support: the grassroots amateur levels of rugby league. Although it received little coverage in the media, beneath the top layer of two dozen or so professional clubs, rugby league was also played extensively in its heartlands for recreation and enjoyment. Indeed, the show-piece occasions of the amateur game were often significant local events. Over 10,000 turned out for the final of the Wakefield works competition in 1933 and 7,000 spectators saw the 1939 final of the Halifax Workshops tournament. Schoolboy finals could draw similar numbers. The 1924 *Daily Dispatch* under-fourteens cup final between Wigan St Patrick's and Widnes St Bede's drew over 17,000 spectators. In 1936 10,000 turned out for the final of the St Helens schools cup, while 5,000 did so for the equivalent Leigh tournament.[39] Indeed, as the secretary of the rugby section of the Hull Works Sports Association exasperatedly commented in 1938, it became something of a frustration to supporters of the game to have to point out that there was much more to the sport than professionalism.[40]

As with the professional game, the first years after the war had seen the amateur side of the sport boom. From just forty-two teams registered with the RFL in the 1919–20 season, the number leapt to 318 in 1924–25. St Helens Recreation, Featherstone Rovers, Wigan Highfield and Castleford all graduated from the game's junior ranks to become fully fledged professional clubs. The growth in amateur clubs peaked in 1929 and the depression in the early 1930s drastically reduced the number of clubs. Indeed, it appears that its impact was far more severe on amateur rugby league than on the professional game. A 1933 report into the state of the amateur rugby league noted the devastation that had occurred to the sport. There were no amateur clubs in Bradford, no adult clubs in the Dewsbury/Batley area, just two in Huddersfield and a mere seven in Leeds.[41] By the end of the decade numbers had begun to rise again, especially through the increasing number of work-based clubs formed through employers' recreation schemes.

The depression hit amateur rugby league in a variety of ways. Some teams suffered simply because their players left the locality to find work. In 1932 it was reported that the club in Kinsley, a mining village south of Wakefield where Billy Batten had been born, was £40 in debt and about to disband because 'employment [was] bad in the village and players left the club to join others where work was better'.[42] The cost of renting pitches on which to play and equipment with which to play often proved to be beyond the reach of amateur enthusiasts, especially in the depression years of the early 1930s. In December 1932 a Mr Ramsden of Halifax found his attempts to organise a side floundering and appealed to the RFL for help:

We have all managed to obtain boots, socks and tights but we can see no way of obtaining shirts. ... Then there is the question of a ball. The one we at present use is patched all over and the bladder is out of a soccer ball. I feel certain that as a sportsman, you will help us to obtain both ball and shirts.[43]

Although there is no record of whether this appeal was successful, the RFL at the time did, in fact, have an informal policy of paying for rugby shirts for amateur clubs and schoolboy teams. As early as February 1921 it gave fourteen amateur clubs grants of up to £5. By 1928 it supported fifteen part-time district organisers across the sport's heartlands. It made regular grants and loans to clubs and district leagues, although the amounts disbursed rarely exceeded £10, a stark contrast to the tens of thousands of pounds loaned by the RFU to its clubs during the same period. However, by the end of the 1930s it had ceased to provide grants directly to clubs, preferring instead to give money to district leagues to distribute. It also helped out with the other most important expense facing a team, that of pitch rental. This often proved to be an insurmountable difficulty for clubs, as the Huddersfield & District League pointed out in their report for the 1931–32 season: 'Field rents are as usual the big drawback. There has not been a great difficulty in getting them but the excessive rent asked for is a very big load for clubs to shoulder. £10 for the season is as little as any owner seems to think of asking.'[44] To deal with this problem, the RFL had set up the British Playing Fields Society before the First World War as a charity to purchase and maintain pitches for the use of the sport as a whole but by 1930 it owned only five pitches, one in Cumberland and two each in Lancashire and Yorkshire. In fact, the Society mainly functioned in order to provide grants to amateur clubs so that they could rent pitches, a subsidy that totalled £200 in 1930.[45]

These were not the only financial hurdles facing the amateur league enthusiast. Even if a club could procure a pitch and equipment, players still had to find the money to pay for insurance. The cost of insurance premiums could vary from threepence to sixpence a match, depending on the age of the player, for which they would receive between ten and twenty shillings per week for a specified period, usually four weeks. This in itself was a double deterrent to playing the game. Not only was the cost of playing prohibitive but the benefits received by an injured player would not cover his wages while injured. This was the fate that befell Thomas Barton, a Dunscroft amateur player in 1935, whose injury led to him being off work for four months, for which the RFL granted him an extra £5 to help keep his family of six children. The fact that soccer was perceived to be less dangerous, cheaper and easier to play also meant that amateur rugby league was not necessarily the participant sport of choice even for those who were supporters of their local professional league club – for example, in York in 1936 there were approximately 350 amateur rugby league players, compared to almost 1,400 soccer players, despite the fact that the city's league and soccer sides both attracted average crowds of around 4,000.[46]

But to some degree the problem faced by amateur league clubs was more fundamental. Few working-class people had the time, finances or the administrative experience to organise a club. A 1930 enquiry highlighted the problem; a speaker from Dewsbury noted that the biggest difficulty 'was committees losing interest, especially when their team was losing matches. Working men could not be expected to shoulder financial responsibility [for clubs]'. A spokesman from York pointed out that in his area 'the lads who wanted to play had little money to spend on the game, and had no idea of how to raise funds or run clubs'.[47] The final report of the 1933 enquiry reiterated the problem, identifying the 'root causes' of the precipitous decline in the number of clubs as being:

(a) the inability of those who want to play to form, finance and manage clubs.
(b) the absence of older men to undertake the work mentioned in (a).[48]

Unfortunately it could offer no solution to these problems, although the growing number of works-based clubs were relieved of the burden of paying for pitches and some organisational duties because of the facilities provided by employers. Nevertheless, the combination of financial hardship and lack of administrative experience goes some way to explain the huge number of clubs that fell by the wayside in the 1930s. Of the 318 amateur rugby league clubs listed in the 1924–25 *Official Guide* of the RFL only sixty-three were still listed in the 1934–35 edition, a survival rate of slightly less than 20 per cent. This compares sharply with the experience of rugby union clubs in the same period, almost all of which survived. As we saw in the previous chapter, sports clubs played different roles in working- and middle-class communities. Whereas a union club was a nodal point in a social network, an amateur rugby league club existed simply for the purpose of playing rugby league. With a handful of exceptions, no league clubs had clubhouses that could act as a social centre or as means of raising finance. And the business contacts that allowed even humble union clubs to negotiate loans to finance the running of clubs were practically non-existent.

One partial exception to this, as the 1933 report noted, were those clubs that were 'attached to districts, small towns or villages, where the local people take an interest, and where the club is run by a properly constituted committee elected annually' and were the focus for the locality's civic pride. This was the case in Cumberland, where the game was entirely amateur throughout the inter-war years. Indeed, the RFL's only chairman from an amateur club was Millom's Edward Brown in 1931. For towns on the Cumbrian coast such as Egremont, Maryport and Whitehaven the chance to play a professional side in the first round of the Challenge Cup was almost as much an event as playing at Wembley itself. The results in these games veered wildly from the narrowest of heroic defeats, such as Great Clifton's 6–5 loss to Keighley in 1930, to shattering destruction, as in Flimby and Fothergill's 116–0 loss to Wigan in 1925. But despite their sides invariably losing, these games were occasions on which the forgotten third county of rugby league could demonstrate not only its playing skills but also its commitment to the sport, as a dialect poem written about Great Clifton's 1930 encounter with Keighley illustrates:

Clifton went ta Keighley, beat six points ta five,
They landed back fra Keighley, an ivery yan alive
The meade a glorious story 'at Keighley won't forgit,
Thurteen Clifton heroes chock full o' Clifton grit
…
Clifton com fra Keighley, just beaten bi a point,
Ah bet 'at sum war riddy ta eat their Sunday joint,
Wat they'll win in Cumberlandhed best be left untelt
Thear's menny a slip 'twixt cup an' club, an' heeds can suen be swelt.[49]

This sense of community was also expressed by local amateur clubs, who organised fund-raising games for strikers and those locked-out by employers during industrial disputes. For example, in May 1921 local Wigan side Ince All Blacks played a charity match to raise funds for striking miners, and in October 1926 the St Helens sides Gartons Lane and Clock Face staged a match in aid of miners' relief funds. Unlike soccer, there are no examples of strikers playing rugby league with policemen during the General Strike – hostility between strikers and the police was also probably too strong in rugby league-playing industrial areas.[50]

The two other exceptions to the general lack of organisational resources in the game were the supporters' clubs of professional sides and works-based teams. As we have already seen, supporters' clubs organised local workshops competitions in Batley, Bradford, Hunslet and York, and the Yorkshire Inter-Town Boys League was administered for many years by the county's Federation of Supporters' Clubs.[51] But it was the growth of employer-provided recreational facilities that was probably the most important factor in the formation and survival of most new clubs in the 1930s. Throughout the decade, the number of works teams grew while locality-based teams declined. By 1939 works teams made up over a quarter of all amateur sides. As many historians have noted, much of working-class culture was centred on the workplace and the tremendous increase in employer-provided recreation facilities in the inter-war years sought to use this to bolster company loyalty among employees. No company, wrote a publicist for the brewing industry in 1929 'can afford to neglect welfare work for its employees. For, as health means good work, and recreation means fitness and contentment, welfare is a very efficient synonym for prosperity in every sense of the word'.[52]

Works sides were traditionally of two types; those formed specifically for end-of-season competitions and those that were permanent sections of factory recreation systems. Teams entered in workshop competitions tended to be scratch sides formed especially for the tournament. These could be quite numerous. In 1909 forty-four sides entered Huddersfield's workshop competition while eighty entered Broughton Rangers' 1911 competition.[53] In those towns where rugby league was the dominant code of football, the level of works-based organisation could be extensive. By 1938 the Hull Works Sports Association had over 700 registered players, twenty teams and five different competitions. St Helens not only had numerous works sides, such as United Glass Bottle Manufacturers, Ravenhead Glass and the

mysteriously titled Uno's Dabs, but Pilkington Brothers, the town's major employers, had their own league comprising teams from the various sections of the
company's factories.[54] But the extent to which these clubs were successful in
cementing employee–company loyalty must be open to question. Certainly many
workplace teams soon dropped any commitment to fielding only those players who
worked for the company. Some, such as Warrington's Orford Tannery works side,
did not even bother with an employee-only rule, ostensibly because the firm did
not have a large enough workforce.[55] A team like Hull's British Oil and Cake Mills
side, which had been formed in 1911 and regularly played professional opposition
in the first round of the Challenge Cup from the 1920s to the 1970s, rapidly lost
its reliance on employees, instead becoming a magnet for the city's better amateur
players, with the company's involvement amounting to little more than providing
pitches on which to play.[56]

Perhaps somewhat paradoxically, along with the slow economic recovery of the
mid-1930s, one of the biggest boosts to the amateur game was the establishment
of rugby league in France in 1934. As well as international matches and reciprocal
tours by professional sides, a number of cross-channel tours by amateur league sides
from both countries took place. St Helens' schoolboys blazed a trail when they
visited France in the 1934–35 season and the following season four amateur clubs
played a touring side of Paris students. Most notably, in 1935 the first-ever amateur
rugby league international match took place between the two countries.[57]

Although the amateur game continued to be a reliable conveyor belt for the production of new professional players – for example, in the 1932–33 season thirteen
of the 538 registered players in the Wakefield and District Amateur League were
signed by professional clubs – there was ongoing friction between amateur and
professional clubs. Few if any of the clubs that signed amateur players bothered to
pay their amateur clubs the requisite signing-on fee of £10. Indeed, the league's
local organiser complained that he had written fifteen letters during the season to
three West Yorkshire clubs asking, to no avail, for the money. The issue continued
to be a source of intense friction in the game, as was the fact that the senior clubs
could pay hundreds of pounds for Welsh or Antipodean players while neglecting
their obligations to the game's grassroots. Writing in 1930 Harry Sunderland
wondered if

> wealthy clubs like Leeds and others are willing to spend sums like £1,000 on
> a junior competition – or in aiding schoolboy football – in the enthusiastic
> way in which they have paid out big sums to buy a finished player who has
> been moulded and made in someone else's workshop.[58]

Amateur rugby league was just as competitive and subject to gamesmanship as it
was at the professional level. Although statistics are almost non-existent, in 1932–33

the Wakefield Intermediate League, composed of clubs for players between the ages of fifteen to twenty-one years, saw thirty-nine players sent off in 184 matches; in five cases that the sending-off was judged sufficient punishment, although the nature of the offences were not recorded. This represents an average of a player being sent off every 4.7 matches, a much higher frequency than in the professional game that season where the average was a player being sent off every 7.1 matches.[59] At the higher levels of the game, players were also paid – for example, even before they joined the professional ranks in 1926 Castleford paid its players seven shillings and sixpence for a win and five shillings for a loss.[60] Clubs bending the rules were commonplace. A 1927 cup-tie between Askern Miners' Welfare and Kirk Sandal in West Yorkshire was ordered to be replayed when it was discovered that the Welfare team included a certain Billy Batten in its ranks, contrary to the competition's rules forbidding professional players. In 1937 the RFL's Amateur sub-committee found that the game was being stifled by too many clubs complaining about the administration of the game, appealing against the results of matches and failing to fulfil fixtures.[61]

Despite, or perhaps because of, the naturally intense competition with which the sport was played at all levels, the game's leadership did try to imbue a moral dimension that emphasised the building of character and the inculcation of sporting values. In 1925 the RFL issued *Speakers' Notes* for local organisers, point three of which was:

> To play in the true spirit of the game, and not put too much importance on the winning of matches. Cultivate the open game as this is more enjoyable to players and likely to attract more spectators. Players to support captain and committee.[62]

This was reiterated again in 1937 when the RFL insisted that steps be taken to instil 'the lessons of good sportsmanship and to try and raise generally the tone and standing of the whole amateur rugby league game'.[63] To some extent this keenness to emphasise sportsmanship was a defence mechanism against the accusations of rugby union and its adherents that league was a game which placed winning at all costs above all else. But there was also genuine belief that the sport could play a moral role in society. Although, as can be seen from Appendix 2, church-based teams were in a small minority – and usually connected to a local YMCA or Sunday school – many of the more committed organisers of amateur rugby league saw the game as having a broader pastoral role, especially for younger players. Wakefield organiser Tony Bland exemplified this attitude in his dealings with young players who had been sent off during matches:

> In some cases I write a letter to the boy, & in this case not only does the boy see it but also his parents as well & this does show to them that we are out to do our best in trying to teach the boy to play the game & be a sport, & may I add that on more than one occasion it has been said to me that I was doing more good than the parson's do. [sic][64]

Bland's belief in the lack of significance of the church in socialising young players could probably also apply to other semi-official agencies of socialisation, and especially to the intended lessons imparted through the stories and comics produced for boys at this time. Although huge numbers of stories about rugby union and soccer were written for schoolboys in the inter-war years, few dealt with rugby league. One of the handful to do so appeared in *The Boy's Realm* in 1914. *The Thirteenth Player* featured crooked directors, a cynical New Zealand player, a loyal but dim Cornish forward and the hero Roy Hunter, a Welsh rugby union import forced to switch to league owing to financial problems at home. Thanks to Roy the directors' plot to ruin the club was thwarted, the New Zealander turns over a new leaf, one of the directors exposes his crooked colleagues, and together with the Cornish player, the principals become firm pals. The story ended after several weeks with the genre's most recognisable cliché: 'very happy, the four friends arm in arm, walked out of the cafe.'[65] The remarkable feature of the story was that none of the northern players played any positive role whatsoever. They were portrayed as out of condition and drunken, easily manipulated by the directors or, as the story develops, led equally easily by the hero. The sympathetic characters were the Welsh and Cornish players, who obviously received their moral training in rugby union, whilst the worst features of the New Zealand player had been exacerbated by playing league. It would be difficult for a rugby league-supporting schoolboy to empathise with any of the characters or to identify any positive characteristics in their own sport. If anything, the story would underline how difficult it was for boys of his class to be, in the words of Tony Bland, a 'sport'. The story was actually written by rugby union journalist Trevor Wignall, suggesting that its purpose may have been to confirm the pre-existing prejudices of a rugby union readership. But, in fact, most stories written for working-class schoolboys at this time were similarly dismissive of working-class characters. And, as Dave Russell has pointed out, the rare fictional heroes from the working classes often discovered at the end of a story that their 'true' origins were from the middle or upper classes. To the extent that young people read these stories, it appears that they either ignored their overt propaganda or took it as one more example of the bias faced by rugby league and, by extension, the working classes in general.[66]

It may well have been that the biggest impact of these images of moral turpitude was not on boys but their teachers. Throughout the inter-war years the fortunes of schoolboy rugby league fluctuated even more than the other branches of the amateur game. To some extent this was because its playing was dependent on individual schoolteachers with the personal enthusiasm to initiate and sustain school sides. The fact that only the tiniest number of teachers would have played rugby league at their secondary school meant that, unlike soccer or union, there was no steady stream of experienced masters flowing from schools and universities back into the education system. The task of those who did want to play was made doubly difficult by the fact that few elementary or 'modern' schools of the time could afford to play league as well as soccer, the sport of the vast majority of non-private and grammar schools in rugby league areas. And it is safe to make the assumption that no private or grammar school would have even considered playing league. In 1938 there were 126 schools fielding 205 teams in the towns of the eleven clubs that responded to an RFL survey on the schoolboy game – with the Leeds/Hunslet area recording thirty-nine schools and Wigan just eight – a figure which could be extrapolated to suggest that, with twenty-eight clubs then in the League, the total number of schools playing the game at that time would be approximately 320.[67]

Despite the majority's inability to complete such questionnaires, some professional clubs do seem to have been marginally more charitable towards the schoolboy game than they were for amateur clubs. In the 1930s Wakefield supplied local schools with free two-penny tickets for them to sell and keep the proceeds, and during the 1935–36 season Leeds claimed to have given £100 worth of playing equipment to local schools.[68] But, despite these difficulties, some schools, such as Hunslet Carr in south Leeds, east Hull's Courtney Street and Barrow's Risedale School, became as important to rugby league as Sedbergh or Fettes Schools were to union, dominating local competitions (neither Courtney Street nor Hunslet Carr lost a game for ten and five seasons respectively between 1920 and 1939) and producing dozens of future professional players, although few could hope to match Risedale's record of three future national captains.[69]

But there was also much unorganised rugby league played by boys outside of school. In Widnes in the 1920s, recalled future Labour MP Jack Ashley, 'we played rugby with a piece of sacking tied with a string', the kick-off being determined by whether one team captain could guess which hand the opposing captain had secretly moistened with his lips. He and his friends hit upon the idea of saving Oxo coupons to get a real rugby ball. Unfortunately it did not last until the end of its first street match, when it was run over by a passing lorry. These informal boys' matches could range from street kickabouts between boys from the same street to much more elaborately organised games between teams of boys from several streets or whole districts of a town and took place on wasteland or, if lucky, in municipal parks. Growing up in Hunslet, the actor Peter O'Toole established a name for himself as a speedy twelve-year-old back playing for a side known as Raggy-Arsed Rovers against opponents such as Chip Shop Wanderers and the Silly Army. Like the boys in Widnes, their rugby balls were of an inconsistent quality; patchworks of leather pieces were inflated by a bicycle tyre inner-tube, newspapers or just rags. At the worst, an unlucky player would 'volunteer' a shoe. As O'Toole recounted, such games provided the instinctual thrills of folk football in pre-industrial times:

> Two or three matches between teams from various clusters of streets were played simultaneously. One sometimes found oneself straying into others' matches. Goalposts were a premium. If the pair had already been snatched, often a player's younger brother, 'our kid', would find himself elected as a post. Kit was irrelevant. A familiar figure with the ball, you supported him; an unfamiliar, you downed the bastard.[70]

Such scenes were repeated in towns and villages throughout rugby league's heartlands. But for those whose futures would not lead to Hollywood or the Houses of Parliament, the only records of such matches reside in the memories of players who ran, passed and tackled with an equally glorious enthusiasm, unaware of and uncaring about their ultimate destination in life.

Chapter 3

Masters and servants: the professional player 1919–39

Despite the inevitable association of the words rugby, league and professionalism, the full-time rugby league professional was a very rare bird indeed. The overwhelming majority of players had full-time jobs outside of the game and hardly any could afford to live on their rugby earnings alone, as can be seen when we look at the match payments they received. At the start of the 1919–20 season Halifax players received £2 and 10 shillings for a win and one pound less for a loss. By the following season this had increased to £4 for a win and £2 and 10 shillings for a loss. In 1934 the club was paying £4 and 10 shillings for a home win and £5 for an away win. But this was at the higher end of the wage scale. Salford's 1929 payments of £3 for a win and £1 and 15 shillings for a loss were more representative of the average. In 1938 St Helens were paying £2 and 10 shillings for a home win, £3 and 5 shillings for a win in Yorkshire but just £1 and 10 shillings for a loss.[1] Dai Davies signed for Broughton Rangers in 1926 for £3 winning pay and £1 and 10 shillings for a loss. Lower down the scale, throughout the 1920s Featherstone paid just £1 and 10 shillings per win and, during one of the club's regular crises in the 1936–37 season, Leigh players' wages were cut to just £1 per match win, lose or draw. In 1936 the two new London sides paid £4 for a win or an away draw and £3 and 10 shillings for a loss or a home draw. But their players also received £3 and 10 shillings wages for working for the construction company of Sydney Parkes, the owner of the two clubs.[2] For successful players, there could also be perks from supporters in the local business community. In the 1915 Championship final Harold Wagstaff broke through the Leeds defence and was surprised to find forward Fred Longstaff charging up alongside him in support shouting 'suit, suit, suit'. Earlier that week Wagstaff had been promised a new suit by a local tailor if he scored a try. Longstaff complained to the tailor that it was always the backs who got the gifts, to which the tailor replied that Longstaff could also have one if he scored too.[3] It is also noteworthy that the practice of paying higher wages to backs than were paid to forwards appears to have died out by the 1920s, largely it seems in order to avoid the disputes which had arisen over differential pay rates in the pre-First World War era, when strikes by forwards for equal treatment were not unknown.

The more successful a side was, the more its players could expect to receive in bonus payments. During their 1921 run to the Challenge Cup final, Halifax players received £2 for their first round win, £7 for the second, £8 for the third and £9 for winning their semi-final. They missed out on a further £10 bonus by losing to Leigh in the final and had to settle for their standard losing pay of £2 and 10 shillings. Eighteen years later they did lift the cup and their players finally received a £10 winning bonus. For finishing in the League's top four in the 1933–34 season each player received a £6 bonus, but when they finished one position higher in the 1938–39 season the whole squad had to be satisfied with sharing £100 between them. But despite the concerns of club directors, there is little evidence that the sport suffered from wage inflation between the wars. Compared to soccer players of the time, it could be argued that their rugby league counterparts were underpaid; the Football League had set the maximum weekly wage at £8 plus £2 per match win bonus in 1922, a figure rarely equalled in the handling game.[4]

Of course, star players often received more than their less illustrious team-mates. Wakefield Trinity and Great Britain half-back Jonty Parkin asked for and received a fixed £10 per match when he moved to Hull KR in 1930. Australian Dave Brown was reportedly paid £6 per match by Warrington when he joined the club from Eastern Suburbs in Sydney in 1936. Welsh players coming north were also regularly paid higher wages than their native northern colleagues. When George Lewis signed for St Helens from Pontypool in 1922 he was paid £5 and 10 shillings for a win, £4 a draw and £3 a loss. St Helens star winger Alf Ellaby often received almost twice the amount of his team-mates. For a match against Wigan in March 1932 he received £9, £4 more than anyone else, and his match payments generally exceeded those of his colleagues by at least £3. In the 1929–30 season his losing pay was £7, considerably more than the winning pay of the next best paid member of the side. Even so, his match-winning abilities were such that few, if any, members of the side complained about this inequality.[5] Those players good enough to be selected to tour Australia and New Zealand gained more than recognition as players. One-third of the profits of tours were distributed among the players, resulting in bonuses on top of their playing wages of between £100 and £200, which in some cases would be more than a player's annual wage from his non-rugby job.[6]

Players also benefited from signing-on fees paid to them as an inducement to join a club, although these tended to be much lower for home-grown rugby league talent than for established Australian league or Welsh union players. In 1923 Featherstone's standard signing-on fee was just £2 for local players, although a young prodigy could expect £200–£300 from a leading club, roughly the same amount as a Welsh rugby union player.[7] The fact that there was no maximum signing-on fee in the game meant that those players talented enough to be courted by soccer and rugby league, such as England rugby union full-back Jim Brough or the young Gus Risman could benefit financially by choosing league over soccer, at least initially, as Brough explained in 1948 when describing why he had rejected Liverpool FC's approaches:

> What signing on fee would I receive? When told the maximum allowed by the FA was only £10, I immediately lost interest, for it compared very unfavourably with Swinton's recent offer of £350. Of course, there was a guaranteed benefit of £650 every five years, but that seemed a long way off when I could get this amount from a Rugby League club at once.[8]

The attraction of the signing-on fee was aptly described by Salford manager Lance Todd in 1939:

> the money has been paid over into a bank and a banking account opened with the amount paid, so that the player starts with that great and glorious feeling of 'having money in the bank' ... with application to his work and his football, the player's opportunity of getting away from what in many cases might mean a lifetime's grind, is great.[9]

Signing-on fees were both financially attractive and psychologically very persuasive. The standard procedure of the club official was to place a large amount of pound notes in front of the player they wished to sign. Few could resist. When Jim Brough met Swinton secretary Sam Jones in 1924, Jones put £350 in notes on the table in front of Brough and said if he signed there and then he could take it home with him. This was a scene repeated countless times across the north of England and in South Wales. Contrary to RFL regulations, signing-on fees were also covertly paid to players to induce them to transfer to a new club. Dai Davies' 1927 move from Broughton Rangers to Warrington was facilitated by a 'backhander' of £250 from his new club. The hard-headedness of clubs probably meant that the highest signing-on fees during this period were paid to established Australian rugby league players. Dave Brown received £1,000 for signing for Warrington, plus £6 per match and a job paying £3 per week. Vic Hey left Australia for Leeds for £1,400 and a job in an electrical store in 1937, a fee that at the time was higher than the record transfer fee.[10]

As well as the signing-on fee, Welsh, overseas and high profile northern signings were given jobs. In times of economic comfort, jobs on a club's ground staff were readily supplied but these became increasingly rare from the mid-1920s. Close relations with local companies often provided opportunities for players too. The brewers Greenall Whitley in St Helens regularly provided jobs for the club's players, enabling many of them to become pub landlords. The two Hull clubs' links with Hull Brewery also provided similar opportunities for their star players. The long-established connections of Huddersfield with the local textiles industry provided many of their major signings with office or sales jobs. Other than those who were employed in warehouses, few players continued in heavy manual work once they had signed. Indeed, for many Welsh rugby-playing miners who went north, not having to work down a pit was a crucial factor in switching to league. For some, the jobs offered the possibility of a small elevation in social status. When Roy Kinnear signed for Wigan he was given a job as a car salesman. Within six years of signing for Huddersfield in 1933, Australian Ray Markham had risen to become the assistant superintendent of Huddersfield Corporation's markets and fairs department. And those with the talent, commitment and sheer good fortune to play the game for ten years with the same club could also benefit from a testimonial season, in which money would be raised by supporters and the club would allocate a game from which the proceeds would go to the player. For the best-loved, this could be a significant amount. In 1920 Billy Batten, after Wagstaff probably the greatest player of his era, received £1,079 from grateful Hull supporters. Although lower in amount, even the £200 raised for stalwart Huddersfield forward Henry Tiffany in 1936 was substantial enough for him to be able to buy a house.[11] However, the reality was that very few players had a career of ten years in the game, let alone with a single club. An analysis of Wigan players' careers in the inter-war years suggests that less than 6 per cent of players lasted for a decade or more. Conversely, 54 per cent played for no more than two seasons.[12]

The vast majority of northern players therefore had neither the opportunities nor the wages to enable them to change their normal employment or social status. Indeed, much of the economic viability of clubs rested on the fact that the overwhelming majority of their players drew their primary income from outside of the game. At the RFL's 1924 Annual Conference it had been noted that clubs were now encouraging players to take jobs outside of the game so as not to become reliant on rugby. Although this was dressed up with the argument that it was morally unacceptable for a player to earn his living solely from rugby, it was very much an economic necessity. Apart from a handful of leading sides, no club could afford to pay its players when they were not playing, either through injury or during the off-season. Such was the importance attached to employment outside of the game that clause three of the RFL's standard player contract stipulated that 'the player shall have the right to refuse to play when called upon, if by his playing he would jeopardise his position at his ordinary work or be likely to lose such work'. Thus the NU's original belief that rugby should not be a full-time job survived.[13]

Although rugby league wages were unlikely to enable a player to live on them alone – unlike those of soccer players – they did offer a useful supplement to the weekly wages earned in their full-time occupation. The average weekly wage of a mineworker was slightly over £2 and 13 shillings in 1924, which fell to just over £2 and 7 shillings by 1935. A male textile worker could expect to take home an average of £2 and 16 shillings in 1938. Even a skilled worker would only average £3 and 15 shillings in 1936.[14] The addition of an extra two or three pounds a week, especially during the winter, could make a considerable difference to the living standards enjoyed by a working-class family. Not so fortunate were those players who were unemployed. Men registered with a club as a professional player were not entitled to claim unemployment benefit, regardless of whether they actually played for the side, putting those unemployed players who were not selected to play in the unenviable situation of having no source of income at all, although an appeal system later mitigated this.[15]

★

The importance of the rugby league wage in keeping players' heads above the waters of poverty during the Depression has been suggested as a reason for a perceived increase in violence in the game, as players sought to secure a winning bonus, whatever the cost. There appears to be some truth in this claim, as can be seen from Appendix 3. Although the number of players sent from the field of play by referees during matches declined during the interwar years, from ninety-nine in the 1920–21 season to seventy-three in the 1938–39 season, dismissals for violent acts, such as fighting and punching, increased both in number and as a percentage of total dismissible offences. In the 1920–21 season thirty players out of one hundred were sent off for these offences, rising to 54 per cent in 1930–31 and 67 per cent in 1938–39. There is other evidence which also suggests that violent play was becoming more common. In the 1928–29 season John Wilson was forced to warn clubs about increasingly rough play and the RFL's 1934 annual general meeting banned tackling with a stiffened arm extended above the shoulder, a 'stiff-arm tackle', which was used against the head of an opponent and, as the mover of the motion noted, 'invariably leads to a player being completely knocked out'. The stiff-arm tackle had reportedly been taken to Australia by the 1932 Lions tourists and the Australian game also became noticeably more violent during the Depression.[16] There is also reason to suspect that desperation to win matches led players to risk being sent off. In both 1920–21 and 1938–39 almost 40 per cent of players dismissed came from clubs that finished in the bottom eight places of the league. In contrast, the league champions in both 1930–31 and 1938–39 did not have a single player sent off during the season.[17]

Interestingly, this increase in violence was accompanied by a decline in dismissals for kicking and tripping, acts that rugby league culture increasingly felt to be dishonest and unmasculine. The use of the hand or the arm to attack an opponent was seen as fair because the recipient could see it coming and had a chance to respond, either in kind or by avoidance. In contrast, the use of the foot was seen as underhand and therefore more dangerous. It became an unwritten rule during the inter-war years that tripping an opponent meant an automatic sending-off for the perpetrator. The complex relationship of the game to violence was shaped by a wide variety of factors: the traditional English male view, common across all classes, that fisticuffs was a manly way of resolving differences; rugby league's self-image as an open and honest game, in contrast to the perceived hypocrisy of rugby union; a parallel belief, sometimes expressed in relation to soccer, that kicking was a sign of weakness and femininity; and the simple fact that in most cases a broken leg would stop a manual worker from working for a much longer period than a broken jaw.

Because of the close link between the worlds of work and rugby league, the life of the professional player was not wholly dominated by the sport. Most clubs trained only on Tuesday and Thursday nights, when running and sprint training were the main forms of exercise. Training regimes changed little during the period. Spiked sprinter's shoes were used by players as a means of improving their speed. Skipping and punch ball exercises were popular as a way of building strength and stamina. Most trainers recommended hot baths for two days following a match in order to relax and heal muscles, although Huddersfield trainer Arthur Bennett varied this by dousing his players with cold water after training. Deep breathing exercises were also felt to be important and many trainers prescribed a series of breathing exercises for players to follow at home. Excess, whether of food, alcohol or 'careless living' was to be avoided at all costs. In 1939, worried by poor results, Huddersfield banned its players from attending any social events on Thursday and Friday nights before matches. By and large, however, it was felt that the greatest aid to fitness was to be in regular, physically demanding work. 'When fit and playing every week, men following an everyday occupation require very little training', said Huddersfield's Douglas Clark in 1925.[18]

Although methods remained broadly the same, the organisation of training began to change in the 1930s as the concept of the coach began to emerge in the game. Trainers had been responsible only for the fitness of players, whereas, throughout most of the 1920s, tactics and stratagems for matches had been developed by senior players and communicated at team meetings. For example, Huddersfield's forwards had adopted specialist positions in the scrum, instead of the usual 'first up, first down' policy, after it had been suggested at a meeting by Douglas Clark. Well-regarded trainers such as Billy Bennett would still be much sought after by clubs; Bennett enjoyed great success with both Warrington and Halifax in the 1930s. But by the end of the decade, spurred in all likelihood by a number of prominent ex-players becoming trainers and the fame of soccer managers such as Herbert Chapman, it became increasingly common for one person to take charge of both off-field training and on-field tactics. Lance Todd, a star with the 1907 New Zealand tourists, became manager of Salford in 1928 and took responsibility for all aspects of the team, although even then captain Gus Risman took much of the responsibility for organising set moves. Harold Wagstaff became coach of Huddersfield in 1924, followed by a stint at Halifax in 1925, but found little success partly owing to the fact that both jobs coincided with mediocre periods for both clubs. His team-mate, Edgar Wrigley, also became a coach but, as with many who followed him, proved to be both unsuccessful and disliked by players because of his constant references to his own success as a player. In contrast, Halifax's Dai Rees helped raise his side to former glories in the early 1930s before moving to Bradford Northern in 1936, where he led them to an unprecedented three successive Wembley cup finals in the 1940s. Rees foreshadowed many later coaching innovations by studying opponents for weaknesses before matches and imposing a tight disciplinary regime over his players, a template that was subsequently used by many other coaches until Roy Francis revolutionised coaching methods in the 1950s.[19]

Most clubs also had an intricate list of rules that had to be followed by their players. Leeds' *Training Rules and Players Instructions* laid down seventeen detailed instructions. These included rules that injuries had to be reported to the club within forty-eight hours otherwise the player would not receive insurance payments; that match payments would only be made on the Thursday following a match; and that players who would not play for the reserve side would not be picked for the first team.[20] Nor did these restrictions cease when a player had retired from playing. Following the Football Association's precedent, former professionals were not allowed to sit on club or league committees unless granted dispensation by the RFL Council, a source of much annoyance to Harold Wagstaff whose attempts in 1929 to be elected to the Huddersfield committee were initially frustrated by the rule.

Aside from injury or the loss of form, the greatest danger facing a player was the inevitably unstable master–servant relationship between him and his club. The attitude of club directors towards players seems to have been amply demonstrated by Broughton Rangers' and RFL chairman Fred Kennedy, who when asked for a transfer by Welsh half-back Dai Davies turned him down with the words 'We made you. Don't you forget that'. Needless to say, Davies, whose talent was eclipsed only by his distrust of authority, got his way and negotiated his own transfer to Warrington.[21] A similar attitude was highlighted in 1934 when Leeds' Joe Thompson publicly complained about rough play by Hull in a match against the French side Villeneuve, who he was helping to coach at the time, and the RFL Council instructed John Wilson to write to Leeds about 'statements made by one of their servants'.[22] When financial constraints forced St Helens to offer Alf Ellaby for transfer, Ellaby discovered that he had been sold to Broughton Rangers behind his back:

> the Broughton Rangers secretary arrived and said 'We've signed you from St Helens'. I replied, 'Haven't you considered me?' He had a paint business and I said, 'You're not buying a gallon of paint! I'm not going to play for you. I couldn't play well in your team.'[23]

His obstinacy paid off and he eventually moved to Wigan, the club of his choice. At the extreme end of this managerial continuum was London rugby league promoter Sydney Parkes, who openly viewed the players he had signed as his own property, going so far as to demand that RFL pay him £100 to allow George Nepia to play for a Dominions representative side in Paris. For the majority of players who signed for his clubs, Parkes' was both their sporting employer and their day-job employer, having provided players with jobs on his building sites, making their lives doubly precarious. His players' contracts included a clause which stated that, aside from their wages for playing rugby, that they would be guaranteed

> regular suitable employment at £3.10.0 per week for at least two years as long as the aforesaid player does his work conscientiously and is a loyal and honest

servant of the club. (If, however, he knowingly breaks any rules of the Club, or if he refuses to work to the satisfaction of his foreman, this guarantee immediately becomes void).

In other words, to step out of line or fall out of favour either as a footballer or labourer would be to lose one's livelihood. In fact, the reality for many players who signed was somewhat worse. When they arrived in London they found that they were expected to work as self-employed contractors on Parkes' building sites and that the houses promised for their families had to be paid for out of their wages. Inevitably, most players eventually drifted back north or out of the game.[24]

Vic Hey probably reflected the attitude of most players to club directors when he argued that 'many club directors are not very well versed in rugby league football, perhaps never having played the game … they think that a footballer is a machine'.[25] It was this type of belief that animated the formation of the Northern Rugby Union Players' Union (NRUPU) in November 1920. The idea of a players' union had been mooted as early as 1909 and, according to Gwyn Thomas, one would have been formed following the strikes against wage cuts in November 1914 had it not been for the war. It appears that the idea was discussed among players during the 1920 tour to Australia and New Zealand and a few weeks after the tourists returned the new union was founded in Huddersfield under the chairmanship of Harold Wagstaff.[26] In contrast to most players' unions in other sports, and subsequent unions in rugby league, this one was remarkable in that it was initiated and led by players at the very top of the game. Huddersfield players formed the core of the leadership. As well as Wagstaff, the secretary/treasurer was Gwyn Thomas, with Johnny Rogers and Ben Gronow also playing leading roles. The presence of such star names meant that it could not be ignored by the NU and the increasing discontent among significant number of players – in January 1919 Oldham players had struck for higher match fees, in November of that year Halifax players threatened strike action and in 1920 both Salford and Barrow were hit by players' strikes over payments – ensured that its proposals had to be taken seriously.[27]

The increasing militancy of players reflected the dramatic rise in the level of industrial conflict in society as a whole. By the end of 1920 trade union membership stood at 8.3 million workers, more than twice the number in 1913, and 1921 saw over 85.8 million working days lost owing to industrial disputes, almost nine times the days lost in 1913 and over three times those lost in 1920.[28] Uncertainty about the future and fear of working-class unrest, behind which possibly lay the spectre of Bolshevism, affected many employers. The NU leadership was no different. This is not to say that the goals of the union were very militant. Its founding aims sought to promote friendship among players, redress grievances, modify the transfer system to the advantage of the players and guarantee players a benefit after six years continuous service with one club. Despite the moderation of these demands, the NU was unwilling to compromise in any significant way. Much of 1921 was spent skirmishing over recognition of the union by the NU. The latter objected to the words 'trades union' in the union's title and its intended affiliation to the General Federation of Trades Unions (GFTU). In September the NU met with the union's leaders to discuss their demand for £10 wages per player for all representative matches. As it had done over the questions of its name and the GFTU, the union compromised, agreeing to £7 for test matches, £5 for other internationals and £3 for county matches.[29]

Having been successful in its delaying tactics, by February 1922 the NU felt sufficiently confident to deal with the union's substantive demands relating to transfers and benefits. At a special meeting on the sixteenth it turned down the demand for guaranteed benefits or bonuses after six years' continuous service and rejected the key demands that the union had made for the reform of the transfer system. Although the meeting adopted the proposals for fixed transfer fees, rather than the auctioning of players, for clubs to circulate lists of players open to transfer and for the player to be allowed to decide to which club he transfered, it drew the line at transfer fees being based on a player's service and to him receiving a proportionate signing-on bonus that rose to 100 per cent of the transfer fee after six years at one club. And although the NU agreed to the setting up of a board of appeal to decide on disputed transfer fees, it did not allow a representative of the union to sit on the board.[30]

The union responded to the NU's intransigence by announcing that its members would not play against Halifax or Wakefield Trinity because some of their players were in arrears with their union subscriptions. The NU replied by announcing that if the union did not withdraw the threat it would no longer negotiate with it. Its bluff called, the union backed down but then found that the NU refused to meet it anyway. At its conference on 12 August, the union announced that it would call a strike at the beginning of the 1922–23 season if the NU did not re-open negotiations. Its position was further strengthened by threatened player strikes at Barrow, Halifax and Hull over match fees for the new season. Eventually the NU agreed to meet provided that the strike threat was withdrawn, which it was, and the two sides met on 27 September. By this time the union had reduced its demands to just two: that a transferred player receive 25 per cent of the fee and that the union be given a representative on the transfer board of appeal. Three weeks later the NU Council voted 12–10 in favour of the first proposal, although this remained a dead letter as it had to be ratified by a two-thirds majority at the annual general meeting, and unanimously for the second. Ironically, within weeks of the union been giving representation, it had effectively ceased to exist. Gwyn Thomas, the organisation's driving force, suddenly left the country, blaming it in later years on his 'irresponsibility', leaving the winding up of the union's affairs in the hands of Harold Wagstaff, who was increasingly suffering from the ill-health that would eventually lead to his early death in 1939.[31] But the union's demise was not primarily due to the loss of Thomas. It had failed to achieve any of its major aims and had been comprehensively out-manoeuvred by the NU leadership. Unlike in industry, it was also very easy for the NU's clubs to 'divide and rule' by offering players covert payments to undermine collective action. The union's formal dissolution in May 1923 simply underlined its fundamental weakness.

Strikes by players in the inter-war years were much less frequent than in the first two decades following 1895. After the three strikes of 1919–20, the only clubs whose players struck over wages in the inter-war period were Bramley in March 1926 and Leigh in February 1931. In 1929 Bradford players threatened to strike immediately before their match at Featherstone but the fixture eventually went ahead after the directors came up with the cash to make good the players' unpaid wages. The difficulties of going on strike in an economic depression were highlighted by the action of the Leigh players in 1931. Protesting against a cut in match payments, they refused to play in a league match against Bradford. The directors of the club consequently enlisted the reserve team to play, who promptly defeated the luckless visitors 8–0! But collective action was not the only option open to players in dispute with their club. Individual action was also available. After signing for Hull KR in 1923, South African forward George van Rooyen found that the promises made to him by the club about his employment and accommodation were so much hot air and refused to play. He appealed to the RFL, who found that the club had done its best to meet his demands but could not provide a house because of 'the great scarcity of housing accommodation in Hull'.[32] Other dissatisfied overseas players simply packed their bags and headed for home. In 1929 Australians Albert Carr and Sydney Harris abruptly left Huddersfield halfway through a three-year contract. That same year three New Zealanders who had signed for St Helens suddenly informed the club that they would not play in the forthcoming Challenge Cup semi-final unless their grievances about expenses and jobs were redressed. Eventually the town's mayor brokered a deal to enable them to play.[33]

Most English players did not have such room for manoeuvre; walking out on a club or threatening to do so would in all likelihood spell the end of their careers. The option was generally only available to the most gifted and resourceful players. When it came to self-preservation, few players had either the means or the self-confidence to emulate Jonty Parkin, either on or off the field. In 1930 Wakefield sought to reduce their players' wages but Parkin objected and was placed on the transfer list at £100. He paid the fee himself and entered into negotiations with various clubs, demanding a £300 signing-on fee and £8 per match, eventually joining Hull KR. No-one could follow his example because, concerned by the precedent he had set, the RFL promptly outlawed players paying their own transfer fees.

★

Parkin was a product of amateur rugby league in Sharlston, a mining village near Wakefield, and it was similar towns and villages in Cumberland, Lancashire and Yorkshire that supplied the vast majority of players in the professional rugby league. A flash of glamour was provided by the handful of Australian and New Zealanders who came to play in Britain. But a vital leavening agent was provided by the scores of Welsh players who journeyed north to receive the rewards their rugby talents deserved. Names like Jim Sullivan and Gus Risman, who both

went north from Cardiff as teenagers in the 1920s, light up the rugby league fir-
mament to this day, but there were also numerous less talented but equally committed players who made their careers, and often their homes, in the three counties of
rugby league. Indeed, it has been estimated that for every international Welsh rugby
union player who switched to rugby league, of which there were sixty-nine,
another twelve uncapped players would follow, and that around nine hundred players moved from South Wales to play rugby league between 1919 and 1939.[34] But
as Appendix 4 demonstrates, this is a huge over-estimate and the actual figure is less
than half of that. An analysis of the minutes of the Management Committee of the
Northern Rugby Football League, which governed the league competition and
authorised the registration of all professional players in the league, shows that 392
players from Wales were registered as professionals with northern clubs in this
period.[35] Pointing to differences between the economic structures of South Wales
and the Lancashire and Yorkshire rugby league regions, it has been argued that it
was the greater availability of jobs in the northern economy, especially during the
1930s, that attracted players.

In fact, a greater proportion of Welsh players moved north before the worst of
the economic depression took its toll of the Welsh industrial heartlands in the late
1920s and 1930s. If we exclude the 1919–20 season, when many players were still
being demobilised, and the aborted 1939–40 season, the average number of players
going north prior to the 1926 General Strike was slightly over twenty-five per
season, and only in the 1924–25 season did less than twenty players move. In contrast, an average of just under seventeen players went north each year in the thirteen
seasons between the General Strike and the outbreak of war. And in only four of
those seasons did twenty players or more join rugby league, still one season less than
in the much shorter 1920–26 period. But in general terms, rugby players represented
a statistically insignificant proportion of the 430,000 Welsh people who emigrated
in the inter-war years. Those without rugby skills to trade did not go to the north
of England but to the new engineering and services industries of the Midlands and
the South East. 'The accents [of those residents of Slough who turned out to
welcome a Hunger March from Wales in the 1930s] were so thick I thought that
we were in Rhondda, with this difference, instead of silent pits, massive factories
all lit up were in full go', reported a Welsh hunger marcher in 1936. Indeed, one
of the reasons given for the creation of professional league clubs in London in the
mid-1930s was the hope that they would attract support from Welsh migrants who
had moved to the South East in recent years.[36]

Although rugby league clubs paid great attention to talent-spotting in Wales –
in 1938 St Helens paid their Welsh scout £1 and 10 shillings per week, plus £1
travelling expenses, £7 and 10 shillings when a player he signed made fourteen
appearances and 5 per cent of any transfer fee – the reality was that Welsh rugby
union's loss of talent was a self-inflicted wound.[37] The vast majority of Welsh players
went north because they wanted to earn money for their rugby skills, in the same
way that their soccer- and cricket-playing compatriots could do. It was the WRU's
amateur ethos and refusal to pay them that forced players to leave Wales. The

experience of the young Jim Sullivan was typical and illustrates the problems which amateurism caused:

> I was serving my apprenticeship to a boiler-maker, and I seemed to have little prospect of securing another job ... the Cardiff club would have done anything to keep me, but when I broached the subject, officials said that I could have been given a job on the ground, but that would have meant me being classed as a professional.[38]

Nor was it only the lack of employment opportunities which influenced players' decisions. The risk of injury and subsequent hardship, given that rugby union insurance schemes were extremely tightly policed (indeed, many officials saw insurance as tantamount to professionalism), was also powerful incentive to take the money and go north.

Rugby league's appeal to Welsh rugby union players was simple. It offered them the opportunity to benefit financially from their footballing skills. Many were given jobs on a club's ground staff or with companies connected to club directors. For others, clubs guaranteed to make up a minimum wage if the job that was found for the player did not pay an adequate sum. Some were given the tenancy of a pub. Most importantly, hardly any were given the type of heavy industrial work they would do in Wales. And at least some Welsh players, such as Neath's Dai Davies who went north in 1926, saw the union game as a stage from which they could land a league contract.[39] In short, rugby league gave working-class Welsh rugby players the chance to escape from a life spent down the pit, in the steelworks or on the dole.

Of course, there were also limited opportunities to receive money or employment in Welsh rugby union. Before going north, Dai Davies was paid a flat rate of £3 per match regardless of the result when he played for Neath in 1926 and many others doubtless received similar payments.[40] And from the late 1920s, the relatively healthier economic fortunes of some English union clubs in the South West meant that it was possible for Welsh players to 'go South', and receive a job and perhaps surreptitious payments. But for the players who 'went south', there was a world of a difference between a professional contract in league and the sleight of hand of 'shamateurism'. The covert nature of the payments meant that they were unreliable and unenforceable, unlike those made under a contract, and could not provide any guarantees for the future. Nor could players receive large amounts such as bonuses or signing-on fees, which could lift them out of the daily routine. And, of course, the ever-present threat of denunciation and being banned from the sport underlined the insecurity of the paid rugby union player. Indeed, the damage that the WRU's adherence to amateurism did to their own game was exacerbated by the lifetime ban it imposed on players who played rugby league. This ruled out the prospect of anyone ever returning to Wales to play rugby union. A number of players who went north found themselves unsuited to the different demands that league placed on them, yet could not return to their original game – and of the sixty-nine internationals who switched to league, only twelve reached similar heights in their new sport by playing at Test match level. The WRU's amateurism forced it to turn its back on any player who wished to return to union.

In the one hundred years between the founding of the Northern Union in 1895 and rugby union's adoption of professionalism in 1995, the WRU only allowed one player back to play union. Glyn John signed for Leigh as a seventeen-year-old in 1949 but after two matches in league decided that he wanted to return to union and repaid his £450 signing-on fee. Because he was under eighteen when he signed for Leigh the WRU decided that the laws against professionalism did not apply to him and welcomed him back into the fold. In 1954 he played twice for Wales, much to the chagrin of the Scottish Rugby Union, whose protests that he was a professional forced the WRU to cave in and end his international career. Such was the way in which the WRU repaid his loyalty.

Although John was unique in being allowed to change his mind, a great number of those who went north never felt the need to reconsider their decision. Many Welshmen made their homes in the northern towns in which they had become stars and symbols of the community. Like many, Trevor Foster, whose career as a player and an official of Bradford was to last more than sixty-five years, was initially chary of succumbing to the blandishments of the league scout, Bradford Northern's managing director Harry Hornby, in 1938:

> Mr Hornby looked at me and said, 'Are you ready?' I said 'I'm not going.' He went red, white and blue and yellow and tore a strip off me. 'You've brought me all the way from Yorkshire and you're not going to sign – what's the big idea?' I said 'I want a Welsh cap.' He said 'Here. There's £100, £200, £300, £400. Go and buy six Welsh caps.'
>
> Just at that moment my elder sister, who lived a few doors away, came into the bar [of his parents' pub]. My mum said to her 'Trevor's not going.' She walked into the dining room where we were talking and she said 'Mum said you're not going.' I said 'No I'm not. I want a Welsh cap.' She said 'What if you break your leg next Saturday when you play Penarth?'
>
> I picked up the pen and signed. And the greatest thing I ever did was to turn [professional] and play for Bradford Northern.[41]

Chapter 4

Wembley and the road from Wigan Pier

On 24 October 1928 the RFL voted to stage the 1929 Challenge Cup final at Wembley stadium in London. Practically and symbolically, it was its most important decision since the momentous 1906 changes in the game's playing rules, creating both a deep-going tradition within the game and establishing rugby league in the national consciousness for the first time.

Despite the economic depredations of the 1920s, the leadership of the game approached the end of the decade with confidence. Indeed, one of the most pressing reasons for moving the final away from rugby league grounds was the increasing size of the crowds that the match was attracting. Over 41,000 people had crammed in Rochdale's Athletic Grounds in 1924, giving rise to serious concerns for spectator safety, and it was felt that nether Headingley nor Wigan's Central Park, the foremost league stadia, were large enough to cope. But the need for bigger ground capacity could have been satisfied by remaining in the north and using a soccer ground, as indeed happened in the late 1930s when Leeds United's Elland Road and Manchester City's Maine Road grounds were used for Championship finals. The choice of London, and in particular Wembley, to host the match was based on a desire to put rugby league on the national stage.[1]

Although the motion to take the final to London was proposed at the RFL's 1928 annual general meeting by John Leake, the first public call to move the game to the capital was made at a meeting of the Yorkshire Society of Referees in March 1928 by the Reverend Frank Chambers, the former referee and the senior game's last remaining link with rugby's muscular Christian origins.[2] A resident of Huddersfield, he pointed to the tremendous excitement that had been generated in the town by the soccer team's impending visit to Wembley for the 1928 FA Cup final, the first by a soccer side in a rugby league area, and argued that the RFL should take a leaf out of soccer's book. His comments struck a chord in the game, not least because the success of Herbert Chapman's Huddersfield Town in the very birthplace of rugby league had generated renewed fears about the round ball game encroaching once more on traditional rugby areas. Moving the Challenge Cup final to London would emulate, if not neutralise, the tremendous national appeal that the FA Cup final could have in the rugby towns and villages of Lancashire and Yorkshire.

Leake's motion was carried by thirteen votes to ten and the RFL discussed Wembley, Crystal Palace and White City as possible sites for the final. However, as was demonstrated by the closeness of the vote, the decision to move was not without opposition. The cost to supporters of travelling to London was raised, especially in a time of economic depression, and a number of clubs who had staged, or hoped to stage, the final opposed the move. Those who simply objected to the move south, a body of opinion that would only finally be extinguished in the 1960s, were given encouragement in October when Wigan offered to stage the final in opposition to London. Despite this, the RFL opened negotiations with Wembley and Crystal Palace. As ever, the clinching argument against those who doubted the move south was money. The 1928 tourists to Australasia returned home in September with a profit of £10,607 and bolstered by such a healthy bank balance, any financial risk to the game incurred by playing in London was minimised. On 17 October RFL chairman Fred Kennedy and secretary John Wilson were delegated to visit London and return with a recommendation. After inspecting both stadia, including climbing to the top of Wembley's twin towers to ensure that an adequate view would be available to all spectators, Kennedy and Wilson returned north united in their decision. The 1929 Challenge Cup final would be played at Wembley.[3]

Although it was later reported that the choice of Wembley was made because their terms of 15 per cent of the net gate receipts were more favourable than those of Crystal Palace, who allegedly asked for a third of the gate receipts, there were broader reasons for the RFL's selection.[4] The success of the FA Cup final since it moved to Wembley in 1923 was quite obviously something that the RFL sought for itself. But it was also attracted by the national symbolism of Wembley. As Bolton Wanderers, Newcastle United, Sheffield United and Blackburn Rovers had demonstrated in winning the FA Cup at its new home, Wembley was an arena in which northern towns and cities could gain national prominence and significance beyond their immediate regions. Moreover, Wembley's status as a symbol of the British Empire gave its appeal an added resonance. Originally built to house the 1924 British Empire Exhibition and conceived as a showcase for the wonders of the Empire, it owed much to the enthusiasm of the Prince of Wales, the future Edward VIII, who kick-started the project at the 1921 Imperial Conference of Dominions' prime ministers by announcing that the exhibition would house a 'great national sports ground', which the FA was considering as the home of the Cup Final. The exhibition lost around £10 million and the stadium itself was initially viewed as a white elephant, but its importance for soccer gave it a central place in the national sporting consciousness. This had been cemented by the first game held there: the 1923 'White Horse' FA Cup Final with its mythology of the 200,000 crowd allegedly controlled by a single policeman on a white horse – the perfect representation of the peaceful English crowd and its respect for authority in contrast to continental social upheaval.[5]

Wembley's owner, Arthur Elvin, was keen to attract the RFL to Wembley and appears to have viewed his terms of 15 per cent of the gate as a loss leader. The month after the Challenge Cup final he told the RFL that in future his terms would be 25 per cent of any other rugby league matches played at the stadium.[6] For its part, the RFL was determined to use the opportunity 'to make [the Cup Final] an annual event in the sporting calendar' and made strenuous efforts to publicise the game in the south and organise its supporters in the north. Even before the stadium had been selected the RFL circularised all clubs encouraging them to publicise the match and arrange savings clubs to enable supporters to go to London. Posters and leaflets were produced for clubs to distribute and speakers were made available for those who wanted to organise public meetings. For the south, advertising in local newspapers was arranged and, perhaps somewhat provocatively, 15,000 leaflets produced for distribution at England's games against Wales and Ireland at Twickenham. To assure the widest appeal the minimum admission cost was set at two shillings, while the best seats were priced at ten shillings and sixpence. All other matches were cancelled on Cup Final day so that there could be no conflicting attractions.[7]

In many ways the RFL was seeking to revive the pre-split traditions of northern rugby, when savings clubs were set up by supporters to save for day trips to the Yorkshire Cup final or, although much less frequently, for three- or four-day tours to London or South Wales at Christmas or Easter. The sense of occasion and adventure in these events had gradually faded as travelling across the north to important matches became commonplace – certainly by the 1920s the relative ease of train or coach travel meant that a trip to Leeds or Wigan for a final was no longer the journey it had once been. But a trip to London was different. As Ernest Cawthorne wrote in the match programme for the 1929 Cup Final 'thousands of Northern people who in their highest flights of fancy have only dreamt of a visit have made the metropolis their Mecca today'.[8] For that first final an estimated 20,000 northerners took the trip south to see a match that symbolised the state of the sport in 1929. The cosmopolitan all-stars of Wigan, which included five Welshmen, two New Zealanders, a Scot and just three Lancastrians, outshone a hardworking no-frills Dewsbury side, which contained just one player not born in Yorkshire, by 13 points to 2.[9] Despite not being a memorable game, the final was acclaimed as a successful experiment. It generated record receipts and the crowd of 41,500 failed by just 331 people to set a new attendance record.

The journey to the match set a pattern which was to last intact for over half a century. Trains and buses, or charabancs, left the two towns early on the Saturday morning filled with supporters decked out in their team's colours. This was not just confined to supporters of the two finalists; even in the first year the tradition was established for towns and villages in rugby league areas to organise trips to the final. As the final grew in significance, it became increasingly common for employers to allow their employees time off work to go to Wembley – in 1939 Pratt's Engineering in Halifax not only gave their workers the Saturday off to go to the match but also paid the fares for 200 of them, thus helping to swell the ranks of Halifax supporters to 8,000.[10] A further tradition was begun in 1934 when 1,500 schoolboys made the trip south to watch the Hunslet versus Widnes final, thanks to the RFL's decision to allow schoolboys into the match for free. By the end of the decade over 5,000 were going to Wembley and, despite the subsequent withdrawal of free entry, school trips from across the north became a permanent feature of the Cup Final.[11] For the first few years, most towns had at least one hardy soul who would walk all the way to Wembley, or at least claim to have walked all the way. On arrival in London, for the first few years at least, the practice was for passengers to disembark in the centre of London to go sightseeing before making their way to the stadium. A Huddersfield supporter described his trip to see the 1933 final:

> Upon arrival in London the parties split up into their various groups and hurried off in diverse directions, as the fancy took them, each anxious to see the part of London they planned to see, and very quickly the 'Claret and Gold' [Huddersfield's colours] was to be seen all over the City. ... [I went on] a stroll through the streets of the City to the 'hub of the universe', Piccadilly, meeting from time to time groups of rival supporters engaging in good humoured chaff and wisecracks, a quick lunch and then to Wembley.[12]

By the mid-1930s the parades of crowds of supporters through the city on their way to Wembley had begun to wane. As early as 1934 the *Yorkshire Evening Post* bemoaned the fact that organised coach trips had taken much of the spontaneity out of the Wembley excursion: 'Now the trippers are shepherded into motor coaches and whisked away out of sight, and the parade which used to be made at Trafalgar Square and such places, with bells ringing and rattles sounding, is a thing of the past.'[13] Ironically, many of these excursions were organised by the same local newspapers whose reporters disliked the regimented organisation of Cup Final day. Some groups of supporters simply ignored the opportunity to sample London's attractions and looked instead for that which most resembled home. The sociologists who studied Featherstone in the 1950s were amazed to find that many of the club's supporters who travelled down for the 1953 Cup Final sought out those pubs that most resembled those in Featherstone and 'instead of avoiding them, insisted on spending the evening in them'.[14]

As Cawthorne recognised in the 1929 programme, for the majority of northerners at the match it was the first time they had visited London.[15] Indeed, the opportunity to see the capital became one of the biggest features of the many advertisements for trips to the Cup Final throughout the 1930s and 1940s. 'Do you want to see the sights of London? Do you want to see the Rugby League Cup Final? Do you want the trip of a lifetime?' asked a leaflet issued by Wakefield Trinity to advertise their chartered train to Wembley in 1938. The fact that the final was not always sold out meant that, unlike the FA Cup Final, there was also ample opportunity for families to make the trip and for supporters to visit Wembley every year, regardless of which teams were playing, adding to its carnival-like qualities.

For those left behind, the BBC's radio broadcast of the match would be played in shops and sometimes over loudspeakers at the grounds of the participating teams, although in 1934 the BBC tried to curb these unauthorised broadcasts and issued a warning that their match commentary was copyright and could not be played in public places.[16]

The match itself continued the carnivalesque nature of the day. Community singing, accompanied by a military band, preceded the match and featured such regional songs as *My Girl's a Yorkshire Girl, On Ilkley Moor Baht 'at,* and *She's a Lassie from Lancashire,* as well as popular tunes of the day and a smattering of songs from the First World War, such as *Tipperary* and *Pack Up Your Troubles,* as if to emphasise the sense of regional identity within a national framework. If the final happened to feature teams from both sides of the Pennines, neutral supporters would tend to cheer for the side from their county, encouraged by informal singing competitions between spectators from the two counties. The build-up to the kick-off often saw one or two spectators attempt to climb the goalposts and leave their club colours there, the first successful attempt being that of Widnes supporter Abe Duffy in 1930, who amazingly placed his black and white cap at the top of one of the posts.[17] This folk tradition lasted until the 1970s when, fearful of hooliganism, the police ceased to take such a benevolent view of spectators encroaching on the playing area. Although it was estimated that a majority of the spectators at the first Wembley final were new to the game, by the late 1930s the evangelical aspect of the final had almost completely faded away as it became seen as an almost exclusively northern day out. In 1948 the *Manchester Guardian* noted that 'the crowd which came to London for the Rugby League Cup Final yesterday was much more completely Northern than for the Association Cup Final [between Manchester United and Blackpool] a week ago'. By 1951 the notes that explained the difference between union and league rules had been dropped from the match-day programme completely.[18] As future RFL vice-chairman Tom Ashcroft explained, winning new adherents was not the central goal of staging the final at Wembley:

> The playing of our Cup Final in London has never been looked upon as propaganda in the usual sense of the term but rather to give our game a standing of national importance. ... I believe we are living down the hostility and prejudice which in certain quarters operated against us and feel sure we shall win through if we insist on the game being kept clean and free from all objectionable practices.[19]

The fact that the day out at Wembley was a largely self-contained northern event became one of its most appealing features. For many of those who visited the stadium, the combination of big-match atmosphere, the celebration of northernness and the opportunity to demonstrate the superiority of their code of football helped to make it one of the most memorable days of their lives, as summed up by a dialect poem from Huddersfield, whose colours were claret and gold, in 1935:

By Gum, Fowk, it's champion. Yar Claret and Gold assembly,
We've gotten into t'final, we're gooin ageean to Wembly.
Tha remembers what Ah telled thi, tha knows just what Ah sed,
If ivver Ah got chance ageean, ther's nubdy goas instead.

Ah've booked a seat on t'chara, where t'brass cums from, don't ask,
For if tha tries ta foind it 'aat, tha's got a bonny task.
An t'cup: all t'fowks are asking, does ta think we shall win?
Ah've gate a sooart o' notion we're baan ta taik it in.

...

So lads, let's rally raand em, all on us do ther share,
When yo go up ta Wembly, just let em know yo're there.
An let t'fowk know in London, dahn in yon Wembly fold,
Ther's one teeam con play football, an that's the Claret an Gold.[20]

This use of dialect, especially in newspaper reports, underwent a revival following the move to Wembley. In this poem it had the purpose of asserting difference but it could also be used to patronise too, even by newspapers based in the north. Writing about Hunslet supporters trip to the 1934 Cup Final, the Leeds-based *Yorkshire Evening Post* reported their speech in dialect ('Ere Robbie, does ta knaw, I wer up at quarter ta fower this mornin'') yet unsurprisingly reported the speech of Lord Derby at the final itself in plain English, despite the fact that Derby's Wellington College and Grenadier Guards accent would have been as alien to its readers as the Hunslet accent was to Londoners.[21]

Using dialect to indicate northern speech was one of the ways in which reports and reminiscences of Wembley trips highlighted the contrast between the north and the south. The word 'invasion' was used frequently by both sides, although this never suggested any hostility or opposition to the status quo.[22] Arriving in London for the 1933 final, one supporter noticed 'a wonderful display of tulips, lovely blooms on long straight stems, standing up proudly like Guards on parade, as if anxious to impress these Northerners'.[23] Very often the journey was described as a 'pilgrimage'. This was partly due to the laziness of sporting vernacular and the ease with which religious and military imagery was used to describe sport, but it also captured something of the spirit with which many supporters travelled to the Empire's capital. Just as the RFL saw the Cup Final as a way to establish rugby league's place in the national sporting pantheon, so too did the narratives of Wembley trips seek to stress an integrative, unifying message. This was the northern-ness of Gracie Fields, distinct and with its own traditions, accents and modes of behaviour, yet symbolising a national unity of classes in which the northern working classes were afforded proper recognition.[24]

Of course, there was also often a mistrust and suspicion of London, and especially of the 'wide-boys' who ran stalls and shops in the tourists areas of Carnaby Street or Covent Garden. In rugby league folklore there are many, often apocryphal, anecdotes about trusting northerners being fraudulently parted from their money or being sold goods that were not quite what they seemed. Stanley Holloway's monologue of the 1930s, *The Beefeater*, in which a cockney guide at the Tower of London adopts a Yorkshire accent to fool tourists from the north, the 'gumps', neatly encapsulates the fears of some of the northern visitors to London. Such was the popularity in the north of Holloway's routines, in which the London-born actor imitated a broad Lancashire accent, that he may have helped to magnify the suspicions of the Wembley-bound travellers.[25]

But these did not amount to overt social or political concerns. In contrast to the Hunger Marchers who marched to London from the north in the early 1930s, rugby league crowds were not there because they wanted to challenge the established order but because they wanted to be accepted in that order. The hours before the match were spent visiting such national landmarks as Trafalgar Square and the Tower of London. Some of the most popular trips were tours of Parliament organised by the local MPs of the cup final teams (although these were not necessarily as popular with the players: St Helens blamed their 1930 loss to Widnes on the fact that their trip to the mother of parliaments had lasted until 1.30am on the morning of the match).[26] In the early years it was also part of the ritual for the teams to place a wreath at the Cenotaph before the match, although this seems to have died out in the 1930s. Above all, it was the stadium itself that embodied national unity:

> The Wembley Stadium with its great sense of spaciousness, its flags, its military bands, its touch of pageantry, all combine to lift a game played there on to a plane out of the ordinary. That is especially the case when the match is played under the patronage of Royalty [the Prince of Wales presented the cup in 1935] – for the hush that suddenly falls upon a cheering multitude, who rise as one, in salute of the Royal representatives, and then the solemnity of the National Anthem, must always be a thrilling moment and one that adds dignity and status to the event.[27]

Indeed, throughout the 1930s the most commonly voiced complaint, other than the defeat of one's team, was the failure of the King to attend the Cup Final. 'This continued absence of Royal patronage to the Rugby League game is very disheartening', wrote a 'rugby league supporter and a loyal subject' in 1938. 'His presence would be a great joy to his loyal subjects in Lancashire and Yorkshire and followers of rugby league football.'[28] Although the RFL had invited George V, a regular visitor to Twickenham, to attend the 1929 Final he did not accept the invitation until 1933. Bad weather on the day led to his cancellation and replacement by the Prince of Wales. He also cancelled the following year.[29] It was not until 1948 that a reigning monarch finally visited the final when George VI saw Wigan defeat Bradford 8–3.

★

The occasion did not finish at the end of the match's eighty minutes. There was the journey back, almost an event in itself as the returnees would invariably disembark with tales of misfortune and stranded companions, as if to emphasise the adventure of the trip. Most importantly, there was the return of the victorious team. Before the ease of coach travel allowed the sides to return on the Sunday, the triumphant team would return on the Monday evening to be welcomed by tens of thousands of the town's inhabitants. The rituals surrounding the returning victors had been established in competitions such as the Yorkshire Cup in the 1880s and were observed before the final was moved south. But now the drama was heightened both by the long journey north and the enhanced national importance of the cup. Crowds would gather at the railway station to greet the team, which would be welcomed by local dignitaries, and then the cup would be paraded on an open-top bus through the town. The more imaginative local authorities would provide lights and fireworks. When Halifax returned home in 1931 after defeating York, twenty-two fog detonators, one for every point scored, were ignited as the train pulled into the station.[30] The journey from the station to the ground itself resembled a carnival parade, as Richard Hoggart recalled:

> I remember Hunslet rugby team bringing the Cup home from Wembley years ago [1934], coming down from the City Station into the heart of the district on top of a charabanc. They went from pub to pub in all the neighbourhood's main streets, with free drinks at every point, followed by crowds of lads prepared to risk staying out hours after their bedtime for the excitement of seeing their local champions.[31]

The victorious 1952 Workington Town team left their train at Scotch Corner in North Yorkshire and travelled home through Cumberland by coach. 'Every village in Cumberland turned out to cheer us home. When we reached Workington you could not get near the Town Hall, where the Mayor gave us a civic reception', remembered the team's captain and coach Gus Risman.[32] As if to underline the link between a town's sporting and business success, winning sides were also sometimes presented with gifts from local businessmen. In 1931 each member of the Halifax team received a tin of Mackintosh toffee, a pipe from a local tobacconist and photograph album from the *Halifax Courier*. The fact that the victorious team often contained few, if any, natives of the town, was not allowed to impinge on the celebrations.

Despite the game priding itself on its local links, it was in fact rare for sides to contain a majority of locally born players. In the 1930 and 1937 finals Widnes fielded twelve locally born players, while in 1934 all of the Widnes and nine of the Hunslet players were home-born. But these sides were unusual. The 1939 Halifax cup-winning side had just a single local player, one more than their opponents, Salford. Even Keighley, the epitome of the struggling small-town team, could not muster a single home-grown player for their 1937 Wembley appearance. The reality was that the lack of players from outside the town generally indicated a club's poverty and inability to attract star players, although Widnes were probably unique in having a 'home-grown' player recruitment policy. Indeed, it was seen as a sign of vitality that a club could bring in players from outside. There was never any hint that a team's success had been tarnished by using imported players. In fact, the opposite may have been the case. Wigan chairman Harry Lowe put up a stout defence for his club's importation policy in 1926: 'we have seven Welshmen, three South Africans, one Cumbrian, one player from the Manchester district and only one local', going on to say that without imported players, 'Wigan would become a second or third rate side'.[33]

Although the crowd at the first Wembley final of 41,500 was surpassed only once before 1936, the prominence that being staged in London gave to the Challenge Cup Final meant that the RFL decided almost immediately to repeat the experiment for the 1930 final. The following season a five-year agreement was reached with Wembley, although the 1932 Cup Final had to be played at Wigan because Wembley, which always gave priority to soccer, could not provide the traditional first Saturday in May owing to the England versus Scotland international. The RFL was helped in its decision by the fact that London-based finals were, with the exception of the 1930 final, far more profitable than those that had been held in the north. At its 1930 annual general meeting only one person spoke against Wembley and, although Warrington had argued that Blackpool should be investigated as a possible cup final venue in 1937, there was little serious opposition in the 1930s. In the main this was because of the prominence that the Wembley final had brought to the sport; to move back would have been seen as a sign of weakness. 'It would indicate that the Northerner was losing his grit', argued Oldham's James Parkinson.[34]

More concerted opposition to Wembley developed after the Second World War, led by Stanley Chadwick, a supporter of the Independent Labour Party, who edited the *Rugby League Review*. Chadwick argued that it was the 'birthright' of rugby league supporters that the final should be held in the north:

> The plain truth is that for many Southerners, the RL Challenge Cup Final has no longer any attraction. … The novelty of the thirteen-a-side code has now worn thin in the South and if future Finals are played at Wembley it will be the fans from the North who will have to pack the stadium. And how much longer are these people going to go to the trouble and expense of undertaking such a long journey to watch a match at which the only thrill is the marching of the massed bands?[35]

His views were given added weight by the development of Bradford's Odsal Stadium, opened by the club in 1934, whose huge capacity had earned it the title of the 'Wembley of the North', especially after it attracted over 64,000 spectators to the Halifax versus Leeds Challenge Cup semi-final in 1939. But the core of Chadwick's argument was his belief that rugby league had no need to seek national recognition by playing at the national stadium. His argument was that it was 'the South' that had to change and pay respect to the north and its culture. 'If Londoners want rugby league football they must henceforth display the same enthusiasm as followers in the North', he wrote in 1949. Like many others in the game, he believed that rugby league was a cultural expression of the 'true England' that was to be found in the working people of the industrial north. But unlike most who held that view he saw no reason for the sport to court national opinion. The fact that rugby league could only achieve national recognition by playing its most important match in London, hundreds of miles from the homes of its supporters, was to him yet another example of the way in which the contribution of northerners to British society was denied by the south. 'However much the desire to win adherents in the South,' he argued, 'rugby league football depends for support on the great mass of working men and women in the industrial North, whose devotion to the needs of the nation has done so much to win new life and hope for our trade in world markets.'[36] He took a similarly dim view of attempts to establish professional clubs outside of the north, arguing that towns outside the north must prove their commitment to the sport before being allowed into the League.

Although Chadwick's hostility to the expansion of rugby league was an important strand of opinion among supporters and administrators, the playing of the Cup Final at Wembley was never seriously challenged. From a financial point of view, a London cup final was far more lucrative for the RFL. The 1932 final, played at Wigan, recorded the smallest profit since the 1920 final, and even the 1954 replayed final at Odsal, when 102,569 people had crushed into the municipal amphitheatre, brought in less money than the previous seven finals. Just as importantly, it was clear that the Wembley ritual was immensely popular with supporters. Like Lancashire Wakes Weeks and visits to the seaside at August Bank Holiday, the trip to Wembley had become part of the annual rhythm of life in rugby league areas. Gus Risman, writing about Workington Town's victorious first visit to the Cup Final in 1952, pointed out that 'many people save up all the year round for the annual pilgrimage to Wembley, and they prefer to have the final played on the premier sporting arena in the country rather than on one of our grounds in the north,' and that the enthusiasm for the match was such that 'it is said that radio and television sets were mortgaged to raise money for the trip'.[37] That the Challenge Cup final was usually the only major match to be played outside the north – only five international games were played in London between 1930 and 1989 – heightened the importance of Wembley as a unique event. Symbolically, the league championship final was always played in the north, which meant that the real business of the season was always decided in the sport's heartland. Indeed, in 1938, 1939, 1946 and 1960 the championship final actually attracted bigger crowds than the Wembley Cup Final.

But if the success of Wembley stirred strong and sometimes conflicting emotions, there could be no doubting its success. For one of the few times in its existence, the RFL had pleased both the vast majority of the game's supporters and put the game in the national spotlight, at least for one day in the year.

★

The success of the Cup Final at Wembley revivified the debate about the expansion of rugby league. As early as November 1921 the RFL Council held a detailed discussion on the prospects for the spread of the game to other parts of Britain, primarily London, the Midlands and South Wales. Before the First World War, the Northern Union had staged international matches in London, Bristol, Birmingham, Newcastle and even Glasgow but, as J. B. Cooke noted at the Council meeting, 'without satisfactory results'. The Council rejected a proposal to employ a press officer and a 'representative to follow-up propaganda games', opting instead for a policy of wait and see: 'any distant venture ... should be considered whenever brought to notice, and dealt with on its merits'.[38] Unsurprisingly, this passive stance came under fire from those sections of the game who favoured a more aggressive policy. 'The Rugby League today is much too parochial. Expansion is essential', declared Fred Marsh, 'Forward' of the *Athletic News* in 1923.[39] In fact, rugby league did expand in the 1920s. Four junior clubs joined the top flight of the game – St Helens Recreation joined in 1919, Featherstone Rovers in 1921, Wigan Highfield in 1922 and Castleford in 1926 – but in the lexicon of the game 'expansion' was merely a contraction of the phrase 'geographical expansion'. The issue was regularly discussed at conferences and annual general meetings over the next two decades. Yet the RFL, dominated by clubs for whom the potential prestige of national expansion could never outweigh the actual pounds, shillings and pence of regional competition, was unable to develop any plan to break out of its heartlands.

When it came to the expansion of the game the Mohammed of the RFL simply waited for the mountain of public opinion to see the light and come to it. As well as being based on a reluctance to speculate to accumulate, it was also rooted in a sense of northern superiority that had no use for the rest of the world. A. J. P. Taylor recalled that his Victorian Manchester grandfather 'felt that London was the enemy; it represented everything he disapproved of and which he supposed, perhaps wrongly, that Manchester had defeated', an attitude of insular self-belief that many in rugby league perpetuated into the twentieth century, often to Gradgrind-esque extremes. The *Rugby League Review* wrote without a trace of irony in February 1948:

> There is much which requires to be done nearer home. Unfortunately it will not bring banner headlines or the spotlight of personal publicity. Rather will it involve hard toil, often without even thanks, in the dreary industrial towns of the North of England.[40]

Indeed, it was only after pressure from Australia that the Northern Union changed its name to the Rugby Football League in 1922.

Expansion was also made more difficult by the RFL's deep-seated unwillingness to come into direct conflict with the rugby union authorities. At a 1910 exhibition game in Plymouth J. W. Wood stressed that there were no intentions of following it up with 'active propaganda' and in 1931 John Wilson reiterated this stance in relation to the crisis in French rugby union: 'The Rugby League does not take the view that malcontents in the Rugby Union anywhere should be welcomed merely for the sake of it ... the first step would have to be made by the French themselves.'[41] Although there was an element of dissimulation in this, it also reflected a deferential view that the game should do nothing to undermine its respectability or the limited social standing that it had gained for itself. If the RFL were seen to be poaching union clubs it would allow rugby union to portray it as an aggressive threat to the status quo, whereas in fact the RFL saw itself as very much part of the status quo in its own social sphere.

But, as was demonstrated by the move to Wembley, these attitudes were not always entirely uniform or consistent. The lure of national recognition was appealing to ambitious clubs and the game itself attracted the interest of a number of commercial entrepreneurs in the 1920s and 1930s. South Wales in particular was the obvious region into which the game could expand. Not only was there a constant stream of Welsh players moving to the north but the relaxing of the rugby union's ban on league players during the First World War meant that many in Wales saw what they were missing. The threat from soccer to Welsh rugby union – in 1922 there were twenty-three professional soccer clubs in South Wales, five of them in the Football League and Cardiff City, the most successful, finished second in Division One in 1924, reached the 1925 FA Cup Final and carried the cup home in 1927 – also gave Welsh union clubs cause for concern about the future.[42] Accordingly, the first moves to establish league in Wales after the war came not from the RFL but from inside Welsh rugby union itself. In December 1920 Thomas Rees of Ebbw Vale RFC wrote to the Northern Union asking for an assurance that his club 'would be received into membership of the Union and League in the event of its members making a declaration in favour of the NU code' and asking that his overture be kept secret. Not for the last time, the game's leaders demonstrated their ability to never miss an opportunity to miss an opportunity by telling Rees that they could not guarantee the confidentiality of his approach because they were obliged to inform their member clubs! Needless to say, that signalled the end of Ebbw Vale's tentative courtship.[43]

Nevertheless, it did not dampen Welsh interest in league, as was demonstrated by the 11,000 who turned out twelve months later to see the Australian tourists narrowly defeat the Welsh rugby league side 21–16 at Pontypridd's Taff Vale Park. The prospects looked even brighter in 1926 when 23,000 saw England overcome the Welsh 30–22. Within weeks of the latter match a consortium of local businessmen had formed a club and had been accepted into membership of the RFL. In sporting terms the circumstances of Pontypridd RLFC's formation could not have been more propitious. The local union team was not only struggling on the pitch but was also being investigated by WRU for alleged extremism (the club secretary was a well-known member of the Miners' Federation) and the town's soccer team, which used the Taff Vale ground, had collapsed after finishing second to last in the Welsh section of the Southern League. But the reality was that the economic conditions could hardly have been worse. As the price of coal collapsed in the 1920s it had sucked the life out the South Wales economy; when the Pontypridd club played its first game in September 1926 miners in Wales and across Britain had been locked out by the mine-owners since 1 May and would not return to work for another two months. John Leake, the moving force behind the club, admitted the severity of the situation at the beginning of November: 'at the present time, owing to 80 per cent of the surrounding population being unemployed, the gates being taken at Taff Vale Park were not quite meeting the expenses of the home and away matches'.[44] This was something of an understatement. In January 1927 the club was forced to ask the RFL for a loan of £300 and by the end of the season it was attempting to renegotiate its terms with Taff Vale Park's owners. On 25 October, having played just eight matches of the new season, the club's owners admitted defeat and resigned from the league, owing £1,393, £700 of which had been loaned to them by the RFL. Unlike those that came after it, however, the Pontypridd venture did have grassroots support. In 1929 eight Welsh clubs applied for inclusion in that season's Challenge Cup and the Pontypridd and District Amateur Rugby League continued until 1930, when the WRU decreed an amnesty for its 'professionalised' players.

Poorer but undeterred, two months later the RFL sought to secure its shaky bridgehead in Wales by voting to accept a team from Cardiff into the league for the start of the 1928–29 season. Marking the start of a promising yet ultimately unfulfilling relationship with greyhound racing, the Cardiff venture was to be situated at the city's new greyhound stadium.[45] The venture folded before a team had even been assembled but Cardiff's league place was filled by a new club in Carlisle, formed by a local greyhound racing company. Fatally hamstrung by the admission of Carlisle United to the Football League in the same season, the club's lifespan barely exceeded that of a mayfly, collapsing after only ten games.[46]

Despite these failures, the attraction of rugby league to greyhound-racing promoters continued to grow. Part of a boom in new, technology-based sports, which also included speedway and ice hockey, greyhound racing had been introduced to Britain in 1926 and had grown at an exponential rate, attracting over five and a half million spectators in its first full season of operation in 1927. By 1932 more than twenty million people were watching it annually. To cover the costs of building or hiring stadia, promoters sought to use other sports to attract spectators. The FA actively discouraged its clubs from staging greyhound racing and the RFU explicitly forbade its members from doing so, which left rugby league as the only mass spectator sport with which the Greyhound Racing Association (GRA) could deal.[47] In 1929 the GRA approached the RFL about the possibility of forming clubs at various greyhound stadia around England. On the morning of first Wembley cup final a delegation from the RFL had met with Brigadier General A. C. Critchley to discuss the formation of a rugby league club in London. Critchley had worked on the government's strike-breaking 'British Gazette' newspaper during the General Strike in 1926 but was now the central figure in the GRA, which owned the White City Greyhound Company, and was seeking an attraction to bring crowds to the White City stadium when there was no racing.[48]

In 1932 Critchley eventually bought the ailing Wigan Highfield club, rechristened it London Highfield and announced that from the start of the 1933–34 season it would play its home games on a Wednesday night under floodlights at

White City.[49] Despite crowds averaging 6,000 and a strong team, which finished fourteenth in the league, the club haemorrhaged cash. Critchley claimed to have lost £8,000 and the team decamped to Liverpool, where it was taken over by the local Electric Hare Greyhound Company.[50] But London continued to beckon. Six months after the demise of Highfield, a letter arrived at the RFL from Sydney E. Parkes, managing director of Modern Homes and Estates Ltd and owner of Wandsworth Greyhound Stadium. He did not beat around the bush: 'I am interested in forming a Rugby League for the South. I have grounds for two teams in London. Would you please send me a book of your rules and advise me what your views are respecting inter-team matches, i.e. London and Counties.'[51] A few weeks later, in February 1935, the *Daily Mirror* revealed that Parkes planned to launch six sides in London with the aim of establishing a southern section of the Rugby League. One of the reasons for his confidence was a belief that migrants from the north would support the game. As another supporter in London noted:

> With the transference of workers to the South during the last few years, many of whom are rugby league enthusiasts, I think that there has never been so good a chance of establishing a rugby league club as now. At Dagenham alone there are now working hundreds of former supporters of the Salford club.[52]

Eventually two sides were formed and accepted by the RFL for the opening of the 1935–36 season: Acton & Willesden and Streatham & Mitcham, based at new stadia at Park Royal and Mitcham.[53] Comprising northern journeymen, young Welsh converts and a smattering of local rugby union players, both clubs started the season respectably, but crowds began to dip noticeably from November. Parkes then pulled a masterstroke by signing, in rapid succession, All Blacks Charlie Smith, Eddie Holder and, most amazing of all, George Nepia, arguably the greatest union player in the world. Strangely, or so it seemed, all signed for Streatham despite Acton being the club most in need of a fillip. In fact, as others have pointed out, it appears that Parkes had used rugby league to establish stadia that could subsequently be used for greyhound racing. Indeed, as soon as the Park Royal stadium obtained a licence for greyhounds at the end of 1935, Parkes moved Acton to the Mitcham ground, which had been refused a licence. Beset by player discontent, inexperienced management and Parkes' egomania, Acton & Willesden closed at the end of the season.[54] Frustrated by the continuing refusal of Surrey County Council to grant a greyhound licence, Parkes put the Mitcham ground up for sale. In January 1937 the club announced that it would not compete the following season and Parkes' venture, which he claimed had cost £60,000, staggered to a close.

Much further north, in Newcastle, a similar story was unfolding. Newcastle rugby league club began its first season in the league in September 1936, again based at a greyhound stadium. There had been discussion about a club on Tyneside, a region with a strong rugby union tradition, as early as 1930 and in 1931 a local syndicate had suggested to Featherstone that they play their home fixtures in the city, but it was not until June 1936 that the RFL gave the go-ahead to a group of local businessmen to join the league. Again, all does not appear to have been quite what it seemed, because four months into the season the club announced that it would be moving to a brand new greyhound stadium at Gateshead. The Newcastle team won just six matches in two seasons and borrowed £1,200 from the RFL. When the club applied for re-election to the league in 1938 it was voted out by fifteen votes to eight. Any new club, the RFL decided, would in future have to lodge a bond of £250 before applying for membership.[55]

Part of the reason for the failure of these expansion clubs was obvious. Their true interests lay with greyhound racing, so when rugby league could no longer help promote or sustain dog racing they abandoned it. The continual struggle to keep a professional side above the waters of debt to which the northern clubs had become accustomed had no appeal for them. Doggedness was not a quality that was valued by greyhound entrepreneurs. At a broader level, there was mutual incomprehension on both sides. The entrepreneurs mistakenly believed that rugby league's professionalism was the same as that of the new commercialised spectator sports that blossomed in the early 1930s. The small businessmen who controlled the RFL saw the game as a vehicle to bring them local prominence and civic standing rather than the profits which the entrepreneurs sought. With the partial exception of Pontypridd, none of the expansion clubs had roots in their local communities. And, as we have seen, it was those roots that kept traditional rugby league clubs afloat in times of hardship. Just as importantly, it was what these clubs meant to local and class identity which motivated people to sustain those roots – in 1938 supporters of Newcastle complained that the RFL had spent far more money supporting Leigh than it had on their club, but the difference was that Leigh could rely on the local community to provide enough support to stop the club collapsing. The reason for this was simple. Without a rugby league team, Leigh, like many other rugby league towns, had no independent presence beyond its locality. While money was crucial, without a broader social and cultural significance rugby league could not survive.

★

It is this that explains the success of the one area in which geographical expansion did take place for rugby league in the 1930s: France. The French had always had an ambiguous relationship with the Anglo-Saxon concept of amateurism. A century earlier Stendhal had remarked that 'who says amateur says dunce' and French rugby's inconstancy was noted and viewed with suspicion by the RFU.[56] In 1911 E. H. D. Sewell had warned that there were already 'breakers ahead in the shape of possible veiled professionalism against which the heads of the game in France must fight while the thing is still in the bud', a fear which appeared to be confirmed the following year by a letter written to the Northern Union from a Monsieur Bureau. 'The French clubs', noted Bureau, 'are run on lines which allow the payment for broken time', before going on to suggest that the Northern Union play an exhibition match in Paris.[57] During the 1921–22 Australian tour of Britain, the RFL had made strong efforts to play a game in Paris at the Stade Pershing, but the active opposition of the Fédération Française de Rugby (FFR), led by its redoubtable Scottish secretary Cyril Rutherford, meant that finding a suitable stadium in Paris proved impossible.[58]

However, the 1920s was a turbulent time for French rugby, as the game became immensely popular, especially in the south and southwest. Accusations of payments to players, violence and over-competitiveness were legion. The game began to resemble rugby in the north of England before 1895 and threatened to burst out of the structures created for it by the Anglophile French middle classes. In January 1931 twelve of the game's leading clubs broke from the FFR to form the Union Française de Rugby Amateur, ostensibly in opposition to the FFR's failure to uphold the amateur ethos of the sport. Disastrously for the FFR, this was followed on 13 February by the decision of the four British rugby unions to no longer play matches against the French because, they noted with characteristic euphemism, of the 'unsatisfactory state' of the game in France.[59]

These events did not go unnoticed in league circles. In May, Harry Sunderland, a Queenslander who had travelled with the 1921–22 Australian tourists and whose enthusiasm for promoting rugby league was matched only by his eagerness to promote himself, wrote unsuccessfully to the RFL asking them to fund him to promote the game in France and in London. There were also intimations that the FFR might open a dialogue with the RFL, but the FFR set its face in the opposite direction, founding the Fédération International de Rugby Amateur (FIRA) in January 1934 and, as if to signal where its political sympathies lay, playing internationals throughout the 1930s against Germany, Italy and Rumania. However, in early 1933 the RFL was approached by two journalists from the French daily sports newspaper *L'Auto,* the forerunner of *L'Equipe,* about the possibility of establishing rugby league in France. A committee was established to explore the project and, it appears, RFL secretary John Wilson, who had cycled for Britain at the 1912 Olympics, contacted an old cycling friend Victor Breyer, the editor of the Parisian *Echo des Sports.* In May the RFL decided to stage an exhibition match in Paris featuring the Australian tourists.[60]

The match took place on 31 December 1933 between the Australians and an England side on a snow-covered pitch at the Stade Pershing in Paris. Such was the response – the Australian captain Dave Brown was carried shoulder high from the field by spectators and the French press expressed amazement at the skills of the players of 'neo-rugby' – that it marked the birth of rugby league in France. Two days later French international forward Jean Galia, who had been suspended by the FFR for allegedly offering money to players to transfer to his club at Villeneuve-sur-Lot, signed a contract with the RFL to bring a team of players to England to play a four-match tour in March.[61] This too proved to be highly successful and in April the Ligue Française de Rugby à Treize was founded. Support, both from players and clubs, sprang up like fresh daisies on a spring morning. By the end of the LFRT's first season it had twenty-nine clubs, 171 in its second, and 225 in the 1938–39 season. The FFR, which had sought to stop league by banning players, officials and grounds associated with it, shrank to 558 clubs from a high water mark of 784 in 1930.[62] Not only was French rugby irrevocably split, but the tide seemed to be turning in favour of the new game.

The tide also seemed to be turning in French society during the same period. Although many of the factors that enabled the partisans of the new rugby to make the transition were already in place – the apparently unstoppable movement towards payment for play, the civic pride that animated the local clubs, and the increasing rejection of the governing body and its class-based amateur ideology – it was the social ferment that engulfed France in the mid-1930s that helped to dissolve the bonds of authority and deference that the FFR exercised over clubs and players. The depression in France had ushered in an era of acute political crises and intense class struggle. In February 1934, at precisely the time that Galia was assembling his team of pioneers, an attempted armed attack on the French parliament by fascists was followed by the trade unions organising a general strike. Tension continued to rise and in October the French Communist Party called for the creation of a 'Popular Front' to bind together working-class and liberal capitalist parties. In May 1936 the Popular Front won the French general election and the following month a huge wave of strikes convulsed society, causing many to ask whether France was heading towards revolution.

Although the initiators of French rugby league played no role in these events, the game as a whole became associated in the public mind with the Popular Front period. Its challenge to the established order of the FFR coincided exactly with the upsurge of class struggle, while its commitment to the equality of working-class players echoed the political ideas of the time. For its part, the Popular Front government showed no qualms about being associated with the rebel sport. The socialist minister for sport Leo Legrange appeared as a guest of honour at a 1936 international match. Nor could there be any doubts about the sympathies of a club such as the Treize Populaire Parisien, which was founded in March 1937. And when the powerful Narbonne club voted to leave the FFR for rugby league in 1938, it merely seemed a logical step for a club whose players had celebrated their 1936 championship victory by singing the *Internationale* after the final whistle.[63] Indeed, although French rugby league supporters did not necessarily identify themselves with the Popular Front, their enemies in the FFR certainly identified the 'Treizistes' with it. And this became a factor of great importance in 1941 when the wartime collaborationist Vichy government banned the playing of league and disposed of the Ligue's assets, possibly to the FFR.[64]

For its part, English rugby league rallied round the French developments. In the 1934–35 season four clubs plus Lancashire and Yorkshire made short promotional tours of France. Much to the pleasure of the RFL, the popularity of the game in France and the appeal to English crowds of the open French style of play meant that the venture was almost entirely self-financing. It was not without problems. Some of the Englishmen who crossed the Channel found difficulties with the language and food, and there were the inevitable complaints that money spent on France should go instead to northern clubs.[65] But despite these differences, there was a remarkable similarity between the culture of the game in its heartlands of the north of England and the south of France. Both were led by local 'notables', small businessmen whose backing of a club helped to heighten their standing in their towns or villages. Both were predominantly played and watched by the working classes. Both had a sense of regional superiority over their perceived metropolitan elites – some of the French expressing this through identification with the Cathars, dissident Christians in the south who were massacred during the Albigensian Crusades of the thirteenth century. And, most of all, both had an overarching sense of historic injustice based on their treatment at the hands of the rugby union authorities. The French proved to be far more zealous about expanding the game's geographic horizons than the RFL, proposing a world cup tournament as early as 1934, twenty years before they hosted the first World Cup in 1954, and attempting to take the sport to France's colonies in Africa.[66] Rugby league's banning by the Vichy regime in 1941 intensified these feelings and its remarkable survival and re-emergence following the Second World War demonstrated the extent to which the sport expressed broader social, cultural and political attitudes.

And therein lay the reason for the success and failure of the English league's attempts to break out of geographical constraints. Whether in Britain or France, rugby league symbolised much more than a set of alternative rules for rugby – a fact that was sometimes more obvious to the indifferent and the hostile than it was to supporters of the game.

Chapter 5

Rugby league in the 'People's War'

Rugby league entered the Second World War with a great deal more confidence about its role than in 1914. Unlike the outbreak of the First World War, this conflict had been anticipated for at least a year, giving the sport's leadership time to prepare their options. At the height of the Munich crisis in September 1938 the League's management committee had met to discuss the 'national situation and the possibility of an outbreak of war' and decided to call another meeting if the situation deteriorated.[1] The fateful meeting was eventually held almost a year later on 11 September 1939 when, in response to the declaration of war on 3 September, the RFL suspended its competitions and set up Lancashire and Yorkshire 'Emergency Leagues'. A ten-man emergency committee was set up and cost-cutting measures introduced to help clubs deal with the inevitable wartime financial difficulties. The one immediate problem that needed urgent resolution was that of the New Zealand tourists, who had arrived on 29 August, defeated St Helens in their opening match on 2 September and then found themselves stuck in the middle of a war the following day. Deciding that there was no alternative but to cancel the tour, the RFL acted swiftly and on 14 September, following a last match in which they defeated Dewsbury, the tourists left for home on the SS Rugitiki, having spent just seventeen days on British soil at an estimated cost of between £5,000 and £6,000.[2]

The outbreak of war necessarily meant a severe curtailment of normal sporting activities. As part of its precautions against the expected German bombings of cities, the government restricted the size of crowds to just 8,000, or 15,000 in stadia such as Odsal, which had capacities exceeding 60,000. A number of grounds were requisitioned for anti-aircraft guns or the billeting of troops. Non-essential travel was restricted to fifty miles and a blackout imposed after dark, which effectively ruled out even short journeys during the winter months. And of course many players and spectators had joined the armed forces or were required to work longer hours for the war effort. The one major difference between September 1939 and August 1914 was the complete absence of the hysteria against professional sport that had been such a feature of the opening months of the First World War. The morale-boosting effect of sport on both military and civilian personnel in the previous war, not to mention the vast outpourings of national and local patriotism that had accompanied sport during the inter-war years, had convinced all but its boneheadedly blimpish opponents that professional sport had an important role to play in maintaining wartime spirits.[3] For its part, the RFL encouraged its clubs to support local fund-raising initiatives for war charities, such as the Red Cross, St John Ambulance and, from June 1941, 'Aid To Russia', through collections and the staging of charity matches. It also gave its backing to the FA's Footballers' Days to raise money for the Red Cross. When the Challenge Cup was reintroduced in 1941 War Savings Certificates were presented to the finalists instead of medals. John Wilson even offered to take a cut in his salary, although the RFL Council thought this unnecessary.[4]

Although the early months of the war had a decidedly different atmosphere to that of 1914, history repeated itself in one significant aspect. As they had done twenty-five years before, the leaders of the RFL again demanded that the players take a pay cut. The 11 September Council meeting had decided that all players, regardless of contractual or other previous agreements, should receive just ten shillings per match and that the only other payments they could receive were third-class rail or bus fares. The penalty for violating this edict was to be expulsion from the game. As with the similar decision in 1914, the ruling generated uproar among players, especially after the first two weekends of wartime matches when attendances were not substantially lower than those in peacetime. On 26 September, four days before the two league competitions were to commence, Huddersfield players led by captain Alec Fiddes said that they would not play for ten shillings. They were joined by Halifax and Bradford players.[5] Two days later Huddersfield and Halifax players backed down and agreed to play under protest but Bradford players held firm, causing the cancellation of the club's opening game with Hull KR. On 2 October representatives of players of almost all the Yorkshire clubs and three Lancashire clubs met to discuss their next steps. Again as in 1914, a number of clubs also began to backtrack, and fourteen called for a reversal of the decision. Bradford's Harry Hornby proposed a compromise in which players would receive thirty shillings or a third of gate money, whichever was smaller.[6] Faced with a solid front of players and dwindling support among its own members, the RFL Council met on 11 October and increased the allowable payment to one pound per player, with an additional five shillings for players involved in away games at Hull or Barrow. To pay for the new arrangements, the minimum admission charge to matches was raised to one shilling, except for women, boys, the unemployed and members of the armed forces who continued to pay sixpence. Although not particularly satisfactory to anyone, the new terms took the wind out of the players' case and the strike threat evaporated.[7]

Thus resolved, the season continued with some success. Bradford won a two-legged Championship final against Swinton and the Lancashire and Yorkshire Cups were restarted at the end of the season. Two representative matches were played before reasonable crowds and in December Wales defeated England at Odsal in front of more than 15,000 spectators, with proceeds from all three games going to war charities. However, as summer approached, the immediate future of the game became increasingly unclear. Partly this was a reflection of the national mood. The evacuation of Dunkirk at the end of May, the fall of France in June and the start of the Battle of Britain in August all contributed to a sense of uncertainty, if not foreboding, about the future. At its annual general meeting, the RFL felt unable to declare whether a new season would be arranged, a feeling that was exacerbated after the Ministry of Home Security admitted that it 'was unable to express any opinion on organised football next season'.[8] There were also increasing problems as players joined the military or were effectively conscripted on non-military war work. In May 1940 Batley, Bramley and Keighley withdrew from the Yorkshire Cup because too many of their players were engaged on war work. In the second round of the tournament Huddersfield and Castleford were locked together at three-all after eighty minutes. However, a number of Castleford players had to report for military or fire duty that evening and were unable to stay for the extra-time period. Castleford left the field but Huddersfield continued, scoring an unopposed converted try to win the match. However, in August 1940 the Ministry of Labour wrote to the RFL stating that 'it desires as much football as possible to be played so as to provide recreation and relaxation to the workers'. Buoyed by this the RFL Council decided to raise player payments to twenty-five shillings winning per match.[9]

Even with the moral support of government, for some clubs the problems were insurmountable. The requisitioning of grounds was beginning to take its toll. Leigh, Swinton, Broughton, Salford and Liverpool Stanley were all commandeered in 1940. Rochdale Hornets struggled through the 1939–40 season before bowing to the pressures of wartime and withdrawing for the duration. Their problems, spelt out by the club chairman, were typical:

> The whole of the players on the retained list are of military age and are either serving in the forces or are working long hours in work of national importance, which makes it very difficult to raise a team. Also the ground and part of the buildings have been taken over by the Army authorities and are being used for training purposes and sports.[10]

They were joined at the end of the season by Hull KR and over the following months a steady stream of clubs gradually succumbed. By 1943 the War Emergency League, which had been formed by amalgamating the two county leagues in 1941, numbered only fourteen clubs, exactly half that had competed in the last peacetime season. The decisions to stop playing did not always meet with the approval of supporters. In September 1942 Hunslet supporters forced a special general meeting of the club to reverse the committee's decision to close for the duration. Despite gaining a majority to continue, problems over finance meant that the club could not play. For many of the clubs that carried on, existence was often hand to mouth. The increase in Entertainment Tax during the war – by 1945 it amounted to ten and a half pence out of every minimum admission of one shilling and sixpence – put considerable strain on finances. The fact that gate money from matches had to be divided equally between the two competing clubs was a mixed blessing. Poorer clubs such as St Helens welcomed this arrangement, reporting in 1945 that their 'deficit would have been larger but for the sharing of gates, which has proved an advantage at a difficult time'. In contrast, Bradford, which attracted high attendances throughout the war, decried the fact that 'the war-time division of gate receipts has worked to the detriment of the club and has in fact diverted many thousands of pounds of what would have been club income'.[11]

Clubs were further disadvantaged by the rationing of clothing, which was introduced in June 1941. In September the Manufactures and Industries department of the Board of Trade told the RFL that clothing coupons would not be issued for football kit, but that clubs were free to appeal to the public for donations of coupons. Like many others, Oldham wrote to all their members and season-ticket holders asking for them to donate any spare coupons. By November 1943 the situation had eased sufficiently for the Board of Trade to grant a special allowance to the RFL of 870 coupons, 75 balls and 150 bladders. Even so, the temptation to resort to the black market was always there. In September 1944, an official of Barrow was fined £20 for illegally obtaining football clothing from an RAF officer. His barrister claimed in mitigation that his client had merely been over-enthusiastic in responding 'to the appeal of Mr Bevin that the workers should be provided with relaxation, and that sport should be encouraged in every way'.[12]

If the war presented insuperable difficulties for some clubs, for others it offered new opportunities, especially for player recruitment. By necessity, the circumstances of the war loosened the ties between clubs and their players. At the most obvious level, this occurred when a player joined the armed forces and was stationed away from home. But the problems of civilian travel – in November 1941 petrol for private motoring was withdrawn by the government – and increased working hours presented almost insurmountable problems for many players. In recognition of this the RFL allowed players to appear as 'guests' for a club other than the one with which they were registered, provided that the player's original club gave permission. This gave an immediate boost to sides that were located near military camps, such as Bradford, Leeds and Halifax, and those with officials sharp enough to exploit the possibilities of the new situation. Foremost among the latter was Dewsbury, managed since 1936 by a bright young dynamo called Eddie Waring. A trained journalist, Waring had been offered the position because of his success as a youth coach in the town. In peacetime Dewsbury could never hope to compete consistently at the highest levels of the game, but the wartime state of flux created the perfect environment in which Waring's mix of public relations panache, wheeler-dealer flair and deep knowledge of the game could flourish. Aided by the close proximity of the Caulms Wood army camp, he set about recruiting high profile players to the club, paying little attention to RFL's restrictions on payments. Included among the players he persuaded to play for the club were stars such as

Salford's Gus Risman, Alan Edwards and Barney Hudson, Wigan's Hector Gee and Charlie Seeling junior, Leeds' Vic Hey (who eventually signed permanently for the club) and Barrow's Roy Francis. The Dewsbury side that won the 1943 Championship and Challenge Cup final matches had nine guest players. However, probably his most controversial capture was the signing of Wigan's Jim Sullivan.

Although now in his late thirties, Sullivan was still a superb player and team leader. Soon after war broke out, he volunteered for the Police War Reserve in Wigan. Nevertheless, the freedom which the 'guest' rules brought to players meant that he became much sought after, especially by Dewsbury for whom he played most of the 1940–41 and 1941–42 seasons, much to the annoyance of Wigan who refused him permission to play for Waring's team. In October 1941 the RFL Emergency committee held a special meeting to investigate his case, at which Wigan claimed he had demanded more than the twenty-five shillings payment allowed. They had refused to pay him more than the limit, implying that Dewsbury had not been so observant of the rules. Unable to find evidence of 'backhand' payments, the RFL took no action against Dewsbury but severely censured Sullivan for asking for an illegal payment. Dewsbury continued to play him despite Wigan's subsequent protest.[13] Controversy over Waring's recruitment practices continued throughout the war, the irritation of many being encapsulated by Batley's George Smith, who asked provocatively in 1943 'who is running the Rugby League, the [RFL] Council or Dewsbury?'[14] The animosity between Dewsbury and the other clubs reached its height during the 1943 Championship play-offs. Beaten by Bradford in the semi-final, Dewsbury appealed to the RFL that Bradford had fielded a guest player, Sandy Orford, who was ineligible because he had not played four league games for the club. In fact, the semi-final was Orford's fourth game but as the rule stated that the four games had to be played before the play-offs, Bradford were disqualified and Dewsbury took their place in the final, comfortably defeating Halifax to be crowned champions. However, a month later Bradford protested to the RFL that Dewsbury had also played an ineligible guest player, Castleford's Frank Smith, in their semi-final. Although Smith had played in a number of cup-ties for Dewsbury, he had only played three league matches for them. Bradford's complaint was upheld and the RFL Council fined Waring's side £100, stripped them of the title and declared that season's championship null and void. Few outside of Dewsbury shed tears for the club's fate.

The 1943 Championship imbroglio demonstrated the difficulties presented by the system of guest players. As it always had done when new circumstances created loopholes for clubs to exploit, the RFL engaged in a game of catch-up to try and regulate the situation. In July 1942 the RFL Council brought in the requirement that a guest player had to have played a minimum of four league games to be eligible to play in a cup semi-final or final. The rules were further tightened later that year to outlaw 'en bloc' transfers of players from a club that had ceased playing to an active club and to limit the number of guest players from one club to six. Bramley had shut down at the end of the 1941–42 season and simply transferred their playing staff to Leeds, causing some of their players to complain to the RFL that they had been deprived of the right to choose for which club they played. Salford had also transferred all of their players to Dewsbury when they closed in December 1940. In the summer of 1944 the guest rule was further tightened so that all movements of guest players had to be approved by the Emergency Committee as well as the player's original club, in part to offset the fact that the twenty-five shillings maximum match payment had been abolished at that year's annual general meeting.[15]

The guest rules also considerably altered the balance of power between players and clubs. The reduction in the number of clubs meant that journeyman players had to offer their services to clubs – throughout 1943 and 1944 Oldham's committee received dozens of letters from players asking if they could play for the side. In the 1944–45 season Leeds fielded no fewer than ninety players in just twenty-seven matches.[16] At the other end of the scale, the rules gave good players tremendous bargaining power, as they realised that by playing one club off against another they could earn a lot more than the twenty-five shillings allowed by the regulations. The Oldham committee would write to players who asked for more than the legal amount or unallowable expenses curtly informing them 'that it is illegal to pay and ask for broken-time to be paid'. By 1942 the practice of asking for more had become so commonplace that the RFL Emergency Committee wrote to all clubs demanding written details of all expenses paid after each match played. This did little to stop extra payments and in January 1943 broken-time payments were banned completely in order to close the most common loophole used by clubs to circumnavigate the regulations, although this is unlikely to have stopped the more determined transgressors.[17]

As in the First World War, the focus on national unity did little to change the competitive attitudes of players, officials or spectators. In May 1940, days before the evacuation of Dunkirk, ten players appeared before the RFL Council charged with acts of violence during matches. In general there seems to have been little diminution in the physical intensity of the game during the war. In January 1942 Warrington's Mel de Lloyd was banned for life for punching a referee while guesting as a player for Keighley against Hull. At the same time the Emergency Committee issued a circular to all clubs warning them about the increase in 'disrespectful remarks to referees'.[18] In October 1940 a brawl between players and spectators broke out at Hunslet when members of the crowd rushed on to the pitch to attack a player who had been sent off for punching a Hunslet player. Most notorious was the pitch invasion on Boxing Day 1944 at St Helens, when a substantial section of the crowd poured on to the pitch in protest against a decision of the referee, forcing him to abandon the game halfway through the second half.[19]

Indeed, throughout the war years there was a great deal of 'normality' about rugby league. The Challenge Cup final, now played back in the north, attracted crowds comparable to those of the pre-Wembley days, with the 1944 two-legged Bradford versus Wigan final pulling in an aggregate of over 51,000. England versus Wales internationals were played each season, with over 23,000 attending the

March 1945 match. League attendances fluctuated according to the fortunes of individual clubs and, to some extent, the state of the war. Thanks to their imported players, Dewsbury could expect five-figure crowds for important matches.[20] The amateur game began to grow too from late 1942, stimulated in large part by the increased importance attached to the provision of recreation facilities for employees during the long hours of war work. A good example of this trend was the formation of the Risehow and Gillhead Collieries side in Cumberland, which had been created as part of a social club to cater for the large number of Bevin Boys (young men conscripted to work in the mines rather than the military). Eight hundred miners paid threepence a week to support the social club, with the rugby league side being the most prominent section. The team progressed rapidly in the amateur game, winning the two county cup competitions and reaching the first round of the Challenge Cup in 1948. The war also stimulated the formation of non-works sides too; for example, Kells rugby league club in Whitehaven was reformed in 1943 and Wigan's Pemberton Rovers were revived in 1945, having folded in 1928, owing to the efforts of members of the Lamberhead Green Working Men's Club. From the start of the 1942–43 season the RFL started to subsidise eight local organisers and by summer 1943 there were fourteen amateur league competitions up and running in Lancashire. In Yorkshire, the Halifax District League reported that nine new clubs had recently been formed in the area due to servicemen and men engaged on war work. Most significantly for the professional game, in the summer of 1944 the RFL was approached by a consortium of Workington civic notables and businessmen to discuss the formation of a professional club in the town once the war was over.[21]

★

On 14 November 1939 the RFU relaxed its ban on league players in union, allowing rugby league players in the services to play for and against military and civilian rugby union sides. As the *Daily Mail*'s J. P. Jordan pointed out with some relief though, the ban still remained in force for civilian league players, although this tended to be ignored by rugby union selectors when it suited them. The Welsh Rugby Union followed the RFU's lead but the Scots remained steadfast. SRU secretary H. M. Simson told the press 'that his Union would not remove the ban on professionals in the Services playing for or against amateur teams'.[22] In fact, the ban had been broken a month before when Huddersfield had played a friendly match against a local army team at union and league but this was a rare exception.[23] As in the First World War, the RFU's concession allowed its services teams to have their pick of league players, something they did with all the enthusiasm of an evacuated child let loose in an apple orchard. The 1940–41 season saw the Yorkshire Rugby Union raid league teams for the county services' fifteen, so much so that Leeds and Castleford blamed their defeats in the Yorkshire Cup quarter-finals on the fact that they had had key players requisitioned for the Yorkshire Services union team. Five of Leeds first team were included in the Yorkshire union side that faced

Lancashire at Central Park in March 1941. Part of the reason for this was to boost attendances at union matches by including star league players that would, in the words of the *Yorkshire Observer*, make the Yorkshire team a 'box office attraction'. There were also tensions concerning the use of Headingley, which had been requisitioned by the military and staged union matches in contravention of the agreement between Leeds and Hunslet that they would not both arrange home fixtures on the same day. When Hunslet protested Leeds responded by saying even they had to apply to use their own ground.

To some extent the RFL and its clubs took the moral high ground and refused to be drawn into disputes with rugby union, despite the fact that neither they nor the clubs were consulted about the selection of league players, but there was also a degree of self-preservation involved too. Journalist George Thompson noted that 'certain players, and officials too, [were] somewhat of the opinion that if they did not play [for union teams] they might jeopardise their respective positions in the Forces'. Roy Francis experienced precisely this in 1942 when he was picked to play for Wales at league and England in a services union international on the same day. Despite being Welsh and a professional rugby league player he had no choice but to turn out for the England union side.[24] The RFL also felt considerable irritation at the refusal of the Army Sports Council Board to arrange an Army XIII versus Rugby League XIII match in 1941, although the fact that the secretary of the board was RFU vice-president Bernard Hartley meant that the decision was hardly a surprise. Undeterred, a similar game was arranged between the Northern Command and a Rugby League XIII at Halifax in March 1942.[25]

The RFL's equanimity towards its treatment by rugby union during this period reflected its own self-confidence about its role in wartime Britain. Unlike the marginalisation it had suffered in the First World War, it now saw itself and was seen by government authorities as playing a full role in maintaining morale on the home front. Early in the war RFL secretary John Wilson was co-opted on to the Northern Command Sports Board and the RFL dealt directly with a number of ministerial departments over issues such as rationing, kick-off times and fund-raising. Nor was rugby league without some official support. When in 1943 the Scottish Rugby Union demanded a signed declaration that a Northern Command side due to play a Scottish Universities XV would not include any rugby league players, the Northern Command promptly cancelled the fixture.[26] Clubs saw themselves as a focus for community morale by fund-raising and supporting servicemen based abroad. At Christmas 1944 Hull sent presents paid for by fund-raising to all forty-two of their players in the services. Huddersfield raised £488 for Herbert Sherwood's widow and daughter after the forward was lost at sea in 1943.[27] Bradford's Christmas Day match programme for 1943 emphasised the link between rugby league at home and those fighting abroad:

> To-day our first thought must be of those lads who are languishing in prison camps on foreign soil whilst we are free to enjoy our sport. This should make us very thankful of the opportunity presented to us today to show our

appreciation in a full and practical manner by making Odsal's 'Footballers' Day' collection for the Red Cross Prisoners of War Fund ANOTHER GROUND RECORD. [emphasis in original][28]

Even so, as in the First World War, there was little of the deep mourning for players who had been killed in the war, which was still seen in rugby union. Indeed, it is even more difficult to discover the numbers of rugby league players who lost their lives in this conflict than for the previous war. Les 'Juicy' Adams, a veteran of the 1932 'Battle of Brisbane' test match, was killed when the plane in which he was a gunner was shot down in the Far East in April 1945. As well as Herbert Sherwood, Huddersfield lost Ken Gronow. Leeds lost at least three players: John Dixon, Oliver Morris and John Roper. Bradford lost Charles Freeman and Jack Moore. Jack Dawson and Albert Allen never returned to play again for Hull. Swinton never saw Dick Green and Tommy Holland again, while Harold Briscoe did not make it back to St Helens. The most famous death took place at home, when Lance Todd was killed in a car accident in 1942, although this was marked by naming the award for the best player in the Challenge Cup final after him. This matter-of-factness about the depredations of the war was often reflected in match-day programme reports of players serving overseas: 'Stirling is of course a prisoner of war while … Toga was also taken prisoner in the Crete campaign', wrote Eddie Waring matter-of-factly in a March 1942 Dewsbury programme.[29]

The sport's confidence was further bolstered by the performances of its players in rugby union representative sides, which in the eyes of rugby league supporters helped to confirm the conviction that league was the superior sport. In March 1943 the RFL Emergency Committee minuted with pride that league players had scored twenty-three of England's twenty-nine points in their recent win over Scotland in a services rugby union international, although perhaps more significant were the fourteen points scored by league players in Wales' 17–12 defeat of England at Swansea in March 1942. As *The Times*' rugby correspondent noted in 1944, England and Wales 'were ready to make use of any available rugby league talent'. Consequently numerous league players turned out for the two nations in services rugby union internationals, most notably Gus Risman, who captained Wales twice, Roy Francis, who was capped for England seven times, and Alan Edwards, who won six Welsh caps. Countless others turned out for a plethora of union representative teams from various branches of the armed services.[30]

For many rugby league players, their experiences in union were often eye-opening, especially when encountering the 'amateurism' prevalent in Wales. Gus Risman claimed £4 travel expenses after turning out for the Welsh XV but 'my heart stopped when the officials told me that my expenses couldn't be right. But my heart started beating again when I was handed £8!' In contrast, Eric Batten assumed he would have to negotiate his expenses, as would usually be the case in league, and claimed £13 and 10 shillings when playing in a Fire Services international for England in Wales, fully expecting to settle for less. He was similarly amazed to find his 'expenses' reimbursed in full without question.[31] For others, the fact that their rugby skills allowed them to mix with men from public schools and universities in the army, something that would be practically impossible in civilian life, was an impressive achievement in itself. Hull-born actor Tom Courtenay remembered his uncle Pat returning from the war, bringing 'a photo of himself in an army rugby team. I was very impressed. Rugby Union, too. Not common every-day Rugby League.'[32] Unfortunately, the sport was neither common nor everyday in the services, being played on an organised basis only in the north of England. Indeed, it did not become a recognised sport in the British armed forces until 1994 and league matches between services personnel outside of wartime were extremely rare indeed. Given the Army's preference for union and the prominence of RFU officials and supporters, such as Bernard Hartley, in the forces' sports hierarchy, there was little opportunity for league to be played abroad by servicemen. Informal games were organised in Egypt, although a Rugby League XV regularly played under union rules there, and the sport was also played in German prisoner-of-war camps. In the spring of 1943 Stalag 383 in Bavaria organised two England versus Australia matches and a Lancashire versus Yorkshire match.[33]

Yet even these difficulties seemed unimportant when compared to the success of rugby league and its players during the war. Its most talismanic moments came in 1943 and 1944, when rugby league sides twice defeated rugby union sides under rugby union rules. In January 1943 the Northern Command Sports Board organ-ised a rugby union match between a Northern Command Rugby League XV and a Northern Command Rugby Union XV at Headingley. Some of the league side were former Welsh union players but others had barely played the game. Scrum-half Billy Thornton of Hunslet had played his first game of union the previous weekend. The league side overcame an 8–3 half-time deficit to win 18–11, outscoring the previously unbeaten union side by six tries to one. The second game, this time between fully fledged Combined Services League and Union sides, was staged at Bradford's Odsal stadium in April 1944 and proved to be a much tighter affair. The League side again coming from behind at half-time to win 15–10, thanks to a set move from a scrum that saw stand-off Stan Brogden exchange passes with Roy Francis to scorch away from the union defenders. In between these two full-scale games, a rugby league side had also won the Northern Command rugby union seven-a-side tournament in May 1943, defeating a union side that contained seven internationals, five from union and two from league. These results surprised nobody. Union commentators blamed the defeats on weak union sides and the professional training of the league players. For league support-ers the matches simply confirmed their belief in the superiority of their sport. The suggestion by the secretary of the Northern Command Sports Board that there should be an annual league versus union fixture was predictably ignored by the RFU.[34]

More instructive was the social make-up of the two sides in these games. The union teams fielded nine and ten officers respectively in the 1943 and 1944 sides. Neither of the league squads contained a single officer. While officially portrayed as a 'People's War', the fact was that the essential boundaries of social relations between the classes were maintained during and after the war. With the exception of Gus Risman, it appears that no significant British rugby league player of the time served as an officer, in contrast to the handful who gained commissions in the First World War, such as Hull's Jack Harrison, Wakefield's W. L. Beattie and Wigan's Billy Seddon. The increased importance of sport between 1939 and 1945 did allow a number of league players to join the army as non-commissioned physical training instructors – for example, Trevor Foster, Alan Edwards and Roy Francis – but the rise to sergeant was usually as far as the opportunities went. This lack of real change in social relations was also demonstrated by the RFU's rush to reimpose its ban on league players as soon as the war ended. In June 1945 the issue was high on the agenda of the first meeting of the RFU committee since 1939, when Major R. V. Stanley was among many members who believed that 'the time had come to revert to our Rules as to Professionalism'. The matter was raised again at the RFU's June 1945 annual general meeting. A delegate from Manchester demanded that 'something be done to remove the concessions granted in 1939' but the committee deferred a decision until the matter was clarified with the Armed Forces, who preferred not to have their forthcoming international services tournament stripped of its league players.[35] Once the services internationals had been played, the RFU reinstated its restrictions on league players at the end of the 1945–46 season:

> That so long as there is National Service any man enlisting or called up under 19 years of age may play Rugby Union football as an Amateur during his period of service provided he does not play Rugby League after enlistment. Should he do so he shall be debarred from all Rugby Union football except inter-unit.[36]

The ease with which the RFU reimposed its quarantine on rugby league – in 1947 it banned union clubs from allowing the New Zealand rugby league tourists to train on their grounds, and also barred union players from playing in league workshop competitions – suggests that any dissolving of the social hierarchies of everyday life that might have occurred during the war was extremely limited and temporary, and that they were reinstated with not a little enthusiasm by their supporters following the war's end.[37] In contrast, the RFL's self-confidence occasionally blinded it to the fact that the wartime détente was no longer possible. For example, in 1947 it sought to organise a national collieries knock-out cup for the newly nationalised National Coal Board, and expressed the naive hope that the RFU and WRU 'might extend to miners the same privileges which were extended to servicemen during the war and allow them to participate in the competition without prejudice'.[38]

★

They did not, but it did little to puncture the assurance that the RFL had found during the war. It had had a 'good war'. Unlike 1914–18, when the sport had been marginalised and ignored, the Second World War had seen rugby league play its full part in the national effort. This was not just confined to its successes on the rugby pitch. Rugby league's ethos of northern democratic egalitarianism dovetailed perfectly with the mood of the war years, especially with the official rhetoric and popular belief that portrayed the conflict as a 'People's War'. Perhaps the most striking examples of this change could be heard on the radio, now the most important mass communications medium, in which accents previously seen as inferior by the BBC attained a new found prominence. The radio broadcasts of Bradford-born J. B. Priestley, in which his flat Yorkshire vowels delivered a message of inclusive and social democratic Englishness, gave an authority to a worldview that a large proportion of the population, along with rugby league and its followers, shared. The legitimacy Priestley brought to northernness was underlined by Wilfred Pickles' success as a newsreader, where his slightly softened Halifax accent was contrasted favourably by many listeners to the somewhat strangulated vowels of the regular newsreaders' received-pronunciation accents.

Buoyed by its sense of national worth, the RFL began to plan its peacetime role as early as the summer of 1943, when it had become clear that the tide had turned in favour of the Allies.[39] Relations were re-established with the re-formed French Rugby League in late 1944 and the first peacetime season for seven years kicked-off with the addition of the brand new Workington Town club. Such was the progress that the sport seemed to be making that at its first annual conference since the end of the war the chairman was moved to proclaim that

> to have survived two world wars and emerged virile was a sure indication of the strength of the rugby league movement. ... rugby league was the first national game to put its house in order and play a full post-war league and cup programme.[40]

This sense of new-found national importance was nowhere more clearly demonstrated than in October 1945, when for the first time in its history the RFL Council was addressed by a senior government minister, albeit an Australian one. Dr H. V. Evatt, the Australian Minister of External Affairs. He had travelled to Manchester to persuade the RFL to send a touring team to Australia and New Zealand the following year. A high court judge at the age of 36 and a future leader of the Australian Labour Party, Evatt was shortly to become the first president of the UN's General Assembly. He was also a staunch rugby league supporter of many years' standing. He told the meeting:

> The close relationships that have been built up between Australia and New Zealand and the North of England is in the nature of a history and the building up of this history ought to be resumed as soon as possible, in the best interests of rugby league football and of the Empire.[41]

The Council had turned down a request from the Australian Rugby League Board of Control earlier that year, but, after receiving assurances of government assistance for the journey, they voted overwhelmingly to tour in the summer of 1946. Evatt's presence at the meeting was an acknowledgement of the important role that rugby league believed it could play in post-war reconstruction both at home and abroad. Cricket excepted, no other sport was as well-suited to help re-cement the imperial bond between the British and Australia as rugby league.

The confidence that it was now a national game, in importance if not geography, also led the RFL in 1947 to change the name of the national side from England to Great Britain. Justified on the grounds that the side had almost always included British players who were not English, the move was also a reflection of the times. As Norman Davies has pointed out, the sense of belonging to a specifically British national community and a form of patriotism based on Britishness reached its height during the Second World War.[42] At last, it seemed that the tide of society was flowing in the same direction as rugby league. The game greeted the post-war world on the crest of a wave, more popular than ever before and more confident about being able to play its full role in a Britain that appeared to reflect the demo-cratic, popular sentiments that it had always upheld.

Chapter 6

From boom to bust 1945–70

The tremendous success of the immediate post-war years appeared to all in the game to indicate that a bright future was opening up for it. Attendances reached record levels, club coffers were overflowing and the sport was playing a significant national role, touring Australasia in 1946 and welcoming New Zealand and Australia in 1947 and 1948. The total number of spectators rocketed to a peak of 6.8 million in the 1948–49 and 1949–50 seasons, with crowds at league matches reaching a record 4,982,160 in the latter. Wigan, in particular, led the way; their average gate topped 20,000 throughout this period, helping them to record huge profits, topped by a £17,000 surplus in 1950.[1] Challenge Cup attendances also grew dramatically. In 1949 a record 846,000 people went to cup matches, an increase of over 50 per cent on the last full season before the war. Attendances at the Wembley final ballooned to over 95,000 in 1949, selling out for the first time in 1948 and eclipsing even the records set by Ashes test matches in Australia. In the same season, an unprecedented 75,194 crammed into Maine Road to watch Huddersfield win the League Championship final.

The sport's affluence in an era of austerity was also highlighted by a rising spiral of transfer fees. In the first full season after the war, a new record transfer fee of £1,650 was set when Dewsbury bought full-back Bill Davies from Huddersfield. This was broken five times in the next two seasons, reaching a height in 1951 when Leigh bought the ageing, yet still incomparable, hooker, Joe Egan, from Wigan for £5,000. In the same season it was reported that twenty players were transferred listed at fees of £1,000 and over.[2] Similar largesse was spent on importing Australian players in the two years following the war, culminating in the £12,500 Workington almost spent in their thwarted bid to bring Clive Churchill over from South Sydney.

The amount of money available in the game did not go unnoticed by the players. In 1947 Leeds players had threatened to strike for a £15 winning bonus for their Challenge Cup semi-final against Wakefield. At the start of the following season Hunslet players went on strike for higher match fees, the dispute only being settled two games into the new season. These two actions had coincided with the formation in January 1947 of a new union, the Rugby League Players' Union and Welfare Organisation, led by Leeds' Chris Brereton. Although not as prominent a player as those who had formed the first union in 1920, Brereton was a skilled and enthusiastic organiser who enlisted the involvement of such respected players as Bradford and Great Britain captain Ernest Ward. By 1950 the union claimed 800 members out of 1,300 registered professional players and was turning its attentions to recruiting players in the amateur local leagues.[3] Its programme called for a minimum weekly wage of £5 during the season, a minimum signing-on fee, a superannuation scheme and a 15 per cent share of transfer fees. These were accompanied by calls for representation on RFL and club committees, and consultation on rule changes and coaching schemes. Most far-reaching, they also wanted an end to the 'retain and transfer' system, whereby a player remained a club property at the end of his contract regardless of whether a new contract had been agreed. The union also sought to encourage the growth of the sport and donated a trophy for the newly created Welsh Rugby League Challenge Cup.[4]

As in 1920, the RFL were extremely wary about dealing with the union, yet the government's rhetoric of 'partnership' between labour and management at this time made it difficult for them to ignore it. In March 1948, the RFL Council grudgingly agreed by just one vote to meet a delegation. A sub-committee to examine the union's demands was created but of the eight demands, it rejected six outright and two were promised further investigation. Undeterred by this rejection, Brereton again contacted the RFL Council in June 1950 to discuss the creation of a new insurance scheme and the introduction of a minimum weekly wage. The Council unanimously rejected his proposals but in April 1951 he requested the establishment of an agreement on wage rates and conditions of employment. Instinctively, the Council again turned down the approach – and walked straight into the trap that Brereton had set for them. Under Ministry of Labour regulations of the time, a dispute over wages or conditions could be referred to an arbitration tribunal if requested by one of the involved parties. Faced with the prospect of appearing before a tribunal the Council quickly reversed their position and met the union in June 1951. The RFL again agreed to investigate the players' demands but, realising that this was just a delaying tactic, Brereton invoked a compulsory arbitration order. But when the arbitration tribunal published its findings the following April, it dealt the union a body blow from which it would not recover. The tribunal opposed the union's key demands for a minimum wage, a share of transfer fees and a standard signing-on fee. Brereton's tactical astuteness had been undone by his naiveté in believing that the tribunal would support the union and it rapidly disappeared from the game.[5]

But the lack of a union did not stop players from taking strike action. In 1950 Hull players unsuccessfully struck for better winning bonuses. In 1952 Doncaster players all requested transfers in protest at a £2 reduction in match fees, winning a compromise of a £1 reduction. The following season Castleford players refused to play their match at Workington in support of their demand for a £1 increase in losing pay and the start of the 1955–56 season saw Halifax players strike for better pay. The 1957–58 season began with Oldham players refusing to play unless they received £12 winning pay and that October Hunslet's match with, ironically,

Oldham was cancelled after the Yorkshire club's players demanded higher match fees.[6] None of these strikes or threatened strikes was wholly successful, in large part because of the hostile actions of club directors. The Hull dispute ended when the club suspended the players and forced them to apologise, while the Oldham board simply refused to negotiate. This reflected not only the attitudes of club directors towards players but also the fact that the game's growing financial difficulties in the 1950s were increasingly blamed on a combination of declining attendances and high wages.

Indeed, these two issues came to dominate the game throughout the 1950s. As with all spectator sports, crowds fell steadily throughout the decade, dipping below four million in the 1952–53 season and below three million for the first time in the 1959–60 season. Between 1950 and 1960 the average league match attendance fell from 9,600 to 4,829.[7] Challenge Cup crowds fell at an even quicker rate, to just over 441,000 in 1955, below even their 1935 level. The RFL's initial response to the problem was to attempt to control wages. In 1954 RFL secretary Bill Fallowfield – who had been appointed in November 1945 following the retirement of John Wilson – outlined a plan for a maximum match fee of £6 plus a maximum win bonus of £2.[8] Although that season's annual general meeting accepted the proposals 'in principle' no action was taken. Another package of proposals to curb winning bonuses paid to players was presented to an extraordinary general meeting before the start of the 1955–56 season. It too failed to get any practical support.

Such measures had little chance of being implemented because the clubs that comprised the RFL would always safeguard their own individual interests first, often in disregard of any wider responsibility to the sport.[9] In 1959 it was revealed that Oldham had been making illegal loans as large as £600 each to its players. The club claimed that the monies were merely advances on the benefits that players would receive after ten years' service but few, if any, of the players concerned had bothered to make any repayments on the loans. The RFL expelled ten members of the club's committee, forced the players to start making repayments and suspended scrum-half Frank Pitchford until he had repaid the whole of his loan. Similar difficulties were experienced at Halifax in 1964 when the club was caught making illegal payments to star winger Johnny Freeman. The Oldham case also highlighted the way in which club officials dealt with players. Although they refused to discuss with the players collectively during their 1957 strike, they were prepared to make illegal payments to buy their loyalty and maintain a policy of 'divide and rule'. Episodes such as these and the failure of the clubs to agree on common action fatally undermined any prospects of effective wage control.[10]

★

However, it was not just player payments that were putting club coffers under strain. Since its introduction in 1916, Entertainment Tax had taken, in the eyes of most sporting organisations, rather too large a slice of the money which spectators paid to watch matches. In the 1952–53 season the thirty professional league clubs paid £49,172 in Entertainment Tax out of an aggregate attendance income of £301,073 – in other words, over 16 per cent of their gate receipts went to the Exchequer. The way the tax was charged also led to some iniquitous anomalies. St Helens, that season's champions, paid 15 per cent of their £48,255 gate receipts but Doncaster, which finished fourth from the bottom of the table, handed over more than 19 per cent from their meagre £3,882. Insult was added to injury in 1953 when cricket and rugby union was exempted from the tax, the former because it had, in the words of Chancellor of the Exchequer R. A. Butler, a 'special place among sports', the latter because it was amateur. The increases in the rate of the tax in 1952 were felt to be particularly harsh; any increase in gate receipts was severely penalised by the duty payable. The RFL had raised the minimum standard admission charge by threepence to one shilling and sixpence to offset the increase but although income rose, crowds fell by over 12 per cent.[11] In 1955 the Exchequer tightened the screws even more when it was announced that the Inland Revenue would henceforth levy income tax on the previously tax-free signing-on fee paid to players, which inevitably meant clubs paying more money to players in order to compensate for the deducted tax. Following numerous appeals, the Inland Revenue decided that a signing-on fee would not be taxed if the player receiving it was an amateur. British tax law deemed the loss of amateur status to be so grievous that the poor denuded player could only be compensated by receiving an even larger amount of money than a professional team-mate.[12]

Clubs were also beginning to face financial problems caused by the poor state of most rugby league grounds, despite the efforts of the supporters' clubs to improve them through donations or voluntary labour. Writing in 1955, the Halifax three-quarter Tommy Lynch had argued that one of the reasons for the decline in attendances was the fact that

> many of the grounds leave much to be desired for the comfort of the people who make professional football possible. The paying spectator should be able to watch a match knowing that if it is wet he has a chance of being able to stand without being subjected to the weather, and not at the expense of a grandstand ticket either?[13]

In 1953 Bill Fallowfield had calculated that ground improvements costing over £135,000 were necessary for the professional clubs, including new terracing, the covering of stands, the erection of new stands and the improvement of toilet facilities. By and large, if such work was not funded by the supporters' clubs, it did not get done, partially because the primary purpose of a club's income was to secure and retain players, but also because the poor state of repair of grounds meant that increasing amounts of money were being spent simply on day-to-day maintenance costs. Doncaster, which had only become a professional club in 1951, found that it was caught so badly in this spiral that in 1960 it sold its ground to the RFL and rented it back at £100 per year. As visitors to the aptly named Tatters Field discovered, even this did nothing to enhance what would later become known as the 'spectator experience'.[14] It was not only money that was drying up. So too was the voluntary labour on which the clubs relied. Fewer people going to matches meant that fewer still were willing to volunteer for the menial tasks required to maintain their team's ground. If such work was carried out at all, clubs were finding that labour that was once volunteered now had to be paid for.

Some of the direct financial pressures were relieved by the abolition of Entertainment Tax in 1957 and by the introduction in 1956 of the Small Lotteries and Gaming Act, which allowed sports clubs, among others, to organise lottery competitions for fund-raising purposes. The latter provided an important boost to club finances. Wakefield Trinity's 1957 annual report noted that the 'dominant factor' in the club's profitability was their new football pools-style competition. For clubs further down the league ladder, such income rapidly became the difference between bankruptcy and viability. Featherstone Rovers' profit of £2,031 in the 1962–63 season was entirely due to their 'development fund' income of £6,007, which accounted for almost 30 per cent of the club's total income. But even the large amounts raised by many clubs through lottery activities were often not enough to keep them out of the red. In the 1962–63 season Leigh raised almost £32,000 yet still recorded a loss of £20,000 on the season's activities.[15]

Such fund-raising successes were due almost entirely to the enthusiasm and commitment of club supporters. Despite their declining numbers, they continued to provide the infrastructure and personnel for the daily slog of club fund-raising. Even before the 1956 Act, supporters' clubs were playing a vital role in raising extra cash for their teams. In 1955 Featherstone supporters' club spent £2,300 on building new dressing rooms and improving terracing. The following year Halifax received £4,500 from their supporters' club. By the early 1960s most supporters' clubs had become crucial in keeping the wolf of insolvency from the door, by organising raffles, weekly draws, pools, dances and bars at matches. The organisation of players' testimonials inevitably fell to supporters. In the twenty-five years following the Second World War Huddersfield supporters' club raised over £12,500 for fourteen players. Not that these efforts were always appreciated by club directors. In 1965 Bradford demanded, and were given, control of their supporters' club's weekly prize draw. In 1973 Halifax withdrew recognition from their supporters' club and demanded all monies from its social club. But by and large most supporters' clubs maintained a reasonably harmonious relationship with the directors of their teams, if only because the latter recognised the importance of unpaid labour to the club's fortunes.[16]

Nevertheless, the end of Entertainment Tax and the arrival of new sources of funds provided only a temporary respite from financial distress. Attendances fell by another one and half million between 1959 and 1964, leaving the sport caught in an ever-sharpening scissors of rising player payments and dwindling income. The split of the league championship into two divisions in the 1962–63 season – a change which had been called for by many clubs at different times since the 1920s – did nothing to halt the fall despite the supposed extra interest created by promotion and relegation. Another attendance slump the following season caused a panicked scramble back to one division for the 1964–65 season, but this turned out to be similarly ineffective in halting the slide. The scale of the problem was highlighted by the financial collapse of Bradford Northern in 1963. In the 1952–53 season the club had been watched at home by an average of 17,169 spectators per match. Ten years later the average was a mere 1,257. On 23 November 1963 just 324 people watched the game against Barrow and less than three weeks later the club announced that it could not fulfil its fixtures. Its debts totalled more than £11,000, not as great as that of some other clubs, but the collapse of attendances and the consequent drying up of its cash flow had caused its bank to refuse to lend any more money.[17]

Even though the fall of Bradford had not been entirely unexpected, especially in the light of the club's pathetic recent playing record, the plummeting attendance figures elsewhere suggested that it could be the first of many. As early as January 1960 the RFL held the first of a number of wide-ranging discussions on the reasons for the decline in fortune. Members pointed to changing leisure habits, the availability of cars, hire purchase, the popularity of television and the way the game was played.[18] Featherstone Rovers called for a switch to a summer season and by the mid-1960s the realisation that change was necessary gradually overcame the ingrained inertia of the sport's leaders.[19] In late 1966 it was decided to allow the professional sides to play on a Sunday – amateurs had been allowed to do so from 1954 – although the first matches did not take place until December the following year. Within a short space of time most clubs had abandoned the traditional Saturday afternoon for Sundays or, for those with floodlights, Friday nights. On the field, substitutes were allowed for the first time in 1964 and, as will be outlined in Chapter 7, the four-tackle rule was introduced in 1966.

The vehicle for a number of these innovations, such as the start of limited tackle rugby league and the installation of floodlighting, was the BBC2 TV Floodlit Trophy. Begun with just eight clubs in 1965, the RFL sought to encourage support for the new competition by offering loans to clubs for the installation of lighting – only Bradford and Leigh had used floodlighting before 1965 – and over the next two years seventeen clubs took the opportunity to upgrade their grounds, leading to probably the biggest collective investment in stadia since the 1890s.[20] Although never attracting huge crowds or viewing figures, the competition became a staple of BBC2's Tuesday night programming until the corporation withdrew its support in 1979.

The Floodlit Trophy was one of the least controversial aspects of rugby league's relationship with the BBC, a relationship that had come under intense scrutiny in the 1960s as the sport sought to understand and escape from the crisis which engulfed it. Problems had emerged almost as soon as the BBC had begun radio broadcasts on rugby league in 1927, when E. G. Blackwell had provided commentary for the Oldham versus Swinton Challenge Cup final from Wigan. There was a widespread belief in the game that the BBC was biased against rugby league and that it positively favoured rugby union. 'Many of us in the North have a suspicion that someone with an 1895 complex rules in a high place at the BBC', protested the Huddersfield Supporters' Club in 1946, but there was some cause for this mild paranoia. As early as December 1927 the RFL Council had written to the BBC to complain that rugby league results were not read out alongside soccer and rugby union scores on the Saturday teatime news bulletin. The matter arose yet again in 1948 when complaints from supporters led to the RFL asking the BBC why no league scores were given on the Light Programme's Saturday evening news programme. Feelings ran sufficiently high for the RFL to circulate the BBC's dismissive reply to clubs to encourage supporters to write directly to the BBC. In 1951 the weekly *Rugby Leaguer* organised a 25,000-name petition to support the demand. Neither initiative had the desired effect, and the issue was still being raised in 1954. The BBC was usually impervious to such demands; indeed, it was reported in August 1948 that a 'prominent' BBC administrator – the implication being that it was Head of Sport, Alan Clarke – had said that 'rugby league got far more space than the game warranted'.[21]

While there may have been an element of exaggerated self-importance in these criticisms of the BBC, the Corporation clearly did have problems presenting the sport. As Asa Briggs has noted, rugby league 'was treated very cautiously as a socially inferior local sport'. Drawn entirely from the public and grammar schools, the BBC's sports broadcasters in the 1930s had little real knowledge of rugby league, and the reporting of the game was often left to rugby union reporters such as Frank Shaw. More generally, the BBC's attitude to rugby league was a symptom of its wider inability to engage with the working classes without being condescending. Nor did professional sport gel easily with the Reithian ethos, especially when it appeared to be in direct opposition to amateurism. As late as 1948 an internal BBC document stressed its commitment to the values of 'humble endeavour … good sportsmanship and no transfer fee' and its desire to reflect 'the reputable sports world' of golf, lawn tennis, rowing and rugby union. Despite this, by the late 1930s the Challenge Cup final had become part of the BBC's national sporting schedule, even if its reporting was shot through with class and regional stereotypes.[22]

These problems came under even greater scrutiny with the advent of television. The BBC broadcast its first live league match in 1948, somewhat incongruously restricted to the Birmingham area. In the 1951–52 season it broadcast four games nationally, including a test match and the Cup Final at Wembley. But in 1953 the RFL refused permission to televise the following year's final because it believed that the 1952 attendance, which was 22,000 down on 1951, had been affected by its live coverage. Nevertheless, the RFL realised that some form of accommodation had to be reached with the new medium. In an unusually prescient insight, RFL Council member Barney Manson had predicted that 'there is no doubt that sooner or later all opposition, every stumbling block, every form of reluctance will be swept aside' by television. For the next two decades the game was torn by the suspicion that live television coverage reduced attendances at matches and the conflicting desire to use it to spread interest in the game. This schizophrenia was highlighted in 1955 when the League management committee decided that no league games would be televised, only to be overruled a month later by the clubs at a general meeting.

The initial evidence seemed to favour the view that live coverage damaged crowds. When the 1953 England versus France international was broadcast, league attendances on the same day dropped by 50 per cent and the live screening of the inaugural World Cup final between Britain and France saw league crowds on the same day fall by a third, although the obvious solution to this problem was not to stage club matches on the same day as internationals. But by the late 1950s it became clear that there was no simple causal link between television coverage and attendances at matches. Bill Fallowfield, always a firm supporter of television, monitored crowd figures for the 1958–59 season and found that there had been no 'adverse effects on gate receipts and attendances' compared to the previous season when no live league matches had been on television. Indeed, he noted that attendances at some of the televised matches were actually higher.[23] But this did not end the controversy. Warrington organised a successful campaign to stop live television coverage during the 1960–61 season. Contrary to expectations, attendances fell during the season with no live television coverage but rose when the cameras were allowed back in. This did not convince everyone and in 1965 Wigan were fined £500 by the RFL for refusing to play in a live televised cup-tie against Bradford. Four years later Warrington organised another campaign against live television and gained the support of almost half the professional clubs.

However, by the mid-1960s television broadcast fees had become a vital source of income for clubs. In the 1964–65 season the BBC paid £31,423 for exclusive broadcast rights. Even those clubs that did not feature on television received a payment of £638, a substantial amount for those in the nether regions of the league. In 1967 the contract with the BBC was renewed, providing the game with £200,000 over three years for live league, cup and international matches. This was extended for another four years in 1970, guaranteeing each club £4,000 per season. The RFL's negotiating team wearily recommended the deal by stressing that they could not 'see how clubs could hope to obtain an average of £4,000 per annum or more for four years from any other source'.[24]

This was undoubtedly true, but it ignored what was now seen as the most significant problem in television coverage: the BBC's presentation of the sport. Even in 1952 Bill Fallowfield had noted that 'there is no doubt that the public are not happy with the commentaries on rugby league which are made either on television or sound broadcasts'.[25] An RFL delegation which met with the BBC January 1973 explained that

> there was a feeling that rugby league was being used and games were only being televised when nothing better could be found, rugby union matches being preferred at times, and rugby league always seemed to be hit when very early kick-offs were required ... [sometimes] simply to show a western film.[26]

Tom Mitchell, the Workington Town representative on the RFL Council who had taken over the management of the relationship with the BBC, believed that the sport's problems were due to 'a not inconsiderable body of influence within the BBC who have no real affection for rugby league'.[27]

And then, of course, there was the problem of the commentator. Eddie Waring had been the BBC's rugby league commentator since 1951 and had been an advocate of televising live rugby league since 1950 when he had seen how American football was televised in the USA.[28] As well as his television commentaries, he was also the sport's leading journalist, working for the *Sunday Pictorial* and the *Sunday Mirror*. As early as 1952 reservations had been expressed about his commentary style – many felt he was too jocular in his comments and that his personality tended to overshadow the action on the pitch – and these grew stronger from the mid-1960s as the fortunes of the game subsided and Waring's fame increased.[29] In 1966 he became a presenter of BBC TV's *It's A Knockout* and was to become one of comedian Mike Yarwood's most famous impressions. As the BBC's rugby league commentator he fulfilled all the expectations of the northern stereotype: his sometimes unintelligible accent with broad vowels, his insistence on using humour in almost every situation, even the outdated trilby he was always seen wearing. And as Jack Williams has shown, many of Waring's supporters outside of rugby league praised him in terms that reinforced the stereotype. Geoffrey Mather of the *Daily Express* claimed that Waring's 'lips [were] equipped with tiny clogs'. Ian Wooldridge attacked those who criticised Waring and argued that his image 'was all about slagheaps, Tetley's ale, black pudding, Lowry paintings, busted noses'. The fact that many, such as Michael Parkinson, often incorrectly and unfairly thought that Waring had little understanding of the game, merely added to the stereotype of the unintelligent northerner.[30]

In fact, a great deal of Waring's on-screen persona was an act. One only has to look at his journalism, or his wartime management of Dewsbury, to see how far from the truth his television image was. As a journalist, Waring was extremely talented. Astute, opinionated and well-connected, he helped to fashion the pugnacious style of sports journalism that appeared in the mass circulation dailies in the 1950s and 1960s. His articles and books are full of verve and passion for the game, its history and its culture. Through his career he had helped to raise tens of thousands of pounds for players' benefits, amateur clubs and many other rugby league causes. Perhaps more than any other journalist, it was Waring who also promoted rugby league's egalitarian ethos: 'For years I have been plugging rugby league football as being the most democratic game in the world', he told his readers in 1948.[31]

But by the late 1960s, the commentator seemed to be becoming bigger than the game. 'Eddie Waring is rugby league', said Cliff Morgan, the former Welsh rugby union fly-half who was BBC head of outside broadcasts, in 1980. Rugby league's weaknesses meant that Waring became identified nationally as the embodiment of the sport. His television appearances on *It's a Knockout* and programmes such as the *Morecambe and Wise Show* meant that he had probably had a higher profile than the game itself – certainly one could not imagine soccer commentator Kenneth

Wolstenholme attracting such attention. And when people laughed at him, it seemed to many in the game that they were not laughing with him, but at the north and rugby league itself. It was this that caused many in the game to become antagonistic towards him as a commentator.

The issue came to a head in 1971, when the Manchester-based firm of John Caine Associates was appointed as the RFL's marketing consultants with a brief to look at the problems facing the game. When they published their findings, a substantial section of the report dealt with the BBC's presentation of the game, which, it said, was 'totally detrimental to the life of the game'. Waring's role as a commentator was characterised as 'unfortunate' and his humorous style criticised because 'the laughter is patronising and lends support to the view of rugby league held by midland and southern watchers'. The BBC's response was one of outraged intransigence: 'Eddie Waring is not just a commentator. He is The Commentator and the five million viewers prove it', declared the BBC's Derek Burrell-Davies, who had been the first BBC producer of rugby league in 1951, inadvertently confirming that the BBC did think that Waring was bigger than the game. Waring himself seemed to have little understanding of the criticisms of his commentaries, claiming that 'the BBC would not employ me' if he was not accurately reflecting the language of northern England. The controversy only made the BBC more determined to keep him. In 1976 the 1895 Club, which had been formed by supporters based in St Helens to campaign for an improvement in the sport's image, presented a petition with 11,000 signatures to the BBC, calling for an improvement to its coverage and heavily criticising Waring. The BBC took no notice and Waring carried on commentating until his retirement in 1981.[32]

★

The Caine Report marked a watershed for the sport. Although the press focused on its criticism of Eddie Waring, its real target was not Waring but Bill Fallowfield. Born into a rugby league family in Barrow, he had gone to Cambridge University before the war, played union for Northampton and the RAF, and made two appearances as a wing-forward in two wartime internationals for England. Following his appointment as RFL secretary in 1946, his energy, forcefulness and command of committee work, combined with an ability to exploit the rivalries and jealousies of club officials, gave him an unprecedented level of administrative power in the game. His arrogance was legendary, as was his desire not to let compromise stand in the way of forming a lifelong personal enmity; during his twenty-eight years as RFL secretary he initiated legal actions against journalists, newspapers, amateur rugby league officials and eventually against John Caine himself.

The Report's findings were devastating for Fallowfield. If anything, the sport was in a far worse state than it appeared. Amateur rugby league was in a 'woeful condition'. Relations with the press had broken down; 'it was not sufficient for the press and others to be told that they were too busy to answer telephone calls'. Information about sponsors and television was not passed to clubs by the RFL; 'not one club was aware of the agreement with the BBC'. A sponsorship deal with John Player had undersold the rights by tens of thousands of pounds and the RFL's investments had lost 40 per cent of their original value. Fallowfield was also directly accused of not co-operating with the consultants and of generally having 'tremendous problems in communications'. The report recommended a two-division structure for the league, a full-time organiser for the amateur game, a press office in Manchester and the publication of an official magazine to counter the poor press that the game received. It also suggested that decision-making processes were too unwieldy and proposed a reduction in the size of the RFL Council. Although the Council voted to accept the report, the consultation exercise descended into farce when Fallowfield sued Caine for libel.[33] However, the report and its aftermath had fatally undermined Fallowfield's authority, bringing into the open many of the criticisms made of him over the years. It came as little surprise when barely twelve months later he announced his early retirement.[34] Despite the drama, there was sufficient feeling for two divisions to be re-introduced to the league from the start of the 1973–74 season.[35]

For some, this was the last throw of the dice. In 1971 just 13,351 had watched the three test matches against the Kiwis tourists and barely 36,000 had seen the test matches against the 1973 Kangaroos, including an embarrassingly dismal 9,874 for the first test at Wembley. In the last season of one-division rugby league, crowds had dropped to 1,367,285. The first season of two-division rugby league saw another 200,000 spectators lost. The verdict passed by Hull KR director Ron Chester seemed to be confirmed with each passing day: 'Rugby League is not dying, it is dead.'[36]

But the precipitous decline in the numbers of people watching the game was not unique to rugby league. Soccer crowds fell by almost 32 per cent between the 1949–50 and 1964–65 seasons. Cricket crowds fell even more dramatically, from 2.1 million in 1949 to just 750,000 in 1960, worse than that of rugby league. Speedway, boxing and the other mass spectator sports also slumped in popularity. Two of the reasons advanced for falling soccer attendances do not appear to apply to rugby league. Dave Russell has suggested that rising admission charges may have played some role in deterring football supporters from attending matches. The fact that throughout the 1950s the RFL deliberately set the minimum admission charge at threepence lower than that of the Football League would suggest that rising charges would have less impact in rugby league.[37] In fact, it is more likely that spectator sport became, in economist's terms, an 'inferior good', the demand for which declined as income increased, owing to the availability of higher quality substitutes, in this case other forms of leisure. And, unlike soccer, it is not the case that crowd violence would deter spectators. There were only five instances of crowd trouble reported to the RFL in the 1950s and all of those involved assaults on referees. As will be discussed in Chapter 10, the pattern changed somewhat in the 1960s when thirty-three instances were reported but again most of these were directed at referees, with violence between supporters only appearing from 1967.[38]

The decline in sports attendances was part of a general shift away from collectively based leisure, which began in the early 1950s. The most obvious example of this was the cinema. Like sport, it had also reached unparalleled heights of popularity following the end of the Second World War. In 1946 cinema attendance peaked at 1.6 billion admissions, but by 1970 admissions amounted to just 200 million, an 87 per cent decrease. Pubs too underwent a significant contraction of custom. The same trend could also be seen on a smaller scale in the closures of Miners' Welfare Clubs that began in the mid-1950s, marking the start of a gradual unravelling of the collective culture of coalfield communities.[39] This weakening of 'traditional' collective leisure activities can be attributed partly to the rise of television. By 1961 75 per cent of households had a television; ten years later the figure had risen to 91 per cent. The attractions of watching sport from the comfort of one's armchair rather than on a windswept terrace do not need to be emphasised, yet the growth of television was not the only factor that contributed to the decline. The acquisition of a television set was one of a number of examples of the growing affluence of the late 1950s and 1960s. Car ownership leapt from 2.3 million cars in 1950 to 11.8 million in 1970, offering those who could afford a car a far greater range of leisure activities.[40] Home ownership also grew, from 16 per cent of all housing in 1945 to 47 per cent in 1970, often bringing with it a concomitant enthusiasm for 'do it yourself' home improvements. It has also been argued that the changing position of women in the 1950s and 1960s, especially the growth of female employment, undermined the traditional male-centredness of leisure, making it more difficult for men to simply choose their own leisure activities and ignore domestic tasks at weekends.[41] Indeed, the 'privatisation' of leisure was a much discussed topic among commentators in the 1960s, although many of the trends highlighted as examples, such as the popularity of allotments and gardening, the rise in the number of off-licences and drinking at home, actually had their roots in the inter-war years.

But these factors do not provide a complete explanation. Similar trends were underway in Australia and the United States, yet league in the former and professional gridiron in the latter reached new heights of popularity. The decline of collective leisure in Britain must also be seen in the context of the changing economic and urban geography of industrial England during the post-war decades. Coal and textiles had been in historic decline since at least the end of the First World War, a trend that started to accelerate from the mid-1950s, which was also the point at which the other staple industries also began to struggle. Between nationalisation of the coal industry in 1947 and the end of the 1970, over two-thirds of all coalmines were closed. In 1960 the Lancashire coalfield had ninety-three mines, thirty-one in the Wigan area alone. By 1980 there were just sixteen in the entire northwest area. In the Yorkshire coalfields, traditionally focused on export markets, the impact was to come later; ninety-five pits in 1970 were reduced to just thirty-two in 1990. The number of dockers fell by almost a half between 1951 and 1971, with numbers in Hull declining by a third. An even sharper fall was recorded in textiles. In 1954 some 538,100 people were employed in the cotton and silk industries, with a further 197,200 in wool and worsted textiles. By 1984 numbers had collapsed to just 32,500 and 41,900 respectively.[42] One effect of this accelerated structural decline of British industry was a reduction in recreational facilities provided by employers, brought about by tightening profit margins and the undermining of the paternal-ist attitudes that motivated such schemes. Works-based rugby league teams declined from seventy-eight in the 1949–50 season to just thirty-two fifteen years later, a pattern repeated in many other sports.[43]

These economic changes were accompanied by demographic shifts. Slum clearance and the provision of new homes was viewed as a priority by post-war governments and local authorities. It was well underway by the mid-1950s and brought with it a plethora of soulless housing estates and inhospitable high-rise towers. Combined with the increasing tendency towards home ownership, this resulted in serious population decline in many traditional rugby league-supporting districts. The old necessity for close geographical links between home and work was broken by improved transportation, both public and private, and by the closure of locally based factories or their movement away to new sites. The example of the Bramley and Hunslet areas of Leeds, both of which had their own professional rugby league sides, is indicative of the general trend at work across the north; between the 1951 and 1981 censuses, the population of Bramley fell by 15 per cent, while that of Hunslet shrivelled by almost 53 per cent.[44]

As rugby league and soccer grounds were often the third part of the local trin-ity of home, work and leisure, these social changes also uprooted traditional leisure patterns. In 1948 Stan Chadwick had described, albeit somewhat romantically, how the different strands of social existence intertwined to create the community of rugby league supporters and players:

> it forms part of their very existence, and they would no more dream of miss-ing a match than of absenting themselves from work. Their support dates back to schooldays; to them the players are Tom, Bill or Jack; often they work along-side them in workshop or office, and are members of the same club; their wives meet in food queues and at the child welfare centre.[45]

By the 1960s this scenario was becoming increasingly difficult to locate, even shorn of Chadwick's idealised worldview. Soccer clubs in industrial northern towns were affected no less than rugby league clubs. Between 1959 and 1985 the average attendances at Bolton, Burnley and Preston fell by more than 82 per cent, and the first three clubs to be voted out of the Football League after it reorganised its reselection procedures were Bradford Park Avenue (1970), Barrow (1972) and Workington (1977), all three in rugby league areas.

Rugby league also suffered because of a shift away from regionalism in favour of a greater national-centredness of popular culture that began in the mid-1950s. The rise of television, especially after the introduction of commercial television in 1955, was both a cause and a symptom of the increasing national centralisation of the media that took place over the following two decades. The world of newspapers was transformed by technological advances in printing and the aggressive takeover strategies of media moguls such as Roy Thomson and, later, Rupert Murdoch. It was highlighted most symbolically by the *Manchester Guardian* dropping *Manchester* from its title in 1959, an act that prefigured its subsequent move to London in 1970. By the 1970s, even the production of regional editions of national newspapers was coming to an end.

The centralisation of national media, which was always and inevitably centred on London, tended to undermine the importance of regional identities in sport and other forms of popular culture. A successful soccer club would gain as much coverage in the national media as it would in its local newspaper. Thanks to television, one did not have to live in the same town as a club to see its players regularly – or, indeed, to support them, as attested to by the phenomenon of Manchester United supporters, among others, who had never even visited the city of their chosen club. The increasing importance of international competition such as the Olympics and soccer's World and European Cups, also meant that local sporting heroes necessarily became national ones. To paraphrase Marshal McLuhan, the media was helping to create a 'national village', in which regional geography was not necessarily related to sporting affiliation. Big city soccer sides such as Manchester United, Liverpool and Arsenal acquired national followings, loosening their identities as regional sides. Conversely, clubs in smaller towns with distinct local identities lost much of their national importance. In the 1958–59 season soccer clubs from 'textile Lancashire' provided five of the First Division's twenty-two sides. By 1984–85 those same sides were scattered around the lower divisions of the Football League. This same phenomenon could also be seen in the loss of spectators across the various divisions of the Football League. While crowds in Divisions Two, Three and Four fell by 50, 48 and 64 per cent respectively between 1960–61 and 1985–86, those in Division One fell by the much smaller amount of 30 per cent. Although this could be due to discrimination in favour of higher quality football, it also reflected a decline of interest in local identities and rivalries, traditionally the sustainer of much of the interest in lower division soccer.[46]

The trend can also be seen when we look at the fortunes of Yorkshire county cricket club, arguably the most potent exemplar of sporting regional identity. In 1954, when the club finished second in the county championship paying spectators at Yorkshire's home matches averaged 13,798, with 30,818 attending that year's Roses match at Headingley, without doubt the most important county clash in the sport. By the 1968 championship-winning season, the average was down to 4,456, with just 11,841 paying to see the Roses match. Ten years later, when the county finished fourth, only 7,229 saw the same match, and an average 1,967 watched the home championship games.[47] While some of this decline was offset by the increased importance of one-day cricket, the ebbing of Yorkshire's power to evoke the same levels of interest in the 1960s and 1970s underlined regionalism's decline as a driver of sporting loyalty.

★

Given the importance of locality to rugby league, the impact of this trend towards nationally focused sport was much more severe than on other sports. This intersected, and was exacerbated by, the greater levels of social mobility of the period, largely the result of the 1944 Education Act and the access of a layer of working-class boys to grammar school, and often university, education. The use of education as an escape from a life of manual labour, exemplified by the working-class 'scholarship boy', became a motif of the early 1960s. The phenomenon had an impact on rugby league, most notably in a number of working-class boys with rugby league backgrounds who progressed to the England rugby union side after having played union at their grammar schools, most notably Reg Higgins, Ray French and Fran Cotton. In 1961 the RFL Council discussed the growing problem of boys joining local rugby union clubs after they had left school. This itself had been partly spurred by increased educational opportunities and a weakening of the caste-like barriers to social mobility that prevailed in the inter-war period. And the fact that rugby union could open up life opportunities for those who played it was not lost on rugby league supporters. In 1949 the journalist T. H. Evans Baillie reported how an unnamed rugby league international had told him 'I want my boy to play rugby union', because of the social benefits it would bring his son.[48] The prospect of rugby talent procuring social advancement rather than direct monetary reward could be an attractive alternative to those working-class boys for whom it was now available.[49]

The small but real prospects of social mobility now available also fed into the changing perceptions about what it meant to be northern and working class in the 1960s. The problem for rugby league was highlighted with great force by the 1963 release of the film version of David Storey's 1960 novel *This Sporting Life*. Born in Wakefield in 1933, Storey had won a scholarship to the local Queen Elizabeth Grammar School. After leaving, he somewhat incongruously straddled his new and old worlds by studying at London's Slade School of Fine Art while playing rugby league for Leeds 'A' team at the weekends. The novel describes the relationship between the league player Arthur Machin and his widowed landlady Valerie Hammond, combining a finely wrought understanding of the emotional entanglement of the couple with an accurate, if one-sided, description of the seamier realities of rugby league. Machin is depicted as a young man largely impervious to the world around him, while Mrs Hammond is crushed by the society around her. Many have lazily described Machin as a 'working-class hero' or anti-hero in the mould of Alan Sillitoe's Arthur Seaton (*Saturday Night and Sunday Morning*) or Colin Smith (*The Loneliness of the Long Distance Runner*). But Sillitoe's characters are rebels, kicking against a society that seeks to force them into roles they are not prepared to accept. Machin, in contrast, is not a rebel; his conformity is hampered only by his inability to understand the codes by which he is expected to live his life, not by his rejection of them. Indeed, in contrast to Sillitoe's work, *This Sporting Life* has more in common with the pre-war novel *Love on the Dole*, with its depiction of stultifying conformity and the extinguished hopes of working-class people.

But it was the book's depiction of rugby league that was problematic for the game's supporters. Machin describes how he is 'knocked about, thumped, cut, and generally treated like a piece of mobile refuse, just so that I could have that extra load of cash'. Rugby league, he says, is a 'game played for money, personal prestige, and an enjoyment composed of these two and other elements, [in which] the animal fills most of the ranks'. It is not only the players who are so described. The descriptions of spectators use the same language: 'the crowd screamed and surged like penned animals' and it sounded like 'an animal roar' or a 'maimed animal'. In contrast to Storey's subtle depiction of the emotional complexities of the couple's relationship or the social and sexual gradations of the world inhabited by the protagonists, this is a flat and one-dimensional landscape. The motives of the players are mercenary at best and the crowd simply atavistic. There is no hint of the athletic artistry that could also be seen on the pitch or of the appreciation and enjoyment that spectators could derive from it. In part, this negative portrayal of the game was derived from Storey's own experience playing for Leeds. As the only art school student among a squad of working-class youths he stuck out like a sore thumb and was treated as such by his team-mates. 'I think I handled it extremely badly. I was permanently belligerent', he admitted later, and it is this belligerence which colours his portrayal of the sport.[50]

These themes were at the forefront of Lindsay's Anderson's film adaptation of Storey's book. Filmed in stark black and white and unremittingly bleak in tone, it was dominated by Richard Harris's portrayal of Machin, which derives not a little from Marlon Brando's performance as Stanley Kowalski in *A Streetcar Named Desire*. Its most memorable scenes are the match sequences, filmed at Wakefield Trinity and making full use of the club's players and coaching staff; scenes in which, with the exception of a flowing movement leading to a try mid-way through the film, violence is the dominating feature. Indeed, these images are among the most memorable of the whole film. Lacking the novel's means of portraying the protagonists' emotional and social complexities, the film highlights rugby league as the metaphor for the brutality and inarticulacy of northern, male working-class life.

Coming at the end of the New Wave of British realist cinema, the film was a major success in Britain and America, with Harris being nominated for an Oscar. Although the film was welcomed by many people in rugby league for putting the game in the public eye – Harris was made an honorary president of Wakefield Trinity – it was not welcomed by everyone. At a discussion at the 1963 annual meeting of the Yorkshire Federation of Supporters' Clubs, Hull KR representatives complained that the film was not a fair reflection and was 'detrimental to the rugby league code'. Supporters from Wakefield Trinity claimed that they were not aware of 'the true nature' of the film until it was premiered, presumably not having bothered to read the book. York fans on the other hand thought that it was 'not far from being correct' and that some games did indeed degenerate into 'bloodbaths'. Reviewing the film for the *Rugby Leaguer*, Ramon Joyce commented that 'my worst fears of the film ... were unfortunately realised'.[51] From a broader perspective, the film presented an image of rugby league that was deeply out of step not only with the 'Swinging Sixties' but also with the fashionable young north, a phenomenon described by Raphael Samuel:

the North in the 1960s – anyway the early 1960s, when Harold Wilson made his appearance as a great iconoclast, the Mersey Sound first captured the nation's record players, and Z Cars put Liverpool in the front line of crime-busting – was definitely Mod, and on the side of radical change. It offered itself as an idiom for the degentrification of British public life. In place of an effete establishment it promised a new vitality, sweeping the deadwood from the boardrooms, and replacing hidebound administrators with ambitious young go-getters. In place of the polite evasions of circumlocution and periphrasis, it made a fetish of bluntness.[52]

This new northernness was associated with varying degrees of rebellion and a rejection of the past. It was perhaps most pointedly highlighted in the Beatles' film *A Hard Day's Night*, when the group inadvertently share a railway carriage compartment with a bowler-hatted representative of the southern middle classes: 'I fought the war for your sort', he says indignantly as the four mock him, to which Ringo flashes back 'I bet you're sorry you won!'

In contrast, rugby league's northernness was firmly rooted in the past. It was led by men for whom the Second World War was a defining experience, both in their own lives and for the way in which the sport had become a part of the national culture. The game's immobility in the face of a changing world and inability to escape the past were evocatively captured by Arthur Hopcraft in a 1964 article for the *Sunday Times Colour Magazine*:

> There is an extraordinary anachronism about the setting of League, its grounds bounded by the living museum pieces of the heyday of British heavy industry; a railway line on one side, the eyeless wall of some tired-out old mill, the colour of dried blood, on another, and behind you the bent backs of the terrace rows, built in brutal meanness for men with fears and families; and from their chimneys the soot brushes your forehead like a kiss from a corpse. … Rugby league men give the impression that they know they are tethered somewhere back in the social evolution.[53]

Hopcraft's observations were also shared by some in the game. In 1960 Wigan had argued that the sport 'has literally stood still in a changing world. The structure still remains the same' and urged a radical rethink of the organisation of the league.[54] But there was little that the sport could do to change its image. Life increasingly came to imitate art as journalistic coverage of league drew on the images popularised by *This Sporting Life*. The *Sunday People* in particular regularly entertained its readers with graphic stories of violent play. Mick Sullivan's life story was serialised with lurid descriptions of stiff-arm tackling taking centre stage, and even Billy Boston allegedly claimed in its pages that rugby league 'was the dirtiest of all games'.[55] This national image of rugby league mirrored to some extent contemporary middle-class stereotypes of working-class men. Violent, inarticulate and stubbornly refusing to change with the times; this was a stereotype which was regularly rolled out when dealing with the widespread trade union militancy of this period. It may well have been trendy during much of the 1960s to be *from* the working class but it was not so fashionable to be *of* the working class.

And yet, despite the apparent slide towards an irrelevant death, there still remained a deep residual support for rugby league in its traditional constituencies. Clubs regularly staved off economic collapse through the efforts of volunteers and wider circles of more passive support within their communities. Nowhere was this better demonstrated than at Bradford, where, within five years of their seemingly terminal financial crisis, the club had recovered and increased its average crowds to over 9,000 in the 1967–68 season. And at the sport's highest levels, the Challenge Cup final at Wembley recorded significantly bigger average attendances in the 1960s and 1970s than the 1940s or 1950s (87,356 and 86,622 as against 79,712 and 80,012), hosting capacity crowds three times in the later decades, compared to just once in the post-war years. The continuing success of the cup final demonstrated the two major trends affecting the fortunes of the game. The high media profile of the match, ironically due in large part to BBC TV coverage, gave rugby league an annual prominence on the national stage, allowing it to benefit from the increasing national focus of sport and popular culture. And this exposure also helped to increase the appeal of the annual supporters' excursions to Wembley. The interaction of national prominence and the stimulation of the traditional reservoir of community support were the two factors that were to prove crucial to the sport regaining its health in the 1980s.

Chapter 7

'Chess with muscles': the rules of the game

The move to limited tackle rugby league in 1966 was part of a trend that was as old as the game itself. In contrast to its rival codes, the sport had never been fearful about changing the rules of the game. This was in marked contrast to soccer, which had maintained an extremely stable set of rules since the 1880s, and to rugby union, where the social conservatism of its leaders was matched by their extreme reluctance to tamper with the grandly titled 'Laws of the Game'. To a large extent this capacity for change was rooted in the circumstances of the sport's birth. The movement that led to the Northern Union had been one that sought to make rugby a more open and entertaining spectacle for players and spectators alike. Proposals to amend rugby's rules had been voiced even before 1895; as early as 1891 there had been calls to reduce teams to thirteen-a-side, and the constant scrummaging of the game was seen as a severe disadvantage in the battle with soccer for spectators. As well as reducing the value of goals, the line-out had been abolished by the NU in 1897 and the rules continued to be honed in various ways until the two key changes of 1906 – the reduction of teams to thirteen-a-side and the move to an orderly play-the-ball after a tackle – had made the sport qualitatively different from the union game.

As well as making the game attractive to spectators, there were also fundamental technical reasons for the sport's willingness to change. Like all handling codes of football, rugby league was forced to grapple with the question of what happens when the ball carrier is tackled. Unlike soccer, where the ban on outfield players using their hands made it is impossible to use spoiling tactics by continually holding on to the ball, the problem is one with which all handling versions of football are beset. Rugby union's answer, that a ruck, a maul or a formal scrum be formed so that forwards can struggle for possession of the ball, was seen by the NU and its public as unsatisfactory because it severely reduced the opportunities for open rugby. Nor were they alone. The Canadian Rugby Union had introduced a version of the orderly play-the-ball in 1879, whereby a tackled player had to get up and immediately place the ball on the ground, and in 1882 it followed this up with the abolition of the scrum, replacing it with an American football-type scrimmage in which the centre would heel the ball back to the quarterback. Football in the US had also separated itself from its original rugby rules by replacing the scrum with the orderly scrimmage in 1880 and by introducing the concept of 'downs' two years later. Although Michael Oriard has claimed that the latter changes were manifestations of American cultural exceptionalism, the fact that these were only marginally different answers to questions that were also being asked by rugby players in the north of England suggests that the mechanics of playing a handling code of football was a crucial factor in the evolution of those codes that rejected rugby union rules.[1]

Both American and Canadian football solved the question of the struggle for the ball by abolishing it. Rugby league sought to control it and make it secondary to the running, handling and tackling features of the game. Consequently, for the half century following the end of the First World War, the sport was involved in a continuous assessment and revision of its scrum and the play-the-ball rules, as it attempted to steer a course between union's domination by scrums and North American football's uncontested scrimmages. The first major gathering of rugby league officials after the First World War was a special conference in 1921 to discuss the problems of scrums. In what was to become a familiar refrain, scrummaging was identified as a major blight on the game. Not only was it felt that there were too many with an average of between fifty and sixty a match, but it was also agreed that they were disorganised, causing the ball to have to be put into the scrum several times, and that the ball rarely came out cleanly from them. Hookers – a title that was just coming into common parlance, in preference to striker or centre-forward – were accused of trying to get an unfair advantage by putting their legs across the tunnel formed by the scrum. Props, the two front-row forwards who supported the hooker on either side, were also accused of the same offences, while scrum-halves were criticised for their inability to put the ball into the middle of the scrum in order to allow both hookers to have an equal chance of striking for it with their feet. Rather than changing the rules, the conference suggested five 'guidelines' for referees to implement.[2]

This did little to alleviate the problems and similar discussions occurred throughout the inter-war years. There were rule changes to prevent the more obvious reasons for scrum problems, such as the 1930 rule forcing forwards to pack down with three in the front row, two in the second row and a loose forward binding the second row – designed to prevent teams having four in the front row and unbalancing the scrum – and the 1932 ban on the hooker having a loose arm in the scrum. These changes usually resulted in an initial spate of dismissals of hookers for breaking the new ruling (six were sent off on one Saturday following the ban on loose arms), followed by a period in which the status quo ante bellum gradually reasserted itself and the same problems arose again. As many speakers at the RFL's 1935 Annual Conference noted, there was little wrong with the scrums if the rules were implemented correctly by referees. The problem, as pointed out by Hull's Harry Dannatt, was that scrum-halves and hookers continued to attempt to break the rules to their advantage. Indeed, rule-breaking was almost inherent in the very nature of the scrum – when Australian hooker Ken Kearney arrived to play for Leeds in 1948 he asked a referee what were the best tactics to use in English scrums. 'Cheat' was the one-word reply he allegedly, but quite believably, received. The cycle of clampdown, dismissals and eventual reassertion of the norm continued into the 1970s, when the introduction of limited tackle rugby league meant that struggle for possession, and consequently scrums, lost much of its previous importance.[3]

The fact that it seemed that the scrum could not be reformed led many to advocate that its importance should be reduced. As early as 1928 there had been proposals from Batley's chairman J. F. Whittaker to revert back to a punt out from touch following a kick over the touch line, instead of a scrum. The debate became more intense in the late 1930s, when it was not uncommon to see matches of between eighty and a hundred scrums. In 1935 a long debate about scrums at the RFL's Annual Conference reached the verdict that something should be done, even though no-one knew quite what. At the 1938 conference John Wilson proposed a soccer-style throw-in from touch, whereby a ball kicked out of play would not lead to a scrum but would be thrown-in as in soccer, with the caveat that it could not be thrown forward. This was unanimously approved in principle but stalled because of the logistics of discussing it with Australia, France and New Zealand, a problem that became insurmountable with the outbreak of the Second World War.[4] The idea was raised again after the end of the war and a handful of experimental games were organised to test the rule. But it failed to capture the imagination not only of players and spectators but also of the Australian and New Zealand leagues. After watching an experimental game at Bramley in 1947, the New Zealand touring team's managers argued that 'we must never lose sight of the fact that the scrum-mage is part of the rugby game and that it would be wrong to do away with it and thus lose the advantage of having big strong men in our game'.[5] The following year Australian Board of Control secretary Keith Sharp saw Hunslet 'A' play Wakefield Trinity 'A' under the rule and was even less enthusiastic, seeing 'no real need for the introduction of this suggested innovation'. He thought that it could easily be used for time-wasting and would probably eventually become identical to the line-out. He was, he reported back to Australia, 'unconvinced' that the throw-in was 'either desirable or necessary'.[6]

Indeed, both of the Antipodean authorities were reluctant to fundamentally alter the rules of the game. In their eyes, provided that the rules were properly imple-mented by referees and adhered to by players, there was little wrong with the way the game was played. Although differences in interpretation of the rules had been a source of contention on tours – for example, the Australian insistence on pun-ishing a forward pass with a penalty for off-side (because the catcher was in front of the passer) rather than a scrum (as in Britain) was a continual source of friction for almost seventy years – these were the result of the 'tyranny of distance' between the league-playing nations rather than deep-rooted differences about how the game should be played. It may even have been the case that Australian and New Zealand players were more inclined to play to the spirit of the law – Ken Kearney's shock at being told to cheat on his arrival at Leeds was matched by the surprise of British fans to find that the 1948 Australian tourists got up quickly from tackles and played the ball cleanly back to their waiting team-mates, in marked contrast to the slow and ragged play-the-balls common in the English game.[7]

Although the throw-in proposal died, it was not the end of the RFL's attempts to make basic changes to the rules of the game. For the next twenty years the leadership of the league expended much time and energy trying to find alternatives to the play-the-ball rule. The fact that the play-the-ball after a tackle was still regarded as having an element of the struggle for possession meant that it was fraught with difficulties. The original idea was that the play-the-ball would be a kind of two-man scrum, in which a tackled player had to get to his feet, put the ball on the ground and then try to heel it back to a team-mate, known as the acting half-back or dummy half. This was complicated by the fact that the tackler was also allowed to strike for the ball with his foot and that other players could gather around the play-the-ball. Needless to say, the opportunities for breaking the rules in order to gain an advantage were legion.[8] Despite its problems, however, the play-the-ball was regarded by all in league as a qualitative improvement over rugby union's rucking and mauling, and the quickness with which it usually allowed the ball to be passed to the backs was one of the reasons why French journalists in the 1930s nicknamed the sport 'lightning rugby'.

This was a view that came under serious pressure in the 1950s, thanks in large part to the efforts of Bill Fallowfield. In 1946 he proposed experimenting with a rugby union-style method of releasing the ball in the tackle.[9] This was not taken too seriously at the time, partly because no-one expected it to be adopted – in 1942 John Leake, supported by Wigan, had unsuccessfully made a similar proposal on the grounds that it would make it easier to convert Welsh union clubs to league – but also because it was merely one of numerous ideas that had been floated since the late 1930s as a way of cutting down on teams having continuous possession of the ball for long passages of a match.[10] Particularly in important matches or those in which the scores were close, teams would minimise the risk of losing possession by having the acting half-back pick the ball up from the play-the-ball and run forward without passing time after time. Nicknamed the 'creeping barrage' by *Yorkshire Post* journalist Eric Stanger, one of the most notorious examples occurred during the 1951 Championship semi-final at Central Park, when Workington Town, reduced to twelve men owing to injury, defended an 8–5 lead against Wigan with fifteen minutes left to play.[11] Gus Risman, Town's captain and coach, ordered his players not to pass or kick the ball:

> They would be tackled, play the ball to the acting half-back, who would move forward two yards and then go down in a tackle. He would then play the ball to the acting-half back, who would move forward two yards and then go down in a tackle. And so it went on ad infinitum.[12]

At the October 1954 meeting of the Rugby League International Board, Fallowfield and Leigh chairman James Hilton proposed using the rugby union method of playing the ball as a way of reducing problems at the play-the-ball. The other three nations rejected it out of hand. Australia argued that there was nothing wrong with the rule providing that the referee enforced it properly, while French secretary Antoine Blain captured the significance of the debate when he stated that 'to adopt the rugby union method [of playing the ball] would be to step back fifty years, which would be bad'.[13] Nevertheless, this did little to dampen Fallowfield's enthusiasm for the idea. In the RFL's 1954–55 annual report he blamed the play-the-ball rule for the decline in the sport's attendances since the 1940s. He also received support from a very unlikely source in the shape of the Duke of Edinburgh, who had presented the cup at the 1955 Challenge Cup final and told Lord Derby that he did not like the league method of playing the ball because it had 'all the disadvantages' of American football.[14]

The receipt of the royal seal of disapproval was treated as the tocsin to commence battle and in June 1955 Fallowfield persuaded the RFL Council that all pre-season friendly matches and the Lancashire and Yorkshire Cup competitions should be played using the rugby union method of playing the ball. But Prince Philip's opinions counted for little among those who were expected to play under the rules. Wakefield Trinity flatly refused to consider the union rule and cancelled their pre-season friendly with Castleford in protest and both the Lancashire and Yorkshire county committees refused, arguing that it would bring the game into ridicule.[15] In June 1956 a questionnaire was circulated to clubs about changing the play-the-ball rule. Of the twenty-four that replied, just three wanted further trials of the union rule.[16] Two experimental matches were staged in October 1956 but both were unsurprisingly characterised by the press as 'a farce'.[17] This did not stop Fallowfield's campaign, however. At the RFL's 1958 annual general meeting the idea was again raised but rejected by twenty votes to seven and in 1961 a slightly revised version of it was again thrown out, although it led to yet another experimental trial match being played, this time between specially selected British and French sides in Paris. The players were chosen for their familiarity with rugby union, yet it made little difference to the outcome. Ray French, who had won four England rugby union caps before joining his home-town club St Helens, recalled that 'the game was a disaster and many of us spent the whole evening scratching and scrambling on the floor for the ball'.[18]

Justifying his reputation as a man impervious to criticism, Fallowfield raised the issue again in November 1963 when he circulated a memorandum on the subject to the RFL Council. Testily denouncing 'dyed in the wool Rugby Leagueites' who wanted to retain the traditional play-the-ball, he stated baldly that 'this particular law has given trouble ever since the tackled player was first allowed, in 1907 [it was actually 1906], to rise from the ground with the ball in his hands'. Furthermore, he argued, the rugby union method of releasing the ball in the tackle had 'stood the test of time' and that the play-the-ball 'reduces the chances of the rugby league game appealing to a much wider public'.[19] He therefore arranged a specially created competition to test his ideas, the 'Bottom Fourteen Play-Offs' for those clubs finishing in the wrong half of the league table. This time the rule was changed to allow a team one tackle with a standard rugby league play-the-ball but on the second tackle they had to release the ball rugby union-style. The latter, claimed Fallowfield haughtily, was 'a method which was readily understood by all rugby supporters throughout the world', ignoring the fact that rugby league supporters' understanding was not matched by a corresponding enthusiasm for it, as the abject crowds for the competition demonstrated.[20] Voicing the general criticism both of the play-off idea and the new rule, four clubs refused to take part and those that did demanded that matches be subsidised by the League. To no-one's great surprise it went down in the annals of rugby league as possibly the most meaningless tournament ever staged. Even Fallowfield later described it as 'unsatisfactory', not least because it cost the RFL several hundred pounds to compensate clubs for the poor crowds at matches.[21] Whatever shred of credibility the tournament may have had was destroyed three weeks before it kicked-off when an emergency meeting of the clubs voted against any change to the rules. The competition therefore became a trial of a rule that could not be implemented.[22] Yet again, rugby league appeared to the public to be a sport whose administrators appeared to be constantly changing their minds and altering the rules of the game. David Watkins, who signed for Salford from Welsh rugby union in 1967, later looked back on his first years in the game with bewilderment: 'there were confusions and anomalies under the Fallowfield regime which made Rugby League football hard for spectators to follow and, let me add, for players to play!'[23]

Why was such a state of affairs allowed to happen? In large part it must be seen in the context of the severe financial problems facing the game from the late 1950s. As we saw in the previous chapter, there was also a growing sense of anomie among many in the leadership of the game. Fallowfield was able to fill the vacuum of leadership with a vision of rugby league that appears to have been essentially that of professional thirteen-a-side rugby union. In 1963 he wrote to RFU secretary Robin Prescott about the play-the-ball rule saying 'I can never see why it was instituted in the first place'.[24] As well as wanting to adopt the rugby union play-the-ball rule he was also an early enthusiast of the throw-in from touch proposal. In 1973, long after the play-the-ball controversy had been settled, he gave a stout defence of his position:

> top class [rugby union] matches are attracting large crowds who are showing great enthusiasm. One advantage accruing from adopting the rugby union play-the-ball would be that rugby league clubs would not be wasting money on signing-on fees because if a player was good at one game he would automatically be good at the other. Furthermore a broader section of physical specimen would be required and all the team need not necessarily be super athletes or expert ball handlers, the forwards would be used for the purpose for which they were originally intended, i.e. securing possession for the backs.[25]

Of course, the irony of Fallowfield's position was that it was rugby union that was taking rules directly from rugby league. In 1948 the RFU had reduced the value of the dropped goal from four to three points. In 1970 kicking the ball directly into touch was allowed only from behind the kicking side's twenty-five yard line, a variation on the league rule and one that had operated for decades in Australian union. The following year the value of a try was increased to four points, the first time in the history of union that a try had been worth more than a dropped or penalty goal, and was again raised in 1992 to five points. A regular drip feed of rule changes continued from the early 1970s, aimed at speeding the game up and encouraging handling movements and the scoring of tries. And from the late 1980s, as the howling gale of incipient professionalism battered at its doors, numerous rule changes were introduced to make the release of the ball after a tackle quicker and more fluid, causing numerous commentators to note that 'the suspicion is growing that the new laws are making rugby union appear more like rugby league'.[26]

Although Fallowfield's statements about the merits of union to the detriment of league were anathema to most of the game's players and supporters, they did find a degree of support among club directors and members of the RFL Council. Fallowfield himself had played for Moortown RUFC until the early 1950s despite his position as RFL secretary. Like him, a number of the game's leading figures had strong links with rugby union, most notably Leeds' director Edwin Airey, who was one of the founders of the reformed Bradford RUFC as well as being a long-standing RFL Council member, and Keighley's John Smallwood, who had been Skipton RUFC's secretary and who at the time of his election as RFL chairman in 1967 was also a vice-president of two union clubs.[27] To some extent this was indicative of the interlocking nature of sporting loyalties among the local middle classes where top-class league, union and soccer were all available during the winter months. But Fallowfield's views were also indicative of a frustration on the part of some club directors that rugby league was not able to escape from its working-class roots and image, and that a change in the rules might make the game more acceptable to rugby union's traditional constituency. He himself was dismissive of those who disagreed with his views: 'It is difficult for [rugby league supporters and officials] to look at the game objectively. Their interest is primarily in winning rather than being entertained', he argued in 1966. Similar views were sometimes expressed privately by club officials, although it was left to a vicar from Cumberland to express them on paper:

> there is [sic] far too many drawn from one social order who are intimately connected with the management of our code. We must have at least a sprinkling of a class with a superior intelligence and if it be correct to say so, men who have climbed a rung or two higher up the social ladder. We want toning up, and so a little of the plus four lads would be of immense gain to the game.[28]

The fact that Fallowfield was not disinclined to disguise his belief in his own 'superior intelligence' was a not insignificant factor in his failure to gather support to adopt the rugby union play-the-ball rule. But there were also more important objective reasons. The outright opposition to it by the Australian and New Zealand leagues meant that the RFL could not unilaterally implement it without doing severe harm to the international game and consequently itself. This was not merely a question of prestige, the reciprocal tours still provided the RFL with its most significant source of revenue after the Challenge Cup final. Secondly, and possibly more importantly, there was widespread opposition to such a move throughout British rugby league. Echoing the Australian position, Dewsbury's George Oldroyd had argued that the problems of the play-the-ball could be placed at the door of players trying to gain an unfair advantage. It was also noted that the problems did not occur in amateur and schoolboy rugby league and that it was the gamesmanship of professional players that was to blame.[29] At a conference of former players and officials called to discuss standards of play in 1954, which included Jim Sullivan, Alec Fiddes and John Wilson (all of them highly familiar with union as well as league), not one mentioned the rugby union rule.[30] Writing in 1955, Joe Egan, the then Leigh coach and probably the sport's greatest-ever hooker, argued that it was negative tactics by teams, rather then the play-the-ball rule, which was to blame for declining attendances.[31] Indeed, outside of Fallowfield and one or two club directors such as Leigh's James Hilton, no-one in the game made any public statement in favour of a return to the union rule. This should not be surprising. The idea that rugby league should revert to a rule which it had decisively rejected in 1906 cut to the very marrow of the sport's culture. It was an article of faith to rugby league followers that the play-the-ball was superior to union's method of releasing the ball. The union rule offended every technical instinct of the rugby league player and every aesthetic feeling of the supporter. The first principle of playing rugby league was to keep hold of the ball. The greatest crime was to lose it. Players who had spent their entire sporting lives adhering to these principles could not easily or willingly abandon this truth.

Indeed, those rugby league followers interested in such questions have argued that the play-the-ball is fundamental to the underlying philosophy of the game and is the unique distinguishing feature between it and rugby union. French historian Robert Fassolette has argued that, because of the play-the-ball, 'rugby league gives the decisive role to the individual ... by restoring a clear and fair man-to-man duel in every blocked situation, rugby league is a true modern game', in contrast to the 'frustration' and 'irresponsibility' of the tackled ball-carrier in union.[32] True or not, the fact that similar if unarticulated beliefs were common throughout league demonstrates that cultural traditions of sports are not merely embodied in team colours, nostalgia, sense of place or shared experiences of supporting a club. They are also embodied in the rules of the chosen sport. The way the game is organised and played becomes the template upon which cultural meanings can be written and expressed. Rugby league without the distinctive rules that differentiated it from other sports would cease to be rugby league, and it would consequently forfeit both its support and the cultural meaning that it has within its communities.

The debate over the play-the-ball rule was finally settled by a decision to move further away from rugby union rules and borrow from American football. The British, represented by Fallowfield and Hull KR director Wilf Spaven, who appeared to contribute little to the meeting, once again put reform of the play-the-ball rule on the agenda of the July 1966 International Board meeting. And once again the Australian and New Zealand delegates opposed any major change to the nature of the play-the-ball. However, this time the Australians were also seeking a solution to a domestic problem: the fact that one side, St George, had won the Sydney premiership ten consecutive times and showed little sign of relinquishing the title (they were to make it eleven later that year). Although there is no evidence to suggest, as St George supporters believed, that the rules were deliberately changed to stop them winning, their total domination of Australia's leading competition meant that the Australian representatives were more open to ideas which would make the game more competitive. On the first day of the International Board meeting Fallowfield referred to the experience of American football and its introduction of the rule that dictated a transfer of possession after three downs. Why he did so is not clear. It may have been a warning as to the future direction of the game or as a possible way out of the impasse. The following day, the New Zealand delegates requested that the discussion be continued and proposed the idea that a side should have three play-the-balls, following which a scrum should be formed if they were tackled in possession. For the first time in two decades of discussion, all four countries agreed and a decision was made to experiment with the four-tackle rule and report back before it was adopted.[33]

Back in England, the new rule was trialled in the BBC2 Floodlit Trophy competition in October 1966. Within the first few matches it was clear that it encouraged attacking play and speeded up the game considerably. Flushed with success, the RFL Council decided in the middle of October to allow it to be used in League matches if both teams agreed. This meant that League matches were being played under two different sets of rules and that clubs could decide which set to play against which opponents. For example, Leeds chose to play the four-tackle rule against a weak Doncaster side but the old rule against the Challenge Cup holders St Helens, much to the annoyance of the latter. Caught in a mess caused by their own enthusiastic lack of foresight, the Council met on 26 October and announced that from 31 October all matches would be played under the four-tackle rule, giving clubs one week to prepare.[34] Fortunately, the success of the rule overcame the abruptness of its introduction and within weeks it was being hailed as a turning point for the game, as Norman Gaulton reported in the *Rugby League Magazine*:

> Few will deny that it has produced an improvement. It has ended the forward domination which was killing the game as a spectacle. ... Skill and enterprise have been given far more rein during these last few months, and the variety of tactics and the spirit of adventure which have been so sadly lacking has been reintroduced again.[35]

A similar verdict was delivered by the three other nations, Australia's Bill Buckley telling the RFL Council that it had 'revitalised' the game down under. Although Buckley did not know it at the time, the rule also helped to bring about the end of St George's amazing premiership run when Canterbury finally ended their streak with a 12–11 win in the 1967 preliminary final. For teams like St George who built their game around continuous forward drives to give their backs a platform for attack or who lacked a strong tactical kicker, the new rule created tremendous difficulties.[36] It was partly in recognition of this and the belief that more tackles would allow a more structured attack to develop that the rule was extended to six tackles in 1972, following two trials in Sydney, marking a further move away from union's contest for possession.[37] Over the next ten years rugby league continued to abandon the last semblances of its rugby union heritage. In 1974 the value of the drop-goal was reduced from two points to one, the problems of the scrum were gradually solved by the expedient of allowing, albeit informally, the scrum-half to feed the ball to his own forwards, and in 1983 a handover of the ball to the opposing side, rather than a scrum, was introduced when the attacking side was tackled in possession on the sixth tackle. The final break with the past came with a series of changes in the early 1990s to the play-the-ball rule that removed the last vestiges of the struggle for possession and made it simply a device for restarting play. In the continuum occupied by the handling codes of football, rugby league had never been so far away from its rugby union roots.

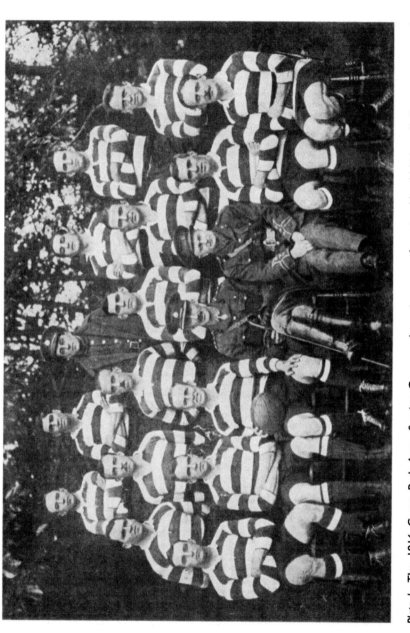

Plate 1 The 1916 Grove Park Army Service Corps rugby union team, featuring Harold Wagstaff (front row, second from right) Ben Gronow (middle row, third from right) and Douglas Clark (back row, far right).

Credit: RFL Archives

RULES AS TO
PROFESSIONALISM

The Rugby Union Committee deem it advisable, as the game spreads in all parts of the country, to draw the attention of all players to these rules.

THE PRINCIPAL RULES AS AFFECT THE INDIVIDUAL ARE AS FOLLOWS:—

1. Professionalism is illegal.

2. Acts of Professionalism are:—

   Asking, receiving, or relying on a promise, direct or implied, to receive any money consideration whatever, actual or prospective, any employment or advancement, any establishment in business, or any compensation whatever for :—

   (a) Playing football or rendering any service to a football organisation (provided however, that the Secretary and Treasurer of a Club who has definitely ceased playing football may be excepted under special conditions).

   (b) Training, or loss of time connected therewith.

   (c) Time lost in playing football or in travelling in connection with football.

   (d) Expenses in excess of the amount actually disbursed on account of reasonable hotel or travelling expenses.

   Playing for a Club while receiving, or after having received from such Club, any consideration whatever for acting as an official, or for doing or having done any work about the Club's ground or in connection with the Club's affairs, unless such work was done before the receiver became a football player.

   Remaining on tour at his Club's expense longer than is reasonable.

   Giving or receiving any money testimonial. Or, giving or receiving any other testimonial, except under the authority of this Union.

   Playing on any ground where gate money is taken :—

   (a) During the close season (that is between 21st April and 1st September, except when the Tuesday in Easter Week falls later than 21st April, when the close season shall commence from the Wednesday in the Easter Week), except where special permission for the game has been granted by this Committee.

   (b) In any match or contest where it is previously agreed that less than 15 players on each side shall take part (except where, in exceptional cases, this Committee may have granted special permission for less than 15 players aside to take part).

   Knowingly playing with or against any expelled or suspended player or Club, or with or against any professional player or Club.

   Refusing to give evidence or otherwise assist in carrying out these rules when requested by this Union to do so.

   Being registered as, or declared a professional, or suspended by any National Rugby Union or by the Football Association.

   Playing within 8 days of any accident for which he has claimed or received insurance compensation, if insured under these rules.

   Playing in any benefit match connected with football (except where this Committee has given permission for a *bona fide* charity match).

   Knowingly playing or acting as referee or touch judge on the ground of an expelled or suspended club.

   Receiving money or other valuable consideration from any person or persons as an inducement towards playing football.

   Signing any form of the Northern Union (Rugby League).

   Advocating or taking steps to promote Northern Union (Rugby League) or other professional football.

   The penalty for breach of these Rules is suspension or expulsion. (Expulsion carries with it the formal declaration of professionalism).

   This Union shall have power to deal with all acts which it may consider as acts of professionalism and which are not specifically provided for.

   October, 1924.   *BY ORDER OF THE COMMITTEE.*

IGNORANCE OF THE RULES IS NO DEFENCE.

Plate 2 A 1924 RFU poster for display in rugby union club houses warning players of the dangers of 'professionalism' and contamination by the Northern Union.

Credit: Museum of Rugby, Twickenham

Plate 3   Wigan's triumphant team parade the Challenge Cup through the streets of the town in 1929 after their victory in the first Wembley cup final.

Credit: RFL Archives

Plate 4 The 1929–30 Australian tourists in the garden of 10 Downing Street as tour manager Harry Sunderland shakes hands with Prime Minister Ramsey MacDonald.

Credit: RFL Archives

Plate 5 Gracie Fields in the kit of her home-town team Rochdale Hornets shakes hands with Hornets' Victor Armbruster and St Helens Recreation's Billy Greenall in the early 1930s.

Credit: RFL Archives

Plate 6 Handbill produced for the first-ever rugby league versus rugby union match at Headingley in January 1943. Playing under union rules, the league side won 18–11.

Credit: Museum of Rugby, Twickenham

Plate 7 Mrs Minnie Cotton is escorted from the pitch at the 1966 Challenge Cup semi-final after rushing on to defend her lodger, St Helens' forward John Warlow.

Credit: RFL Archives

Plate 8 League meets the swinging sixties. Star of the *Avengers* TV series and 1960s icon Diana Rigg is interviewed at Headingley in 1965 while Leeds play Oldham.

Credit: RFL Archives

Chapter 8

The Kangaroo connection: Anglo-Australian rugby league

The debate over the introduction of the four-tackle rule highlighted the extent to which the sport was now completely intertwined between Britain and Australia. Locked as it was into the geographical straitjacket of three counties in the north of England, the spread of the game to Australasia in 1907 was crucial to the consolidation of rugby league's distinct identity. As well as the interest generated by the regular visits to and from the Antipodes, a significant amount of cosmopolitan glamour for the game was provided by the regular signings of star Australian and New Zealand players by British clubs. Just as importantly, it gave rugby league a deep sense of self-confidence – after all, it was proof that the sport was capable of expanding beyond its northern boundaries – and allowed it to register a small presence as one of the sports of the Empire. As the *Athletic News* pointed out in 1923, 'one phase of the game attracts interest even outside Lancashire and Yorkshire ... the periodical visits of British teams to Australasia and Australasian teams to England'.[1]

Although A. H. Baskerville's 1907 pioneer Kiwi tourists had established the sport in the southern hemisphere, the New Zealanders struggled against the behemoth of union in their country. Rugby league there remained an entirely amateur sport until the 1980s. The infrequency of New Zealand tours to Britain and the perceived weakness of their sides when compared to the Australians meant that Australia was always a bigger attraction for spectators and a greater challenge for players. By the mid-1920s Anglo-Australian test matches were unrivalled as the pinnacle of the sport, as well as being hugely profitable. In 1920 Australia had regained the 'Ashes', as the contests had been known since the first tour, surprising the star-studded British touring side. The following year the symbolic trophy had been snatched back in a series which had thrilled the crowds and which did more than anything to cement the attractiveness of Australian touring sides, thanks to the wonderful ball-handling skills of the Kangaroos. A solitary Jim Sullivan conversion ten minutes from time in the second test of 1924 had kept the Ashes in British hands and the 1928 series had been a similarly close affair.

The 1929–30 Kangaroo tour was even closer; echoing Bob Deans' famous disallowed 'try' for the New Zealand rugby union tourists against Wales in 1905, Australian scrum-half Joe 'Chimpy' Busch seemed to have won the Ashes with two minutes remaining in the third test at Swinton in Manchester. With the score tied at 0–0 Australia won a scrum against the feed twenty-five yards from the England tryline. Busch picked the ball up from the base of the scrum, evaded a couple of would-be tacklers and darted to the corner like a hawk hunting a sparrow. As he dived to ground the ball and win back the Ashes, England's Fred Butters, who had chased Busch from the scrum, lunged across, grabbed his legs and tried to roll him into touch before the ball hit the ground. As Busch, Butters and the ball hit the corner flag, the referee Bob Robinson went to signal a try only to see touch judge Albert Webster standing motionless with his flag in the air, indicating that Busch had knocked the flag over before grounding the ball. In Australian folklore, Robinson allegedly said to Busch 'Fair try Australia, but I am over-ruled', although Busch's team-mate Victor Armbruster recalled the referee's words as 'Tough luck son'. Busch never wavered in his belief that he had scored a legitimate try, claiming that he was getting up after placing the ball down when Butters hit the flag. In later years Jonty Parkin, the English captain that day, said that he agreed with him. In the few seconds remaining of the match, Butters left the field covered in blood after ripping open an ear on either the corner flag or Busch's boot – accounts varied according to the allegiance of the observer – and Kangaroo full-back Frank McMillan was poleaxed in a tackle on the final whistle.[2]

The pulsating drama was almost matched by the controversy that ensued after the match. Left with a tied series, the management of the Kangaroos, led by the ever-publicity-conscious Harry Sunderland, called for a deciding match to be arranged. Most British commentators pointed out that the draw meant that the Ashes stayed with England, who were the current holders, but faced with a huge amount of public interest and the possibility of a highly lucrative game, the RFL decided to stage an unprecedented fourth test match. Fear of losing the Ashes mingled with a distaste for the obvious money-making at work in the minds of many British supporters; Harry Waller, the founding chairman of the Northern Union, was so outraged he sent a telegram protesting to the RFL that 'Mammon has won' and arguing that the Ashes would be 'worthless' if a fourth test went ahead.[3] In fact, the bumper crowd envisaged did not materialise but almost 17,000 spectators saw an enthralling match in which the deadlock was broken only by Stan Smith's solitary unconverted try for England after seventy-three minutes – and so the Ashes remained where they had been after the third test match.

The third test was noteworthy not merely for the result. It was, according to all contemporary accounts, an unremittingly brutal match. 'To call it a game is a misnomer', wrote the *Yorkshire Post*. 'War is a more appropriate term.'[4] Nevertheless, it was far from the most violent test match staged before or after. From the first British tour in 1910 until the late 1970s, Anglo-Australian matches were marked not only by the great skills and athleticism of the participants but also by the ferocity of the combat and the level of violence that was often attained. The first test match between the two countries following the First World War set the tone for what was to come: 'the contest was not characterised by anything striking in sportsmanship: that is, the striking things done were with fists or boots', wrote one reporter.[5]

The tone intensified even more in the 1930s. The 1932 tour became notorious for the second test match, the 'Battle of Brisbane', which Australia won despite being reduced to ten men at one point because of the injuries sustained during the course of the match, and both the first test and the match against the Queensland representative side were also characterised by violence and fighting throughout. Claude Corbett, probably Australia's leading league journalist of the time, described the Brisbane match as 'hard all the time, rough most of the time and foul frequently' and called for the sport's officials to clamp down on violent play 'otherwise there will be a fatality on the field which will not be accidental'.[6] There was to be no let up in subsequent years: in 1936 Australian forward Ray Stehr achieved the unprecedented feat of being sent off twice in the same test series.

The experience of soldiering alongside each other in the Second World War did little to bring the two sides together; less than half an hour into the first test of 1946, Bradford schoolteacher Jack Kitching was sent off for punching Australia's captain, Joe Jorgensen. Clive Churchill's abiding memory of the 1948 Kangaroo tour to Britain was the violence meted out by the English club sides they played in the early part of the tour. Bradford's Ken Traill described the third test of 1952, known as the 'Battle of Bradford' as the roughest game he had ever experienced. Perhaps the depths were finally plumbed in the 1954 Britain versus New South Wales tour match, which was abandoned by the referee after just sixteen minutes of the second half owing to incessant fighting among the players. But even this salutary experience was not heeded; the 1960s saw more players sent off for violence in test matches than in any other decade, culminating in the 1970 World Cup final at Headingley, when vicious fighting between the players did not end when the referee sounded the final whistle.

Yet such behaviour was never once used as a reason to question, let alone break, the relationship between the Australian and British rugby league authorities. Indeed, it appears that the officials were often as culpable as the players. Alf Ellaby blamed the tour managers for 'indoctrinating' players in the dressing room before test matches and remembered as 'disgusting' the speech given before the first test match of 1928 in Brisbane. Some support for this view was provided by Claude Corbett, who claimed in 1932 that British players had told him that 'they acted in a way which would not have permitted them to stay five minutes in the game at home'. Post-war British RFL secretary Bill Fallowfield certainly had little truck with those who criticised the exuberance of touring teams: 'rugby league players are not supposed to be cissies', he told journalists in 1952 in response to criticisms that the Kangaroo tourists were overly physical in their approach to the game. In 1958 Ray Stehr, who graduated from hard-hitting player to hard-hitting journalist, noted that it was not only the players who felt it necessary to resolve their differences through fisticuffs when he recalled, perhaps exaggeratedly, a fight in the team hotel between Australian tour manager Wally Webb and Bradford chairman Harry Hornby in 1934.[7]

★

This apparently unbreakable bond between the two rugby league organisations stood in marked contrast to the reaction to the Bodyline cricket tour by England to Australia in 1932, when Douglas Jardine's intimidatory bowling tactics appeared to threaten the future of Anglo-Australian cricket. Far worse misdemeanours than Jardine's were committed on the rugby league pitch by British players just a few months earlier without a hint of diplomatic embarrassment. Partly this can be explained by the importance of cricket to the Empire and to the higher echelons of society. Few members of the British elite would know of a rugby league tour and fewer still, if any, would care. Even so, the 1932 league test series in particular created massive interest in Australia, being watched by almost 150,000 people, and press coverage, especially for the 'Battle of Brisbane' test, often moved from the back to the front pages of the newspapers. The opportunity certainly existed for at least the more sensationalist sections of the Australian press to question the relationship between the two countries' rugby league authorities.

But this did not happen, because of two interconnected reasons. First, the fact that Australian rugby league officials were fundamentally loyal to the Empire and, second, the cultural affinities between the predominantly working-class constituency of the sport in the two countries. 'We are just as British as you are', protested Harry 'Jersey' Flegg, the president of the New South Wales Rugby League, in 1950 during a dispute with British tour manager George Oldroyd.[8] At a dinner in honour of the 1928 British tourists in Sydney, Harry Sunderland, speaking this time as president of the Victorian Rugby League, told the visitors to 'remember Captain Cook; if he hadn't planted the Union Jack here, Australia might have become a Dutch dependency'.[9] 'Australians look to England as the mother country in war, in industry and also in rugby league football', said Kangaroo tour manager E. S. Brown in an address to the RFL Council in 1954, explaining that 'there is a strong desire in Australia to get along with England from every point of view'.[10] This view was more than backed up by the sporting press; the 1914 third test in Sydney was named 'the Rorke's Drift Test' not by British journalists but by Australians and even as late as 1958 the Australian *Truth* could begin its report of the second test, again a landmark British victory against overwhelming odds, by quoting Shakespeare: 'This happy breed of men, this little world … this England.'[11]

Given the working-class composition of the Australian game and its very close ties with the Australian Labour Party, the experience of Anglo-Australian rugby league relations must also cast a doubt over the widely accepted narrative that following the First World War sport became an arena for the expression of Australian nationalism and the desire to break the chains of the Empire. This reading of current nationalist feelings back into the past is obviously helped by the simple win–lose logic of sport, yet the history of Australian sport is one in which the maintenance of imperial links was paramount. This is demonstrated by the fact that the Bodyline crisis was triggered by the intransigence of Jardine and the attitude of the MCC, rather than any separatist actions on the part of the Australian cricket authorities, who believed that it was Jardine who had departed from the imperial ethic. Whatever his feats on the field, Bradman was no Bolivar. The great weakness of Australian Rules football, pointed to by some as an expression of cultural nationalism, was captured precisely by its name: it was played nowhere but certain areas of Australia. In contrast, rugby league in Australia drew a significant proportion of its strength from its links with Britain. The regularity of incoming and outgoing tours gave the sport an international importance with which only cricket could compare. Indeed, the short-lived proposal to merge Australian Rules and rugby league in 1933 never got off the ground in large part because of the threat it would pose to the link with British sport.[12]

But this loyalty to the Empire was also tempered with a hostility to many of the social mores of British society, especially its deference and class snobbery. Whereas Jardine, and English cricket captains in general until the late 1960s, were the embodiment of the English imperial elite, rugby league players manifestly were not. British rugby league tourists were not seen as representatives of a distant, and perhaps alien, government. In fact, they had far more in common with Australia's self-image as a country of the (white) working man than with the privilege and class discrimination that English cricket represented. Much of the hostility towards Australia from the British upper and middle classes was based on social snobbery – best encapsulated by the Lady Bracknell-ish comment of the novelist Angela Thirkell in the 1920s when she described the country as 'an entire continent peopled by the Lower Orders' – which was equally directed at the working classes in Britain.[13] Jardine's tactics were unacceptable to Australians to a great extent because of what he represented. Yet physical intimidation and worse by a British rugby league side that shared the same social background and suffered similar frustrations as the great mass of Australians was, to put it colloquially, a 'fair dinkum' part of the game.

Rugby league perfectly encapsulated the two seemingly contradictory attitudes of imperial loyalty and hostility to privilege. And Anglo-Australian test matches provided an arena in which both aspects of this relationship could be demonstrated. Captained and led by workers from the industrial heartlands of Britain – almost certainly a unique phenomenon among imperial travellers of the time – the British players were working men just as the Australian players and spectators were. They presented an image of the Empire that resembled Australia more than it did Britain: ostensibly working-class, democratic and meritocratic. This sense of shared identity was sometimes reflected by the combatants on the field. When Nat Silcock and Ray Stehr were sent off for fighting in the first test match of 1936, they shook hands as they left the field. During the 1958 Brisbane test Australian captain Brian Davies forbade his players from attacking British captain Alan Prescott's broken right arm (although this decision was later questioned by some of his team-mates). Even Vince Karalius, who pointedly refused to shake hands with Australian players before test matches, became an honoured and much sought-after guest in Australia when his playing days were over. Most tellingly, following the 1954 abandoned match between the British tourists and New South Wales, the players met the same evening at a dance and, according to Clive Churchill, 'had a good laugh' about the match. In contrast, Aub Oxford, the referee who had abandoned the match in disgust, was never given another match to referee in Sydney.[14]

This shared identity had its roots in the cultural meanings attached to rugby league. The working classes both of the north of England and Australia faced the contempt of imperial rulers in southern England and responded by developing a sporting culture which was ostensibly more democratic, at least for white-skinned people, than that of the London-centred establishment. Rugby league's self-image as 'the working man's game' embodies many of the common elements of British and Australian working-class culture, and it was this that underpinned the bond between these two distant heartlands of the sport. This was also a relationship which stood in marked contrast to that which English rugby union had with Australia: the snobbishness exhibited towards the 1908 Wallaby tourists to Britain meant that many of them had 'developed a dislike for everything English' by the time they returned to Australia, according to captain Herbert Moran.[15]

This is not to say that there was no conflict between the two governing bodies in Britain and Australia. In particular, the British jealously guarded their position as the game's ultimate decision-making body. In 1927 a motion to establish an Imperial Rugby League Board to oversee the rules of the game was voted down by the RFL, despite the fact that they would have three representatives on it and the Australians and New Zealanders only one each. The subject was raised again in 1935, partially spurred by the growth of the game in France and the keenness of the French to promote the game internationally, but the RFL felt that 'the time had not yet arrived for this to be seriously discussed'. Further pressure from Australia and New Zealand in late 1936 led to the RFL agreeing in principle to the formation of an International Board but a disagreement with Australia over the ban on international transfers led to the idea being shelved until after the Second World War. Eventually, at the end of New Zealand's 1947–48 tour to Britain and France, the RFL sanctioned the formation of an International Board (IB) composed of one representative from each of the four league-playing countries, with the provisos that the RFL secretary have the same role with the IB and that the RFL remain 'the paramount body controlling the laws of the game but the IB should be empowered to make recommendations for submission to the RFL Council'.

The Australians baulked at this latter stipulation and held back from joining, stating that they could not see the advantages of forming such a body if it did not have law-making powers. Eventually in late 1949 they agreed to join on condition that the IB alone and not the RFL was responsible for the laws of the game and that all IB decisions had to be unanimous in order to be binding. In reality this meant that the IB remained a largely ceremonial body as all four nations had their own interpretations of the rules, which they were not inclined to change. In fact, it was not until the 1966 vote to introduce the four-tackle system that the IB made any unanimous decision on the game's laws. Sniping over the laws continued between the British and the Australians throughout the 1950s, exacerbated in part by Bill Fallowfield's increasing opposition to the play-the-ball rule and, one suspects, by his personality, which was a little too near that of the arrogant English colonial administrator for some of the Australians. Feelings against him ran sufficiently high for the Australians to stop subsidising his travel expenses for IB meetings in 1955.[16]

Fallowfield himself admitted that the relationship between the two leagues had deteriorated since the Second World War, noting in 1954 that the Australians tended to view any RFL initiative with suspicion, despite continuing protestations of their loyalty to Britain. In 1961 the RFL threatened to play just three test matches and 'one or two other games' on the following year's Lions' tour in protest against the Australians' decision to reduce Britain's share of the tour revenue, although a compromise was eventually reached.[17]

This changing relationship between the British and Australian authorities after 1945 reflected the fissures that were emerging between the two countries at a political level, generated partially by Australian suspicion of the British during the war owing to Churchill's unwillingness to commit major forces to the defence of Australia. The relationship was further weakened in 1961 when the Macmillan government declared that it would apply to join the European Common Market regardless of its impact on the Australian economy and also ended free entry into Britain for all Commonwealth citizens, including those from Australia. To a large extent forced into doing so by the actions of the British government, Australian society in the 1960s had begun to question its deferential attitudes towards the mother country, and this new self-confidence was also reflected in Australian rugby league. The British game was no longer regarded as being inherently superior and Australian coaches began to look to American football for inspiration. The dissolving of the colonial relationship was demonstrated at a symbolic level by the end of the pre-match Australian 'war cry' in the late 1960s. It had been performed by all touring Kangaroo sides since the pioneering 1908 tour but, unlike the Maori haka of New Zealand's league and union sides, was created to emphasise an artificial colonial exoticism for the original tourists. But by the 1967 Kangaroo tour it had become a joke among the players who could not see its relevance to modern Australia.[18]

Ultimately these changes would reverse the balance of power between the two leagues, but until the early 1960s the chief source of antagonism between British and southern hemisphere rugby league was the poaching of Antipodean players by the wealthy English clubs. This had begun during the first New Zealand tour and had helped to bring to the British club scene a cosmopolitan glamour unheard of in other sports, with the partial exception of league cricket, and to offset the appeal of soccer's national competitions and rugby union's social cachet. Six of the first New Zealand tourists and ten of the first Australians joined English clubs, some of them, such as Wigan's Lance Todd and Huddersfield's Albert Rosenfeld, becoming household names in rugby league communities. But, however much this benefited the English, it did little to increase the appeal of the fledgling Australian and New Zealand Rugby Leagues at home. In response to protests from down under that their best players were being looted, in November 1909 the British authorities introduced the first regulations governing player transfers between the hemispheres – any player wishing to sign for an English club now had to have the permission of both his home league and club. This effectively meant that international transfers were banned. A revolt of British clubs at the start of 1912 led the NU to cancel the ban but furious threats from Australia forced its re-imposition in February 1912.[19]

British clubs again tried to remove the ban after the First World War and the RFL succumbed to this pressure in the summer of 1923, only to reinstate the restrictions a few weeks later after protests from Australia.[20] However, by 1927 the British clubs' desire to boost their attendances through Antipodean glamour proved too strong and in June of that year they forced the removal of the restrictions on international transfers. This marked the beginning of a new golden age, providing a temporary respite from the gloom of the depression years for the mining villages and mill towns across Yorkshire and Lancashire. Ernest Mills and Ray Markham at Huddersfield, Vic Hey, Eric Harris and Jeff Moores at Leeds, Hector Gee at Wigan – a departure from their then traditional policy of signing New Zealanders – and Bill Shankland at Warrington, were merely the most prominent of the Australians who lit up the football fields of northern England in the 1930s. Not all were successful, however. Dave Brown, one of Australia's greatest-ever players, made little impression at Warrington, and 'Chimpy' Busch never fulfilled his potential at Leeds.

But, however much these stars delighted English spectators, it brought no pleasure to Australian rugby league. By the mid-1930s such was the player drain that it was becoming commonplace for journalists to wonder if Australia would ever beat Britain in a Test series.[21] The problem of weakened Australian teams could have largely been solved by the simple expediency of allowing players contracted to English clubs to play for their country when touring Britain. But once signed to an English club, a player's contractual obligations meant that he was no longer eligible for international selection. The precedent had been set following the attempt of Dan Frawley, the 1908 Kangaroo, to play for the 1911 tourists despite being contracted to Warrington. The club refused to let him play for Australia, but his contract was sufficiently ambiguous to allow him to eventually play later in the tour. Alarmed by this precedent, British clubs made sure that there would be no similar ambiguity in the future: a player's responsibility was to his club and his club alone. Even so, the lack-lustre performance of the 1937 Kangaroo tourists underscored the importance of a competitive Australian side to both the credibility and the coffers of British rugby league. Consequently, in December 1937 the RFL imposed a ban on international transfers and the one-way traffic from the Antipodes dried up.

The ban lapsed in 1940 and no attention was paid to it until the RFL received a letter in early 1946 from the New Zealand Rugby League, complaining that Wigan had breached the agreement by signing Ponsonby winger Brian Nordgren. Although the British authorities somewhat cynically dismissed the complaint because neither New Zealand nor Australia had requested a new agreement, they were sufficiently concerned to instruct the managers of the 1946 British touring side to Australasia to discuss the issue when they arrived down under.[22] Partly this was motivated by rumours that the British players would themselves be targets for Australian clubs. In fact, a number were approached when they arrived but none were tempted. For example, Wakefield Trinity forward Harry Murphy was offered £300 to sign for Balmain, plus a three-year contract paying £9 per match. He turned it down because, as the Wakefield secretary explained, 'he was brought up on the Trinity ground. He has been with us since he was sixteen and in his job as a marine engineer he has prospects which will develop as he grows older'.[23] Balmain's terms were barely more than what Murphy received at Wakefield and offered little incentive to move. Although more prominent players were probably offered more money, it is unlikely that Australian clubs at that time had the finances to match the wages offered by English clubs. British insularity probably also played a role in players' reluctance to move, as it also often did with English soccer players. Returning from the 1946 tour of Australasia, Eddie Waring lamented this cultural resistance to life abroad when he sadly recounted the response of a returning Lions tourist in the 1930s who, when asked what was the best part of the tour, replied 'getting home!'[24]

The opportunities offered by the booming British game did not go unnoticed by Australian players. The international transfer ban was not renewed until 1947, giving a vital window of opportunity to British clubs to take their pick of Antipodean talent.[25] If the 1930s were a golden age for overseas players, the players signed in 1946 and 1947 helped raise the British game to even greater heights, among them being Brian Bevan, Harry Bath, Arthur Clues, Lionel Cooper, Pat Devery and Johnny Hunter. Possibly even more than the preceding two generations of Australian exiles, this group indelibly marked the sport with a resonance that remains today. Bevan became the most prolific try-scorer ever, with 796 touchdowns. Hunter, Devery and Lionel Cooper especially became the crucial triumvirate in Huddersfield success of the early 1950s. Arthur Clues and a complete three-quarter line of fellow Australians raised Leeds back to the heights they had conquered under their previous generation of imports.

Following the 1947 ban, British clubs sought ingenious ways to lure Australian players. In 1948 it was announced that Australian full-back Clive Churchill was emigrating to England to advance his 'position in life with speciality training for a professional job in private life' – and that he had also signed to play for Workington Town for £12,500. His passage to England had even been booked for January 1949 but the Australian Rugby League Board of Control stepped in to halt the move at the last minute, realising that not only would they lose their best player but also that an unstoppable juggernaut was about to be driven through the international agreement. Deprived of the opportunity to earn such a huge sum, Churchill, who was working in a Sydney sports shop at the time, declared that the ban was 'a denial of human rights for a man to better himself'.[26] No sooner had this loophole been closed than British clubs realised that the ban did not apply to rugby union players. Rochdale Hornets hit upon the idea of persuading league players to switch temporarily to rugby union, thus becoming free to transfer to England. In 1950 Rochdale managed to sign five junior rugby league players using this subterfuge until the Australian Board of Control found out and protested to the RFL that:

agents scour our junior ranks for players of promise and approach them to sign contracts for English clubs which they represent. If the prospect is interested, these agents advise the lads to forsake rugby league and transfer to rugby union (sometimes under fictitious names). After playing a few matches in rugby union these players are then signed up for English clubs under the guise of being rugby union players.[27]

British scouts also turned their attentions to bona-fide Australian union players such as Wallaby captain Trevor Allen and future league TV commentator Rex Mossop, both of whom signed for Leigh at this time. Under heavy pressure from the Australians, in 1951 the RFL agreed that all overseas signings, whether from league or union, had to be sanctioned by the player's domestic rugby league authorities. Finding all doors to Antipodean talent locked, British clubs' focus for overseas signings turned to South Africa – as had happened in the 1920s – and, to a lesser extent, Fiji.

The success of Australian players in Britain during the post-war years once again highlighted the shared identity of league in the two countries. The vast majority of those Australian players who played for English rugby league clubs quickly became part of the local communities which nurtured the game and a number settled in those towns after they had stopped playing. While it is unlikely that they went as 'native' as Rex Mossop claimed of Harry Bath (Bath allegedly told his fellow Warrington forwards to 'Get this convict Australian bastard Mossop!' when the latter made his debut for Leigh), those that did stay slipped easily into the culture of the north of England.[28] Albert Rosenfeld, who came over with the first Australian tourists in 1908, lived in Huddersfield until he died in 1970, working for most of his life as a dustman. The peerless winger, Brian Bevan, has a statue erected to his memory in Warrington. Arthur Clues, who made his reputation through ferocious assaults on the 1946 British tourists, settled in Leeds, becoming one of its most prominent sporting celebrities. When he died in 1998, the church had to close its doors, such were the numbers wishing to attend his funeral. As Jeff Hill has also argued in relation to overseas cricket professionals in the 1930s, the Australian rugby league star 'was respected as a man who somehow carried the reputation of the local community on his shoulders'.[29]

The esteem in which Australian players were held by British rugby league supporters was almost without exception reciprocated. No biography of an Australian player who spent time with a British club is complete without a comment about those who watched them play. In a reversal of national stereotypes, Steve Roach found them less reserved than Australians. Ken Thornett, who played for Leeds in the early 1960s, encouraged fellow players to get out and meet them. Even players who, like Brett Kenny, had little liking for the British way of life, praised the British supporters. Rex Mossop's comments about Leigh in the 1950s seem to be representative of most: 'I loved these loyal supporters, the way they'd cheer and sing at matches and shout you a pint in their cosy, friendly pubs. They made you feel part of a community.'[30] A similar observation was made in 1990 by Australian journalist Adrian MacGregor:

To east coast Australians, Yorkshire and Lancashire towns are more relevant to their education than the Tower of London. England and Australia have cricket in common but nobody pretends that singular game, by its very nature, possesses the camaraderie of rugby league. It may sound naïve to refer to an international brotherhood of rugby league, yet hundreds of Australians have come to England to play, many to stay. I found that, in the North, to be Australian was to be welcomed, to be an Australian on the rugby league trail ensured a hospitality bred of an intangible bond.[31]

For the British, the major argument in support of the transfer ban was the damage to international rugby league that would occur because of the importation of southern hemisphere players. Writing in the September 1947 issue of *Rugby League Review* Alfred Drewery said he had little sympathy with Australian clubs but 'those who look upon rugby league football from an international point of view cannot help but be perturbed at this wholesale drain on Australian talent'. In fact, the Australians were gaining ground. In 1950, thirty years after they had last won them, Australia finally regained the Ashes on a muddy Sydney Cricket Ground when winger Ron Roberts found himself the extra man on an overlap and dived over in the corner fifteen minutes from full-time to give his side a series-winning 5–2 victory. Normality was restored in 1952 when Britain retook the crown but they faltered in 1954 when, in one of the most thrilling and free-scoring series, Clive Churchill once again captained the Australians to success. Britain retained the Ashes for the rest of the decade but in the 1963 series in England, in what subsequently proved to be a portent of what was to come, Australia shocked even themselves and took the Ashes by winning the first two matches by 28–2 and 50–12. The latter score in the second test at Swinton was the first time either side had scored fifty points in an Ashes match. For the remaining years of the 1960s the balance of rugby league power was for the first time ever to remain with Australia.

Ironically, one of the reasons for this shift in power was the large number of Australians who had honed their skills playing in England. As they returned home in the 1950s, they took back new approaches to the game. Future Australian national coach Harry Bath left Warrington to play for St George in 1957 and was shocked at the poor skills of his new team-mates: 'I couldn't believe the bash and barge way Saints played the game. Blokes knocking themselves stupid. I thought "Christ! This is for me".' Dick Huddart, the British second-row forward, who moved to St George in the 1960s, credited Bath with revolutionising Australian forward play:

Before Harry showed them how to play, Australian forwards were called pigs, and that's how they played. ... all they'd do was put their heads down, get tackled and die with the ball. Harry taught them that there was much more to forward play than that.[32]

Much of the success of St George's record-breaking eleven consecutive premierships was due to the influence of British defensive techniques learned by Bath and captain-coach Ken Kearney, who played for Leeds from 1948 to 1952.

But rugby league in Australia in the 1950s was also undergoing a financial and social revolution, which gave an additional impetus to the increasing skilfulness and tactical awareness of its players. The legalisation of poker machines in New South Wales in 1956 opened up extensive sources of revenue for clubs, whose associated Leagues Clubs could use the money raised through gambling to subsidise the on-field activities of their side. Coupled with the abandonment of the residential qualification for players in 1959, which meant that players no longer had to live in the immediate catchment area of their club, and the development of a formal contract system, Sydney rugby league clubs were now able to match the financial benefits of playing in England, both for Australian players and, for the first time, those from Britain. Indeed, the international transfer ban was renewed quickly in 1957 not least because of British fears that 'there might be a one-way stream of players being transferred from this country to Australia'.[33]

This was a fear that came close to realisation by the mid-1960s, when the lure of Australia became irresistible for many British players. This was not simply due to the new opportunities available in the game. This was also the era of the 'Ten Pound Poms', whereby, thanks to the measures of the 1946 British Australian Migration Agreement, which became known as the assisted passage scheme, emigration to Australia from Britain was open to anyone for just £10. Over a million British citizens made the trip between 1947 and 1970, a number of whom were also rugby league players. In 1960 Phil Jackson, the Barrow centre who had starred on the 1958 British tour of Australia, accepted an offer to captain and coach the Goulburn Workers club, although injury had forced him to retire from playing in Britain before he moved. He thus became the first British player of the modern era to move down under to play; the only previous example was Huddersfield's Welsh forward Ben Gronow, who moved to Grenfell in New South Wales in 1925 as their coach but returned two years later.[34]

In March 1963 Derek Hallas became the first active player to move when he went from Keighley to Parramatta. However, because there was no transfer fee system yet in place – the Australians had opposed such a system in order to protect their own players from British poaching – Keighley did not receive the £3,000 transfer fee they had been asking for Hallas.[35] Even so, the floodgates had been opened and a steady stream of highly rated players made the trek down under. Test match stars such as Huddart, Dave Bolton, Cliff Watson and Tommy Bishop, together with a range of top club players, migrated in the 1960s. These were followed in the 1970s by an even greater number of British internationals, attracted by better wages, the Australian lifestyle and the star treatment accorded them by being high profile names in Sydney's biggest sport.[36] Ironically Britain's 1970 Ashes series victory – the last time that they were to be won by Britain in the twentieth century – accelerated the exodus down under, as Australian clubs clamoured to sign the victorious British stars.

By the mid-1970s it would have been almost possible to select a full-strength Great Britain side from British players in Sydney. In 1971 Manly paid a world record £15,000 to Castleford to sign their awesome loose forward Malcolm Reilly. As with the Australian players who returned from Britain in the 1950s, the wave of British imports of the 1960s and 1970s also brought new skills and approaches to the Australian game. Wigan's Dave Bolton went to Balmain and redefined stand-off half play. Reilly brought a whole new combination of all-sided technical ability and uncompromising ferociousness. His Manly team-mate, Hull KR's Phil Lowe, built on Dick Huddart's legacy as a free-running second-row forward: 'as the aircraft carrier made the battleship obsolete, Phil Lowe established that the lumbering forward was about to join the mastodons in extinction', wrote an admiring Thomas Keneally.[37] If the Australian game had suffered in the past because its talents were siphoned by British clubs, the reverse was now true. British rugby league had become seriously weakened at international level and the 1977 World Cup, in which Great Britain was forced to field a drastically understrength side owing to the loss of numerous leading players to Sydney clubs, was the final straw for the RFL, who successfully lobbied for a new international transfer ban. The rugby league boot was now firmly on the other foot – and things were about to get much worse.

Between 1979 and 1988, Great Britain did not win a single test match against the Australians. Indeed, such was the gulf between the two sides that the British found it extremely difficult to score a try – in the 1982 Ashes series they managed just one in the three matches. The chasm that had opened between the two countries was shocking. One of the most overused journalistic expressions about the 1982 and 1986 Kangaroos was that they were 'from another planet'. The Australians' improvement in skill, athleticism and all-round awareness was equalled only by the concomitant decline of the same in the British game. To some extent, the introduction of limited tackles in the mid-1960s had played into the Australians' hands; British dominance had been built on forward domination exerting continuous pressure on their opponents. The fact that the ball could now only be held for six tackles meant that it was impossible to build such dominance and that the emphasis was now on fitness and speed, qualities which the Australian game had always possessed. It was not until the emergence of a new generation of British players in the mid-1980s – such as Ellery Hanley, Martin Offiah, Andy Gregory and Garry Schofield – that the gap began to narrow. Yet even then the British side could not wrest back the Ashes. Throughout the 1990s a pattern emerged whereby Britain would win one match in a three game series but not be able defeat the Australians in the deciding test match.

By the mid-1990s, it was clear that this inability to win when it mattered most was partly a psychological problem. Brought up with the idea of the invincible Kangaroos, it was almost impossible for modern British players to imagine they could win a series. But this was a manifestation of much deeper structural changes, which meant that Australian hegemony over rugby league appeared impregnable. The most obvious difference was immediately apparent to any visitor to Sydney or Brisbane: rugby league dominated the sporting life of Australia's eastern seaboard.

This gave it advantages about which the British could only dream; a huge pool of schoolboy and amateur players from which to draw, significant wealth owing to their leagues' clubs, and, because of huge media interest, an intensity of competition which meant that players were accustomed to playing regularly in high-pressure matches. Australian coaches were also willing to learn from other sports and other countries. Many of the innovations that coaches Terry Fearnley and Jack Gibson brought to the game in the 1960s and 1970s were taken straight from American football. In contrast, the British game suffered from an insularity and unwillingness to learn which was common to all British sport. Even among those who knew better, there was a parochial bravado in the face of the Australian challenge: 'we have nothing to fear', said former Great Britain coach Colin Hutton shortly before the arrival of the 1982 Kangaroos, despite the fact he privately thought that they were light years ahead of the British.[38] Fitness levels and competence in the basic skills of the sport lagged far behind. Many of the Australian players who played for British clubs in the 1980s were appalled at the poor tackling and lack of defensive technique of their native team-mates.

To some extent these problems were the result of the crisis in the game in the 1960s. The late 1970s and early 1980s belong to the generation of players which began playing as boys in the 1960s, when the amateur game had shrunk and coaching had been almost non-existent, leaving them ill-equipped to face their more skilful and tactically astute Australian contemporaries. This was linked to what might be termed the 'Ryan Giggs Problem'. The abolition of soccer's maximum wage in the 1960s and its tremendously high national profile meant that rugby league could no longer compete with it. As was seen in Chapter 3, soccer's maximum wage could make rugby league financially more attractive to young players talented at both games. But from the 1960s, the changes to soccer meant that the most talented young athletes would almost inevitably be drawn to the round-ball game, whereas in Australia it would be league to which they would be attracted. Perhaps the best example of this was Manchester United's Ryan Giggs, whose father played for Swinton and who himself played rugby league for Lancashire schoolboys. In an earlier era he may well have followed the family tradition but his soccer skills brought him a professional contract as a teenager and he was lost to the game.[39]

Yet, despite the inability of the British side to compete effectively, Australia's success helped to raise rugby league's profile on the national stage. The 1982 Kangaroos earned the plaudits of even rugby union journalists and their tours attracted national coverage throughout the 1980s and 1990s. In 1990 Mal Meninga even went where no other rugby league players had gone before and picked up the BBC's overseas sports personality of the year award. For many British rugby league supporters the Australians brought a new affirmation of the sport's self-belief. In some circles a cult of all things Australian developed – like Sidney and Beatrice Webb's view of Stalin's Russia in the 1930s, Australian rugby league seemed to represent 'a new civilisation'. A minor industry sprang up importing Australian rugby league videos, books, magazines and playing kit. By the late 1980s it was a sign of an enlightened rugby league fashion sense to wear an Australian replica club shirt to matches. In one sense, the continual cycle of defeat for the British came to be of secondary importance to the committed rugby league fan because Australian players were demonstrating to the world what they had always believed: that their game was the greatest game of all. Even in the reduced circumstances of the British game, the 'intangible bond' remained as strong as ever.

Chapter 9

'Sporting apartheid': rugby union's war against rugby league

Ever since 1895 the RFU had policed the border between league and union with merciless vigilance. Those who transgressed the boundary were banned not only from playing rugby union for life but also from any other type of involvement in it. The catechism that laid down the dividing line was contained in RFU's 'Rules as to Professionalism'. Like all sacred texts that sought to separate the elect from the damned, it laid out a precise code of practice. Its essence was defined in section one and the sixteen clauses and six sub-clauses of section two:

1. Professionalism is illegal.
2. Acts of professionalism are –

    (1) By an individual –

        A. Asking, receiving, or relying on a promise, direct or implied, to receive any money consideration whatever, actual or prospective; any employment or advancement; any establishment in business; or any compensation whatever…[1]

And where there was ambiguity, section eight of the Rules – 'this Union shall have power to deal with all acts which it may consider as acts of professionalism, and which are not specifically provided for' – provided the RFU with the arbitrary powers of Lewis Carroll's Humpty Dumpty: 'when I use a word … it means just what I choose it to mean, neither more nor less.'

Although technically the rules forbade contact with any professional sportsman, the definition of professional encompassed all forms of rugby league, professional or amateur. It was an offence to sign a rugby league form, play with or against a rugby league player or 'advocate or take steps to promote' rugby league, regardless of whether any money was received. Although the RFU formally claimed that the regulations also covered professional soccer players, the reality was that this was window-dressing. In 1924 the RFU reinstated a Mr Whittle of Hartlepool as an amateur despite the fact that he had played soccer as a professional.[2] The plain truth was that the rules on professionalism were only ever intended to apply to one sport: rugby league. In private, rugby union administrators were quite explicit about this fact, as a 1958 International Board resolution revealed:

in keeping with principles underlying the Rules as to Professionalism, persons who are or have been associated in any capacity with a Rugby League club should be regarded as being ineligible to participate in the affairs of Rugby Union clubs or teams. The Board also agreed that, while this must in practice be a matter for each Union to determine in the light of its own local problems, *there is in general no objection to persons who are or have been ranked as professionals in games other than Rugby League football being permitted to play Rugby Union football or to participate in the affairs of rugby union clubs.* [emphasis added][3]

This visceral hostility to league also explains why, after the Second World War, the majority of the leaders of rugby union tolerated the semi-professionalism of their game in European countries such as France, Italy and Rumania. As former Welsh captain and prominent judge Rowe Harding explained to a Foreign Office official about Rumanian rugby union in 1956, the rugby union authorities were prepared to bend their rules for such countries, because if they were to 'pull down the iron curtain' and expel them, 'I have no doubt that the Rumanians will turn to rugby league, which will be a tragedy'.[4]

In public, however, the RFU's attitude to rugby league was one of disdainful dismissal, rather like a headmaster preferring not to mention his troublesome pupils because it would draw attention to them. But behind the scenes its leading committees spent a considerable amount of time discussing their attitude towards rugby league. In the 1920s, 'professionalism' was formally discussed at twenty-two of the RFU's first thirty committee meetings following the end of the First World War. Immediately after the Second World War, league was constantly discussed by the RFU Committee. Between 1948 and 1950 it also heard reports about rugby league's progress in the Army, the Midlands, Surrey and even Canada. In 1968 its Executive Committee discussed the alarmingly titled 'Rugby League Infiltration', although this turned out to be nothing more than an advertisement in a Durham newspaper inviting players for a trial with a rugby league club.[5]

After the sporting flux of the First World War, the RFU Committee expended considerable energy dealing with applications from players who had played league but who now wished to return to union. Each was met, as recorded in the RFU minute books, with the summary response 'Declined'. In 1920 Lieutenant-Colonel A. Brown was refused permission to play union because he had played amateur league as an eighteen-year-old. In 1928 a player called Armstrong, who played for Seaton in the North East, signed professional forms with a league club. He almost immediately decided that he had made a mistake and sent the forms back to the league club asking to be released from his obligation. He then informed the RFU of his transgression. It was to no avail. On receiving his confession, the RFU committee promptly banned him for life. In 1935 a referee from Manchester was banned when it was discovered that he had played rugby league as a seventeen-year-old in 1924. That same year a nineteen-year-old schoolboy called Drinkhall was banned because he had chosen to play rugby league outside of school when he had the opportunity to play union at school.[6] Most famous, or infamous, was the case of England and Bristol full-back Tom Brown in 1933. He had travelled to Lancashire for a discussion with officials from either Warrington or Broughton Rangers (reports differ) and, after declining their offer, had accepted a cheque in payment of his travelling expenses. Rumours that Bristol players were considering switching to league got into the press and the RFU set up a committee of inquiry to investigate. Brown was banned for life, much to the despair of Bristol, whose representatives appealed to the RFU for a lighter sentence. They appealed again in 1934 only to be told that the case would not be reopened. Brown, who never even saw a game of rugby league until he bought a television set in 1954, was posthumously reinstated as an amateur in 1987, some twenty-six years after his death.[7]

The RFU paid particular attention to the danger of schoolboys being contaminated with the league virus. As early as 1919 a Lancashire representative on the RFU committee raised the question of whether boys at rugby league-playing schools could be allowed to play union, inadvertently underlining the fact that it was the playing of the game, rather than money, which was at issue. After much deliberation the committee decided that 'boys under nineteen playing Northern Union football at any school where only the NU game is played shall not be considered disqualified'. Although seemingly lenient, the ruling actually meant that any boy who chose to play league at a school where both games were played or who chose to play league when at a union-playing school, would be banned, as the unfortunate Drinkhall discovered in 1935.

The RFU was also concerned that union-playing teachers might also become infected. In February 1936 it set up a sub-committee to discuss the status of teachers who taught rugby league in elementary schools – the state schools in which the majority of working-class children were educated. According to RFU rules, anyone teaching rugby league automatically 'professionalised' himself, which would mean a significant number of teachers in the north could be banned from playing union. Former RFU president James Baxter wrote to the Board of Education complaining that teachers were being forced to teach rugby league against their will and asking if the Board had any discretion about which sports were played in schools. 'We naturally do not want to ostracise these people', he explained, in the hope that the Board would dig the RFU out of a hole of its own making. The hypocrisy of the RFU's stance was once again underlined by the fact that it had no objection to its players teaching schoolboys to play soccer, a sport far more 'professionalised' than league. The Board replied that the choice of games was a matter for the schools and that it hoped all teachers felt 'a strong sense of obligation' to promote school sport. Unmoved, the RFU responded by sending the Board a copy of the sub-committee's terms of reference, asking if teachers could be contractually compelled to teach league and, somewhat paranoically, if local education authorities could force teachers to become professional rugby league players. The Board replied with the adept neutrality of seasoned civil servants. Forced to resolve its own problem, the RFU decided that as long as coaching rugby league was a part of official school duties teachers would not be banned from playing union. There was, however, a body of opinion on the committee that unsuccessfully proposed that teachers who taught league in elementary schools should simply be banned from union.[8]

Then there was also the question of teachers who had been union players but had switched to league. In 1938 one such player wrote to the RFU to ask their permission to accept a teaching position at Wade Deacon Grammar School in Widnes, where his duties would include coaching rugby union. This situation became increasingly common in the 1950s and 1960s. For example, when England fly-half Tom Brophy signed for Barrow in 1966 he wrote to ask the RFU if he could continue to coach union at Rossall School. The RFU allowed this to happen if it was part of the teaching duties of the player but forbade him to train with or act as coach to any union side other than those at his school.[9]

Following the Second World War, the RFU once again spent considerable time re-establishing its boundaries. In March 1947 it set up a Northern Counties sub-committee (NCSC), a saloon-bar star chamber to deal with accusations of professionalism in the north of England. The necessity of such a body was demonstrated a few months later when Ilkley RUFC asked the RFU if the forthcoming New Zealand rugby league tourists could borrow its pitch for training sessions. Led by Sir Wavell Wakefield and seconded by Adrian Stoop, the RFU committee refused permission, as it had done when a similar request had been made for the 1921 Kangaroo tourists.[10] The same meeting, concerned at possible backsliding in attitudes towards rugby league in areas other than the north, also voted to send out a 'Warning Notice Circular' advising all clubs on the rules relating to professionalism. Much of the 1947 RFU annual general meeting was taken up with discussion about rugby league. It reiterated its bans on players who took part in rugby league workshop competitions and on schoolboys who chose to play league when at union-playing schools. It allowed league players to play unrestricted union when serving in the armed forces, provided they had no contact with their league clubs while serving in the forces, in which case they could only play for their immediate unit. In its only concession, the 'Rules as to Professionalism' were deemed not to apply to players under the age of eighteen, although this was subsequently amended in 1958 to exclude youngsters who had been paid money.[11]

Much of the NCSC's work dealt with applications for reinstatement from players who had dabbled in league, which naturally were turned down, but it also sought to provide advice to the RFU about precise definitions of amateurism in various contexts, especially as it related to players in the armed forces. In 1953 it successfully advised the RFU to stop league players in the Territorial Army, Army Reserve and RAF Auxiliary from playing union. Despite being based in rugby league territory, the NCSC was no less zealous than its southern-based counterparts. In 1951 it organised three hearings to investigate accusations that a young Orrell player, J. F. Hurst, had played for Wigan. He finally cracked at the third meeting when he confessed to having played ten matches for Wigan's 'A' team. A tip-off that a union player was working for the RFL resulted in a letter being fired off to Bill Fallowfield demanding to know, without explanation, whether his assistant Peter Gaunt held an executive position with the League. In fact, he had a minor clerical role and so escaped sanction. One of the NCSC's last actions was to produce a warning poster for distribution to the armed services in 1959.[12]

The RFU's strictures extended beyond the mere playing of the game. In 1923 it forbade former rugby league players from being involved in coaching union teams, a ban which was reiterated in 1948. Although it did not become an issue until the 1950s, the RFU also banned ex-league players from becoming non-playing social members of rugby union clubs. 'Past or present rugby league players could not be admitted to membership of a rugby union club' it decreed in 1962, although it graciously allowed such individuals to join clubs connected with their employment, provided that they did not sit on any committees.[13] Some clubs, especially those in the north, even had declarations attached to their membership application forms which in true McCarthyite style invited the applicant to declare that 'I have not taken part in rugby league football, either as an amateur or a professional, nor have I signed any rugby league form, after reaching my eighteenth birthday'.[14] Of course, the reality was that few 'defectors' would be allowed into union clubs anyway. Devon County representative on the RFU Committee Ted Butcher was quite typical in his attitude, as described by his daughter: 'throughout his life, if he ever suspected a "Scout" or even a player from Rugby League of being on a Union ground he would have him thrown out'. Even in the late 1960s Bev Risman, who had played union for England and the British Lions before switching to league with Leigh in 1961, found himself threatened with removal from a fancy-dress party at Broughton Park rugby union club simply because he played rugby league.[15]

Although the policies of the RFU had serious consequences for transgressors, the impact went much deeper, helping to create an atmosphere of fear within union itself and of contempt towards rugby league. Using a variation of the Catholic Church's concept of culpable ignorance, the fear of inadvertently transgressing the union's amateur code was encouraged by the posters distributed by the RFU for display in dressing rooms and clubhouses from the 1920s to the late 1950s. These outlined seventeen different ways in which the amateur rules could be violated, two of which were outlined in thick bold type: asking for or receiving any form of remuneration for playing and 'signing any form of the Northern Union (Rugby League)'. And if the detailed clauses and sub-clauses did not engender sufficient paranoia, the poster ended with an ominous warning of retribution against the unwitting, the unwary and the simply naïve: 'Ignorance of the Rules is no Defence'.[16] This manufacture of paranoia had a major impact on rugby league's attempts to expand beyond its heartlands. It meant that those players and spectators most familiar with a form of rugby were also the people least likely to show any interest in league. The fears of union people were recalled by the great Welsh union scrum-half Gareth Edwards: 'there was tremendous amount of stigma related to [rugby league] ... which made you petrified that you were even going to be approached because even conversation or discussion with rugby league clubs meant that you could have a lifelong ban'.[17] After all, why would anyone risk being banned from playing their sport, entering their local club and participating in its committees – in short, suffering not only sporting but social ostracism – just for the sake of trying out another sport?

The magnitude of such a fate for most middle-class men can only be gauged when the importance of the rugby club as a focus for social and business life is understood. As Margaret Stacey and others have pointed out, the rugby union club, like golf and tennis clubs, was an important hub in a complex web of middle-class male sociability; it was a place where one could maintain and renew personal friendships and business links; in which young men could undergo rites of passage and entry into the world of employment; and, for some its most important attribute, where men could gather without women. Not for nothing did rugby union supporters regularly refer to their sport as 'a wonderful freemasonry'. And for those raised in this environment, ostracism was, as Philip Trevor pointed out in his 1922 *Rugby Union Football*, 'the supreme penalty'.[18]

In such a culture working-class rugby union players were viewed rather ambiguously. On the one hand, supporters of rugby union claimed that their sport was free of class distinction and was a 'game for gentlemen of all classes'. It was not, wrote Frank Ludlam, the secretary of Sheffield RUFC, in 1932,

> a game confined chiefly to those whom for want of a better term we describe as public school men. … working men (are we not all working men?) play and mix on equal terms in every respect both on and off the field.[19]

But the reality was that they played little role at the forefront of the sport. They were woefully thin on the ground at international level. Of 513 England internationals between 1902 and 1971 whose occupations are known, only thirty-three (6.43 per cent) were manual workers, but 89 per cent belonged to social classes I and II.[20] Within its own ranks rugby union had developed a nuanced pyramid of club hierarchy, with Harlequins, Richmond, Blackheath and the Universities (by which was meant Oxford and Cambridge) at the apex and the rest positioned below them according to social status. Especially in the inter-war years, these divisions were rigidly enforced, reflecting a widespread fear among the middle classes of the threat represented by the working classes, illustrated in a particularly sharp fashion by the Cutteslowe Walls, which were erected in Oxford in 1934 to physically separate a private housing estate from council houses.[21] In schoolboy rugby, the line of demarcation was even more pronounced. The chances of an elementary or secondary modern school player ever meeting a public school boy on the pitch were approximately zero. Separate international sides were formed for public and state schools. The English Schools Rugby Union, which had been formed in 1904, was restricted to overseeing the sport in board and elementary schools, and allowed absolutely no jurisdiction over the public schools, who formed their own union in 1948. For years the RFU even refused to allow the ESRU permission to stage its annual England versus Wales match at Twickenham. Even a relatively liberal rugby union journalist like T. H. Evans Baillie would let his anti-working class prejudices appear on occasions, such as in 1949 when he criticised league for recruiting 'the manual-labour type who, while strong and fit enough to learn technique, is often, though by no means inevitably, liable to fall short on tactics'.[22] The RFU idealised the working man who knew his place – and that place certainly was not in the front ranks of rugby union.[23]

This attitude underpinned the RFU's view of the overwhelmingly working-class rugby league game. The problem was not that working-class players played rugby, but that they played the league game free of the guidance of those who felt obliged to offer appropriate moral leadership. The fact that this leadership was rejected by those seen as their social inferiors was an affront to traditional middle-class male identity. 'What are called the upper classes (how I dislike the term!) have, as matters stand, an advantage over what are called the working classes in the matter of moral education', admitted Philip Trevor frankly in a discussion of the centrality of the 'public school spirit' to rugby. 'Of course, we cannot define the term "public school spirit" any more than we can define, by any amount of elaboration, the term "gentleman". But we all know exactly what we mean by both.' The circular argument that this spirit was self-evident only to those who understood it necessarily meant that those from the public and grammar schools must control the game. Left to their own devices, the lower orders would undermine 'purity and sportsmanship in the conduct of all matters affecting the best of games'. In 1924 RFU Committee member and president of the Eastern Counties union F. C. Potter-Irwin expressed what many others in the sport no doubt thought and baldly stated that 'Rugby football was never intended as a recreation for those to whom Nature has denied the high privileges of gentlemanly instinct'.[24]

Although this distrust of mass working-class sports extended to professional soc-cer – in 1931 the union writer Glyn Roberts proudly asserted that 'I visit a soccer match once a season to keep my disgust fresh' – it was rugby league which was portrayed as uniquely inferior and aberrant, and its heresy caused it to be treated differently to all other sports, including soccer. At best it was portrayed as a safety valve where working-class rugby players could indulge their mercenary instincts – 'an honest get-out to any who feel they can no longer continue to play the Rugby Union game for its own sake' according to RFU historian O. L. Owen – or at worst, in the words of RFU secretary C. J. B. Marriott, an 'incubus'. On the 1930 British tour of Australasia the tourists' manager James Baxter famously replied that 'every town must have its sewer', when asked why league was popular in Auckland. Lewis Jones, who signed for Leeds in 1952, recalled that his union upbringing had taught him that league was 'a game for thugs administered by thugs in which £.s.d [pounds, shillings and pence] was the first, last and only consideration. A game, in fact, in which violence and sharp practice existed in equal proportions.' Even as late as 1993, a sports reporter on the London *Evening Standard* could describe the sport as being one 'for ape-like creatures watched by gloomy men in cloth caps'.[25] This view of rugby league also radiated out far beyond the immediate jurisdiction of the RFU; when David Hinchliffe was elected to the House of Commons in 1987 he was taken aback by 'how many people have been (and in some areas still are) brought up to genuinely believe that playing league is, more or less, on a par with some sort of criminal activity'. As others have pointed out about similar discourses used to describe working-class and colonial peoples, such stigmatisation served both to engender loyalty within the dominant group, rugby union, and to justify its discrimination against the 'other', rugby league. This parallel was inadvertently highlighted by the leader of South African rugby union Danie Craven in 1985 when he approvingly described union's attitude to league as 'the strictest form of apartheid.'[26]

This antagonism was not uniformly intense across rugby union. In the counties where league was dominant, such unremitting hostility could damage union more than it would league, especially from a public relations standpoint. It was actually Ilkley rugby union club's idea to loan their ground to the 1947 Kiwis for training and they again unsuccessfully approached the RFU to let the Kangaroo tourists use it the following year. The secretary of Cumberland and Westmoreland Rugby Union publicly criticised the RFU for its ban on loaning union grounds to league teams. Welsh captain Watcyn Thomas trained with St Helens Recreation when he played for Waterloo in the 1930s.[27] In the early 1950s, the Royal Signals regimental side at Catterick in North Yorkshire took advantage of the numbers of league players doing national service to build a crack side featuring Billy Boston, Phil Jackson and Brian Gabbitas, among others. They carried off the Yorkshire Cup twice in three years before the Yorkshire Rugby Union banned league-playing servicemen from the competition.[28] There was also some cross-over of players back into union after they had retired from league, especially as coaches, something that also took place in Wales. One of the most well-known examples of this was Ben Gronow, who became coach of Morley rugby union club in the mid-1930s, although the need to preserve his anonymity was such that when the club published a brochure on its history he was identified as 'unknown' on a team photograph, despite being the first man to kick-off an international at Twickenham and an all-time rugby league great. Such idiocies continued for decades. When Ray French helped to coach St Helens RUFC in the 1970s he could not be seen to be coaching the team at matches and had to pose as a spectator. Even into the late 1980s Yorkshire rugby union was plagued by accusations of professionalism as former league players, often under assumed names, turned out for union sides. Although a form of modus vivendi emerged in the 1960s, it could be capsized at any time by a zealot for amateurism intervening or, as was often the case with clubs, by someone using the regulations as a way of settling scores with a rival. And ultimately, no local rugby union official would put his relations with rugby league above their loyalty to the RFU. Bob Oakes, the long-time president of the Yorkshire Rugby Union, was on extremely friendly terms with many leading rugby league figures, yet led the NCSC and never flinched from rigorous implementation of the amateur code.[29]

The response of rugby league to the war waged against it by rugby union was largely to ignore it. In general the social gulf between the two sports was so great that there was little direct contact between them in the inter-war years. This began to change in the 1950s with the opening up of grammar schools to academically bright working-class boys, but it was not until the late 1960s that the RFL formally questioned union's discrimination against its players. In the 1947–48 season Bill Fallowfield had fought a short campaign on behalf of French rugby league to high-light the hypocrisy of French union over their wholesale poaching of league play-ers, one of whom, Yves Bergougnan, had found his way into that season's French Five Nations team.[30] This was a rarity, however. The RFL's unwritten policy was not to get involved in public disputes with the RFU. It never sought to legally challenge the RFU's ban on league players until the 1990s. There were two rea-sons for this conservatism. First, the leadership of rugby league for all its northern self-confidence was fundamentally deferential to those of a higher social class. To challenge rugby union in the courts would bring accusations of undermining tra-ditional social structures. Second, and apparently paradoxically, this deference sat alongside a deep-going sense of moral superiority towards union; a conviction that not only was theirs a better sport to play and watch, but also that it was democra-tic and meritocratic in comparison to union's exclusivity. Every union ban and restriction simply added weight to that belief. This was not as contradictory as it may appear. The idea that the poor are morally superior to the rich is common across cultures and is perfectly compatible with the maintenance of social hierar-chy, as the history of Christianity demonstrates. With the exception of Stan Chadwick's *Rugby League Review*, which called for union clubs to be banned from league grounds after the RFU banned the Kiwi tourists from Ilkley's ground, there seems to have been little sentiment within league for a fight with rugby union. Indeed, given its treatment at the hands of union, the game as a whole seems to have been fairly benign in its attitude: in 1946 *The Oval*, St Helens' weekly league newspaper, even printed photos of locally born England union international cousins Dickie Guest and Jack Heaton with the caption 'rugby union – but we're proud of them', its civic pride tempered by a conditional but.[31]

If anything, the continuous litany of slights against league helped to strengthen its self-belief. In an echo of Edward Said's observation that story-telling is 'the method that colonised people use to assert their own identity and the existence of their own history', numerous stories entered into league folklore about the way in which it had been treated by union. These were often as much an affirmation of league's positive virtues as they were a critique of union's discrimination. Examples of people being banned from entering union clubhouses or grounds, of being dropped from union teams and never selected again, or of being excluded from school teams because of their league links were legion. One story that turned out not to be true but was assumed to be so by both sides was that concerning W. B Wollen's 1895 painting 'The Roses Match'. Broadly based on the Yorkshire versus Lancashire match of 1893, it was widely but wrongly believed that follow-ing the 1895 split those players who had joined the Northern Union had been painted out. To do so would have removed almost all of the players but the strength of the myth was such that league supporters believed that it demonstrated the perfidy of union and union supporters accepted it as proof of their power over league.[32]

Little was to change until the 1980s, although in 1967 and 1968 Bill Fallowfield informally approached Denis Howell, the Minister for Sport, and Walter Winterbottom, the former England soccer manager who was director of the Sports Council, about the RFU's policies. In 1969, in an apparent concession but which was actually an extension of its own arbitrary powers, the RFU had established a 'Reinstatement Committee' to examine appeals by former players who wanted to be reinstated as amateurs, thus underlining the fact it did not accept an objective definition of 'amateur' and that it alone could determine who was or was not entitled to the title. The formation of the British Amateur Rugby League Association in 1973 saw the start of a long campaign to introduce a 'free gangway' for amateur players that would allow them to play both sports. BARLA's indefatigable Maurice Oldroyd astutely sought to bring public scrutiny to bear not on the RFU but on the Sports Council, which allocated state funding to sport. In the late 1960s and early 1970s rugby union was one of the major beneficiaries of government funds, despite its refusal to put into practice the Sports Council's policy of 'Sport for All'.

Initially, Oldroyd had been brushed off. The Sports Council's early response to his probing was a stout defence of the RFU's policy and a personal letter to Robin Prescott, the RFU secretary, warning him that 'it seems quite possible that Mr Oldroyd will go to the press'.[33] But Oldroyd would not go away, and enlisted MPs and lawyers to challenge the Sports Council's policy. Increasingly embarrassed, the Sports Council started to exert some pressure on the RFU to rethink its policies. In 1984 BARLA's campaign was joined by the Freedom in Rugby campaign and four years later by the All-Party Parliamentary Rugby League Group. During the 1980s the RFU, which was also starting to buckle under the contradictions of amateurism and commercial reality, found itself under real pressure for the first time. The rapid growth of BARLA and the increasing number of schools taking up league was a cause of great concern. Numerous discussions ensued and in December 1983 the RFU even convened a special meeting to discuss the success of BARLA and the threat it represented to union.[34] Eventually, after fourteen years of dismissal and prevarication, the RFU grudgingly conceded in April 1987 that amateur rugby league players should also be free to play rugby union if they so chose.[35] Despite this, union players still found themselves informally barred from playing amateur league. In 1993 Wasps' full-back Steve Pilgrim was banned for a year by the RFU after he had played a trial game for Leeds for nothing but travelling expenses. The following year Ady Spencer was forced to withdraw from the Cambridge University side for the Varsity match with Oxford after the RFU discovered that he had also played rugby league. The letter of the RFU's law had changed but its spirit had not.

But by this time the RFU was being forced to fight the war on several fronts. In 1993 Stuart Evans, the Neath and Wales prop who had signed for St Helens in 1987, began legal proceedings against the rugby union authorities alleging restraint of trade because they refused to allow him to play union again. The Inland Revenue had also begun serious investigations of the taxation of rugby union players' secret earnings and in 1994 David Hinchliffe had introduced his Sports

(Discrimination) Bill, which sought to outlaw union's policies towards league. That same year the Ministry of Defence announced that it was lifting the ban on rugby league in the armed forces and that it would henceforth be a recognised sport with the same rights and privileges as dozens of other sports. Faced with an unrelenting campaign from the union-playing nations of the southern hemisphere to allow professionalism the RFU desperately tried delaying tactics, for example, by allowing, in March 1995, professional league players into union after a three-year 'stand-down' period. But the previously impregnable walls of amateurism were now subject to intolerable strain. On 27 August 1995, they were swept away as union finally legalised open professionalism. It was ninety-nine years and 363 days since the formation of the Northern Union. Rugby union, for whom amateurism had been proclaimed as the very reason for its existence, was now as professional as those it despised.

Chapter 10

The working-man's game: class, gender and race

Who played, watched and administered rugby league? Questions of social and occupational background are among the most difficult for historians of sport. In particular, to what extent is it correct to characterise rugby league as a 'working-class sport'? The paucity of information about the game in the pre-Second World War period means that detailed analysis of players and crowds is virtually impossible. But thanks to the inexorable rise of sports statistics and trivia since the 1950s, we can examine the occupational backgrounds of players over the past fifty years with some confidence.

Using club annuals, match programmes and statistical books, Appendix 6 tabulates the backgrounds of players and allows us to track how these changed between 1950 and 1990. The most obvious fact is the degree of similarity in the occupations of players across the post-war period. Leaving aside the category of the full-time professional player, there are three occupations, engineer, labourer and miner, which appear in the top six occupations of all three samples. Electrician and warehouseman are in the top six for two of the periods and are seventh for another. Bricklayer is in the top six in the 1950s and the top eight in the 1990s. Painter is in the top six for the two early periods and the fifteenth most common occupation in the 1990s. It is also noticeable that building, traditionally an employment sector catering for unskilled manual labourers is among the leading occupations of the latter two periods but does not appear in the 1950s sample. Unemployment is mentioned only in the 1990s.

In contrast, the most noticeable difference between the three eras is the growth in the numbers employed within the game. Not only were there 136 professional players but another twenty-one players were also employed as coaches, ground staff and local development officers. Unfortunately, we have no way of checking the previous occupations of full-time players, but we can be reasonably sure that they would not be significantly different to those of other players. It should, however, be noted that the samples used are not precisely comparable. The sample from the 1950s is taken from players appearing in Challenge Cup and Championship finals, and therefore will contain a bias towards more successful players, and the sample from the 1960s and 1970s is of Leeds players and therefore contains local occupational biases. The final sample for 1990 is taken from the 1991 *Rugby League Who's Who*, which covered every registered professional player in Britain.

Despite these caveats, it is clear that rugby league was, and remains, a solidly working-class sport in composition, heavily dependent on manual labourers for its playing personnel. It is difficult to assess how many players were skilled and how many semi- or unskilled. Categories such as engineer and miner can cover a wide range of skill levels. Nevertheless, it does appear to be the case from this data that the occupational spectrum of players ranges broadly across the working class, encompassing the skilled and the unskilled. This leads to the conclusion that involvement in rugby league is not based on occupational status within the working class but on the geographical location of that working class.

We can also calculate the numbers of players who worked with their hands and those who had white-collar occupations. In the 1950s, almost 17 per cent of the sample had non-manual jobs, in the 1960s/70s, the percentage was just over 20 per cent, and by 1991 it was 26 per cent. Of course, not all white-collar jobs were professional occupations. In the 1950s, just 4.8 per cent of players were professionally qualified (three teachers, two accountants and a draughtsman). In the 1960s/70s the total was 5.9 per cent (four teachers, two accountants and a draughtsman). Yet in 1991 the percentage had actually declined, with just 2.1 per cent of rugby league players being professionally qualified (ten teachers, four accountants, two architects, a civil engineer, a quantity surveyor, a solicitor, a bank manager and a chemist), a figure that was actually one less than the number of players who described themselves as unemployed. It must also be noted that many of the professionally qualified had a background in rugby union – for example, all four of the teachers and both accountants from the 1960s sample were former union players.

This apparent decline of those employed in the professions may suggest a somewhat counter-intuitive trend in which professional rugby league seems to have become more, rather than less, working class in playing composition in the two decades before 1995. This is also reflected in the fact that there appears to have been only marginally more students playing the game professionally in the 1990s than there were in the 1960s/70s, despite the huge increase in the numbers attending further and higher education in the 1980s (and in the numbers playing the sport at student level). The percentage of teachers playing the game also appears to have fallen in the 1990s.

Such findings stand in contrast to the overall change in employment patterns in British society during this period. Between 1964 and 1992 the percentage of the population engaged in manual labour fell from 50.2 per cent to 36 per cent, while those engaged in 'routine' clerical work and in white-collar supervisory roles grew from 28.8 per cent to 40.5 per cent. The 'higher salariat' of the professions and senior management grew from 7 per cent to 11.6 per cent.[1] One should be wary about drawing general social conclusions from limited data in such a geographically confined sport. However, these findings would at least suggest that the idea that social mobility has increased significantly since the 1960s is mistaken, at least in the industrial north of England. It is quite probable that some members of the working class who were socially mobile abandoned their connections with the sport as they advanced up the social ladder, yet the fact that they still felt the need to cut their ties with the sport demonstrates the deeply ingrained patterns of social prejudice that still existed in the latter half of the twentieth century. It is worth noting that of 617 players who appeared for Great Britain up to 1995, only five were privately educated.[2]

Conversely, the data also indicates that rugby league was a resilient, self-replicating culture within its historic constituency. Despite the decline of the traditional industries of the north of England and the shift towards service-based industries, the sport remained part of the cultural world of manual labour. This is reinforced when we look at the post-playing careers of former professionals, although here the data is even more limited. Although there is very little data on what players did after they had finished playing, it is probably safe to assume, because most players had jobs outside of the game throughout their playing careers, that the vast majority of them simply carried on with their 'ordinary' day jobs. The only partial clue we have to post-playing careers is in Ken Dalby's 1989 book, *Nothing But the Best*, a series of biographies of forty-six great Leeds players from the previous sixty years. Of the twenty-eight whose occupations he lists, eleven became publicans and four became teachers, while individual jobs included caretaker, textile factory operative, fish and chip shop owner, foundry worker, gardener, miner, policeman, tiler and tram worker. With the exception of Bev Risman, only those who came from outside of the north of England experienced any form of social advancement. All four of the teachers came originally from rugby union (although one of them, Risman, came from a league family before playing union), the former Springbok winger Wilf Rosenberg became a dentist and Vic Hey and Eric Harris returned to Australia to become a successful coach and sports administrator respectively. The Australian Arthur Clues became the proprietor of one of Leeds' most popular sports shops. But for those who lived in the area and grew up playing league there, the game offered little in the way of social or occupational mobility.

This essentially static nature of the sport's social structure can be seen when we look at the leadership of the game. The occupational distribution of officials mirrors that of the NU leadership before the First World War, which was based on the lower sections of the middle classes and especially on those closely connected with the daily lives of the working classes. Of the forty men who stood for election to the Wakefield Trinity club committee between 1935 and 1960 whose occupations can be traced (see Appendix 7), there is, as one might expect, a bias towards managerial, white-collar and self-employed occupations such as shopkeepers and tradesmen, with the ubiquitous publican again being the most significant occupation. However, it is important to note that few candidates could be said to represent either the industrial bourgeoisie, only two describing themselves as managing directors, or the professions, which boasted just an accountant, a draughtsman and two teachers. As could be expected, many occupations were closely linked with the local mining industry. By and large these men were from what Brian Jackson and Dennis Marsden identified as the 'local' middle classes, made up of 'the self-made businessman, works officials, school masters clinging to their home town. Such a class is part of "them" but in some situations can merge for a while with "us"'.

This local middle class stands in contrast to the 'national' middle class, who were public school and university educated.[3]

Much the same is true when we look at the senior office-holders of the RFL itself. Of the eighty annually elected chairmen or presidents of the RFL who held office between 1895 and 1995, the occupations of fifty-two can be traced. As can be seen from Appendix 8, the dominant occupation is that of publican. Of the three textiles manufacturers, two held office before 1914 and the other in 1927. Only two others can be regarded as representatives of manufacturing industry and one of these was chairman in 1902. The 'self-made man' from working- or lower-middle-class origins predominates. Even those who accumulated substantial fortunes through business success, such as Maurice Lindsay and Rodney Walker who held positions in the 1990s, began their lives in state schools. The only major exceptions to this were Sir Edwin Airey, elected chairman of the RFL in 1951, who was also chairman of Leeds for many years and a member of a prominent local family, and Workington's Tom Mitchell, elected in 1961, who was privately educated and inherited a family farm in Cumbria. The only 'private resident' on the list dates back to 1898 and was Batley's D. F. Burnley, who had private income owing to his family's substantial textile business. None appears to have been prominently involved in either national or local politics, although Mitchell was a Conservative Party supporter. Of the fifty-two, nine, or approximately 17 per cent, were professionally qualified (two accountants, architects, solicitors and teachers, plus a doctor). There are seven shopkeepers (baker, draper, dry cleaner, hatter, jeweller, pawnbroker and sports outfitter), slightly more than 10 per cent of the total, and five in managerial positions. With the exceptions of Lindsay and Walker, the two decades before 1995 were dominated by publicans, teachers, accountants and various representatives of the building trade. It must also be pointed out that all of these officials were men; not until Kath Hetherington in 1995 was a woman elected president of the RFL.

We have very little data about the backgrounds of rugby league supporters, but all anecdotal evidence suggests that they were overwhelmingly, although not entirely exclusively, from the working classes. However, there may be some differences in comparison to the occupations of players. Few who had a grammar school or professional background would play league. To do so would exclude them from the social and business networks of rugby union, but some would watch it. We know slightly more about the backgrounds of the highly committed 'activist' supporters. Of the twelve members of the committee of Leeds Supporters' Club in 1969, seven had manual jobs, two worked in offices, one gave her occupation as 'married woman', one was a chartered secretary and another was the director of a local sheet-metal producing firm. Of the eleven who gave the names of the secondary schools they attended (including the chartered secretary and the company director), all had gone to local state schools with a tradition of playing rugby league; with three attending one school a mile away from the club's Headingley ground.[4] Although this one example is not necessarily representative – but again anecdotal evidence suggests it probably is – it does demonstrate the close and deep-rooted links between the clubs, their locality and traditional working-class occupational patterns.

What of the behaviour of supporters? During the 1950s there were only five crowd disturbances reported to the RFL, all of which involved a referee being jostled at the end of a match, including one at Warrington in 1958 when the unfortunate official reported that chocolate had been thrown at him. The numbers of reported incidents increased dramatically in the 1960s. Thirty-three incidents were recorded, nine involved assaults on referees or touch judges by spectators, seven involved stones or bottles being thrown at match officials, and five involved officials being jostled after a match. Six involved missiles being thrown at players and the rest related to hooliganism in the crowd. As early as 1961, the Yorkshire Society of Referees said it was 'perturbed' at the lack of protection given to referees at matches and the matter was discussed in depth by the RFL Council the following year. Nor were the assaults on referees confined to the professional game. In 1966 York referee G. A. Smith took court action against a spectator who attacked him during a local amateur game. The first report of hooliganism between opposing supporters, rather than at referees or opposing players, was made in 1967 when there were complaints that a group of young Featherstone supporters were stealing scarves from fans visiting the club's Post Office Road ground, a common occurrence in soccer at the time. This new development was also noted by the supporters' clubs, the Yorkshire Federation discussing the disturbing trend in November 1967.[5]

This trend grew in the 1970s. Of the thirty incidents reported to the RFL, fifteen involved assaults on or stone-throwing at referees, two were directed at players and the rest were hooliganism between fans. In 1975 the RFL Council discussed the problem twice within five weeks and called on clubs to liaise with local police to counteract the problem. Perhaps the most serious outbreak of violence came during the 1981 Good Friday derby between Hull and Hull KR, when rival gangs fought before and during the match, and threw bricks into the crowd, injuring thirty-seven people.[6] But even this serious outbreak was relatively inconsequential when compared with the widespread violence that accompanied many soccer matches at the time. Certainly by the mid-1980s, fights between supporters had declined significantly, partly a result of growing crowds but also because, in general, the culture of supporters differed from that of soccer in that most fans saw themselves as supporters of the sport as a whole, not just of a particular club.

★

But while violence on the terraces proved to be minor and transient, violence on the pitch was not. In terms of statistics taken from the first complete season of each decade, the numbers of players sent off increased following the war, peaking in the 1970s and then remaining steady over the next two decades. As can be seen in Appendix 3 the number of players sent off for punching and fighting remains fairly static in the post-war years but there was a growth in the number of players dismissed for foul play during a tackle. Kneeing, elbowing and butting in the tackle, and stiff-arm, late and high tackling appear to become more frequent from the 1960s. But it is more likely that such practices became more unacceptable in the game, especially with the significant television coverage of the 1960s, and were therefore singled out by the RFL as offences that referees should punish harshly. Tackling around the head became a particular focus for concern. A 1969 article in the *British Dental Journal* noted that in a survey of a hundred players at all levels of the game in Lancashire, over a third had suffered tooth and mouth injuries.[7] In the 1989–90 season, sendings-off almost doubled from 91 to 172, owing to a directive to referees from the RFL that deliberate tackling around the head should warrant an automatic sending-off.

In 1983 the RFL launched a general campaign against violence in the game, somewhat unfortunately titled 'Stamp Out Violence'. This coincided with the introduction of the 'sin bin' at the start of the 1983–84 season, to which players could be banished for ten minutes for lesser or technical offences.[8] But the 1980s also saw the start of a shift in attitudes to violence, brought about by the success of the 1982 and 1986 Australian touring sides. The tourists were far more disciplined and unlikely to concede penalties than previous sides. This changed emphasis in the Australian style of play began to be emulated by British teams, especially by the John Monie-coached Wigan side of the early 1990s, for whom the giving away of an unnecessary penalty was regarded almost a disciplinary matter in itself. By the 1990s, the use of the fist, the arm or the elbow to intimidate an opponent had been replaced to a great extent by a focus on increasing the severity of the tackle, or 'hit' as it had become known, and the game began to describe itself as a high-speed collision sport.

Even with such a reduction in the open violence of previous generations, intense physical confrontation continued to be central to the sport. Much of this aggression was focused on the battles between players in the same position on opposing teams. Indeed, for many, the struggle for supremacy in the one-on-one tackle was one of the most appealing features of the game, as described by Ray French:

> I used to relish looking into the player's eyes, often shouting at him to come at me, talking to him when I had endowed him with a feeling of powerlessness. The ability to stand over your victim and await the next 'play the ball' adds to this feeling of triumph after a good tackle.[9]

It goes without saying that these confrontations often involved more than the legitimate use of force. Up until the 1970s, when the six-tackle rule and the gradual erosion of the importance of scrums reduced the opportunities for violent behaviour, matches often began with a 'softening-up' period, in which the opposing forwards would seek to establish domination through fair means or foul. This was seen as an accepted part of the game by referees as well as players. During his first season at Leeds in 1947, Australian forward Arthur Clues was punched by a Halifax player in the first scrum of the match. Although no penalty was awarded, the referee told Clues: 'I saw what happened Arthur. You've got one free.' Clues waited for his chance and, during the second half, knocked out his assailant, at which point the referee ran over and started wagging his finger in Clues' face: 'The crowd think I'm bollocking you, but I'm not. He bloody deserved it. Now get on with the game!'[10]

These confrontations were not simply about intimidation but were also part of a process by which players would discover, by the response of their opponents to such action, whether a player was worthy of respect as a man. 'It's all about facing-off and respect', an unidentified player told Ian Clayton in 1993.

> If someone is coming full pelt at you and you knock him on his arse, it might make him think twice next time. If he comes at you again and again, you know then that he's got a big heart under his jersey.[11]

A player with heart was someone who played with courage, without fear of intimidation and, possibly most importantly of all, for his team-mates. One without heart (there was never an indefinite article before the noun) was despised and looked down on as someone who could not be trusted or relied upon.

A key reason for this attitude was the fact that players took pride in doing a job well – and their job was winning. 'I hold strong feelings about what a professional player's approach to the game should be', said Vince Karalius in his 1964 autobiography. 'There's still far too much talk in England about the glory of sport and so on.' In working-class communities professionalism, and the responsibilities it brought, was a badge of honour. In this, it was analogous to the world of the professional black jazz musician in the 1930s and 1940s described by Eric Hobsbawm as 'a milieu that accepted the overriding importance of professionalism, of getting the music right, of the strange marriage between group cooperation and ferocious testing of individuals'. Moreover, for the working-class male who would have otherwise followed a life of manual labour, being a professional was

> a continuous means of asserting oneself as a human being, as an agent in the world and not the subject of others' actions, as a discipline of the soul, a daily testing, an expression of the value and sense of life, a way to perfection.[12]

It is this testing and the struggle to assert oneself in life that explains the importance of violence and intimidation to the game. It was expected that players would give and receive punishment, regardless of their status or age. When teenage prodigy Carl Dooler made his debut for Featherstone Rovers in 1961 he was met with a ferocious tackle from Wakefield Trinity's Derek Turner. Rovers' Terry Clawson protested to Turner: 'Fucking hell, Derek, he's only a kid', to which Turner replied, 'He's getting the same fucking money as us, isn't he?'[13]

This ritual intimidation of the debutant or the inexperienced player (especially when fresh from rugby union) also has parallels with the world of work and the treatment by older workers of those starting their first jobs, especially as part of apprenticeship rites. Certainly players' attitudes towards the money that they were paid for playing the game were identical to those of workers in industrial jobs. Players had an acute sense of their own worth and believed that they were entitled to decent pay for the effort they expended. In 1930 the young Hull KR half-back, Harry 'Scrubber' Dale made his debut for Yorkshire and was shocked at the lack of effort from his team-mates. When he complained at half-time he was told by a senior player: 'do you think I am going all out when we only get as much for winning as losing.' An astonished Dale was then informed that, contrary to the impression he had been given, the Yorkshire players received a flat £3 whether they won, drew or lost the match.[14] This was not, in the eyes of the players, a fair day's pay for a fair day's work. In pursuit of this ideal, match fees often became more complicated than the simple win, loss, draw formula. Geography played a part too. Many teams paid extra for away matches outside of their own county and the introduction of mid-week floodlit games in the 1960s saw a variety of rates introduced to compensate players for travelling during the working week. In 1970, for example, Featherstone agreed to pay players an additional £1 and 10 shillings for mid-week matches in Lancashire or in Hull.[15]

Although negotiations over signing-on fees were an individual matter, players at a number of clubs evolved a form of collective bargaining whereby they would elect representatives to 'settle terms' with the club at the start of each season. Naturally, it was not always easy for the two sides to come to an agreement and, particularly during the 1970s when the prevailing atmosphere of industrial conflict pervaded the sport, the months of August and September were often punctuated by strikes and the threat of strikes by players seeking to improve their playing terms for the forthcoming season. There were seven such strikes in the 1970s, although none lasted more than a week or for more than one match.

During the 1980s the threat of strike action was more likely to be used to extract higher bonuses from clubs on the eve of important cup-ties, although the changing economic circumstances of the game also saw players strike over unpaid wages or pay-cuts, such as at Bramley in 1983, or for a larger share of sponsorship money, as was threatened at Hull KR in 1981. But pay was not the only cause of strike action. In 1975 Huddersfield players successfully struck for the reinstatement of their sacked coach and in 1978 Featherstone players went on strike in protest at the club committee's new RFL Council representative. On the other hand, there were occasions when players agreed to forego wages to help clubs out of financial difficulties, such as at Huddersfield in December 1972.[16] In 1981 yet another attempt was made to form a player's union, the Rugby League Professional Players' Association. Inspired by mine worker and Doncaster player-coach Alan Rhodes and actively supported by a number of leading players, the union was formed as part of the Association of Professional, Executive, Clerical and Computer staffs (APEX). It focused on the issues of players' injury insurance, which was then just seven pounds per week for thirteen weeks only, and on the lifting of the transfer ban with Australia, which it saw as a restraint of trade. Like the other attempts to establish a players' union, it was a short-lived organisation but, unlike the previous two, this was due to its success in winning both of its key aims. The transfer ban was lifted in 1983 and in 1982, following a well-supported strike threat, the RFL introduced a new injury insurance scheme which provided players with up to £70 a week for twenty-six weeks.

A further parallel with the world of work can be found in the constant striving of players to bend the rules or cheat to gain an advantage over their opponents or the referee, the embodiment of authority. Alex Murphy, whose command of the art of gamesmanship and beyond was only marginally surpassed by his genius as a player, commented in 1968 that:

> It's up to any player of recognised top-flight calibre to try and 'get away with a little bit of something' out there on the field. … Rules aren't meant to be broken. But it's a challenge to any player worth his salt to try and get away with bending them a little. And if you don't succeed in getting away with a little bit of something that's not quite in line with the rule book, then you must be prepared to pay the penalty.[17]

This was precisely the attitude that prevailed throughout British industry. Up to the late 1970s much of British shop-floor culture was based on extracting the maximum amount of informal control of the work process from the management or to find ways to earn more money or do less work within current working conditions. Alongside this was a generalised culture of seeking to cheat or 'fiddle' which was common, in different forms, to all classes.[18] In many ways this culture was responsible for a number of the problems faced by the sport on the pitch, with players constantly seeking to circumvent the rules or the referee's authority. 'All players are cheats and always will be,' Jim Sullivan told a 1954 meeting. The RFL's first coaching manual, published in 1948, noted with dismay that matches were often spoilt by 'flagrant attempts to break the laws of the game by "beating" the referee, especially in standing off-side and in scrimmage infringements'. And, as we have seen, this was particularly true at the play-the-ball, which was a problem that largely did not exist in other league-playing countries. In 1947 *The Oval* favourably contrasted the attitude of the French to British sides' reliance on 'beating the rules to as great an extent as the referee will allow. The French show that there is nothing very wrong with our rules, if the players want to obey them.'[19]

The attitudes of rugby league players were therefore shaped and defined by the world of industrial labour, which was intensely physical, often aggressively oppositional to management and, above all, almost absolutely masculine. This was as true in amateur rugby league as it was in the professional game. A 1987 survey of amateur players found that 55 per cent of its sample had been sent off for fighting or foul play at some point in their careers.[20] That close connection between working-class masculinity and manual labour was captured by Walter Greenwood in his 1933 novel *Love on the Dole*. Greenwood himself came from Langworthy, an area of Manchester still noted for amateur rugby league, and also wrote the script for the 1935 film 'Where's George?' a laboured comedy about a rugby league team.

The novel's protagonist, Harry Hardcastle, decides that on leaving school he will give up his part-time clerk's job in a pawn shop and get a manual job at Marlowe's engineering works. As he approaches the works to enquire about a job, 'he felt ashamed of himself, slunk along by the walls trying to make himself inconspicuous. All these men and boys wore overalls; *they* weren't clerks, they were Men, engaged in men's work'. As Paul Willis and later Joanna Bourke have strikingly pointed out, the masculinity of manual labour, with its emphasis on strength, endurance and intimidation (and the ability to stand up against it), was a central feature of working-class men's self-image for much of the twentieth century, and this was reflected strongly in rugby league.[21]

In particular, the ability to withstand extremely high levels of physical pain was ingrained in the ethos of the sport. The two most revered examples of this are the 1914 third Ashes test match and the second Ashes test of the 1958 series. In the former, the British team defeated Australia 14–6 despite playing with only ten men at one stage, while in the latter Britain prevailed 25–18 with only eleven fit players for most of the game. In both, players continued to play well past normal limits of endurance. Douglas Clark played most of the 1914 test with a badly broken thumb before being forced off with a dislocated shoulder. Alan Prescott played with a broken right arm for seventy-seven minutes of the 1958 test. The fact that both games were won against the odds helped to elevate them to almost mythical tales of heroism but, to the majority of players and supporters, these players were only doing what was expected of them. Allegedly Clark cried tears of frustration, but not of pain, when he was finally forced to leave the field in 1914, as if to underline his determination not to succumb. Indeed, this tradition has been passed down to every schoolboy who has ever picked up a rugby league ball, all of whom at some point will have been told by his coach: 'Don't ever let them know they've hurt you'. In this, the actions of the injured players reflected everyday working life in the mines, the docks or the factory. Illness or injury was largely something to be ignored or overcome because it usually meant a loss of wages, which in turn would undermine masculine pride at being able to provide for his family. And this attitude towards pain showed no diminution even after the industries that had given rise to it had long since fallen into terminal decline. Ten minutes into the 1990 Challenge Cup final, Wigan's Shaun Edwards fractured his cheekbone and eye socket but continued to play on because, as he later explained:

> I didn't come off because I didn't want them to know that they could hurt me. I knew that if I'd pulled a muscle or something like that then I couldn't have gone on, because I'd have been a hindrance to the team, but I knew that the injury was only pain and I could put up with it.

Although Edwards was a half-back, it was in the forwards, where the emphasis was on tackling and carrying the ball into the opposition, that the masculine ideal of toughness and imperviousness to pain was the strongest. Castleford and Great Britain forward Brian Lockwood recalled his treatment at the hands of his coach

Derek Turner after winning a man of the match award against Hunslet in the early 1970s:

> I was trooping back to the dressing room with my cheque, pleased as punch, until I saw Turner waiting for me. 'Call yourself a forward?' he bellowed. 'Look at you. Your face is like a bloody choir boy's.' Thump! he cracked me on my nose and I was covered in blood. 'There,' he said, 'you look like a forward now.'

The resilience of this historical thread of masculinity, work and wages which ran through the sport was underscored by the slogan which was prominently displayed in the Wigan team's gym in 1991: 'No pain, no gain; no pain, no train; no train, no play: no play, no pay.'[22]

Of course, the most masculine of all occupations was that of coalmining. 'There used to be a saying that if you wanted a good prop forward you only had to shout as much down the nearest pit shaft and there'd be a good one come up in the next cage', claimed National Union of Miners president Joe Gormley in his autobiography.[23] This link between rugby and mining stretches back to the 1880s when the first teams of coalminers began to play the game in Yorkshire and Lancashire. By the time of the split in 1895, it was commonplace for sides such as Hunslet and Wigan to be composed almost entirely of miners. Many Welshmen who came north were from mining villages in the valleys and it was also noticeable that the short-lived Welsh rugby league clubs of the 1900s were based in the mining districts rather than the larger towns. Throughout the inter-war years, the relationship was highlighted by the success of mining towns such as Wigan.

Rugby league's new sense of national importance following the Second World War dovetailed with the rhetoric of post-war optimism in the coal industry following nationalisation and the creation of the National Coal Board (NCB) in 1947. The NCB's monthly employee magazine *Coal* regularly carried articles on the rugby league careers of miners and the importance of the game to mining districts, often in order to promote harmonious relations between workers and management. Following the victory of Cumbrian pit side Risehow and Gillhead over Keighley in the Challenge Cup in 1948, the NCB's area manager stated that 'undoubtedly the club has helped improve production … I am certain that the social organisation [of which the club was a part] will continue to promote full co-operation between management and men'.[24] The fact that the 1946 Great Britain tourists could field a front row of miners seemed to echo Labour's propaganda about the place of the miner in the engine room of post-war reconstruction. Five of the 1950 British touring side were miners, three of whom were from Wigan. The two new professional sides in Cumberland, Whitehaven and Workington, drew much of their playing strength and support from local pit communities. Whitehaven's principal officials were Wilson Walker and George Farquhar, surface yard manager and pit manager respectively at the local Haig Colliery. In the 1949–50 season, miners at one pit in Whitehaven began their shift early at two o'clock in the morning so that the later shift could finish work in time to go to the Whitehaven versus Warrington match. Such was the importance of the industry to the game that in 1953 even a side such as Liverpool City, which was not located in a mining area, had a forward pack who were all miners, plus a coach who was also a miner, drawn from the St Helens coalfield.[25] These links continued into the 1960s and 1970s, especially in the coalfields of West Yorkshire, with the mining towns of Castleford, Featherstone and Wakefield all winning the Challenge Cup, and the latter two also winning the Championship, between 1963 and 1977.

From the 1980s, the link between mining and the sport tended to be emphasised in the past tense, as the decline of the sport both on and off the pitch was linked by many to the decline of the coal industry. In 1996, in the wake of the introduction of Super League, David Storey explicitly linked the decline of what he sees as 'traditional' northern values in the game with the collapse of the coal industry:

> I used to think of rugby league as an extension of the coalmining industry, not just in terms of geography, but it has the same mechanical, repetitive process. Tackle, play-the-ball, tackle – it has a similar rhythm to chipping away at rocks. But now, of course, the coalmining has gone, and so has the confederacy that infused the game in the Fifties and Sixties, the camaraderie that came from a united struggle, whether it be against nature or the class system.[26]

More specifically, former Wakefield player and Castleford coach Dave Sampson argued that Britain's eclipse by Australia was due to the decline of hard manual labour:

> Years ago men worked down the pit then came up to play rugby. We don't appreciate this when comparing eras of rugby and making analogies of hard physical training. My contention is that the toughness of the mind and body was made by repetitive hard work and tough occupations that the people of the past had to endure, ... it's no surprise that we haven't won the Ashes since the 1970s, before the mines and the factories started to close.[27]

As with all generalisations, these beliefs contain a mixture of truth and myth. Nostalgia is the over-riding sentiment but, as we have seen, the 1960s were a period in which the game was in a seemingly inexorable decline. And, as the occupational analysis of players demonstrated, the proportion of miners playing professional rugby league also appears to have remained fairly constant from the 1950s to the 1980s. When it comes to Australia, similar problems of de-industrialisation and de-population in traditional league heartlands, especially in Sydney itself, have also occurred, yet have not affected the national side's playing ability.

Nevertheless, the bond between coalmining and rugby league remained strong into the 1990s, even where, as in the case of Wigan, there was no longer a living link.

The reasons for this were not simply due to historic and geographic circumstances, but also to a shared conception of what being a miner and being a rugby league player represented. Both were viewed as the most masculine expressions of work and sport; both were viewed as the embodiment of collective teamwork; and both were viewed, as Storey hints above, as embodying a somewhat greater degree of class-consciousness, even if it was often expressed in broad social rather than explicitly political terms. There was also a shared sense of separateness from, and moral superiority over, other occupations and sports. The idea that miners somehow represented the moral core of rugby league was generally accepted within the game. Perhaps the only challenge to it came humorously in the 1980s, when supporters of the two Hull clubs would taunt fans from mining districts with the chant 'we all agree, dockers are better than miners', more in ironic comment on a lost industrial age than an attempt at a serious confrontation.

It was these factors that made rugby league's relationship with coalmining more profound than that which other sports had with the industry. Although soccer in Scotland and the northeast of England had deep links with mining, it had neither the intense physicality nor the shared sense of social exclusion of rugby league. Nor were its fortunes so closely identified with the industry. Cricket, which had a tradition of fast bowlers who came from mining areas, most notably Harold Larwood and Fred Trueman, was essentially a sport of individual endeavour and had none of the shared social consciousness of mining and league; throughout the 1970s and 1980s Trueman seemed to go out of his way to criticise National Union of Mineworkers leader Arthur Scargill. Rugby union in South Wales, while it shared with league both overt masculinity and collectivity on the pitch, was certainly not a repository of any form of working-class consciousness. Many Welsh international union players who worked in mining were most definitely on the other side of the class divide in the industry. Idris Jones, who captained Wales against Ireland in 1925, was the NCB's first director of research, and Billy Cleaver, who played fourteen times for Wales following the Second World War, was the manager of Celynen North pit when he played for Wales and the British Lions in 1950.[28]

The difference between the two sports' relationships to mining was highlighted in 1950 over the organisation of a rugby union match between miners from England and Wales. Promoting the game in the NCB's *Coal* magazine, Idris Jones had claimed that 'Rugby football has not gripped the imagination of coalminers in England and Scotland to anywhere near the same extent it has in Wales', to which a furious miner from Tyldesley, near Leigh, replied that 'apparently [miners in the north of England] do not count in the eyes of the purist since their adherence is to the rugby league game.' He went on to point out that

> in our mining district of Leigh there is one professional club and approximately thirty junior clubs – who are more genuinely amateur than many rugby union teams. Local collieries, such as Astley and Tyldesley, Bedford and Bickershaw, compete with other mill and workshop teams in the Leigh Amateur League.

And ended with the challenge that 'if the "old school tie brigade" is unwilling to recognise the fraternisation of rival amateur codes, why not hold a second rugby international under League auspices?'[29] Needless to say the challenge was not taken up, and the union international, which resulted in a tedious 0–0 draw, was not repeated. The fact that it was a senior management figure who was promoting rugby union and a miner from a traditional mining town defending rugby league seemed to highlight the difference between the two sports.

★

What of those who did not meet the masculine imperative of rugby league? As in all intensely male environments, there was an undercurrent of self-conscious fear of femininity and homosexuality within the sport. The insults 'You tackle like a girl' and the more general 'you big woman', shouted at a player who drops a ball or misses a tackle, show how the culture of league, like that of all major team sports, based much of its self-esteem on its hostility to femininity. In 1952 Bill Fallowfield had claimed that the game had no place for 'cissies' and in 1967 the RFL Council sent out a circular to clubs warning players not to indulge in 'kissing and cuddling' after scoring a try, which they believed was becoming common in soccer, and expressing pride in the fact that 'players, for the most part, behaved in a manly rather than an over-demonstrative fashion when congratulating a colleague who had scored'.[30] Even the RFL's 1980s marketing slogan 'A Man's Game for all the Family' could be seen to be overly concerned to proclaim the masculinity of the game. Of course, there were varying degrees of homo-eroticism within the game. Storey's *This Sporting Life* accurately captured some of this element in the relationships between the players and the club scouts and directors, a theme amplified in Lindsay's Anderson's film version. Rumours of players thought to be homosexual circulated at least as early as the 1940s, and certainly by the 1980s at least one reasonably well-known player in England was quite open within the game about being gay. In 1995 Australian prop-forward Ian Roberts became probably the world's highest profile male sportsman to come out and publicly declare that he was homosexual.[31] The attitude within the sport towards Roberts and others was markedly different to the furious hounding and ostracism of gay soccer player Justin Fashanu, who eventually committed suicide. Even homophobic bigots within league were quite prepared to accept Roberts as a player as long as he was good enough to play, a somewhat grudging echo of league's self-identification as an open and democratic sport.

This democratic spirit was most severely tested when it came to women in rugby league. Women spectators had been common at rugby in the north from the 1880s and were clearly not an insignificant proportion of crowds. They were occasionally arrested for hooliganism at matches, although the prominence given to such incidents by the press probably tells us more about their rarity than anything else. In 1930 a woman was escorted from Hunslet's Parkside ground by the police after she had rushed on to the pitch to hit Oldham forward Jim Addison over the head with her umbrella. The woman with an umbrella became something of an irregular feature at some grounds. In the 1940s a St Helens woman supporter would hit unsuspecting visiting players over the head as they came on to the pitch. In 1954 the referee George Phillips complained that 'women spectators are largely to blame' for shouting at players and inciting rough play. In 1973 a Warrington woman was arrested and fined for attacking referee Gerry Kershaw after a match. Most famously, Minnie Cotton of St Helens achieved a degree of fleeting notoriety in 1966 when she twice rushed on to the pitch to defend her lodger, Saints forward John Warlow, from unwelcome attentions during a Challenge Cup semi-final and Championship final. In 1986 a woman supporter was accused of hitting Australian full-back Gary Jack over the head with an umbrella during the tourists' match with Hull.[32]

In schools' rugby league, there was a tradition of women coaching schoolboys in the game, women such as Winnie Powell at Wakefield's St Austin School in the 1940s, who later became a Carmelite nun, and Adriel Collinson at Hunslet Carr School in the 1960s.[33] But although women had long been involved in the running of supporters' clubs it was not until 1970, when Betty Haile was elected to Whitehaven's board of directors, that a woman took an official position in the leadership of a club. In 1984 Barbara Close became the first woman to lead a board of directors when she became chairperson of Fulham, and the same year the RFL Council was breached for the first time when Kath Hetherington became Sheffield Eagles' representative on it. The late 1980s also saw women physiotherapists join professional clubs, led by Widnes's Viv Gleave.[34] Before the 1980s, however, the most prominent women in rugby league tended to be the 'Rugby League Queens' selected each year at supporters' clubs beauty contests. One aspect of women's involvement in rugby league, which like that of wives of professional male players in other team sports has received little consideration outside of North America, is the role played by players' (and referees') wives in maintaining and supporting their husband's involvement in the game. This is very probably incalculable and, certainly, anecdotal evidence suggests that for a number of players, it is the direction and astuteness of their wives that has enabled them to develop a successful career both on and off the field.

Women playing rugby league began in earnest in the 1970s, although there had been an unsuccessful attempt to establish the game for women during the First World War. Certainly women in Featherstone had attempted to play the game in 1919 but had been told by local men that it was more appropriate for women to play soccer. However, they did play league during the 1921 miners' strike and the 1926 General Strike to raise funds for locked-out miners. It is worth noting that the popularity of women's soccer in the Lancashire coalfields in the early 1920s can to some extent be ascribed to the fact that in rugby league-playing areas soccer was always seen as being a less masculine sport and therefore more acceptable for women.[35] In 1978 BARLA allowed thirteen-year-old Elisabeth Beal to play for her local under-fourteens side, after the local league had banned her, although it hoped that a girls side would be formed so she did not have to play with boys. By 1980

'Ladies' clubs had been formed at Huddersfield, Leeds and at Pilkington Brothers in St Helens. In 1984 Julie Fitzpatrick became the game's first woman referee when she took up the whistle in the West Yorkshire amateur league, although stalwart referee Billy Thompson complained that 'I can't see rugby as a game for women to get involved in … it's not a woman's world'. His views were not entirely shared by everyone in the sport. In 1987 Peter Corcoran, the former Australian director of coaching then advising the RFL, told the *Huddersfield Examiner* that 'I would like to see rugby league divorce itself from the macho image and get more women involved', although his remarks were directed more at women filling administrative and coaching roles than actually playing.[36] Nevertheless, by 1994 there were twenty-one women's clubs playing the game, largely based in traditional rugby league towns, in contrast to the even greater growth of women's rugby union, which was largely based on existing men's clubs and higher education. Despite a greater openness, women players and referees in particular still had to face significant levels of male chauvinism, fuelled by the deep belief that, in contrast to Peter Corcoran's comments, rugby league was indeed predominantly a man's game.[37]

★

But was it also a white man's game? Black players had first played professional league before the First World War, appeared at international level in the 1930s, and from the 1960s were such a common sight on rugby league pitches that it almost ceased to be a matter for comment. The first black athlete to play rugby league appears to have been Lucius Banks, who signed for Hunslet in 1912.[38] Banks, a US soldier, was spotted playing American football by a former member of Hunslet's management committee living in New York. The club bought him out of the US Army and over to England, but the strength of Hunslet's back division limited his opportunities and he soon faded from the scene.[39] In 1913 Barrow signed the first black Englishman to play the game, James Peters, a dockworker from Plymouth. Peters played five times at fly-half for England at rugby union between 1906 and 1908, but was in his early thirties when he switched to league and was never able to make his mark.

However, the first significant minority group that found prominence in rugby league were the Jewish communities of Hull, Leeds and Manchester. As early as the 1890s, Jewish spectators had been prominent at rugby matches in the north, so much so that the Leeds Parish Church side became known as 'the Jewish team' because of its large-scale support from local Jewish immigrants. There were also local Jewish players, such as Bramley's Edward Jacobson, and it was perhaps not coincidental that the two most famous Welsh players to 'Go North' at this time, the James brothers, who were of Jewish origin, went to Broughton Rangers, a club which also had a large local Jewish following. Albert Rosenfeld, Huddersfield's Australian try-scoring phenomenon, was the most prominent Jewish rugby league player, and the inter-war years also saw a number of local Jewish players rise to prominence, such as Hull KR's Louis Harris, Rochdale's Sam Birkinshaw and a number of Broughton Rangers' players. Rangers' Lester Samuels, one of the few qualified doctors to play rugby league, played the game as an amateur because that allowed him to play on Saturday, the Jewish Sabbath. Like Hull and Leeds, Broughton also had significant Jewish representation among club directors and officials. The popularity of rugby league among Jews in Leeds was bemoaned by a number of more orthodox Jews, most notably the mathematician and Zionist leader Selig Brodetsky, who lived in Leeds and was disturbed by the numbers of Jews he saw making their way to Headingley on the Sabbath. Reputedly Yiddish songs were sung on the terraces at Leeds during the 1930s. The game was not free of anti-Semitism, however. 'But we don't bring supporters from Jerusalem' was the alleged response of one St Helens supporter to criticisms by Salford fans of its importation of players from New Zealand in 1929, and anti-Semitic comments against Leeds could occasionally be heard at matches.[40]

This sprinkling of Jewish players – which although not great, was still significantly more than the four Jews identified by the *Jewish Chronicle* in 1935 who had ever played professional soccer – was a small indicator of rugby league's willingness to recruit on the basis of merit rather than social status.[41] At a time when black boxers where barred from fighting for British championships and black sportsmen rarely achieved prominence in any sport, black players began to make their presence felt at the highest levels of rugby league.[42] In 1935 Wigan stand-off George Bennett made the first of three appearances for Wales in their first match against France. Oldham loose forward Alec Givvons missed only two of Wales's eight matches between 1936 and 1939. In 1937 Broughton's Jimmy Cumberbatch became the first black player to be selected for England when he scored two tries against France at Thrum Hall. His brother Val played for Barrow and he scored a try on his debut for England against France in Paris in 1938.

Roy Francis signed for Wigan as a seventeen-year-old in 1936 but was transferred to Barrow after just twelve matches by the club's new manager, Harry Sunderland, who appears to have been a racist. Francis played for Great Britain in 1947 and then moved to Hull, where he became probably the first-ever black person to coach a professional sports team in Britain. He turned a mediocre Hull side into championship winners and brought to the game motivational techniques, scientific fitness regimes and tactical innovation.[43] The 1950s saw a significant presence of black players in the game. Leeds-born Cec Thompson played for Great Britain in 1951, and in 1960 was appointed as coach of the Barrow club. In 1953 Wigan signed winger Billy Boston, who was such a phenomenon that he was selected for the British tour of Australia a matter of months after making his debut, becoming the youngest-ever tourist. Clive Sullivan, who was signed by the Hull club in 1961, became the first black captain of a major British sports team in 1972 and led the British side to victory in that year's World Cup final. This roll-call of black players achieving at the highest levels of rugby league continued through the 1980s and 1990s. Des Drummond, Henderson Gill, Roy Powell, Martin Offiah, Phil Ford, Sonny Nickle, Alan Hunte, Carl Gibson and Jason Robinson all appeared for Great Britain. But no player dominated British rugby league in this period like Ellery Hanley. Born in Leeds, Hanley rose to prominence as a stand-off in the early

1980s, when he became the first player since Billy Boston to score fifty tries in a season. Transferring to Wigan in 1985, he switched to loose forward and as captain of the side helped steer it to become league's world club champions. In 1987 he was appointed Great Britain captain, a position he held until his retirement from international football in 1992, and in 1995 he became British coach, the first black person to coach a major British national sports side.

This level of racial equality was partly due to rugby league's self-perception as a sport open to all, which allowed it to welcome players who would be excluded from other sports or whose opportunities would be severely restricted. This emphasis on merit meant that racial barriers did not carry the same weight in the game as they did in other, more socially conservative, sports. And, of course, there were also elements in rugby league quite conscious, and in some cases proud, of their aberrant position in relation to middle-class sporting norms. Despite the RFL's attempts to establish the sport in South Africa in the late 1950s and early 1960s, there was overt opposition to collaboration with the apartheid regime from within the sport, as exemplified by a 1957 article in the *Rugby League Gazette*:

> [The South African government's] racial discrimination will reap its own whirlwind someday. In the meantime, our game should confine itself to playing Rugby League. We have no colour bar, we judge a man as a man irrespective of colour, and anyone good enough is eligible to play for the country of his birth. That is as it should be, and anyone who tinkers about with this in order to 'fit in' with South African standards is dealing a death blow at every civilized concept of sportsmanship.[44]

Moreover, there were also precedents for working-class identification with the oppression that black people faced. During the Second World War black American troops stationed in Britain appear to have been given a much warmer welcome from the working classes than from other sections of British society. In his book, *A Rising Wind*, the black American journalist Walter White argued that this was based on the hardships of life that were shared by British workers and black GIs. The great black American singer Paul Robeson became something of a folk hero among South Wales mining communities in the post-war years, and Australian aboriginal activist Charles Perkins also noted in the 1950s the common oppressions faced by workers in the north of England and those of a dark skin colour. In *Coal is Our Life*, the authors commented that in Featherstone, 'propaganda about inequality and injustice has a strong appeal to working people; in all sorts of ways these are the marks of their situation in life'. This is not to suggest that life in working-class communities was free of racism, but that elements of a broader social consciousness were sufficiently strong and widespread to allow a predominantly white sport, albeit one with an egalitarian ideological stance, to accept black players in positions of prominence and even authority. The boyhood lessons in equality and respect taught to Doug Laughton, who signed Martin Offiah for Widnes, were not uncommon in working-class homes:

We never thought that people with different coloured skin were inferior to us. My grandmother used to say: 'There's nobody better than you and there's nobody worse'. The 'nobody worse' bit would prompt me to ask: 'Am I that bad?' I was taught to treat people with respect. We were raised that way even if we never had a great education.[45]

This basic belief in equality was reinforced by the commercial necessities that obliged the sport to seek talented players from wherever it could find them. If a player was good enough to attract more paying spectators through the turnstiles, rugby league officials did not worry about the colour of his skin. And to a limited extent, the game also carried a sense of exclusion from society that was shared by those who suffered from racial oppression. This intersection of race and class status was captured by Cec Thompson when he remembered the problems he faced as a young man: 'It was bad enough being black ... How much lower down the social scale could one go than be seen as a black, uneducated rugby league player ...?'[46]

Rugby league therefore stood somewhat apart from the sporting mainstream and offered a relatively open and meritocratic alternative to those sports more tightly bound to the racist status quo. This certainly played a role in attracting black Welsh players, who knew that no black rugby union player had ever worn the red shirt of Wales until the 1980s. Similarly, a small but significant number of black South African rugby union players escaped apartheid by moving to play with English league sides in the 1960s and 1970s. One black South African, Bradford's Dave Barends, became the first and only non-British player to play for Great Britain when he was selected for the 1979 tour of Australasia. Possibly the most spectacular example of this sense that rugby league did not march in lockstep with other sports was Wakefield Trinity's unsuccessful attempt to sign John Carlos, the American 200-metres bronze medallist at the 1968 Olympics, whose black power salute on the victory rostrum led to him and Tommie Smith being vindictively banned from international athletics.[47]

However, although black league players had greater opportunities to rise to prominence, the positions in which they played were restricted by racial stereotypes. In general, black players have been confined to positions that emphasise speed and strength, a phenomenon known as 'stacking' or positional segregation.[48] This is illustrated by the Great Britain side between 1984 and 1994. In sixty-five games, thirteen black players made an aggregate total of 152 appearances. But over 68 per cent of these appearances were in the wing or centre positions, traditionally those in which speed is the most important factor. Even more tellingly, not a single black player appeared in the critical playmaking positions of scrum-half and hooker. All of the stand-off half and loose forward appearances were made by one man, Ellery Hanley, and, of the other twelve black players, only three appeared in any position other than winger or centre. Similar findings have been found at club level by Long *et al.*, who discovered that 63 per cent of black players in the top two English divisions were wingers.[49] The extent of these stereotypical views was highlighted by Barry Maranta, former owner of the London Broncos, when he announced in 1995 that his club was aiming to recruit local black players: 'They can't play soccer because of their size, but ... they're Wendell Sailors. They can sit on the wing and bust through tackles.'[50]

Off the field, there is little evidence to suggest that the sport posed a conscious challenge to prevailing attitudes to race. Throughout the 1950s there were accusations from senior figures in the game, such as leading journalist Eddie Waring and former Great Britain captain Gus Risman, that racism on the part of the selectors was responsible for keeping Cec Thompson out of the British side.[51] In 1988 Des Drummond was left out of the British touring party to Australasia after defending himself from a supporter who rushed on to the pitch shouting racist abuse. Although not on the widespread and horrific scale of English soccer, racial abuse of players by spectators was not unknown. Even in the 1950s, Billy Boston, a universally popular player, was occasionally subject to racist taunting. Racial abuse between players has also been a problem. In 1978 Doncaster had complained about racial taunts directed by opponents at their black players – despite finding this 'unsavoury' the RFL Council decided that this was part of the game and should be treated with 'a low profile' – and incidents continue to be reported.[52]

Crowds at rugby league matches have remained overwhelmingly white, despite the changing racial profile of many northern towns. In 1995 researchers from Leeds Metropolitan University discovered that there were more black people, thirty-eight, playing professional rugby league than watching it, a total of just twenty-four.[53] Despite the success of black players in the sport, there appears to be little incentive for black people to become supporters. Rugby league's continuing lack of status means that it is not perceived as a method of social integration. More to the point, league is perceived by black and Asian communities as being an exclusively white sport. Indeed, the insularity and parochialism of 'northernness' could often by translated into a racial exclusionism. For example, many working-men's clubs had racial exclusion policies until the 1970s and even in the 1980s it was a common sight in many pubs in Lancashire and Yorkshire to see 'No Travellers' signs, banning gypsies and other travellers. This is also graphically highlighted by the almost non-existent links between rugby league clubs and their local Asian communities. In the early 1960s many Asians emigrated to take jobs in the textiles mills of the north of England. By the 1970s, large numbers of rugby league clubs found themselves in towns and cities with significant Asian populations. Some, such as Halifax and Keighley, found that the working-class housing areas surrounding their stadia had become the centres of local Asian communities. However, the sport has done little to attract Asian players or spectators to the game. In contrast to the success of players with an Afro-Caribbean background, only two Asian players, the brothers Ikram and Tony Butt, have played professional rugby league, with Ikram Butt playing for the English rugby league side in 1995. Three others, Safraz Patel, Gurjinderpal Pahal and Junaid Malik have played international amateur rugby league. Just as racist stereotypes have helped to confine black players to particular positions in league, stereotypes about Asian people not being physically strong enough for the game are often used to explain the lack of Asian participation in the game.

Rugby league's contradictory record on racial issues raises the broader question of whether sport can be a force to overcome racism in society. Even a sport with league's record of on-field integration has proved largely incapable of confronting deeper aspects of racial stereotyping and institutionalised discrimination. Moreover, its history of racial equality often serves as a self-congratulatory barrier, preventing it breaking out of its traditional white working-class constituency to build support among local black and Asian communities. In short, rugby league demonstrates that having a significant number of black players in prominent positions does not necessarily mean that a sport is free of racism. Nevertheless, as a sport that was marginalised in its relationship to British society, it is undeniable that for those who also felt themselves marginalised by society, rugby league has historically offered more opportunities than other British sports.

Chapter 11

The other amateurs: beyond the heartlands

The fortunes of amateur rugby league in the post-war years fluctuated as widely as those of the professional game. Indeed, by the late 1960s similar doubts were being expressed about the long-term viability of the amateur game. But by 1990 amateur rugby league had not only consolidated and developed its popularity in the game's heartlands but had established itself as a national sport, played in towns and by people far away from the sport's traditional constituency. In this it differed sharply from the professional game, which, despite strenuous efforts, struggled vainly to expand its horizons.

The game's expansion in the 1970s and 1980s was the culmination of work that had begun after the end of the Second World War, when amateur rugby league had gained a toehold in both London and South Wales. The self-confidence imbued by the sport's 'good war', coupled with the huge boom in attendances, had reinvigorated its expansionist spirit. In 1949 Leigh chairman James Hilton had articulated this optimism in terms that were to become a familiar mantra of the game:

> we all believe it to be the greatest game on earth. We steep in its glorious traditions and its very character comprising speed, virility and attractiveness … we believe that if it is presented to a wider public in the right setting, it cannot fail to capture the interest'.[1]

For once, the signs seemed to be propitious. The establishment of professional sides after the war in Workington (1945), Whitehaven (1948), Doncaster (1951) and, to a lesser extent, Blackpool (1954), were part of an organic growth of the game in its heartlands. More ambitiously, in May 1947 a 'London Rugby League Supporters' Association' had been founded to promote the game in the capital and Harry Sunderland announced that he would help them to form 'a London working-class rugby league team of thirteen amateurs' in readiness for a forthcoming tour of an amateur French side. The same month saw Barrow and Leigh play three missionary games in Cornwall, although disappointing crowds aborted any possibility of developments in the South West. Nevertheless, there appeared to be bright prospects for development in London, so much so that in August 1947 the RFL Council offered Sunderland a three-year contract to be the full-time London organiser.

Typically, however, when told that he would have to give up his journalism if he wanted the position, the great self-publicist's expansionary zeal disappeared, somewhat undermining the RFL's plans.

Nevertheless, the scheme to establish amateur rugby league in London continued to attract support and in April 1948 the RFL gave its backing to a planned London workshops competition to begin the following season. This was supported by none other than Sidney Parkes, who offered to provide four grounds for the competition. When it was launched a few months later, the London Amateur Rugby League was very different from what had been originally envisaged and consisted of teams from Brixton, Mitcham and the Third Regiment of the Grenadier Guards, based at the Wellington Barracks, later to be joined by teams from Slough and Southampton.[2] The fledgling league struggled on to 1953, handicapped by its distance from the game's amateur heartlands and the active opposition of local rugby union; members of the Grenadier Guards team were all disciplined by their regimental authorities. The hope that industrial migrants from the north and Wales would provide a ready-made audience for the game was not realised, no doubt because integration into local communities was best facilitated by these migrants sharing the sporting preferences of their new environment. And the belief that there was a pool of working-class support for rugby union in London was also a chimera. Unlike in Bristol and certain others areas of the South West, London rugby had no working-class support that would be sympathetic to league.

This was in direct contrast to South Wales, where the RFL had more realistic expectations of expansion. The late 1940s was a period of considerable unease within Wales about the league threat, best exemplified by the comment of Rowe Harding at the WRU's 1950 annual general meeting that 'rugby league is only an infant, but it wants strangling'.[3] High hopes, and corresponding deep concerns, had been generated by the tremendous response of the Welsh public to the Welsh national rugby league side in the 1940s. Wales versus England at Swansea in November 1945 had attracted 30,000 people, followed by around 20,000 for the next two internationals. To capitalise on this, and to support the league evangelists in South Wales – 400 of whom attended a meeting at Neath to relaunch the game in Wales in March 1949 – the RFL voted the following month to appoint a full-time Welsh organiser, allocated a budget of £1,000 to Welsh efforts and arranged for Huddersfield and St Helens to play three exhibition matches. Filled with optimism, the new Welsh league kicked off in September 1949 with eight teams. However, even before the games had been played, the RFL had received complaints from the Welsh sides that not only were northern clubs poaching their best players but also that a number of Welsh union players had refused to sign for local clubs, preferring instead to play union until a northern club approached them. The Welsh sides wanted a ban on northern clubs signing Welsh league players but this was never likely to be agreed. Eventually a compromise was reached whereby a northern club signing a Welsh league player would pay £120 to the club and £80 to the Welsh league. The issue was raised again in December when the Welsh called for a ban on northern clubs signing Welsh union players, in order to force converts to play league in Wales. Again it was rejected, although it was agreed that £300 would go to the Welsh league for every union player signed, although it is unlikely that this was ever honoured.[4]

The WRU was as hostile as the northern league clubs were unhelpful. Consequently most of the teams struggled to find suitable grounds, although the Bridgend club outbid the local union side to rent the town's Brewery Field stadium. It also quickly became clear that, although the Welsh public would flock to see the top league sides, going to watch lower quality local sides was another matter entirely. The RFL therefore invited the Cardiff and Llanelli league sides to join the league as professional clubs for the start of the 1951–52 season. Llanelli failed to make it to the starting post, apparently owing to the withdrawal of their backer, but Cardiff duly began the season. Unfortunately the campaign started inauspiciously and went downhill from there, as the club won just five of its thirty-six matches that season, thus compounding the problem of attracting spectators to watch second-class league. By the end of the season it was clear that the club was not going to survive, and the last rites were accordingly performed on 28 April 1952 when the club resigned from the league with debts of £866. The Welsh league itself struggled on until it finally folded at the end of the 1954–55 season.[5] To some extent, the saga was a repeat of the experiences of Pontypridd in 1926 and the earlier Welsh clubs in the pre-First World War period, when short-term financial difficulties overwhelmed the initial fervour of local businessmen backing the new clubs, and the commitment of enthusiastic volunteers was ground down by public apathy and rugby union hostility. But the crucial difference was that by 1951 the social democratic consensus that had been generated during the war, in which rugby league had flourished, was at an end. Union had re-established its hegemony in Wales, in large part owing to a renewed success in the Five Nations championship, which included Grand Slams in 1950 and 1952, and the space in Welsh sporting culture which league had hoped to occupy had been closed.

This turn in the fortunes of the sport was also reflected in the north. The success of the game in the mid-1940s had led to the creation of hundreds of new clubs and by 1949 there were 352 amateur clubs playing the game, the highest-ever total. It was probably at its strongest level on the pitch too, with professional sides being beaten twice by amateur opponents in the first round of the Challenge Cup. Sharlston Red Rose defeated Workington 12–7 in 1946 and Risehow and Gillhead beat Keighley 10–2 in 1948, the first time that this had happened since 1909. In 1952 Warrington's Rylands Recreation drew nine-all with Whitehaven. The number of new clubs could have been even higher but, as one speaker pointed out at a 1949 RFL conference, the post-war building boom and the lack of government support for playing fields meant that there was a shortage of pitches on which to play the game. National service was blamed for some of the problems of continuity faced by clubs and the continuing austerity of the early 1950s was also pointed to as making it difficult for potential players to afford the necessary playing equipment. As in the inter-war years, it was also recognised that the amateur game continued to suffer from a lack of people with organisational and administrative experience.

The gradual withdrawal of large companies from employee sports' provision, which had begun in the mid-1950s and was reflected in a decline in the number of works-based sides, increased the administrative burden on local clubs and leagues. By 1970 the only remaining works-based leagues were those in Hull and Leeds. And, as we have already seen, the growing dissonance between the image of rugby league and the social changes of the 1960s also undermined the appeal of the sport at an amateur level. By 1964 the number of amateur clubs had fallen by a third from its 1949 total, mirroring the fall in attendances at professional matches.[6]

Many of these problems had been faced in previous decades and were chronic rather than terminal aspects of the sport's health. However, the changes to the educational system, brought about by the 1944 Education Act, which effectively led to the division of secondary education into grammar and secondary modern schools, were also exerting a new and disconcerting influence on the game's fortunes. The problem had first been identified in a 1954 report on schoolboy rugby league in Cumberland, when it was noted that academically bright boys who had played league at primary school or for a local club were being lost when they passed their eleven-plus exam and went to grammar school, all of which without exception played union and occasionally soccer. This was a pattern that was repeated throughout Lancashire and Yorkshire too, although it was not without opposition from boys themselves, as the sociologists Brian Jackson and Dennis Marsden noted in their study of working-class education in 1950s Huddersfield:

> A recurring situation at Marburton College seems to have been the desire of working-class boys to play rugby league football (the northern professional game) instead of soccer. When this reached the state of groups of boys organising themselves into something like unofficial school or house teams, then the school might put out feelers for compromise, and suggest the difficulty of catering for *rugby union* as well as soccer – difficulties say over fixtures of the better kind. The whole point, of course, of the rugby-playing was lost on this, for the school had failed to see that whereas rugby league was very close at heart to northern working-class life, and whereas soccer could occupy a kind of neutral and classless position, rugby union was almost as remote as lacrosse, and not what was wanted at all. [emphasis in original][7]

There was little that the RFL could do to alleviate what was a social rather than a sporting question. Even those grammar school boys who wanted to play league for a local club found themselves being threatened with expulsion from the school side by zealous grammar school games masters. From 1958 the RFL provided free playing kit to all under-nineteen teams and in 1961 it had reorganised youth rugby league into under-seventeen and under-nineteen age groups in order to provide a structure for the sport for school-leavers, although it was also claimed that some talented league schoolboys had been advised to switch to union by their parents or other advisers because they believed that, as a union player, they would receive a higher signing-on fee from a professional league club than as an amateur league player.

Even so, the RFL's encouragement did have an effect. According to a 1964 census the number of players aged between seventeen and nineteen increased by 28 per cent, and those under seventeen increased by 90 per cent in Lancashire and 38 per cent in Yorkshire. In 1965 the organisation of the sport in schools was taken over by schoolteachers who formed the English Schools Rugby League 'to foster the physical, mental, social and moral development of the schoolboys of England in every type of school through the medium of rugby league football'.[8]

Somewhat paradoxically, the problem of playing the game in 'every type of school' was exacerbated by the introduction of comprehensive schools in the late 1960s and early 1970s. The assumption within the game that the egalitarian ethos of the comprehensives would lead to a wider dissemination of league was badly misplaced. In fact, a number of league-playing schools switched from league to union in order to arrange fixtures with those former grammar schools that had become comprehensives, thus demonstrating the residual higher social status both of the ex-grammar schools and of schoolboy rugby union. It was only in the 1980s, when league's public profile had increased, that it regained ground in comprehensive schools. Indeed, such was its popularity at the time that a small number of northern grammar schools, such as the union stronghold of Cowley School in St Helens, began to play union and league. By 1980 an unprecedented 423 schools played rugby league, a total that had more than doubled to 865 by 1990.[9] This was not simply due to the heightened awareness of the attractiveness of the sport. It was also a result of the extension of higher education from the 1960s, which had led to rugby league-loving schoolboys progressing up the educational ladder to become teachers and pass on their enthusiasm for the game.

Indeed, although it was not appreciated at the time, it was the social changes of the 1960s and 1970s that provided the seedbed for the recovery and expansion of amateur rugby league. The failure of the RFL to halt the decline in amateur rugby league had been a cause for concern among many in the game throughout the 1960s. Much of the blame was laid at the door of the professional clubs, whom it was felt did little to promote the game at a grassroots level and, in a grievance which dated back to the 1920s, rarely paid amateur clubs the signing-on fee to which they were entitled when recruiting an amateur player. The crisis of self-confidence of the 1960s had also affected the amateur game deeply. By 1965 the number of amateur sides had shrunk to its lowest level since before the First World War. It had also generated a sense of alienation from the RFL, which still nominally governed the amateur side of the game, a feeling aggravated by Bill Fallowfield's abrasive inapproachability. Fallowfield himself had little time for those at the grassroots. In 1967 he criticised the RFL Council for pandering to:

> those who think they are doing rugby league a favour by either playing rugby league or indulging in the hobby of looking after an amateur team. At other sports, one finds that the attitude is that people are playing the game or organising clubs because they like to do it and are prepared to pay a little for their hobby.[10]

By 1973 a group of amateur league officials in Huddersfield, led by Maurice Oldroyd and Tom Keaveney, had begun to raise the idea of forming an association that would promote the amateur game and safeguard their clubs' interests. The formation of the Sports Council in 1972 had also helped to focus minds. The new body was responsible for providing grants to amateur sports organisations but, because it was controlled by the ostensibly professional RFL, amateur rugby league was not eligible. Despite Fallowfield's opposition, the rebels' idea garnered considerable support and in May 1973 the British Amateur Rugby League Association (BARLA) was formed. Fallowfield responded by ordering professional clubs to stop BARLA teams from using their facilities, withdrew RFL support for any amateur side joining the new body and issued a libel writ against the *Hull Daily Mail* for publishing letters supporting BARLA. Despite this, or perhaps because of it, support for BARLA snowballed and by May 1974 the RFL Council had abandoned the fight and recognised the rebels as the amateur game's governing body.[11]

After its first two seasons of operation, BARLA claimed 300 member clubs organised in twenty district leagues, had 114 clubs competing in its first national amateur knock-out competition and had drawn up a five-year plan not only for the amateur game in the north, but also for the South of England, the Midlands and at all levels of education.[12] Fuelled by the not inconsiderable drive of Maurice Oldroyd and the enthusiasm of hundreds of unpaid evangelists for the sport, BARLA grew rapidly, recording more than 400 clubs, for the first time in rugby league history, by 1985 and over 500 by 1990, making it the second largest 'rugby' organisation in the British Isles after the RFU.[13]

From the outset, BARLA had prided itself on the word amateur in its title. On its 1978 tour of Australia, New Zealand and Papua New Guinea, each team member had to raise their own costs of travel; the only things which members of the tour party were given were an official tie, a holdall and a tracksuit. This, and many other examples of sacrifice by officials and players, allowed BARLA to proclaim itself the 'most amateur rugby organisation in the world'. To some extent, the success of BARLA's amateurism was made possible by the rise in working-class living standards. Until the 1960s it would have been impossible for significant numbers of working men to raise sufficient sums of money to allow them to travel long distances to play sport. It was also a product of increased national and local government funding for sport. Without the financial backing of the Sports Council, BARLA itself would have struggled to exist and its network of development officers spread across the north of England, and later in parts of the south and Wales, was heavily subsidised by local authorities.

BARLA's amateurism was of a very different stripe to that of the middle-class amateur. For rugby league, 'amateur' was descriptive rather than prescriptive; an adjective but not a noun. The only meaning that amateur had within the sport was that the player did not get paid, nothing more and nothing less. In contrast to the twelve pages of regulations by which rugby union's International Board sought to define amateurism, BARLA's definition had just ten words: 'Players shall not receive payment for playing amateur rugby league'.[14] There was no belief in the moral superiority of sport without money and no attempt to separate those who had been professionals from amateurs.

There was, however, one section of society to which BARLA and its amateurism did feel itself superior. That was rugby union. From its inception BARLA had called for a 'free gangway' for amateur league and union players. Central to this campaign was the demonstration that amateur rugby league was more faithful to the idea of play without pay than rugby union. As the 1970s progressed and successive episodes of union 'shamateurism' unfolded, BARLA chalked up a series of impressive propaganda victories against Twickenham. The fact that amateurism, which had been used by rugby union for decades as a club with which to beat rugby league, was now being used against the RFU was an irony appreciated by many beyond the confines of the rugby league world. Despite this, BARLA's campaigning had only a marginal impact on the RFU's attitude to amateur rugby league, largely because it was rugby league, paid or unpaid, to which the RFU objected and no amount of evidence of the piety of BARLA's amateurism would change their minds. But the campaign did play an important role in buttressing rugby league's self-image as a democratic and egalitarian sport that was discriminated against by a hypocritical establishment RFU. The often-repeated description of BARLA as 'the genuine amateurs' carried with it echoes of the late nineteenth-century idea that the moral 'true nation' of England, unadorned by privilege or sullied by humbug, was to be found in the working-class north.[15]

It was this self-confidence that enabled amateur league enthusiasts to develop the sport outside of its traditional bases in the 1960s and 1970s. Although there had always been small pockets of evangelist exiles, it was the expansion of higher education in the 1960s, and the social and geographical mobility that it brought to its beneficiaries, that provided BARLA with a volunteer cadre who took the game to fresh fields. In 1965 a London Amateur Rugby League Association had been founded, the first of many such local associations, and in 1967 the first university side was formed at Leeds. By 1980 there were almost two dozen student sides, including at the hitherto undreamt-of Oxford and Cambridge, which were often formed in the teeth of determined opposition from the student rugby union clubs. By 1990 student rugby league had become one of the most vibrant and geographically extensive branches of the sport. Indeed, the growth of clubs outside of 'non-traditional' areas grew disproportionately in the 1980s and 1990s, so much so that by 1990 they represented 10 per cent of the 502 amateur clubs, a percentage which had risen to almost 15 per cent five years later. And by 1995 almost a quarter of the total number of amateur rugby league clubs were drawn either from outside of the heartlands or from higher education, two categories of club which did not exist thirty years previously. This growth was largely geographical rather than social, insofar as most of the 'expansionist' clubs were formed and led by those who had a previous attachment to rugby league (although the bulk of the playing memberships of these clubs did not), and who were more often than not exiles from the north of England who had moved to new areas for reasons of employment or education.

The narrowness of the social strata from which the sport drew its organisers and evangelists was a problem that also had an important impact on the game's attempts to expand at a professional level. Amateur expansion had inevitably re-ignited the hopes that league's geographical straitjacket could be broken and these seemed to be about to be fulfilled in September 1980 when Fulham kicked off the season in Division Two, becoming London's first professional rugby league side since Streatham folded in 1937. With a team based on a solid phalanx of experienced players determined to enjoy the sunset of their careers and bolstered by considerable media interest in the apparently incongruous notion of a northern sport being played in the capital, the club surged to promotion in its first season, with average crowds topping 7,000. However, as the ageing side struggled to repeat its success and crowds declined, the board of Fulham FC, which had bankrolled the club, began to lose interest. In July 1984 it put the rugby league club into liquidation.[16] For the next decade the side led a nomadic, evangelist existence, changing its name to London Crusaders before being bought by the Brisbane Broncos, transformed into the London Broncos and earning a place in the Super League by virtue of its geographic importance. Nevertheless, the initial success of Fulham led to a wave of soccer clubs expressing an interest in bringing rugby league to pastures new: over the next eighteen months, soccer clubs ranging from Portsmouth to Hearts, Crystal Palace to Grimsby, floated the idea of rugby league. Although most of these ideas never got beyond the idle braggadocio of the soccer club boardroom, over the next five seasons Carlisle United, Cardiff City, Maidstone United and Mansfield Town either formed their own rugby league sides or were involved in ground-sharing ventures with an expansion side. At the start of the 1985–86 season rugby league had thirty-six professional sides, its highest total since 1903.

This expansion was not simply due to rugby league's burgeoning popularity and higher public profile. The sport was also benefiting from the deep crisis confronting soccer. The failures of the national side, declining crowds and, above all, the prevalence of fascistic hooliganism led many to believe that the game was 'set on a course of self-destruction', in the words of the editor of the 1984–85 edition of *Rothman's Football Yearbook*. Rugby league was seen by soccer club directors as a way of boosting income through diversification – 'we want to make some brass', Fulham soccer chairman Ernie Clay told the press in 1980 – and the non-segregated, unthreatening atmosphere at matches, at least off the pitch, was a welcome change for soccer supporters normally used to crowds scenes that resembled a Brownshirt rally as painted by Hogarth.[17] For a number of the clubs involved with rugby league, their interest in the new game coincided with a fall in the fortunes of their own side. This was especially the case with Fulham FC, who had been relegated to Football League Division Three the season before the launch of their rugby league side. The obvious danger was that the soccer clubs would lose interest in rugby league as soon as their own fortunes improved. And this happened in every case. Fulham rugby league club lost £307,000 in its first season and continued to make a loss, and the soccer side's promotion in 1981–82 eventually led to a loss of interest in rugby league. When Ernie Clay realised that the league side would not make any 'brass' he pulled the plug. Exactly the same happened at Cardiff City and Carlisle United, causing the RFL's David Howes to remark: 'The Carlisle board seemed to view the rugby league club like a publican might view a jukebox. Install it. Watch it twinkle. Enjoy the music but take it out the moment it shows signs of losing money.'[18]

In fact, once the soccer clubs had withdrawn their funding, the survival of these expansion sides was, like that of the amateur clubs, dependent on the voluntary work of supporters. The Fulham/London club survived because of a small but committed cadre of supporters, comprising both native Londoners and exiled northerners, plus, most propitious of all, the largesse in the mid-1990s of a millionaire Australian rugby league supporter, Barry Maranta. Indeed, the formation of the club itself in 1980 was entirely the idea of Warrington director and former Widnes player Harold Genders, whose belief in rugby league expansion was persuasive enough for Ernie Clay to put up the initial £100,000 capital for the club. And the importance of a London side to the sport as a whole also helped it survive crises which others would not have. Of the other clubs who joined the league in the 1980s, only Sheffield survived with any distinction, again thanks to a dedicated band of volunteers and the city's proximity to the game's heartland. Carlisle survived until the mid-1990s, largely for the same reasons, until the financial weight of running even a semi-professional side finally forced the club under. As in the 1930s, entrepreneurs who set up a rugby league club to make money were always disappointed, because the long-term investment of money and personal commitment necessary to establish a position in local civic culture were economically unjustifiable to the speculator. But rugby league was not alone in this. Even at the apex of soccer, few clubs were consistently profitable, underlining the fact that professional team sport is almost an entirely loss-making business activity. Without a broader social commitment to sport a professional sports club could not survive.

It is worth contrasting the fortunes of the 1980s expansion clubs with that of Doncaster. Doncaster had been admitted to the league in 1951 and, as was painfully exposed in the 1970s BBC documentary 'Another Bloody Sunday', had stumbled from one cash crisis to another, uninterrupted by any hint of success on the field. Nevertheless, the club continued to survive, both because of indefatigable voluntary support and also because of the roots that the club had in the town. Although within the hinterland of soccer-playing Sheffield, amateur rugby league had always been played in the area, especially in the mining villages to the north, making the club, along with Doncaster Rovers soccer club, an integral part of local culture, as well as an organic part of the game's northern constituency. Thus – as was the case with clubs like Rochdale and Featherstone in the 1930s – successive financial calamities were met, if not exactly solved, by donations from the public and local businessmen, for whom the team represented not a profit-making exercise but an important part of the fabric of local pride.

If the spread of amateur rugby league demonstrated how much Britain had changed over the last third of the twentieth century, conversely the failure of the professional game to expand showed how little the country had changed. Greater geographic, educational and occupational mobility for working-class people allowed the amateur game to establish a presence across Britain, but the identification of the sport with the industrial working-classes, reinforced by its treatment in the media and by the active hostility of the RFU, made it extremely difficult to attract mass spectator support in new areas. In short, rugby league had neither the national glamour of soccer nor the social cachet of rugby union. And at a deeper, structural level, the geographic and social template of modern spectator sport which had been set in the Edwardian era proved to be immensely durable, a fact which was itself an indication of the underlying resilience of the class structure of Britain.

Chapter 12

From slump to Super League 1975–95

'No club will ever again pay its way through the turnstiles alone', declared David Oxley in 1975 shortly after he replaced Bill Fallowfield as the RFL secretary.[1] Coming to terms with that simple truth was to dominate rugby league for the next twenty years and was ultimately, although not necessarily inevitably, to lead to the momentous events which led to the formation of Super League in 1995. But even recognising this fact had been difficult for the sport. Most of the debate in the 1960s about the slump in crowds focused on schemes for changing the game in order to bring back the crowds of the early 1950s. Like the cargo cults of Melanesia who believed that great riches would be miraculously delivered to them, at times it appeared that some in the game believed that the glory days would return if only they could please the god of rule changes. In fact, as Oxley implied, the beginning of wisdom was to accept that the 1950s were over and that other sources of income were needed to keep the professional game alive.

This was to prove a slow process, but the decline in gate money began to be gradually offset somewhat in the 1970s by the growth in commercial sponsorship of clubs and competitions. Rugby league had been one of the first organisations to benefit from the surge of sports sponsorship from breweries in the early 1960s when, in 1961, Whitbread promoted their Mackeson brand by awarding gold watches to players of the club scoring the most points against the touring New Zealanders. The following season the Mackeson Trophy was introduced for the side with the season's best scoring record.[2] But sponsorship remained a largely untapped source of income throughout the 1960s, not least because the RFL did not possess the commercial skills to pursue opportunities but also because, as was also the case in soccer, there was also a lingering disquiet, especially from Bill Fallowfield, about the game appearing to be too overtly commercial. As late as 1971 the RFL had turned down an offer from a chewing-gum company, which would have involved free samples being distributed at matches.[3] Nevertheless, some of the more commercially minded clubs had begun to foster relationships with local businesses and develop promotional activities to supplement their gate-money income. Salford, in particular, led by the energetic hotelier Brian Snape, had leveraged significant income from their ground by opening a successful night club in 1966, the profits from which helped to finance the side's high-spending raids on stars from other clubs and rugby union, most notably Wales and British Lions captain David Watkins in 1967. Successes such as these fuelled the frustration felt by some clubs with the RFL's lacklustre attitude and in the summer of 1970 Wakefield Trinity circumvented the governing body and sent a circular to all of the professional clubs alerting them to the benefits of commercial sponsorships.[4]

Partly in response to this discontent, but also because they were being pursued by an enthusiastic suitor in the form of tobacco manufacturers John Player, in March 1971 the RFL decided to arrange a new knock-out competition to be played in the first half of the season, specifically designed to attract sponsors by offering BBC TV coverage of the tournament. John Player, which had sponsored man-of-the-match awards previously, jumped at the opportunity to have one of its flagship brands advertised on the BBC's Saturday afternoon Grandstand show and in November 1971 the inaugural Player's No. 6 Trophy competition kicked off.[5] Its relative success gave the RFL a track record with which to approach other potential sponsors. The same year Leeds-based brewers Joshua Tetley began to sponsor the Lancashire Cup, as part of their marketing drive to extend the Tetley's Bitter beer brand beyond Yorkshire. Slowly other forms of sponsorship began to emerge. In December 1973 York staged the first sponsored league match and in May of the following year the RFL agreed to allow clubs to carry advertising on the shirts, something which had been pioneered in the 1960s by French rugby league.[6] The more far-sighted clubs realised that shirt sponsorship income would only be maximised if the BBC allowed teams in televised matches to wear sponsored shirts, something which the corporation was not prepared to contemplate until the 1980s. This gave rise to more accusations of BBC hypocrisy, because its ban on shirt advertising did not apply to athletics, and there were occasional attempts to circumvent the ban, especially by Widnes and Hull KR.[7]

But perhaps the most significant boost to the sport's commercial fortunes was the retirement in 1974 of Bill Fallowfield and his replacement as RFL secretary by the Oxford-educated deputy head of the Duke of York's Royal Military School, David Oxley. Despite his somewhat atypical CV, the Hull-born Oxley was a rugby league man through and through, and with the RFL's first Public Relations Officer David Howes, he began an aggressive campaign to seek out sponsorship. As we have seen, Oxley was sufficiently far-sighted to realise that the sport needed stability both on and off the pitch, and that it could not simply rely on money that came through the turnstiles in order to survive. In the last season of Fallowfield's leadership the RFL's income, excluding TV fees and cup and international gate receipts, was just £4,000. By the end of the 1976–77 season, sponsorship and related activities had raised £28,075. Six years later the figure had risen to £413,350.[8] Although Oxley and Howes were to be subjected to criticism in the 1980s for an apparent over-reliance on brewery and tobacco sponsorship – the 'booze and fags' link being seen as reinforcing the 'flat cap' image of the game portrayed by sections of the national media – the effect of their commercial success in the 1970s was to put the RFL on its firmest footing since the late 1950s and to help boost the sport's hitherto sub-rock bottom self-confidence.

The new regime also saw its role as being one of encouraging clubs to develop their own commercial and sponsorship activities. The Association of Rugby League Commercial Managers had been formed in the mid-1970s, with the aim of sharing the ideas of the more successful clubs. Salford's success was especially admired. In the early 1970s they regularly recorded profits in excess of £20,000, mostly derived from off-field activities, such as their nightclub, restaurant and lottery competitions.[9] However, this type of success was not easy to emulate. Attempts to raise money through non-traditional activities sometimes backfired. In 1970 Halifax sought to alleviate their financial problems by staging a rock festival incongruously featuring hippie bluesmen Chicken Shack and aging chart toppers The Tremeloes. Over £6,000 was lost on the event, deepening the financial pall that hung over the club.[10] Although this was an extreme example of a widespread inability to diversify, most clubs took such lessons to heart and restricted their commercial activities to those directly connected to the sport. Sponsorship of playing kit was enthusiastically extended from the shirt to encompass every item of clothing. In 1990 at least one club, Bramley, even sought sponsors for their players' jockstraps.

But commercial activity of this type was directly related to the on-field success of the club. No-one would pay significant sums to sponsor a losing team or its various items of kit. This meant that those teams with poor playing records found it increasingly difficult throughout the 1970s to bridge the gap between income and expenditure. In 1973 it was reported that one club had an annual expenditure of £6,300 on player's wages but had an income of only £1,800 from all sources.[11] More often than not, the RFL found itself the lender of last resort. In 1972, for example, it had outstanding loans to twenty-five clubs totalling £143,000. In reality such loans had little effect on the long-term viability of the clubs receiving them. Blackpool received £20,000 of loans in the late 1970s, yet were still forced to call in the receivers in 1981. The RFL also sought to provide other forms of assistance to its ailing members. In 1970 it offered to buy the controlling interest in Hunslet and six years later it volunteered to buy Doncaster's stadium to alleviate the club's debt burden.[12] As in the past, clubs also sought to dig themselves out of financial difficulties by issuing public appeals for funds, but the regularity with which some clubs cried wolf at the door tended to diminish the effectiveness of such calls. Huddersfield launched two 'survival' fund-raising initiatives in the early 1970s less than three years apart, undermining both fund-raising and public perception of the seriousness of the club's situation. It is noticeable that the regular donations to ground improvement funds which were a staple of supporters' clubs' activity in the 1950s and 1960s became increasingly rare in the 1970s. The luckier clubs were able to find generous local businesses to bail them out. In 1977 Burtonwood Brewery effectively guaranteed Huyton's short-term future by buying a £12,000 tranche of shares in the club. Halifax's decade and a half in the doldrums was ended in 1983 when the club was taken over by local businessman David Brook, whose money was instrumental in propelling it towards the league championship in 1986 and the Challenge Cup the following year. In the 1980s local councils became a significant source of funding, with a number of them making financial arrangements to benefit clubs, such as the purchase and lease-back of grounds or straightforward donations.[13]

★

Crowds slowly began to increase from the mid-1970s and by the late 1980s attendances were at their healthiest since the early 1960s. Aggregate league attendances topped the 1.5 million mark in all but six of the fifteen seasons before 1995. The Challenge Cup final sold out nine times between 1978 and 1995, compared to three times in the previous years since the move to Wembley in 1929. International matches against Australia attracted unprecedented home crowds, exceeding 50,000 for the first time in 1986 and culminating in the 73,361 who saw the 1992 World Cup final at Wembley. The increased popularity of the game from the mid-1980s could be seen in the fact that there were seventy-three matches that attracted 20,000 spectators or more between 1985 and 1995, compared to just seventeen in the previous decade. But the growth in crowds was concentrated in the upper echelons of the game, among the leading clubs and for showpiece cup and international matches. While average crowds for First Division matches actually exceeded those for Third and Fourth Division soccer for ten of the fifteen seasons before 1995, average crowds in rugby league's Second Division stagnated around the 1,000 mark, and clubs having little prospects of promotion generally struggled by on crowds in the hundreds.

This renewal of fortune was due to on- and off-field factors. The opening of the completed M62 motorway in 1976, stretching from Liverpool in the west to Hull in the east, meant that, apart from those in Cumbria, the majority of rugby league towns were now within easy reach of each other, making it easier for supporters to follow their side to away matches and attend cup finals. The gloom surrounding soccer meant that rugby league was looked at with fresh eyes by some in the media and appealed to disillusioned soccer fans. And the limited social mobility through education that had begun in the 1960s, highlighted by the growth of student and southern-based rugby league, had also begun to undermine at least some of the social prejudices that the game faced. On the field, the domination of the game by Hull and Hull KR in the late 1970s and early 1980s helped raise the profile of the sport. Partly this was because of the uniqueness (outside of Scottish soccer) of a sport being led by two teams from the same city. Between 1979 and 1985, six major finals were all-Hull affairs and the clubs had twice finished first and second in the league together. They had also both been aggressively ambitious, breaking the transfer fee record regularly and bringing in players from New Zealand, and later, following the lifting of the international transfer ban in 1983, from Australia. In doing so, they helped to revive the cosmopolitan glamour of league in the late 1940s when overseas stars had been great attractors of crowds.

This interest in the game was taken to new heights by the 1982 Australian tour, which saw the Great Britain side humiliated as never before yet also brought crowds flocking to see the Kangaroos play. For the first time since the 1950s Australian players became household names across the north of England. Like the England soccer side's loss to Hungary in 1953, the shock at the scale of the 1982 defeat was traumatic and, desperate to learn as much as possible from their conquerors, the RFL called for an end to the international transfer ban. It was lifted in 1983 and in the following ten years, 757 Australian players came to play for British clubs.[14] In the first two seasons clubs were free to sign as many players as they wanted. When Halifax played Leeds in early 1985 they fielded ten Australian players while their opponents fielded five, with another as a substitute. Many imports became local icons: Mal Meninga at St Helens, Peter Sterling at Hull, Brett Kenny and John Ferguson at Wigan. Wally Lewis played ten games for Wakefield Trinity and earned additional immortality by being enshrined in the name of the club's fanzine. The high point of this invasion was undoubtedly the 1985 Challenge Cup final between Wigan and Hull, which brought the sublime skills of Kenny, Sterling and John Ferguson to the attention of a national public. Arguably the greatest-ever cup final, it brought the game possibly the highest public profile it had ever had.

Although undoubtedly popular with the public, the influx of Australian players was not welcomed by all. Halifax's en masse purchase and the sacking of popular coach Colin Dixon to make way for Canterbury's Chris Anderson caused considerable dissension, resulting in the enforced transfer of players' spokesman John Carroll. Hull half-back Kevin Harkin retired from the game in protest after the club signed Peter Sterling. Wally Lewis recalled that only half of his new teammates shook his hand when he arrived at Wakefield Trinity. But there was more at stake than new players. The traditional British view of the game was being challenged by players who came to Britain as representatives of the dominant power in world rugby league. This was perceived by many, especially British coaches, to be a threat to their authority. 'The conventional wisdom in this country is that the Australians play the game at great speed but are stereotyped and lack skill in the finer points of the game', was how *Open Rugby* summed up this attitude in 1983.[15] Others wholeheartedly supported the Aussie invasion. Ironically, it was Halifax coach Colin Dixon, who was shortly to find himself dumped to make way for Chris Anderson, who summed up the attitude when he stated: 'English rugby league must look to the future and now the future is Australia.'[16]

Alongside finance, the quest to regain parity with Australia came to dominate the British game in the 1980s. Successive whitewashes in the 1984 and 1986 Ashes series were followed by tighter series over the next decade; yet a fundamental gulf remained. Although overseas players were eventually restricted to three per club, few teams did without them, partly because of the public interest they created but also because it was generally believed that Australian players would raise British standards. However, it was not at all clear if the importation of Australian players brought success to the clubs using them. If success is measured by the winning of the Championship or the Challenge Cup, the evidence would suggest not. In the ten years after the lifting of transfer restrictions only eighteen Australians appeared for sides winning the Championship, and seven of those played for Halifax in the 1985–86 season. Of the ten sides that won the Challenge Cup in the same period, five of them fielded a total of ten Australians, six of whom played for, yet again, Halifax in 1987. It is also worth noting that Halifax's success was quickly followed by near bankruptcy and relegation. In fact, New Zealanders were far more prominent in Championship winning sides and it was they who provided one of the pillars for Wigan's long dominance of the game from the late 1980s – just as they did during the club's rise to prominence before the First World War.

Even so, it was Australia and its influence that came to dominate British rugby league from 1982. Whether it was players, coaches – such as John Monie at Wigan, Chris Anderson at Halifax or Brian Smith at Hull – or Tina Turner's *Simply the Best*, the theme song of the Australian game, which blared out of every British club's public address system in the 1990s, the British followed in the Antipodean wake. And it was this that was to turn the British game upside down in 1995.

Paradoxically, the renewed success of the game in the 1980s intensified its financial problems, especially among the less successful clubs. The increased profile of the sport, the rise in attendances at the upper reaches of the game and the inclusion of new clubs (by 1985 there were thirty-six professional clubs, six more than in 1980) all helped to increase the pressure for higher wages. However, this was not reflected in significantly higher attendances in Division Two – only in the 1980–81 season did crowds average more than 2,000. In 1983 six clubs were reported to be in 'serious financial difficulties' and over the next two years Rochdale, Workington and Whitehaven scrapped their reserve teams, Bramley, Keighley and Blackpool were saved from liquidation by last-minute takeovers, Dewsbury launched a public appeal for funds and Huddersfield simply announced that the club was looking for new owners.[17] These financial problems were not only caused by players' expectations of higher wages but also by the accumulated costs of neglecting the maintenance and improvement of grounds. The majority of clubs had effectively run down, rather than invested in, their grounds, sharing the belief of Dickens's Mr Micawber that eventually 'something will turn up' to relieve the problem. By the mid-1980s the former test match venues of Huddersfield's Fartown and Swinton's Station Road had become decayed and vandalised husks, municipal skeletons of former grandeur for which the running costs had risen to levels beyond their occupants' means. But the increasing regularity of financial crises, and the failure to provide any long-term solutions for them, had effectively become a crisis in itself by the mid-1980s. And at that point, tragically, something did turn up.

The catastrophe at Bradford City's Valley Parade ground on 11 May 1985, which saw fifty-six people burned to death, was commonly agreed to be a disaster that was waiting to happen. It could just as easily have happened at a rugby league stadium. Valley Parade had actually been a rugby league ground until 1903 and the state of disrepair of the stand that burnt down was no worse than those at many league stadia. Its impact on rugby league was financially devastating, as it forced clubs to confront the legacy of neglect of their grounds. The shockwaves reverberated for the next decade at least and were an important contributory factor in the move to Super League in 1995. The Popplewell Inquiry's report into the fire, published three months later, brought the majority of rugby league grounds under the juris-diction of the 1975 Safety of Sports Grounds Act, which had hitherto applied only to leading soccer clubs. But, as David Oxley pointed out, most clubs could not even afford the minimal safety regulations that the Act had specified for soccer grounds a decade previously. Consequently, the RFL set up a special fund for ground improvement loans, using its offices as collateral to borrow from the banks. A further corollary of the disaster was an astronomical rise in fire and storm insur-ance premiums paid by clubs. In June it was reported that one insurer had raised its premiums by 500 per cent. In its defence, the company pointed out that it was responding not only to the fire but also to the fact that in the previous four years it had received £67,000 in premiums from rugby league clubs yet had paid out over £728,000 in claims. Such was the impact of the rise in premiums that Doncaster were forced to sell their star half-back Kevin Harcombe to cover the increase. In the two and a half years following the fire the RFL loaned its clubs almost £700,000 and Oxley estimated that the clubs themselves had spent over £3 million on ground improvements.[18]

But the limited resources of the RFL and its clubs were inadequate to meet the financial demands of accumulated decades of disregard. In 1987 Hull KR, Keighley and Blackpool announced that they could no longer finance the improvement of their old grounds and would move to new sites, although Keighley eventually stayed put. The following year York and Rochdale made the same decision. Bradford and Wakefield avoided a similar fate owing to their local councils buying their grounds. Even more clubs had stands closed as fire risks and their crowd capacities severely reduced. Wigan's Central Park capacity was slashed from 30,000 to 12,000, less than their average crowd at the time.[19] The situation went from dire to calamitous in April 1989 following the horrific catastrophe at Hillsborough when ninety-six Liverpool fans were crushed to death at an FA Cup semi-final. The Taylor Report into the tragedy resulted in yet more cuts to ground capacities, along with the need to install electronic turnstiles, closed circuit television systems and police control centres.[20] There was significant resentment towards the Taylor Report within rugby league because many of the problems it addressed, such as endemic hooliganism and overcrowding on terraces, were those of soccer, with little relevance to league. The fact that the Inquiry team visited just one league ground, Salford, only reinforced the suspicion that the game was being unfairly bracketed with soccer. Nevertheless, the increased levels of expenditure required by the Report were enough to capsize a number of clubs. As a result, Huddersfield, Swinton, Dewsbury and Bramley all sold their grounds in the early 1990s. Ultimately, it was to prove the final straw to those small clubs who had led a hand to mouth financial existence before 1985. Blackpool, Bramley, Huyton and the remaining expansion clubs, with the exception of those in London and Sheffield, eventually collapsed under the burden.

The changes caused by the Bradford and Hillsborough catastrophes led to the greatest transformation of the landscape of the game since the 1890s. And, although the smaller clubs had walked a delicate tightrope, the leading and mid-ranking clubs also faced a series of complex financial problems, caused to a great extent by their own successes. The rise in the popularity of the game from the late 1970s was reflected in rising attendances at First Division league games. This in turn gave the top clubs the self-confidence to buy players, thus pushing up transfer fees. The end of the 1970s saw the first significant rise in the value of transfer fees since Salford's spending sprees of the late 1960s and early 1970s, led by the two Hull clubs. Hull set a new record in the 1978–79 season when they signed Castleford's Clive Pickerill for £20,000. The two clubs then leapfrogged each other with successive rises in the record over the next two years until Hull KR astonished the sport in 1981 by paying Wigan £72,500, almost twice the previous record of £40,000, for full-back George Fairbairn. In 1985 Wigan paid £150,000, made up of cash and two other players, for Ellery Hanley, followed shortly by deals of £100,000 or more for Joe Lydon and Andy Gregory. The concomitant rise in wages had also been fuelled by the influx of Australian and New Zealand players in the 1980s. Clubs offered premium rates of pay, a trend led by struggling Wakefield Trinity, who paid Wally Lewis £1,300 a match in a vain attempt to avoid relegation in the 1983–84 season.[21] For a four-month stint in England during the Australian close-season, representative players could expect to pick up between £15,000 and £20,000. For clubs like Halifax and Leeds, who signed over a dozen Australians each before restrictions on imported players were introduced, this resulted in sizeable increases to their wages bill. Naturally, the high fees paid to overseas players led to British players demanding higher wages too.

Along with the increasingly high profile of the game, the demands for higher wages were also given impetus by a radical restructuring of the relationship between the clubs and the players. Traditionally, the game had replicated the 'retain and transfer' system of the Football League, whereby clubs effectively owned their players until they decided to transfer them to another club or the player ceased to play the game. A player would sign for a fixed number of years, after which the club had the option to retain the player or transfer him. In the worst cases the club could reduce a player's wages without recourse, transfer him without his consent, or refuse his request for a transfer. Even outside of the players' unions, not everyone in the game was comfortable with this treatment of players. In 1957 the former Hull secretary Wilf Ward had argued that it meant that players were 'bought and sold like cattle'.[22] But in the main the system was justified by the claim that it brought stability to clubs and allowed them to plan over the long term. In 1951 Bill Fallowfield had somewhat cynically dismissed the Players' Union complaint that the system was an infringement of individual liberty by arguing that 'a player prior to the commencement of a season can either accept or reject the terms offered by the club, and he is then free to play for any club outside of the Northern [Rugby Football] League'.[23] Of course, there were no other professional clubs in Britain and an international transfer ban was in existence at that time, so the freedom to sign for another club did not exist.

The system stayed intact until the summer of 1984 when the Fulham club went into liquidation owing to the double burden of debt and expulsion from their original Craven Cottage home. Warrington had signed two of the club's leading players, Hussain M'Barki and Steve Diamond as free agents, on the not unreasonable basis that as Fulham no longer existed, the players were not under contract to it. However, the club was revived within weeks by Roy and Barbara Close, who claimed that the players' registrations still belonged to the club. A legal battle ensued and in November 1984 the case reached the High Court where the judge found in favour of the players, on the basis that the original club had been liquidated so it could not legally own their registrations. At an RFL Council meeting in December 1984, Bramley's Ronnie Teeman spoke for most club directors when he described the judge's finding as 'an attack on the entire fabric of the game which would have far-reaching effects for everyone'. Although the judge declined to comment on the 'retain and transfer' system as a whole, the writing was clearly on the wall. In August 1985 a correspondent for the *Financial Times*, hitherto not noted for its coverage of the game, said that 'the relationship between players and their clubs is almost feudal'. Forced to come up with options for the future, the RFL set up a working party to explore options for the future.[24]

In June 1987 the RFL introduced a new contract-based system for players. It specified that a player was free to arrange a contract with any club he chose but was not bound indefinitely to that club, as had previously been the case. A transfer fee would still be payable to the player's club if the player chose to move to another club at the end of his contract. If the two clubs could not agree a fee, an independent tribunal would fix an appropriate one. In some ways the new system foreshadowed the changes that would come into soccer in the 1990s following the Bosman case. At the time, it was seen as a bold and prescient move that anticipated the future development of relations between professional sportspeople and their employers. Within the game it was hoped that it would help to curb spiralling transfers fees and, by creating a more open market in players, allow clubs to control wages more effectively.[25]

In fact, it led to the opposite. The relative freedom it gave players led to increased player mobility. Clubs could no longer simply refuse to sell a player and players themselves had a greater sense of their own worth. It increased the opportunities for players to sell their rugby league labour power and saw clubs scrambling to offer higher wages to attract the best players. In 1991 Tim Wilby, a much travelled player involved in setting up a players' union, estimated that top internationals could expect to receive over £25,000 per season, with leading club players getting between £15,000 and £20,000. Players at Wigan, from 1986 the only club to employ players as full-time professionals, could probably expect double those amounts. Between 1991 and 1994 the sport's gross income increased by 3 per cent, but its expenditure on wages grew by 10 per cent. Another indicator of the pressure on club finances could be seen in the fact that in 1991, 136 players were employed in some capacity or another by clubs compared to a mere handful ten years previously.[26]

Transfer fees also rose significantly. In 1987 Leeds paid successive record fees of £150,000 and £155,000 for Hull's Lee Crooks and Garry Schofield. They again raised the bar to a quarter of a million pounds to bring Ellery Hanley back to his home town from Wigan. This in turn allowed Wigan to pay Widnes £440,000 for Martin Offiah in early 1992. In the 1993–94 season there were nine transfers of £100,000 or more, topped by Wigan's purchase of St Helens' Gary Connolly for £250,000. As Wigan chairman Maurice Lindsay observed the following year, with all the sagacity of the reformed alcoholic preaching temperance, the contract system 'caused panic and unrest in the British game' as clubs offered 'ridiculous money for average players. It was the road to ruin.'[27]

One of the clubs that had travelled a considerable distance down that road was Lindsay's own. In 1993 Wigan announced a loss of £300,000 on a turnover of £3 million and the following year reported a wage bill in excess of £2 million.[28] Not withstanding the team's awesome record of success in the late 1980s and 1990s, their income had reached a plateau. Between 1988 and 1995 the club's average attendance had stuck at between 14,000 and 14,500, despite its increasing success and glorious playing style, while the costs of running such an extraordinary side kept rising. Alongside its huge wage bill, Wigan was also falling victim to the accumulated costs of maintaining its Central Park ground. In fact, all the sport's dominant sides of the 1980s and 1990s were brought to their knees by the same problems. In 1987 both the Hull clubs found themselves in deep crises, the catalyst for which was the need to improve their grounds, which in the case of Hull KR proved impossible and resulted in a move to a new, and deeply unloved, stadium. Widnes, the form team of the mid- to late-1980s thanks to an often breathtakingly off-the-cuff style of play, were confronted with financial meltdown in the midst of the 1992–93 season. Despite the record sale of Martin Offiah and a Wembley Challenge Cup final appearance at the end of the season, the problems proved intractable. The club's survival was eventually only ensured by the sale of its ground to the local council and the transfer of the vast majority of its players. In October 1994 it was reported that only four of sixteen First Division sides had made a profit and that seventeen professional clubs were technically insolvent.[29]

By the early 1990s, rugby league had come face-to-face with the fact that gate money was not enough to pay for the playing of the game at a professional level. David Oxley's strategy of maximising sponsorship and extending television coverage had been pushed to the limit but had still not solved this basic problem. In large part this was due to the fact that the sport, despite its haphazard and unplanned attempts at expansion, was largely locked into a region that had suffered severe economic difficulties and whose traditional base of support had borne the brunt of the effects of de-industrialisation. Culturally too, its inability to break out of its stereotypical image as a northern sport, often the result of unsympathetic media coverage, undermined its attempts to reach a wider audience. By the mid-1980s, some clubs had recognised that radical measures were needed to survive, although no-one was quite sure what such changes should be.

Much of the impulse for change came from successful clubs seeking a larger slice of the game's revenue at the expense of the smaller clubs. Although there had been rumblings of discontent from the top sides in the 1970s about the financial support given to the smaller clubs, the first real moves to uncouple the leading clubs from those less fortunate came in 1983. Bradford and Widnes proposed abolishing the 15 per cent levy on gate money, which First Division clubs paid into a fund that was distributed equally between all clubs at the end of the season. The levy dated back to 1939, when it had been introduced as part of the package that headed off the players' strike over forced wage cuts. It was originally fixed at 5 per cent, raised to 10 per cent in 1950 and to 15 per cent six years later. As part of the deal that saw the introduction of two divisions in 1973, payment of the levy had been restricted to clubs in the First Division. In 1986 twelve of the leading sides formed an unofficial group to demand a greater share of the game's revenue and a reduction of the First Division from sixteen to twelve clubs. In response to their threat to break away from the RFL, the levy was reduced to 8 per cent. The rebellion was also notable, in hindsight at least, for being the first time the words 'Super League' had been used in the game, Wigan director Jack Robinson calling for a 'Super League' of twelve top sides in January 1986.[30]

What animated the big clubs was a desire to take a greater slice of the television money that was coming into the sport. By 1990 rugby league was being shown on the BBC, Granada and Yorkshire regional independent television, the British Satellite Broadcasting (BSB) network and a short-lived satellite channel for pubs and bars run by British Aerospace. The takeover of BSB by Rupert Murdoch's Sky TV to form BSkyB at the end of 1990 saw rugby league, alongside Scottish soccer, briefly become one of the flagship sports of Sky's as yet under-populated sports channel. The interest in rugby league shown by these TV companies, and in particular the imminent signing of a £3 million deal with Murdoch, prompted another grouping to be formed in early 1992 by seventeen leading clubs, again to demand a larger slice of television money. The appointment of Maurice Lindsay of Wigan in November 1992 as David Oxley's successor was another reflection of the increasing pressure from the leading clubs for radical change. The energetic and resourceful Lindsay made his money from a plant-hire business and became a rails bookmaker. His audacity in bringing the very best talent to his club was admired and envied in equal measure, and when he took over the leadership of the RFL he was widely viewed as a potential visionary with the drive to take the sport to a higher level, just as he had done with Wigan. Superficially, he fitted the Thatcherite archetype of the times, that of a self-made man seeking to refashion society in his own supposedly meritocratic image, but in fact he was merely the latest in the long line of nouveau riche small businessmen who had controlled the clubs and the RFL since 1895.[31]

Under the Lindsay regime the pace of change quickened. A study group was set up to look into switching the season from winter to summer, something which had first been proposed by Lance Todd in the early 1930s and had subsequently been raised sporadically, most notably by Featherstone Rovers in the 1960s and 1970s.[32]

The following season a blueprint for the game's development, 'Framing the Future' was published, calling for a sixteen-team 'Premier League', mergers of clubs, improved stadia and a salary cap, the main proposals of which were endorsed by the clubs in October 1994. Ironically, however, the main exemplar of change in the sport in the mid-1990s was not a major club at all but the perennial strugglers of Keighley. Based in a town that had been hit hard by the collapse of the textiles industry, the club had narrowly avoided being wound up by the Inland Revenue in 1987 and had struggled by on average gates of less than a thousand for most of the 1980s. In 1991, following a takeover by a group of enthusiastic local businessmen, it renamed itself Keighley Cougars and introduced a panoply of pre-, post- and during-match entertainment featuring cheerleaders, mascots, loud music and many other techniques borrowed primarily from American football and Australian rugby league, all of which were to become a staple of Super League in the future. Underpinned, yet again, by the risky strategy of buying a winning team, the side's crowds jumped to an average of around five thousand. The Keighley directors were attempting to deal with the problem of how to promote the game in an age when its traditional industrial base had all but disappeared, a question that underlay many of the discussions that prefigured the formation of Super League. If Wigan led by example on the pitch, the Cougars had become the yardstick against which clubs measured themselves off it – although their exemplary work eventually counted for nothing when, despite finishing top of the Second Division in the 1994–95 season, they were excluded from the newly formed Super League.

In a sense, Keighley's fate symbolised the power of the juggernaut that hit British rugby league in April 1995. There had been a palpable sense for the previous eighteen months that the sport was approaching some kind of denouement, highlighted by the seemingly permanent financial crises gripping most of its clubs, and much of the debate in the game focused on the probability of a switch to a summer season. The visit of the Australian Kangaroos in October and November 1994 brought with it reports of a possible breakaway league in Australia. In December the jaw-dropping announcement that Jacques Fouroux, a name hitherto synonymous with French rugby union, was to set up a new summer rugby league competition in France, gave rise to new rumours of major changes to come. And by the new year the more reasonably well-informed journalists were accurately predicting the formation of a Super League and its likely composition.[33]

But when the expected storm broke it had little to do with the problems facing the British game. The increasingly high profile of rugby league in Australia, attested to by its ever-increasing popularity with television viewers, had made it a valuable commodity for the television networks, and especially for Rupert Murdoch and Kerry Packer, who were both seeking to establish pay-TV networks. The expansion of the New South Wales Rugby League and its transformation into the Australian Rugby League (ARL) had also led to growing friction between the traditional Sydney clubs and its new members, especially the board of the Brisbane Broncos, who saw themselves as thrusting entrepreneurs held back by the deadwood of historic clubs caught in Sydney's declining population centres. In March 1994 the Broncos' chief executive, former Australian winger John Ribot, met Rupert

Murdoch and proposed the formation of a 'Super League' tailored to suit the needs of his television network. Locked into a weak bargaining position some years earlier by guaranteeing Packer the first call on its pay-TV rights, the ARL found itself slap-bang in the centre of a battle between the two media barons with little means of self-defence.[34] Following the rejection of Ribot's plan by the ARL in February 1995, Murdoch's men began to sign up players for their new Super League, largely through the simple expedient of offering them more money than they had ever seen in their lives. The war was on.

Such was its intensity that Murdoch was quickly compelled to open a second front. To undercut the ARL's appeal to players to stay loyal because only it could award international honours, his generals decided to sign up the other rugby league-playing countries, primarily Britain, so that the ARL would have no-one to play against. Murdoch executive David Smith had met with Maurice Lindsay to outline the Super League concept in 1994, but on the evening of 4 April 1995 Lindsay met hurriedly with BSkyB chief executive Sam Chisholm to discuss a deal.[35] On Saturday 8 April at Wigan's Central Park the British clubs voted unanimously to accept a deal worth an unbelievable £77 million over five years. In exchange for such riches, the club chairmen agreed to set up a summer European Super League of fourteen, consisting of six existing clubs (Bradford, Halifax, Leeds, London, St Helens and Wigan), six merged clubs (Calder, Cheshire, Cumbria, Humberside, Manchester and South Yorkshire), plus Paris and Toulouse. Journalist Dave Hadfield reported that:

> I have rarely met as dazed a collection of individuals in my life as the chairmen who were hit over the head by the promise of [£77 million] a couple of weeks ago. I believe they would have agreed to anything – indeed, several of them voted for things with which, it later emerged, they profoundly disagreed.[36]

In fact, everyone at the meeting knew they had no choice but to sign. Not only was the money a guarantee of survival for many clubs but a refusal to sign would in all probability have meant that Murdoch would have simply set up a British Super League over their dead bodies.

The meeting was barely over when Keighley announced that they were considering legal action over their exclusion from Super League. Over the next few days the deal began to unravel. Amidst widespread demonstrations by supporters, one by one the clubs that had backed mergers at the meeting began to back away from them. Amid increasingly virulent recriminations, three weeks later a new Super League plan was issued, abandoning the planned mergers (and the Toulouse club) and announcing a twelve-team league of Bradford, Castleford, Halifax, Leeds, London, Oldham, Paris, St Helens, Sheffield, Warrington, Wigan and Workington, effectively the top ten clubs from that season, plus London and Paris. To sweeten the deal BSkyB threw in another £10 million, bringing the total paid to £87 million. On the eve of its centenary, the RFL had once again crossed the rubicon into a brave new world.

Chapter 13

A proletariat at play

Fourteen minutes into the 1994 Challenge Cup final, Wigan's Martin Offiah picked up a loose ball about five metres from his own try-line. He looked up, swerved to his right past two defenders and set off downfield. Within a couple of strides a collective shiver of anticipation ran through the crowd. Something was about to happen. By the time he had reached the thirty-metre line everyone in the stadium sensed that Offiah knew he could score one of Wembley's greatest tries. As the winger lengthened his stride, Leeds full-back Alan Tait twisted, turned and desperately tried to line up a tackle. It was pointless. Offiah side-stepped and imperiously sped past the tortured full-back. A blink of an eye later, he dived across the Leeds tryline to score one of the most breathtaking tries in rugby league history.

Wigan went on to win 26–16 and Offiah unsurprisingly won the Lance Todd trophy as the man of the match. It was the club's seventh consecutive Wembley triumph and their fifth consecutive league and cup double. No club had dominated the sport so comprehensively since Wagstaff's Huddersfield had prevailed before and after the First World War. The historical symmetry extended beyond statistics and trophies. Both teams were made up of stars from Britain, Australia and New Zealand. Like Huddersfield, Wigan's success had been built by some of the greatest players of their times, none more than Ellery Hanley, as inspirational to his team-mates as Wagstaff had been to his. And where Huddersfield had the try-scoring genius of Albert Rosenfeld, Wigan had Offiah. There were many memorable scenes in Wigan's domination of the game – the 1985 Wembley triumph over Hull, the victory over Australian champions Manly in 1987, Joe Lydon's sixty-one yard drop-goal to win a cup semi-final against Warrington in 1989, the 1994 World Club Challenge win over Brisbane Broncos in Brisbane – but Offiah's try at Wembley on the sport's annual day in the national sporting consciousness was perhaps the most glorious individual moment. And, in hindsight, the 1994 Challenge Cup final also marked the passing of an era. It was the last to be played before the outbreak of the Super League war.

The storm that greeted the Super League proposals was perhaps unprecedented in British sport. The announcement that clubs would be merged to form new teams for the summer competition was met with supporters' protests and rallies in town centres, at grounds and even on pitches to demonstrate their opposition to the plans. As an expression of popular discontent and opposition to authority, nothing like it had been seen in the north since the end of the 1984–5 miners' strike. Indeed, this link between the sport and a wider social struggle was constantly referred to by demonstrators. 'They've taken our jobs, now they want to take away our leisure', one speaker argued at a protest meeting in Wakefield, while another summed up the problem as being that 'this sport always belonged to the working man. Now it belongs to the businessmen'.[1]

Although the sheer intensity of the demonstrations was a new and unexpected development, the sentiments expressed by supporters were not. The identification of rugby league with alienation from the status quo, albeit usually in an inchoate and largely non-political way, was part of the sport's genetic code. Excluded from decision-making, subject to forces beyond its control and occupying a distinct and largely self-contained social sphere, rugby league was part of a narrative continuum through which working-class people in the north made sense of the world. It was not simply a reflection of how the impersonal forces of a hostile society acted upon working-class people. The sport was also a means by which its followers could demonstrate their own sense of sporting, cultural and moral superiority over the forces that sought to control their daily lives.[2]

The interplay of sporting loyalties and residual working-class consciousness can be seen in the story of how Wigan and its supporters became known as 'pie-eaters'. Although it is often assumed to refer to an excessive fondness in the town for meat pies, it has its origins in the final phase of the seven-months long 1926 miners' lock-out. Miners in Wigan were accused, particularly by those in St Helens, of returning to work early and being forced to eat humble pie by the mine-owners. There is some truth in the accusation. By the second week of October 1926, miners at five pits in the Wigan area had voted to return to work (although some in the Leigh coalfield had returned as early as 28 September). In contrast, St Helens miners were almost entirely solid until the very end. The local newspaper reported in mid-October that only ninety men out of ten thousand had returned to work. As Charles Forman discovered when he wrote an oral history of the town, this steadfastness continued to be a source of pride fifty years later: 'nowhere was more solid than St Helens', one old miner told him. 'It was organised here to the last moment.' The intensity of the rivalry was exacerbated by rumours that Wigan captain Jim Sullivan had encouraged miners in the town to go back to work.[3]

The fact that players had full-time jobs outside of sport and were members of the communities that they represented on the pitch meant that there was probably a greater degree of political consciousness among them than among soccer players. In 1930 the Communist Party claimed that 'at least one international' in the Wigan area was a member and that other players were sympathetic to the party. Dai Davies, a Welshman who went north to play for Batley, and Joe Latus, a prominent Hull FC supporter and perennial candidate for the club's board of directors, fought with the International Brigades in the Spanish Civil War. At least one other, Bramley and Bradford player John Clynes, was also rumoured to have fought against Franco. Davies also claimed that his politics, and those of fellow Welshman Evan Phillips, who played league for Broughton Rangers, meant that they would never be selected for the Welsh rugby union side. This left-wing political tradition continued after the Second World War, most notably by Stan Chadwick, who combined the editorship of *Rugby League Review* with membership of the Independent Labour Party, and Norman Berry, a Communist Party member who edited the *Rugby League Gazette*.[4]

These politically conscious rugby league players and activists clearly comprised a very small minority within the sport. But this was also true of political militants within the working class as a whole. They represented the sharpest end of a continuum of social consciousness that encompassed both a sense of working-class separateness and distrust, if not downright hostility, to authority. As Ross McKibbin has pointed out:

> there was [in the inter-war years], especially in heavy industry, a pervasive suspicion of 'them' and the economic system 'they' operated. Even the commendation 'nobody bothers us' was a negative one. Many working men and women held to a kind of folk-Marxism quite independent of actual party-political allegiances.[5]

Some of this was captured in J. B. Priestley's description of a rugby league crowd of the 1920s: 'stocky men with short upper lips and jutting long chins, men who roll a little in their walk and carry their heads stiffly, twelve stone of combative instinct'. This defiance of authority was not confined to the working classes in the north of England. In 1933 Alex Fiddes, then a nineteen-year-old Hawick rugby union player, was instructed by the Scottish Rugby Union to sign a declaration denying that he had spoken to rugby league scouts. Outraged at being told what to do, Fiddes signed immediately for Huddersfield. A similar rejection of authority often underpinned Welsh players' motives when switching to rugby league. Indeed, it required some degree of opposition to authority, or at least a stubborn contrariness, to face the ostracism and hostility that transgressing the authority of the Welsh Rugby Union would bring.[6] In a world that was sharply divided into them and us, rugby league was 'our game', which represented 'us' not least because 'them' were opposed to it.

In this context it is worth re-examining the long-running debate as to whether sport, and particularly the football codes, were a factor in reducing working-class political consciousness and making working people less hostile to the existing capitalist social order. This was certainly the opinion of some, but not all, socialists, and it was also held by supporters of the status quo. Three months after the end of the General Strike a local St Helens newspaper greeted the start of the new season with the observation that 'if there is one unproven thing upon which one may safely "bank" it is the statement that football goes a long way to keeping British working men sane and contented: if not contented, at least mildly philosophic.'[7] In fact, reality was not quite so straightforward. As even the limited examples above demonstrate, playing or watching rugby league was clearly no bar to political activity. Within a few months of the newspaper's observation, St Helens could record, alongside its two professional rugby league teams, eight branches of the Communist Party. More broadly, rugby league's position in society and its own class-based self-identity was part of a generalised working-class outlook that saw the world as divided between 'us and them'. In this, the sport provided a supplementary narrative to, rather than a diversion from, those offered by the labour and trade union movement.

In fact, for many in the game, the sport itself had a political dimension. The emphasis on democracy and equality, which dated back to the debate over broken-time payments in the 1890s, was a constant of rugby league's self-image. Although this was originally expressed through the Liberalism that had been the politics of a significant section of the early leadership of the Northern Union, like much of radical liberalism after the First World War this merged with Labour social democratic ideology. In 1926 RFL chairman Ted Osborne told a banquet in honour of the visiting Kiwi side that league and union should remain separate because 'I believe rugby league is the more democratic body and that the game is the better of the two'. From the 1940s Eddie Waring would regularly promote his belief that the sport was 'the most democratic in the world'. This was also a continually recurring theme in rugby league newspapers and magazines. As the sociologist Brian Jackson noted of rugby league in 1968, 'there is a missionary feeling about "the movement"' and many supporters viewed the game as a cause for which they would seek to recruit others. As an official of the National Coal Board in the 1960s, Geoffrey Lofthouse, who later became a Labour MP, was sent to the Fife and Durham coalfields to recruit miners for the Yorkshire pits and spent part of his recruitment presentations showing slides of rugby league in, as he described it, 'an attempt at missionary work'. Perhaps the best encapsulation of this belief in rugby league as social metaphor was expressed by Terry Wynn in a presentation to the Department of Culture, Media and Sport in 1999:

> Rugby league is more than a sport, for those in its heartland in the north of England it is a cultural identity, a passion, a way of life. Its history is one of determination to succeed against the establishment, to fight discrimination and intolerance and to be an honest sport.

The impact of the year-long struggle of the miners against the Thatcher government in 1984–5, based as it was on many towns and villages in which rugby league was the dominant sport, helped to heighten the sense that the sport was part of a wider social confrontation. These attitudes were increasingly expressed in the late 1980s, especially following the emergence of self-produced fanzines and campaigning supporters' organisations in the latter half of the decade. Unlike the fanzines of soccer, which focused mainly on the affairs of local clubs, most rugby league fanzines had a broader agenda, campaigning about the bias of the BBC and national newspapers, the hostility of the RFU and the failures of the RFL to develop the game. Although the more ideologically committed supporters were a small minority of the game's followers, their views were held to some degree by a considerable number of supporters, as the protests against the merger proposals of Super League demonstrated. This stands in marked contrast to soccer, a sport with far greater working-class support but which lacks a similar quasi-political, oppositional ideology.

Rugby league also differed from soccer in its attitude towards patriotism and in its conception of England. As we have seen, particularly during the First and Second World Wars, rugby league was no less patriotic than any other sporting body. But its Englishness was not unambiguous. Perhaps this was, and remains, most noticeable in the reluctance of many rugby league supporters to offer any support to the England rugby union side. Dual international winger John Bentley recalled in his autobiography how shocked he was by the widespread hostility to the England union team, which sprang from both a resentment of union's treatment of league but also from a refusal to identify with a group of players that were from such a different social class. If Norman Tebbit had used rugby union for his test of loyalty to Britain instead of the England cricket team, he would have consigned even greater numbers of people in the north to the category of his prime minister's 'enemy within'.

This was not the only example of the way in which people in rugby league did not always respond in conventional ways to the normal triggers of national sentiment. So, for example, in 1933 the crowd at Bradford's match against the touring Australians responded to the visitors' war-cry by singing the Yorkshire anthem *On Ilkley Moor B'aht 'At*, rather than with *God Save the King* or a similar patriotic song, as an expression of their identity.[8] The RFL's 1947 decision to change the name of the national side from England to Great Britain was not only a reflection of the national post-war mood of Britishness but also had a democratic component. The name change was justified because 'it seemed rather incongruous that Welshmen and Scotsmen should be invited to represent England', an incongruity that did not seem to concern either the English rugby union side nor the national cricket side.[9] This same tendency can be seen in the fact that in the 1990s the one song that was communally sung at the Super League Grand Final was not the national anthem, although this continued to be sung at the Challenge Cup final, but *Jerusalem*, a favourite poem of northern radicals for a century and a half. The song was invariably introduced to the crowd as 'the rugby league anthem'. In this, rugby league demonstrates a distinctive strand of separateness from the 'English nation' – by which is meant a southern-dominated England – that can be found in other aspects of northern working-class culture. George Formby senior, like his more famous son a leading music hall comedian of his day, would open his shows in the south with the catchphrase, 'I'm George Formby fra' Wigan, I've not been in England long', the implication being that Wigan was not part of the same England to which his audience belonged. Richard Hoggart has also spoken of 'not feeling fully at home in England' because of its hierarchical social structure and the accompanying sense of exclusion felt by people of his background.[10]

But the social democratic impulse of rugby league's northernness also had its unattractive side. It could be deeply parochial and hostile to those outside of its culture. This duality was captured by the slogan that appeared on the masthead of the first issue in 1949 of the *Rugby Leaguer*, the sport's first weekly newspaper, 'By Rugby League People – For Rugby League People'. Although this was an attempt to proclaim its independence from what was perceived to be an anti-league national media, it also inadvertently underlined its insularity. We have already seen how throughout the 1940s *Rugby League Review* editor Stan Chadwick was opposed to any attempt to spread the game beyond the north. In 1951 the *Review's* Vincent Firth welcomed the collapse of the Cardiff rugby league club because it demonstrated that the Welsh were bad losers who 'prefer an inferior brand of rugby to enable them to win'. This local chauvinism could also extend to those from other towns within the game. In 1967 the Featherstone Rovers committee declined to make a donation to support the first-ever English schoolboys' team tour of France; the following week they reversed their decision after being informed that a boy from Featherstone was in the touring party![11] Suspicion of outsiders was also manifested in the selection of players for the Great Britain team. Other than black South African Dave Barends, no non-native British player has ever been chosen for the national side. In contrast to rugby union or cricket, there were never any attempts to 'naturalise' Australian players so that they could play for Britain. In the early 1990s Widnes's Australian hooker Phil Mackenzie married a British woman, took out citizenship and declared his desire to play for Britain, but it became an open secret that the selectors would never pick him because he was 'really' an Australian.[12]

Similar levels of parochialism could also be seen in some of the responses to the announcement of the formation of Super League in 1995. 'I do not care whether rugby league is a success in the south of England or in France. It has been and still is part of the life-blood of Northerners', said one protester, voicing a common opinion.[13] This insularity, which, as we saw in Chapter 9, made it difficult for local Asians to become involved in the sport, and the game's strident masculinity demonstrate the limits of the concept of 'community' within rugby league-playing areas. Some of the attitudes associated with the game could reinforce existing prejudices: as Bourke and others have pointed out, the romanticised local northern community, famously portrayed in the fictionalised Salford of TV's *Coronation Street*, never existed.[14] Most visibly stratified by class, these communities were further divided by gender and, from the 1960s, often by race. 'Community' was not a homogeneous or static entity, and rugby league reflected its ambiguities.

The centrality of class to rugby league's sense of northernness is highlighted when we compare it to rugby union's version of northern identity. Whereas league's northernness was urban, industrial and proletarian, union's was based on the suburbs and market towns of the north. The names of many of union's leading northern clubs illustrate this point well: Otley, Harrogate and Vale of Lune from market towns, Sale and Headingley from the middle-class suburbs of Manchester and Leeds. This version of northernness looked back to the pre-industrial north, the north of the rural, pastoral 'Deep England' evoked in H.V. Morton's 1928 *Call of England.* Indeed, the *Yorkshire Post*'s rugby union and cricket correspondent of the 1930s, J. M. Kilburn, deliberately invoked the sensibility of Morton's work when he named his 1938 book *In Search of Rugby Football*, in homage to Morton's more famous *In Search of England.* This was a northernness based on observance of the hierarchy of England, perhaps best expressed in the writings of people like Kilburn's predecessor at the *Yorkshire Post*, A. W. Pullin (Old Ebor) and the *Manchester Guardian*'s Neville Cardus. Cardus's use of fake dialect to represent the speech of working-class professional cricketers is perhaps the best example of northern journalists' narratives of imagined patterns of deference in English society. Pullin's rugby writings yearned for the days of rugby before the 1895 split, when the social order of his idealised England was reproduced in the English rugby side: brilliant Oxbridge-educated backs swooping in for tries, ably supported by stout-hearted, brawny northern working-class forwards. This imagery reappeared during the Super League crisis when accusations of league 'selling its soul' to Murdoch were as common among union journalists as they were from protesting league supporters. Images of northernness that reinforced stereotypes of the industrial working class were drawn upon to suggest that rugby league should know its place, as exemplified by the *Mail on Sunday*'s Patrick Collins:

> Great mastodons, [the players] are; grappling, grunting, utterly conclusive evidence of Charles Darwin's theory. ... Rugby League is different, which is precisely why precipitate change must be resisted. It is bound up with those muddy images of winter afternoons in small towns off the M62. Northern, you see; not for export. ... So why should anybody want to change the desirable status quo?[15]

For commentators such as these, northernness was part of an ordered England in which everyone knew their place: the rich man crossing the tryline, and the poor man in the scrum. And on a more general level, the re-emergence of this type of imagery underlines the fact that northernness had more to do with class perceptions than it did with geography and location.

★

A few weeks after the seismic shock of the Super League proposals, the sporting world seemed to tilt even further over on its axis when rugby union's International Board announced the abandonment of 109 years of amateurism and its embrace of professionalism. Unlike in league, union's dumping of what had been seen as its most prized attribute caused no protests or demonstrations, despite the fact that the adoption of professionalism was a far more radical step than the Super League proposals had been to league. In the north it gave rise to the fear that union's greater monetary and institutional power would lead to league's best players being bought up. Even worse, union's professionalism was largely being financed by

Murdoch's News Corporation, especially in the southern hemisphere, leading to rumours of a master plan to merge the two sports in the interests of his global television network.

Neither nightmare came to pass. A mere handful of league players switched to union. For a number of those who took the opportunity to play union, the game was neither as easy as they had expected nor as satisfying to play, highlighting that the two codes were indeed two different sports. Some even felt uncomfortable in the different social setting of rugby union. The greatest impact was at the technical level, with a flow of league coaching staff to union. Of the eight teams in the quarter-finals of the 2003 Rugby Union World Cup, only New Zealand did not have a former rugby league coach as part of their coaching team.

Nor did Murdoch's media network make any move to merge the sports or develop a third, hybrid, game. A quick glance at viewing demographics for the two sports would be enough to show that they catered for two quite different markets. Much of the merger talk was killed off in 1996 by the Murdoch-financed 'Cross-Code Challenge' between Wigan and Bath. To no-one's surprise, Wigan trounced Bath 82–6 under league rules, despite taking it easy at the request of their opponents, and then lost 44–19 under union rules. More telling perhaps was Wigan's easy victory in that year's Middlesex rugby union sevens tournament, which highlighted that in skills common to both sports league had the definite edge. But in truth these matches merely demonstrated once again that the only thing league and union had in common was the type of ball and the shape of the goalposts.

Eventually, league found itself benefiting from union's professionalism. As the taboo on playing league began to break down in union, significant numbers of union players began to try their hands at the previously forbidden game. The formation of the amateur league Summer Conference competition in 1998 attracted many of these players and by the turn of the century there was, for the first time ever, at least one rugby league club in every county of England. The sharing of grounds and training facilities, both at an amateur and professional level, also began to benefit both sports. And, as many predicted, the professionalisation of union accelerated its appropriation of rules and tactics from league, a process aptly termed 'treizification' by Robert Fassolette.[16]

But fundamentally the post-1995 period continued to demonstrate that, despite both sports now being professional, the social gulf between them had not narrowed. For rugby league followers, one of the problems presented by the RFL's deal with Murdoch was that it seemed to deprive them of the moral high ground in relation to rugby union. This was eased slightly by union's corresponding dependence on Murdoch television money – and banished entirely by the realisation that the marginalisation of league by the national media would continue and by a belief that rugby union's use of league players, coaches and tactics was yet one more example of that sport's hypocrisy. Few league supporters abandoned their suspicions of the fifteen-a-side game. The RFL's experiment of using Twickenham for the 2001 Challenge Cup final lasted only one season following a low attendance and disquiet among fans about the use of the stadium. Attempts to form dual-code clubs were also viewed with distrust by supporters. Leeds's attempt to persuade league fans to watch their union side by staging a double-header of league and union matches was greeted by protests, including a streaker who ran the length of the Headingley pitch to demonstrate his opposition.

It may even be the case that rugby league's sense of injustice grew rather than diminished, as the period since 1995 has seen an inexorable growth in the media coverage and place in the national consciousness of rugby union. To a large extent, this is also due to social factors. Union's rise in popularity since the 1980s can be seen in the context of the resurgence of middle-class self-confidence in the English-speaking world. It is perhaps not coincidental that the beginning of the rise in English rugby union's fortunes corresponds with the time of the 'Big Bang' in the City of London financial sector, traditionally one of the sport's bastions. As in the City, the gentlemen became players. The rise of Thatcherism and its equiv-alents, the defeats suffered by the trade union movement, the implosion of the Soviet Union, and the hegemony of 'free-market' ideology have all helped to mar-ginalise traditional working-class cultures and to strengthen the middle classes' belief in their right to lead. Many social commentators, echoing Francis Fukuyama's declaration of the 'end of history', have claimed that this represents the 'victory of the middle class', in the words of Tristram Hunt. Despite public state-ments to the contrary, this triumphalism still appears overtly in rugby union. 'We are still two nations, and determined to remain so. Aren't you glad you are middle class?' wrote Michael Henderson in *The Spectator* after watching the 2003 Ireland versus England rugby union international, a theme which would be echoed after England's win in that year's Rugby Union World Cup.[17]

And ultimately it is this that will answer the perennial question of whether rugby league and rugby union will merge. For even though union increasingly continues to borrow from league and move down the path of 'treizification', the two sports have maintained their separate and contrasting constituencies and cul-tural meanings. A visit to Castleford's Wheldon Road is a world away from a visit to Leicester's Welford Road, regardless of the rules of the game being played. Isaac Bashevis Singer once noted that Yiddish had never been the language of a ruling class; likewise league, wherever it has been placed, has never been the sport of choice of the middle or upper classes. Far from being a weakness, rugby league's roots in the northern working class have been its strength and will continue to be so. As this book has sought to show, without the belief of ordinary people that this is a sport in which they have some form of stake, whether it be social, cultural or even moral, the game would have gone the way of the pit-heads and mill-chimneys which once provided its backdrop. In a Britain that remains as rent by class divi-sion as ever, in which the gap between rich and poor continues to expand and where the opportunity for social mobility and improvement is diminishing, rugby league continues to be an example of the creativity, passion and the instinctive distrust of authority of working people. For those for whom it is 'our game', it will remain, in the words of Thomas Keneally:

> a cosmology, a perfected model of an imperfect world. Rugby league was a game whose laws had been codified by workers in the forlorn north of England; [who] were invaded by that peculiar genius which concerns itself with the serious business of human games, and produced what was to Delaney the supreme code, a cellular structure composed of thirteen players which mimicked life and art and war so exactly that it became them.[18]

Appendices

Appendix 1 Challenge Cup crowds: 1921–39

Round	1921	1926	1931	1935	1939
1st	181,070 (12)[a,b]	153,627 (16)	118,150 (16)	194,282 (18)	171,137 (18)
2nd	136,496 (8)	130,300 (8)	98,323 (8)	114,114 (8)	138,682 (8)
3rd	96,000 (5)	78,735 (4)	55,369 (4)	83,106 (4)	90,525 (5)
Semi-final	43,500 (2)	35,983 (2)	54,093 (2)	61,619 (2)	104,453 (2)
Total	457,066	398,645	325,935	453,121	504,797
Cup Final	25,000	27,000	40,368	39,000	55,453
Average (excluding final)	16,928	13,288	10,864	14,160	15,296

Sources: *Athletic News, Leeds Evening News, Rugby League Challenge Cup Final Programmes, 1934–9, Yorkshire Post.*

Notes
a   Figure in brackets indicates number of games played in each round.
b   Four first round matches missing from figures because they involved amateur clubs.

Appendix 2 Amateur rugby league clubs: 1914–95

	1914–15	1919–20	1924–25	1929–30	1934–35	1939–40	1949–50	1954–55
Works	19	3	30	62	53	82	78	57
Church (inc.YMCA)	5	5	22	15	13	10	6	3
Sunday schools	7	–	–	–	–	–	–	–
Youth clubs	–	–	–	–	–	–	28	31
College/university	–	–	1	–	1	3	–	–
Old Boys	–	1	13	8	13	8	3	5
Pub names	–	2	3	8	3	1	7	3
Political	1	1	–	2	3	–	3	3
Military	2	2	2	4	2	3	3	2
Locality-based	174	26	243	217	205	175	215	181
Others – WMC/Supp clubs	2	2	4	8	2	7	9	6
Non-traditional area	–	–	–	–	–	–	–	–
Total	210	42	318	324	267	289	352	291

	1959–60	1964–65	1969–70	1974–75	1979–80	1984–85	1989–90	1994–95
Works	46	32	44	49	45	51	56	32
Church (inc. YMCA)	3	3	1	1	2	–	–	–
Sunday schools	–	–	–	–	–	–	–	–
Youth clubs	32	42	28	9	36	24	5	4
College/university	1	1	8	19	21	29	34	49
Old Boys	2	2	1	–	1	–	1	2
Pub names	1	1	14	28	45	74	71	33
Political	–	–	2	1	2	1	–	–
Military	2	–	2	–	–	–	–	1
Locality-based	150	147	148	141	156	219	275	329
Others – WMC/Supp clubs	4	5	12	10	19	9	10	14
Non-traditional area	–	–	6	5	5	15	50	79
Total	241	235	266	263	332	422	502	543

Source: Rugby Football League, *Official Guide*, passim. British Amateur Rugby League Association, *Handbook*, passim.

Appendix 3 Dismissals of rugby league players: 1920–91

	1920–21	1930–31	1938–39	1950–51	1960–61	1970–71	1980–81	1990–91[a]
Tripping	9	1	5	4	5	2	1	
Kicking	17	15	7	6	9	14	11	
Punching	19	40	45	29	35	38	26	
Fighting	11	—	4	8	30	32	28	
Scrum/technical offences	17	3	5	4	24	4	2	
Foul charging of kicker	12	4	—	—	—	—	—	
'Foul/rough play'	4	2	2	6	—	2	—	
Stiff-arm tackle	—	—	—	2	3	13	13	
Retaliation	4	—	—	1	—	2	1	
Arguing with referee	2	—	2	—	6	9	6	
Kneeing in tackle	—	—	2	—	3	1	4	
Head-butting	—	—	—	—	2	8	6	
Late tackle	—	—	—	—	—	3	3	
High tackle	—	—	—	—	—	12	7	
Elbowing	—	—	—	—	—	2	6	
Stamping	—	—	—	—	—	—	2	
Pulling hair	—	—	—	—	—	—	1	
Unspecified misconduct	4	3	2	—	1	—	—	
Total sent-off	99	74	73	60	118	142	117	115

Source: Northern Rugby Football League Management Committee minute books.

Note

a. Data not available for individual offences.

Appendix 4 Welsh and 'colonial' players in inter-war British rugby league

	1919–20	1920–21	1921–22	1922–23	1923–24	1924–25	1925–26	1926–27	1927–28	1928–29	1929–30
Wales	5	24	34	23	21	18	31	29	9	13	12
Australia	–	–	–	–	2	–	–	–	5	–	–
New Zealand	–	–	1	–	1	–	–	–	5	–	5
South Africa	–	–	1	1	2	1	1	1	–	–	–

	1930–31	1931–32	1932–33	1933–34	1934–35	1935–36	1936–37	1937–38	1938–39	1939–40
Wales	10	16	14	16	21	40	24	12	13	7
Australia	1	4	3	1	–	1	1	3	–	–
New Zealand	1	–	1	1	2	4	1	2	–	–
South Africa	–	–	–	–	–	–	–	–	–	–

Source: Northern Rugby Football League Management Committee minute books. I have excluded those players who signed for the short-lived Pontypridd rugby league club in Wales in 1926 and 1927, as they did not 'go north', but included those who were signed by the two London clubs, Acton and Willesden and Streatham and Mitcham, between 1935 and 1937, as they obviously did leave Wales, albeit in a southeasterly direction.

Appendix 5   Attendances at rugby league and soccer matches: 1949–95

	1949–50	*1954–55*	*1959–60*	*1964–65*	*1969–70*
Rugby league					
League aggregate	4,950,000	3,608,064	2,752,868	1,815,474	1,434,422
Average crowd	9,482	6,466	4,829	3,560	2,812
Soccer					
Football league					
aggregate	40,517,865	34,133,103	32,538,611	27,641,168	29,600,972
Div 3N/4 average	9,612	7,339	7,281	6,362	5,302

	1974–75	*1979–80*	*1984–85*	*1989–90*	*1994–95*
Rugby league					
League aggregate	1,106,193	1,472,301	1,403,925	1,689,502	1,658,915
Average crowd	2,641	3,489	2,700	3,549	3,456
Soccer					
Football league					
aggregate	25,577,977	24,623,975	17,849,835	19,445,442	21,856,020
Div 3N/4 average	3,610	4,257	2,519	3,430	3,384

Sources: RFL attendance records and annual reports; *Rugby League Review; Rugby League Magazine; Windsor's Rugby League Annuals; Eddie Waring Rugby League Annuals; John Player and Rothman's Rugby League Yearbooks;* Brian Tabner, *Through the Turnstiles,* 1992; *Rothman's Football Yearbooks.* I am grateful to Robert Gate and Cathy France for their help with compiling these figures.

Note
The final category 'Div 3N/4' is the average attendance at Football League Division Three (North) matches between 1949 and 1958, when it was merged with the new Division Four.

Appendix 6   Occupations of professional rugby league players

1950–60		1965–74		1991	
Engineer	15 (12.0%)	Builder	15 (12.8%)	Pro player	136 (13.9%)
Driver	14 (11.2%)	Engineer	13 (11.1%)	Labourer	52 (5.3%)
Fitter	10 (8.0%)	Miner	9 (7.6%)	Engineer	44 (4.5%)
Bricklayer	6 (4.8%)	Electrician	5 (4.2%)	Joiner	42 (4.3%)
Electrician	5 (4.0%)	Plumber	5	Fitter	42
Labourer	5	Student	5	Student	42
Miner	5	Teacher	4 (3.4%)	Builder	38 (3.9%)
Publican	5	Telephone engr	4	Miner	27 (2.7%)
Painter	4 (3.2%)	Clerk	4		
Warehouseman	4	Joiner	4	Warehouseman	26 (2.6%)
Clerk	3 (2.4%)	Textile worker	3 (2.5%)	Electrician	25 (2.5%)
Grocer	3	Labourer	3	Sales Rep	25
Industrial chemist	3	Painter	3	Bricklayer	22 (2.2%)
Student	3	Printer	3	Unemployed	22
Teacher	3	Accountant	2 (1.7%)	Driver	21 (2.1%)
Accountant	2 (1.6%)	Butcher	2	Clerk	16
Docker	2	Driver	2		
Joiner	2	Farmer	2	Welder	12
Printer	2	Publican	2	Factory	
Welder	2	Sheet metal wkr	2	Process wkr	11
		Stonemason	2	Plumber	11
Basket maker		Warehouseman	2	Sheet metal wkr	11
Blacksmith's striker		Blacksmith		Policeman	10
Butcher		Bookmaker		Teacher	10
Caterer		Brewery worker			
Draughtsman		Bricklayer		Publican	9
Fish worker		Car salesman		Painter	8
Foundry worker		Casemaker		Plasterer	8
Gardener		Depot Manager		Printer	8
RL gound staff		Docker		RL ground staff	8
Insurance agent		Draughtsman		Telephone engr	8
Laboratory assistant		Fitter		Financial	
Leather worker		Mechanic		consultant	7
Pattern maker		Motor mechanic		Machinist	7
Paver		Plater		Mechanic	7
Plasterer		Postman		Shop worker	7
Plumber		Power station worker			
Policeman		Professional cricketer		Gardener	6
Rigger		Railway worker		Milkman	6
Salesman		Sales Rep		RL coach	6
Self-employed		Tailor		Roofer	6
Shipyard worker		Tailor's cutter			
Sports shop owner		Warp twister			
Timekeeper		Welder			
Water inspector					
Weighbridge attendant					

(Continued)

Appendix 6 (Continued)

1991 (continued)		1991 (continued)		1991 (continued)
Designer	5	Glass worker	2	Health worker
Draughtsman	5	Green grocer	2	Heating engineer
Manager	5	Lab technician	2	Hospital porter
Sports instructor	5	Market trade	2	Leisure Centre manager
Window cleaner	5	Moulder	2	Lift engineer
		Paint sprayer	2	Locksmith
Accountant	4	Pest Controller	2	
Admin assistant	4	Plant Operator	2	Materials manager
Bank clerk	4	Production asst	2	Meat Inspector
BNFL worker	4	Slater	2	Mining Surveyor
Chef	4	Steel worker	2	Motor engineer
Farm worker	4	Technician	2	Nurse
Fireman	4	Textile worker	2	Office manager
Forklift driver	4			Pipe layer
Insurance agent	4	Antiques dealer		Planner
Paver	4	Apprentice		Plastic fabricator
RL club marketing	4	Artificial-limb maker		Polisher
Scaffolder	4	Baker		Printing engineer
Surveyor	4	Bank manager		Prison officer
YTS trainee	4	Barman		Production manager
Civil Servant	3	Betting shop manager		Project Engineer
Coachbuilder	3	Blacksmith		Quality Controller
Council worker	3	Boilermaker		Quantity surveyor
Cutter	3	Carpet maker		Scrap metal merchant
Glazier	3	Caterer		Self-employed
Hod carrier	3	Chargehand		Shift supervisor
Plater	3	Chemist (not shop)		Shipwright
Postman	3	Civil Engineer		Shoe factory manager
Rigger	3	Coalman		Site manager
RL Development	3	Coppersmith		Snooker club manager
Shop owner	3	Customer Service mgr		Social worker
Stone mason	3	Day Centre officer		Solicitor
Tyre fitter	3	Debt collector		Taxi driver
		Drayman		Tiler
Architect	2	Ducting Operator		Tool maker
Brickmaker	2	Financial Controller		Travel agent
Carpet fitter	2	Fleet Control officer		Upholsterer
Company director	2	Florist		Vehicle dismantler
Computer techn	2	Foreman		Window maker
Dustman	2	Golf club maker		Works manager
Electronic engr	2	Handyman		Works manager

Appendix 7 Occupations of members of, and candidates for, Wakefield Trinity club committee: 1935–60

Candidates elected to the club committee	Candidates not elected
Publican (3)	Builder (2)
Managing director (2)	Accountant
Teacher (2)	Accounts clerk
Bedding Manufacturer	Butcher
Clerk	Club steward
Colliery agent & merchant	Coal merchant
Colliery under-manager	Colliery under-official
Co-op secretary	Commission agent
Draughtsman	Contracts manager
Electrician	Decorator
House furnisher	Engineer
Newsagent	Garage owner
Painter and decorator	Grocer
Shoe shop owner	Hotel manager
Wholesale fishmonger	NHS finance officer
Works superintendent	Publican
	Storeman
	Welfare Officer
	Wine and spirit salesman

Source: Wakefield Trinity *Annual Report and Accounts*, passim.

Appendix 8   Occupations of Rugby Football League Presidents and Chairmen: 1895–1995

Publican (10)	Fruit machine owner
Textile/rug manufacturer (3)	Gasworks manager
Accountant (2)	Hatter/tailor
Architect (2)	Hospital administrator
Builder (2)	Hotelier
Builders' merchant (2)	Jeweller
Farmer (2)	Leisure entrepreneur
Solicitor (2)	Local Government Officer
Teacher (2)	Packing case manufacturer
Baker	Paper manufacturer
Bookmaker	Pawnbroker
Cattle dealer	Private resident
Coal merchant	Salesman
Doctor	Scrap metal merchant
Draper	Sports outfitter
Dry cleaner	Works foreman
Engineering company director	Works manager
Fish merchant	

Notes

Preface

1 George Orwell, *The Road to Wigan Pier*, Harmondsworth: Penguin edition, 1972, pp. 112, 154, 75 and 43. Orwell later claimed that he didn't say that the working class smelled, but the book pointedly does not answer his question on page 114: 'do the "lower classes" smell?'. For the comments of those who showed Orwell around Wigan, Barnsley and Sheffield, see Bernard Crick, *George Orwell, A Life*, Harmondsworth: Penguin edition, 1980, pp. 278–82. A diary of Orwell's journey can be found in *The Collected Essays, Journalism and Letters of George Orwell, Volume 1, An Age Like This, 1920–1940*, Harmondsworth: Penguin edition, 1968, pp. 194–247.
2 In March 1936 Orwell stayed in Leeds with his sister, whose house was less than one hundred yards from the entrance to Headingley rugby league and cricket ground.
3 Richard Hoggart, *A Local Habitation*, London: Chatto, 1988, p. 11.
4 Eric Hobsbawm, *Worlds of Labour*, London: Weidenfeld & Nicolson, 1984, p. 206. Brian Jackson and Dennis Marsden, *Education and the Working Class*, London: Routledge, 1962, pp. 106–7.

Introduction: the origins of rugby league

1 What follows is a highly compressed synopsis of my earlier book *Rugby's Great Split. Class, Culture and the Origins of Rugby League Football*, London: Frank Cass, 1998. The NU changed its name to the Rugby Football League in 1922.
2 Talbot Baines, *The Industrial North in the Last Decade of the Nineteenth Century*, Leeds: Jowett & Sowry, 1928, p. 18. Recent historical writing on the north of England includes: Neville Kirk (ed.), *Northern Identities: Historical Interpretations of the North and Northernness*, Sutton: Ashgate, 2000; H. M. Jewell, *The North–South Divide: The Origins of Northern Consciousness in England*, Manchester: MUP, 1994; Frank Musgrove, *The North of England. A History from Roman Times to the Present*, Oxford: Blackwell, 1990, and Charles Dellheim 'Imagining England: Victorian Views of the North,' *Northern History*, 22, 1986. Dave Russell's outstanding *Looking North: Northern England and the National Imagination*, Manchester: MUP, 2004, appeared after this book had gone to print.
3 *Yorkshire Post*, 11 October 1886.
4 All quotes from this meeting are from the *Leeds Mercury* 5 October 1886.
5 *The Yorkshireman*, 29 October 1886.
6 A Londoner, 'Metropolitan Football' in Rev. F. Marshall (ed.) *Football – The Rugby Union Game*, London: Cassell, 1892, p. 329.
7 *Leeds Daily News*, 22 September 1893.
8 *The Yorkshireman* 27 September 1893.

9   These figures are from *Report of the Chief Labour Correspondent on the strikes and lockouts of 1896*, London: Board of Trade, 1897.

10   Arthur Budd, 'The Past and Future of the Game' in Marshall, *Football – The Rugby Union Game* p. 137.

11   RFU annual general meeting minutes, 20 September 1893.

12   Quotes from the RFU annual general meeting are taken from the *Leeds Mercury* and the *Yorkshire Post*, 21 September 1893.

13   *Yorkshire Post*, 29 and 31 December 1894.

14   *Yorkshire Post*, 31 August 1895.

15   The full text of the regulations can be found in *Athletic News Football Annual*, Manchester: Athletic News, 1898, pp. 198–9.

16   *Ben Gronow Benefit Brochure*, Huddersfield: privately published, 1924, p. 4.

17   The exchange of telegrams between the Northern Union and the NSWRL can be found in the *Yorkshire Post*, 3 July 1914. When Clifford received the NU telegram he resigned as tour manager in disgust, but was persuaded to stay on. *Athletic News*, 24 August 1914.

18   Clifford's speech and Wagstaff's recollections are taken from the *Sports Post (Leeds)*, 4 May 1935.

19   Ron Lock and Peter Quantrill, *Zulu Victory*, London: Greenhill, 2003, reveals that the British forces who relieved the troops at Rorke's Drift also massacred over 800 wounded Zulu prisoners in the aftermath.

20   Douglas Clark, handwritten MSS note on the 1914 Third Test Match, in the Douglas Clark Collection at the Imperial War Museum, London.

21   *Athletic News*, 28 September 1914.

I   Rugby league and the First World War

1   See *The Times*, 1 and 8 September 1914. For correspondence between FA secretary J. F. Wall and the Army Council, see *Yorkshire Post*, 14 September 1914.

2   *Yorkshire Post*, 23 October 1914. Other papers proclaimed their readiness to stop publishing football results but none was prepared to do so on its own; see *Yorkshire Post*, 29 August 1914.

3   *Athletic News*, 10 August 1914.

4   *Athletic News*, 14 December 1914.

5   *Yorkshire Post*, 1 September 1914.

6   *Yorkshire Post*, 15 September 1914.

7   NU General Committee minutes, 8 September 1914.

8   *Athletic News*, 7 September 1914.

9   The 15th Volunteer Lancashire Fusiliers did have a recruitment drive at the Swinton versus Barrow match on 3 October 1914, although with what success is unknown – see the *Souvenir History of Swinton*, Manchester: privately published, 1929, p. 25 and Stephen Wild, *The Lions of Swinton*, Manchester: privately published, 1999, p. 148. NU General Committee minutes, 13 April 1915.

10   *Athletic News*, August and September 1914, passim. For Oldham see Oldham FC Supporters' Club *G. F. Hutchins Memorial Stand Brochure*, Oldham: privately published, 1949, p. 11. Figures from *Athletic News*, 21 September 1914. For a discussion on patterns of enlistment, see J. M. Winter, *The Experience of World War One*, Oxford: Macmillan, 1988, pp. 115–21, and Peter Simkins, *Kitchener's Army*, Manchester: MUP, 1988, pp. 88–173. *Athletic News*, 21 September 1914.

11   *Yorkshire Post*, 1 September 1914.

12   Circular to clubs from J. Houghton, 8 October 1914.

13   *Yorkshire Post*, 12 and 21 October 1914. Northern Rugby Football League (NRFL) minutes, Special General Meeting 20 October 1914. *Athletic News*, 26 October 1914.

14 *Yorkshire Post*, 4–13 November 1914. *Athletic News,* 16 and 23 November 1914. NRFL
   Management Committee minutes, 3 and 17 November 1914.
15 Yorkshire Society of Referees (Northern Union), general meeting minutes, 19
   November 1914.
16 NRFL minutes, Special General Meeting, 24 November 1914. *Athletic News*, 7
   December 1914.
17 *Yorkshire Post*, 9 June 1915.
18 *Yorkshire Post*, 18 January 1915. For rugby union games on NU grounds, see *Yorkshire
   Post*, 23 October 1914 and 26 April 1915.
19 *Athletic News*, 18 January and 18 October 1915. Edmund McCabe, 'Rugby and the
   Great War' in *Stand To! The Journal of the Western Front Association*, no. 52, April 1998.
   Tony Collins, 'English Rugby Union and the First World War' *The Historical Journal*, 45
   (4), December 2002.
20 Douglas Clark MS diary, Imperial War Museum, 90/21/1. *Athletic News* 23 December
   1918 and 22 February 1915.
21 J. G. Fuller, *Popular Culture and Troop Morale in the British and Dominion Forces
   1914–1918*, PhD thesis, Cambridge University, 1988, p. 127.
22 *Athletic News*, 22 November 1915. *Yorkshire Post*, 8 and 10 April 1916. Wagstaff had
   previously seen a union game in Australia on the 1914 tour.
23 *Yorkshire Post*, 8 March and 10 April 1916. *Athletic News*, 11 January 1915.
24 *The Times*, 5 October 1916.
25 See the report in *Athletic News*, 27 December 1915.
26 *Athletic News*, 16 April 1917. For background, see John King, *Grove Park in the Great
   War*, London: privately published, 1983.
27 *Yorkshire Post*, 2 December 1918.
28 *Athletic News*, 11 September 1916.
29 *Yorkshire Post*, 10 and 26 April 1916 and *Athletic News*, 17 April 1916.
30 *Barrow News*, 5 September 1914. *Yorkshire Post*, 21 September.
31 NU annual general meeting 1916, minutes.
32 *Yorkshire Post*, 26 October 1917.
33 *Yorkshire Post*, 19 March 1917.
34 NRFL Management Committee minutes, 23 March 1915. *Yorkshire Post*, 5 December
   1917.
35 For crowd disturbances in the years before 1914, see *Rugby's Great Split*, p. 247.
36 RFU Committee minutes, 14 January 1919.
37 *The Times*, 15 April 1919.
38 *Athletic News*, 16 October 1917.
39 *Athletic News*, 10 and 17 March 1919. Wakefield captain W. L. Beattie, who was also an
   officer, was killed but he is not included in these figures because there is no record of
   the total Wakefield players who served. The Football League lost 44 players during the
   war; see Simon Inglis, *League Football and the Men Who Made It*, London: Harper Collins,
   1988, p. 100.
40 George Mosse, *Fallen Soldiers. Reshaping the Memory of the World Wars*, Oxford: OUP,
   1990, especially Ch. 5. For the RFU during the war and its aftermath, see my 'English
   Rugby Union and the First World War' *The Historical Journal*.
41 NRFU, *Official Guide Season 1914–1915* and *1919–1920*, Oldham, 1915 and 1919.
42 Figures from Jack Nadin, *The Chronology of British Coal Mining*, no place of publication,
   2000, pp. 90–3. Joanna Bourke, *Dismembering the Male: Men's Bodies, Britain and the Great
   War*, London: Reaktion, 1996, p. 35. Brian Jackson, *Working-Class Community*,
   Harmondsworth: Penguin edition, 1968, p. 82.
43 For patterns of enlistment, see Winter, *The Experience of World War One*, pp. 115–21.
44 Cyril Pearce, *Comrades in Conscience. The Story of an English Community's Opposition to
   the Great War*, London: Francis Boutle, 2001, p. 21.

45 Warrington versus Villeneuve match programme, 8 September 1934, reprinted in Louis Bonnery, *Le Rugby à XIII, Le Plus Français Du Monde*, Limoux: privately published, 1996, p. 48.
46 Diary entry of North Sydney player Herman Peters, quoted in Andrew Moore, *The Mighty Bears*, Sydney: Macmillan, 1996, p. 114.
47 *Athletic News*, 21 February 1916.
48 John Osborne, 'To Keep the life of the Nation on the old lines: The *Athletic News* and the First World War', *Journal of Sport History*, 14 (2), Summer 1987, p. 149.
49 See Joanna Bourke, *Dismembering the Male*, pp. 35–6 and Gerald De Groot, *Blighty: British Society in the Era of the Great War*, London: Longman, 1996, pp. 268–69.

2 League on the Dole? The game in the depression years

1 Northern Rugby Football Union, *Report and Balance Sheet 1920–21*, Leeds, 1921, p. 1.
2 John Stevenson, *British Society 1914–45*, Harmondsworth: Penguin, 1984, p. 107. Noreen Branson, *Britain in the Nineteen Twenties*, London: Weidenfield & Nicholson, 1975, pp. 159–60. Ross McKibbin, *Classes and Cultures. England: 1918–1950*, Oxford: OUP, 1998, p. 114.
3 Minutes of the RFL Finance Committee, passim. Featherstone's 1926 loan from the RFL was not paid off until 1960.
4 Branson, *Britain in the Nineteen Twenties*, p. 148.
5 Minutes of the First Annual Conference of the Rugby Football League, 30 June 1922.
6 RFL Finance Committee minutes, 3 September 1930. Ron Bailey, *Images of Sport: Featherstone Rovers RLFC*, Stroud: Tempus, 2001, p. 17.
7 *Kelly's Directory of the West Riding of Yorkshire*, London: Kelly, 1936.
8 Hull FC *Annual Report and Accounts*, 1921 and 1926. Bailey, *Images of Sport: Featherstone Rovers*, passim.
9 Don Pettingale and Keith Nutter, *The History of Barrow RLFC*, Barrow, privately published, 1981, pp. 58–71.
10 Manchester City figures in Stephen Jones, 'The economic aspects of Association football in England 1918–39, *British Journal of Sports History*, 1 (3) December 1984, p. 290.
11 *Yorkshire Post*, 10 August 1917.
12 For wartime soccer see John Bailey, *Not Just on Christmas Day*, Upminster: privately published 1999.
13 Inglis, *League Football and the Men Who Made It*, pp. 124 and 138. Dave Twydell, *Rejected F.C., volume 3*, Harefield: Yore, 1995, pp. 228–54.
14 The *Liverpool Echo* of 14 February 1947 notes that Warrington actually balloted their supporters on the issue; only 143 out of 4,293 voters supported a switch to summer.
15 Dave Russell, *Football and the English*, Preston: Carnegie, 1997, p. 78.
16 RFL Council minutes, 24 June 1933.
17 Quoted in Wild, *The Lions of Swinton*, p. 265.
18 RFL Council minutes, 22 December 1921. For Barrow AFC, see Inglis, *League Football and the Men Who Made It*, p. 126. William Garvin, *Warrington RLFC Centenary*, Warrington: privately published, 1979, p. 43.
19 *Leigh Journal*, 17 September 1926. Northern Union All Black Tour sub-committee minutes, 8 September 1926.
20 *St Helens Reporter*, 17 September 1926.
21 RFL annual general meeting 1932, minutes.
22 For 1895–1910, see Collins, *Rugby's Great Split* p. 247.
23 NRFL Special General Meeting minutes, 21 December 1932.
24 *Yorkshire Post*, 22 June 1934. *News Chronicle*, 16 December 1938 and 30 January 1937. Bailey, *Images of Sport: Featherstone Rovers*, p. 17. RFL annual general meeting 1935, minutes.

25 NRFL Management Committee minutes, 15 April 1939.
26 RFL Finance Committee minutes, 25 August 1937.
27 Andrew Hardcastle, *Thrum Hall Greats*, Halifax: privately published, 1994, p. 34.
28 The Featherstone constitution is in the club's Statement of Accounts, year ending 31 May 1963. Liverpool Stanley RLFC committee minutes, 2 November 1950 (RFL Archives).
29 Unemployment figures from Stevenson, *British Society 1914–45*, p. 270.
30 Nigel Williams, *Bradford Northern, The History 1863–1989*, Bradford: privately published, 1989, p. 112. *Yorkshire Evening Post*, 16 July 1927.
31 Yorkshire Federation of Supporters' Clubs minutes, 23 June 1924; 11 February 1929; 23 June and 15 August 1930. Alex Service, *Saints in Their Glory*, St Helens: privately published, 1985, p. 125.
32 Peter Crabtree, *Fartown Supporters Golden Jubilee*, Huddersfield: privately published, 1971, p. 55. *News Chronicle*, 15 July, 1937.
33 Yorkshire Federation of Supporters' Clubs minutes 11 February 1929; 13 September 1935; 15 August 1930; 15 February 1937.
34 Stanley Chadwick, 'Editorial', *Rugby League Review*, mid-February 1949.
35 Yorkshire Federation of Supporters' Clubs minutes 20 April 1925; 13 September 1929; 23 June 1930; 15 February 1937. Wild, *The Lions of Swinton*, p. 180. RFL Council minutes, 28 August 1928.
36 Trevor Delaney, *Lawkholme Lane: 100 Years of Rugby*, Keighley: privately published, 1985, p. 15.
37 Williams, *Bradford Northern*, p. 108.
38 *Yorkshire Evening Post*, 1 July 1926. Bailey, *Images of Sport: Featherstone Rovers* p. 17; Ian Clayton, *One Hundred Years of Featherstone Rugby*, Featherstone: privately published, 1985, pp. 48–54. In September 1939 there were still 800 miners paying subscriptions, *Yorkshire Evening Post*, 18 Sept 1939.
39 T. Bland, *Report on Wakefield & District Leagues*, 1 July 1933, unpaginated (RFL Archives). Andrew Hardcastle, *The Thrum Hall Story*, Halifax: privately published, 1986, p. 83. *Wigan Observer*, 15 June 1926. *Open Rugby*, October 1991. RFL Annual Conference 1936 minutes.
40 W. A. McCausland, 'Amateur Rugby League Football' in *Sport in Industry*, July 1938.
41 Yorkshire Amateur Enquiry sub-committee, *Report* (1933) p. 1 (RFL Archives).
42 Yorkshire Amateur Enquiry sub-committee, 19 February 1930.
43 E. Ramsden to John Wilson, 10 December, 1932 (RFL Archives).
44 Huddersfield & District Rugby League, *Report,* 24 June 1932 (RFL Archives).
45 British Playing Fields Society, accounts to the year ending 31 May 1930.
46 Details of insurance are in the minutes of the Yorkshire Amateur Enquiry sub-committee 5 February 1930 and the RFL Amateur sub-committee 19 September 1938. The Barton case is in the Amateur sub-committee minutes of 7 September 1935. On soccer being cheaper than league, see RFL Yorkshire Amateur Enquiry sub-committee minutes, 5 February 1930. For York see B. Seebohm Rowntree, *Poverty and Progress. A Second Social Survey of York*, London: Longman 1941, p. 387.
47 Yorkshire Amateur Enquiry sub-committee, 4 and 17 March 1930.
48 Yorkshire Amateur Enquiry sub-committee, *Report* (1933) p. 2 (RFL Archives).
49 Reprinted in Delaney, *Lawkholme Lane: 100 Years of Rugby*, p. 27.
50 *Wigan Observer*, 7 May 1921. *St Helens Newspaper & Advertiser*, 26 October 1926.
51 Yorkshire Federation of Supporters' Clubs minutes 11 February 1929; 13 September 1935; 15 August 1930; 15 February 1937.
52 McKibbin, *Classes and Cultures,* p. 162. Mitchell and Butlers, *Fifty years of Brewing 1879–1929*, Birmingham: M&B, 1929, p. 101.
53 *Huddersfield Rugby News*, 27 January 1909. *Northern Union News*, 11 February 1911.
54 *Sport in Industry*, August 1938, March and May 1939.
55 *News Chronicle*, 21 January 1958.

56 For the origins of BOCM, see *Sport in Industry*, November 1938.
57 Amateur league internationals between England and Wales were proposed by John Leake at the RFL's 1929 annual general meeting.
58 *Sports Post* (Leeds), 4 October 1930.
59 For a comparison with amateur soccer in Birmingham, see Tony Mason, *Sport in Britain*, London: Faber, 1988, p. 23.
60 Len Garbett, *Castleford RLFC, A Sixty Year History*, Castleford: privately published, 1986, p. 10.
61 Bland, *Report on Wakefield & District Leagues*. RFL Cup Committee minutes, 2 November 1927. RFL Amateur sub-committee, 6 January 1937.
62 RFL Cup Committee minutes, 26 January, 1927.
63 RFL Amateur sub-committee, 6 January 1937.
64 Bland, *Report on Wakefield & District League*. Spelling and punctuation as in original.
65 *The Boy's Realm*, 12 December 1914.
66 Russell, *Football and the English*, pp. 108–13.
67 RFL Amateur sub-committee minutes, 5 March 1947.
68 RFL Annual Conference minutes, 22 June 1936.
69 Bev Risman (ed.), *The Rugby League Football Book No. 2*, London: Stanley Paul, 1963, pp. 60–2. R. W. Smalley, *Recollections of Rugby League*, Hull: privately published 1999, pp. 72–3. Hull KR, *Report & Accounts*, 1939–40. The three captains were Bill Burgess, Willie Horne and Phil Jackson, see Mike Gardner, *Willie, the Life and Times of a Rugby League Legend*, Barrow: privately published 1996, pp. 29–30.
70 Jack Ashley, *Acts of Defiance*, London: Reinhardt & Evans, 1992, p. 7. Peter O'Toole, *Loitering with Intent: The Apprentice*, London: Macmillan, 1996, p. 113.

3 Masters and servants: the professional player 1919–39

1 Hardcastle, *The Thrum Hall Story*, pp. 64–5 and p. 78. Gus Risman, *Rugby Renegade*, London: Stanley Paul, 1958, p. 20. St Helens committee minutes, 12 July 1938.
2 Letter from Sidney Parkes to the RFL, 20 November 1935 (RFL Archives, London Correspondence file).
3 Harold Wagstaff, 'Four Cups Season at Fartown' *Sports Post* (Leeds), 3 March 1935.
4 For soccer wages, see Nicholas Fishwick, *Association Football and English Social Life*, Manchester: MUP, 1989, Ch. 4.
5 Interview with George Lewis in *Code 13*, no. 1, September 1986. St Helens wages books, 1930–33. St Helens committee minutes, 15 July 1929.
6 RFL 1922 Annual Conference minutes.
7 Featherstone Rovers RLFC, ledgers 1922–24 (Wakefield Archives, C414/1-14).
8 *Rugby League Review*, January 1948.
9 Lance Todd on BBC radio, 29 April 1939 (typescript in BBC Written Archives, Caversham).
10 *Rugby League Review*, November 1947. Bough eventually signed for Leeds for 'nearly £1,000'. Phil Melling, *Man of Amman: The Life of Dai Davies*, Dyfedd: Gomer, 1994, p. 30.
11 Stanley Chadwick, *Claret and Gold*, Huddersfield: privately published, 1946, p. 77 and p. 68.
12 Source: Rugby Football League Players' Registers 1919–1939; Robert Gate and Michael Latham, *They Played for Wigan*, Adlington: privately published, 1991.
13 An example of the standard contract can be found in the RFL Archives, York file, between York RLFC and Leslie Dennis, dated 22 September 1938.
14 G. Routh, *Occupation and Pay in Great Britain 1906–79*, London: Macmillan, 1980, pp. 101 and 120. B. R. Mitchell, *British Historical Statistics*, London: HMSO, 1988, pp. 173–9.

15 See RFL Council minutes, 14 March 1927, 11 March 1929 and 9 December 1931.
16 NRFL Management Committee minutes 12 December 1928. RFL *Report & Balance Sheet* 1933–34. For Australia, see Moore, *The Mighty Bears*, p. 148.
17 RFL minutes for the inter war years record only five deaths of players attributable to playing in a match at either professional or amateur level. This compares to twelve deaths between 1895 and 1910; see Collins, *Rugby's Great Split*, p. 248.
18 Lance Todd talk on BBC radio programme *In Britain Tonight*, 1 December, 1939. *Douglas Clark: Footballer and Wrestler*, Huddersfield: privately published, 1925, p. 36.
19 Interview with Albert Gear, *Open Rugby*, May 1982. Chadwick, *Claret and Gold*, p. 34. Melling, *Man of Amman*, pp. 34–5. Hardcastle, *Thrum Hall Greats*, pp. 29–30.
20 Leeds Cricket, Football and Athletic Club Co., Ltd. *Training Rules and Players Instructions*, August 1938.
21 Melling, *Man of Amman*, p. 76.
22 RFL Cup Committee minutes, 4 October 1934.
23 Alf Ellaby interview, *Open Rugby*, November 1982.
24 Letter from Ivor Halstead to John Wilson, 16 April 1936. Contract of Abraham Johnson, dated 1 July, 1935. Letter from R. B. Farrar to John Wilson, 26 October 1935 (RFL Archives, London Correspondence file).
25 Vic Hey, *A Man's Game: Ten Years in English Rugby League*, Sydney: Market Printery, 1950, p. 12.
26 For the pre-history of the Players' Union, see *Athletic News* 23 August 1909, 23 November 1914 and 5 March 1917. Chadwick, *Claret and Gold*, p. 62.
27 *Athletic News*, 6 January 1919. Hardcastle, *The Thrum Hall Story*, p. 64. NU Council minutes and NRFL Management Committee minutes throughout 1920.
28 Figures taken from tables in Branson, *Britain in the Nineteen Twenties*, pp. 161–2.
29 *Rules of the Northern Rugby Union Players' Union*, PRO FS 11/286. NU Council minutes, 19 January, 24 February, 23 June, 28 July and 20 September 1921.
30 NU Council minutes, 16 February 1922.
31 NU Council minutes, 11 March, 24 August and 19 October 1922. Thomas, who subsequently became a vice-president of the Pepsi-Cola Bottling Company in Jacksonville, Florida, was later accused of dishonestly using union funds to leave England, a charge he strongly denied. The union's final accounts state that there was only £4 cash in the hands of the treasurer; see the documents relating to the union at PRO FS 11/286. For Thomas's account see his letter to John Wilson, 13 September 1940 (RFL Archives).
32 RFL Council minutes, 7 November 1923 and Emergency Committee minutes, 12 November, 1923.
33 St Helens committee minutes, 16 and 21 October, and 11 November 1929.
34 Gareth Williams, 'The Road to Wigan Pier Revisited: the migration of Welsh rugby talent since 1918', in John Bale and Joseph Maguire (eds), *The Global Sports Arena: Athletic Talent and Migration in an Interdependent World*, London: Frank Cass, 1994, p. 26. For Welsh internationals switching to league see Robert Gate, *Gone North*, vol. 1, Ripponden: privately published, 1986, pp. 170–2.
35 NRFL Management Committee minutes, passim.
36 On Welsh emigration see Kenneth O. Morgan, *Wales 1880–1980*, Oxford: OUP, 1981, pp. 230–1. The quotation is from Stevenson, *British Society 1914–45*, p. 115.
37 St Helens committee minutes, 17 May and 23 August 1938.
38 Jim Sullivan reminiscing in 1936, quoted in Gate, *Gone North*, vol. 1, p. 28.
39 See Melling, *Man of Amman*, pp. 21–2.
40 Melling, *Man of Amman*, p. 27.
41 Trevor Foster interviewed on *Gone North – The Story of Welsh Players in Rugby League*, BBC Radio Wales, 2000.

4 Wembley and the road from Wigan Pier

1 A proposal had been made to play a club match at Crystal Palace in 1926: RFL Council minutes 3 November 1926. Finding a suitable ground for the final had been raised at RFL's 1922 Annual Conference, although London was not mentioned as a possibility.

2 RFL Council minutes 15 March 1928. Chambers had been a rugby league referee since the 1900s. Coincidentally, he was also the BBC's commentator for the first Wembley final.

3 1928 RFL annual general meeting minutes, RFL Council minutes of 21 September, 3 October, 17 October 1928 and RFL Emergency Committee minutes 24 October.

4 John Huxley, *The Rugby League Challenge Cup*, London: Guinness, 1982, p. 54.

5 See Jeff Hill and Francesco Varrasi 'Creating Wembley: The Construction of a National Monument', *The Sports Historian*, 17(2), November 1997, and Steve Purcell (ed.), *Wembley: Venue of Legends*, London: Wembley, 1998.

6 RFL Emergency Committee minutes, 5 June 1929.

7 RFL Council minutes, 17 and 24 October, 28 November and 6 December 1928.

8 'First Final at Wembley' in the *1929 Rugby League Challenge Cup Final Programme*, p. 9.

9 Estimate from the *Wigan Observer*, 6 May 1929.

10 Andrew Hardcastle, *The Thrum Hall Story*, p. 82.

11 RFL Council minutes 19 April 1933. *Yorkshire Evening Post* 4 May 1934. For numbers going in the late 1930s see *The Times*, 8 May 1937.

12 Quoted in Crabtree, *Fartown Supporters' Golden Jubilee 1921–71*, p. 23.

13 *Yorkshire Evening Post*, 5 May 1934.

14 Norman Dennis, Fernando Henriques & Cliff Slaughter, *Coal Is Our Life*, 2nd edn, London: Tavistock, 1969, p. 152.

15 The author counts himself among their number.

16 *Yorkshire Evening Post*, 3 May 1934.

17 Huxley, *The Rugby League Challenge Cup*, p. 61.

18 Estimate from the *Daily Mail*, 6 May 1929. *Manchester Guardian*, 3 May, 1938.

19 Minutes of 1934 RFL annual general meeting.

20 Huddersfield Cricket, Athletic and Football Club, *Rugby League Jubilee Cup Final Souvenir*, Huddersfield: The Club, 1935, unpaginated. Huddersfield lost the 1935 final to Castleford.

21 *Yorkshire Evening Post*, 5 May 1934.

22 *The Times* described the 1929 Cup Final crowd as an invasion, 6 May 1929.

23 Crabtree, *Fartown Supporters' Golden Jubilee*, p. 23.

24 In 1975 the playwright Alan Plater wrote *Trinity Tales,* a series of plays based on Chaucer's *Canterbury Tales,* in which the protagonists told their stories on a fictitious trip to Wembley. On Gracie Fields and northernness, see John Baxendale and Chris Pawling, *Narrating the Thirties*, London: Macmillan, 1996, pp. 70–8.

25 Stanley Holloway, *The Classic Monologues*, Audio CD, London: Avid AMSC686, 2000.

26 For the full story, see Alex Service *Saints in their Glory*, St Helens, 1985, p. 125.

27 *Huddersfield Examiner*, 13 May 1935. See also Jeff Hill 'Rites of Spring: Cup Finals and Community in the North of England' in Jeff Hill and Jack Williams (eds) *Sport and Identity in the North of England*, Keele: KUP, 1996, p. 106 and Russell, *Football and the English*, pp. 115–16.

28 Letter in *The Scrum: the magazine programme of Broughton Rangers*, Manchester, 9 April 1938.

29 The Prince of Wales himself had acquired a certain notoriety in rugby league due to his non-attendance at the 1926 Halifax match with the New Zealand tourists. As he was visiting the town the match had been brought forward specially so that he could go to the game but at the last minute he sent a note saying he could not attend. *Yorkshire Post*, 18 October 1926.

30 Hardcastle, *The Thrum Hall Story*, p. 75.

31 Richard Hoggart, *The Uses of Literacy*, Harmondsworth: Pelican Edition, 1962, p. 109.

32 Risman, *Rugby Renegade*, p. 80.

33 *Wigan Examiner*, 16 October 1926. In the 1925 Lancashire Cup final, the victorious Swinton side had more Wigan-born players (three) in their team than their opponents: Wigan (two).

34 *News Chronicle*, 30 January 1937.

35 *Rugby League Review*, May 1949.

36 *Rugby League Review,* March 1949 and Mid-February 1949.

37 Risman, *Rugby Renegade*, pp. 57 and 78.

38 RFL Council minutes, 4 November 1921.

39 *Athletic News*, 18 June 1923.

40 A. J. P. Taylor, 'Manchester' in *Essays in English History*, Harmondsworth: Penguin, 1976, p. 319.

41 For Plymouth see Graham Williams, 'How the West Was (Almost) Won!' *Open Rugby*, March and April 1983. For France see Mike Rylance, *The Forbidden Game: The Untold Story of French Rugby League*, Brighouse: League Publications, 1999, p. 25.

42 See Martin Johnes, *Soccer and Society, South Wales 1900–1939*, Cardiff: UWP 2002, especially pp. 54–75.

43 Northern Union Council minutes, 2 December 1920.

44 RFL Council minutes, 3 November 1926, 26 October 1926 and 26 January 1927. RFL Finance Committee, 30 October 1927. Peter Lush and Dave Farrar, *Tries in the Valleys: A History of Rugby League in Wales*, London: LLP, 1998, Ch. 5, and David Smith and Gareth Williams, *Fields of Praise*, Cardiff: UWP 1980, pp. 225–7.

45 NRFL Committee minutes, 21 December 1927.

46 RFL Council minutes, 2 April, 15 August, 17 October 1928.

47 RFL Council minutes, 22 June 1929. Mike Cronin, 'Arthur Elvin and the Dogs of Wembley', *The Sports Historian*, 22 (1), May 2002.

48 For Critchley see Dave Farrar, Peter Lush and Michael O'Hare, *Touch and Go A History of Professional Rugby League in London*, London: LLP, 1995, pp. 76–7.

49 RFL Council minutes, 16 November 1932.

50 RFL Emergency Committee, 7 June 1934.

51 Parkes to John Wilson, 10 December 1934 (RFL Archives).

52 Parkes to John Wilson, 17 December 1934 (RFL Archives). *Daily Mirror*, 2 February 1935. Letter from J. Steel to John Wilson, 3 January 1935 (RFL Archives).

53 RFL Emergency Committee minutes, 11 February 1935. RFL Council minutes, 5 July 1935.

54 See George Nepia, *I, George Nepia,* revised ed. London: LLP, 2002, p. 126. For Parkes' use of rugby league as a Trojan horse for greyhounds, see Farrar, Lush and O'Hare, *Touch and Go*, p. 87. Following protests from the Acton supporters' club, Parkes moved the club back to Park Royal for the last three months of the season; see Parkes' letter to supporters' club members, 15 January 1936 (RFL Archives).

55 RFL Council minutes, 10 March 1930 and 18 May 1938. Trevor Delaney, 'Rugby League on Tyneside', *Code 13*, no. 4, August 1987.

56 Stendhal, *Love*, Harmondsworth: Penguin, 1975, p. 190.

57 E. H. D. Sewell, 'The State of the Game', *Fortnightly Review*, 89, 1911, pp. 933–48. NU General Council minutes, 12 November 1912.

58 RFL Australian Tour sub-committee minutes, 5 April, 26 May, 8 December 1921. RFL Council minutes, 3 January 1922. See *The Times*, 4 November 1921, for the FFR's official response. For the players, see Moore, *The Mighty Bears*, p. 114.

59 The decision is reprinted in J. R. Jones, *The Encyclopaedia of Rugby Football*, London: Sportsman's Book Club, 1958, p. 41. It was not announced until 2 March. See also Philip Dine, *French Rugby Football: A Cultural History*, Oxford: Berg, 2001, Rylance, *The*

Forbidden Game, and Robert Fassolette, *Histoire Politique du Conflit des Deux Rugby en France*, unpublished PhD thesis, INSEP, 1996.

60 RFL Emergency Committee minutes, 13 May 1931. RFL Council minutes 19 April 1933. RFL Tour sub-committee minutes, 12 May 1933. Breyer worked with the RFL in the 1920s, acting for it in negotiations to hire stadia in Paris; for example, see the RFL Council minutes, 14 March 1927.

61 Handwritten contract between Jean Galia and the RFL, 2 January 1934 (RFL Archives).

62 Figures from Bonnery, *Le Rugby à XIII: Le plus Français du monde*, pp. 58–9.

63 Fassolette, *Histoire politique*, passim. Bonnery, *Le Rugby*, pp. 72 and 81. For the French understanding and adoption of rugby league's ideology see Rylance, *The Forbidden Game*, pp. 118–19.

64 On the disappearance of French rugby league's assets, see Rylance, *The Forbidden Game*, pp. 165–6.

65 For example, former Huddersfield scrum-half Stanley Spencer went to coach Lyon-Villeurbanne but returned within days, claiming language difficulties; see Chadwick, *Claret and Gold*, p. 80. At the 1937 RFL annual general meeting a Mr Howarth objected to money going to France.

66 RFL Council minutes, 21 November 1934.

5 Rugby league in the 'People's War'

1 Northern Rugby Football League Management Committee minutes, 28 September 1938.

2 RFL Council minutes, 11 September 1939. RFL Tour sub-committee, 5 and 7 September 1939.

3 For an outline of the war's impact on sport, see Angus Calder, *The People's War: Britain 1939–1945*, London: Cape, 1969, pp. 431–5, and the reports in the 'Sport 1937–1947' file at the Mass-Observation Archive, University of Sussex. On rugby league, see John Schleppi, *Rugby League in Wartime*, unpublished PhD thesis, University of Dayton, 1979.

4 RFL Emergency Committee minutes, 16 January 1944. RFL Council minutes, 10 July 1940.

5 *Yorkshire Evening Post*, 27 September 1939.

6 *Yorkshire Evening Post*, 3 October 1939.

7 RFL Council minutes, 11 October 1939.

8 Emergency Committee minutes, 10 July 1940.

9 RFL Council minutes, 7 August 1940.

10 J. E. Tweedale to John Wilson, 6 August 1940 (RFL Archives).

11 St Helens RFC Ltd, Report and Accounts, year ended 31 May 1945. Bradford Northern FC Ltd, Report and Accounts for the year ended 30 June 1945.

12 Emergency Committee minutes, 17 September 1941, 24 November 1943. Oldham FC Committee minutes, 25 October 1943. Barrow in Schleppi, *Rugby League in Wartime*, p. 100.

13 Emergency Committee minutes, 1 October 1941. J. F. Barnes (Wigan secretary) to J. Sullivan, 31 March 1942. E. Waring to J. Wilson, 2 April 1942 (Both in RFL Archives).

14 G. Smith to RFL Emergency Committee, 26 July 1943 (RFL Archives).

15 RFL Council minutes, 29 July 1942. Emergency Committee minutes, 9 and 23 September 1942.

16 Ken Dalby, *The Headingley Story, 1890–1955*, Leeds, 1955, p. 118.

17 Oldham FC Committee minutes, 21 February 1944. Emergency Committee minutes, 9 December 1942 and 6 January 1943. RFL Council minutes, 20 January 1943.

18 Emergency Committee minutes, 15 May 1940 and 7 January 1942.

19 Emergency Committee minutes, 9 October 1940.

20 T. Scargill, R. Fox and K. Crabtree, *The Official History of Dewsbury RLFC*, Ossett: privately published, 1989, p. 31.
21 *Rugby League Review*, February and April 1948. J. Gerrard to J. Wilson, 21 May 1943 (RFL Archives). Emergency Committee minutes, 3 March 1943. RFL Council minutes 26 July 1944.
22 RFU Committee minutes, 14 November 1939. [London] *Evening News*, 12 November 1939. *Daily Mail*, 15 November 1939.
23 *Yorkshire Evening Post*, 11 October 1939. Oldham also tried unsuccessfully to organise matches with union clubs, see Oldham FC Committee minutes, 20 May 1943 and 21 January 1944. On 3 January 1943 Salford played an RAF side at union.
24 *Yorkshire Observer*, 8 March 1941. Emergency Committee minutes 10 December 1941. Francis in Schleppi, *Rugby League in Wartime*, p. 61.
25 Letter from Hartley in Emergency Committee minutes, 7 January 1942.
26 *Yorkshire Post*, 25 January 1943.
27 Hull FC Ltd. *Report and Accounts, year ended 31 May 1945*. Huddersfield Cricket and Athletic Club Ltd, *Report and Accounts, year ended 30 April 1944*.
28 Bradford Northern versus Keighley match-day programme, 25 December 1943.
29 For deaths, see RFL Emergency Committee minutes, 15 October 1940, 19 May 1941, and 26 July and 15 November 1944. For Briscoe, see St Helens committee minutes, 16 July 1945. Waring in match-day programme for Yorkshire versus Lancashire, 28 March 1942.
30 Emergency Committee minutes, 3 March 1943. *The Times*, 27 April 1944.
31 Gus Risman, *Rugby Renegade*, p. 35. Robert Gate, 'Eric Batten Obituary', *Rugby League Express*, 13 September 1993.
32 Tom Courtenay, *Dear Tom. Letters From Home*, London: Doubleday, 2000. p. 10.
33 For Egypt, see undated *Yorkshire Observer* article in Correspondence 1932–44 File, RFL Archives. For PoW camps, see BBC producer Alan Dixon's draft script for 'The Story of the Game of Rugby', File N2/113, BBC Archives, Caversham. The Stalag 383 matches are recorded in the PoW diary of Battery Sergeant Hawarden, uncatalogued mss. in the Imperial War Museum, London. I am indebted to Tony Mason for this reference.
34 For details of the matches, see *Yorkshire Post*, 23 and 25 January, 24 May 1943, 1 May 1944 and *The Times*, 25 January 1943 and 1 May 1944.
35 RFU Committee minutes, 22 June 1945 and 7 September 1945. RFU annual general meeting minutes, 22 June 1945.
36 RFU Committee minutes, 19 July 1946.
37 RFU Committee minutes, 11 July 1947. RFU annual general meeting minutes, 11 July 1947.
38 RFL Press and Publicity Committee, 14 August 1947.
39 Emergency Committee minutes, 2 June and 13 October 1943.
40 RFL Annual Conference minutes, 18 July 1946.
41 RFL Council minutes, 10 October 1945.
42 The announcement of the name change was made in the match programme for 'The Rugby Football League versus New Zealand' of 4 October 1947. On 'Britishness' in the 1940s, see Norman Davies, *The Isles: A History*, Oxford: OUP, 1999, p. 1041.

6 From boom to bust 1945–70

1 *Rugby League Review*, June 1949. All attendance figures are compiled from RFL attendance records and annual reports, the magazines *Rugby League Review* and *Rugby League Magazine*, *Windsor's Rugby League Annuals*, *Eddie Waring Rugby League Annuals*, and the *John Player* and *Rothman's Rugby League Yearbooks*. I am especially grateful to Robert Gate for his generous help and assistance with this section and to Cathy France for her help in compiling the figures.

2 *News Chronicle*, 3 August 1951.
3 See the union's Annual Returns to the Registrar of Trade Unions at PRO FS 27/351.
4 RFL Council minutes 31 March, 14 May and 2 July 1947, 15 March 1948.
5 The documents relating to the Ministry of Labour tribunal can be found at PRO LAB 3/938 and LAB 69/101. See also RFL Council minutes 24 June 1950, 17 April, 27 June and 13 September 1951, and 8 April 1952.
6 NRFL Management Committee minutes, 8 April 1950 and 31 October 1957.
7 For attendance figures, see Appendix 5.
8 RFL Council minutes, 26 June and 20 December 1954. NRFL Management Committee minutes 15 October 1954.
9 NRFL Management Committee minutes, 31 October and 10 December 1957.
10 NRFL Management Committee minutes, 29 September and 15 October 1959. RFL Council minutes, 22 May and 24 September 1964.
11 The RFL's discussions about the tax can be found in its *Annual Report* for 1952–53 and at an extraordinary general meeting of 6 May 1954.
12 RFL Council minutes, 11 August 1955.
13 *Rugby League Gazette*, January 1955.
14 Bill Fallowfield, *Memorandum on Entertainment Duty*, 14 January 1953 (RFL Archives). NRFL Management Committee minutes, 18 October 1960. RFL Council minutes, 16 March 1965.
15 Wakefield Trinity Annual Report and Balance Sheet, 1956–57. Featherstone Rovers Statement of Accounts, year ended 31 May 1963. Swinton RLFC Report and Accounts, 1969–70. *Wembleigh – The History of Leigh Rugby Club 1878–1971*, Leigh: privately published, 1971, p. 31.
16 Yorkshire Federation of Rugby League Supporters' Club minutes, 9 September and 11 November 1955, 14 September 1956, 9 October 1964, 11 November 1965, 3 June 1973. Crabtree, *Fartown Supporters Golden Jubilee*, pp. 65 and 75.
17 NRFL Management Committee minutes, 17 December 1963. Williams, *Bradford Northern*, pp. 238–42.
18 RFL Council minutes, 27 January 1960, 26 February 1964, 16 March 1965.
19 NRFL Management Committee minutes, 1 March 1961. Minutes of a meeting of club representatives, 4 February 1960.
20 RFL Council minutes 11 May and 25 June 1965. For a comprehensive view of flood-lighting, and indeed every aspect of grounds, see Trevor Delaney's outstanding *The Grounds of Rugby League*, Keighley, privately published, 1991.
21 RFL Council minutes, 14 December 1927 and 15 December 1948. RFL Cup Committee minutes, 22 February 1932. Special General Meeting, 4 March 1954. *Rugby League Review*, August 1948.
22 Asa Briggs, *The History of Broadcasting in the UK. Volume Four: Sound and Vision*, Oxford: OUP, 1995, p. 778. McKibbin, *Classes and Cultures*, p. 460. BBC document quoted in Mason, *Sport in Britain*, p. 53. Ivor Halstead, *Thirteen a side. A talk on the rugby league game*. BBC national broadcast, 4 April 1936 (Transcript in BBC Written Archives, Caversham).
23 RFL Council minutes, 28–29 June, 1952. NRFL Management Committee minutes, 28 February and 31 March 1955. Trevor Delaney 'Television', *Code 13*, September 1986, p. 42. Bill Fallowfield, *Memorandum on the Televising of Northern Rugby League Games*, 21 February 1959 (RFL Archives). For a broader discussion of the impact of live TV on sports events, see Briggs, *History of Broadcasting*, pp. 796–802.
24 NRFL Management Committee minutes, 8 January 1959, 24 February and 19 July 1966, 21 January and 4 March 1969. RFL Council minutes, 22 March 1967 and 19 August 1969.
25 RFL Council minutes, 28–29 June, 1952.
26 RFL Council minutes of a meeting with BBC representatives, 30 January 1973.

27 RFL Council minutes, 9 October 1974.
28 Waring in *Sunday Pictorial*, 27 August 1950. For a discussion of his role as TV commentator, see Jack Williams, '"Up and Under" Eddie Waring, Television and the Image of Rugby League', *The Sports Historian*, 22 (1), May 2002, from which many of the examples in this section are drawn.
29 See, for example Bill Fallowfield's *Report on Television* for the RFL Council, 3 November 1952 (RFL Archives) and Wakefield Trinity Supporters' Club complaints , Yorkshire Federation of RL Supporters' Clubs minutes, 15 May 1959.
30 Quoted in Williams, *Bradford Northern*, pp. 119–20.
31 *Rugby League Review*, June 1948.
32 *Yorkshire Post*, 13 October 1971. Williams, *Bradford Northern*, p. 121. *The Times*, 14 October 1971.
33 Meeting of RFL Council and clubs, 28 January and 2 February 1972.
34 RFL Council minutes, 19 January 1972.
35 NRFL Management Committee minutes, 3 May, 15 August, 11 October and 5 December 1973. RFL Council minutes, 22 November 1973.
36 RFL Council minutes, 15 December 1970.
37 Russell, *Football and the English*, p. 134. P. J. W. N. Bird 'The Demand for League Football' *Applied Economics*, 14, 1982. NRFL Management Committee minutes, 21 June 1952.
38 Figures taken from NRFL Management Committee minutes, *passim*.
39 *Rothman's Football Yearbooks*. John Hargreaves, *Sport, Power and Culture*, Oxford: Polity, 1987, p. 116. Barry Doyle, 'Return of the super cinema in the United Kingdom', *History Today*, Feb. 1998. Tony Collins and Wray Vamplew, *Mud, Sweat and Beers. A Cultural History of Sport and Alcohol*, Oxford: Berg, 2002, pp. 56–7.
40 Arthur Marwick, *British Society Since 1945*, Harmondsworth: Penguin, 1982, pp. 117–19.
41 Richard Holt and Tony Mason, *Sport in Britain 1945–2000*, Oxford: Blackwell, 2000, p. 124. James Walvin, *The Peoples' Game. The History of Football Revisited*, Edinburgh: Mainstream, 1994, p. 166.
42 Tony Hall, *King Coal*, Harmondsworth: Penguin, 1981, p. 151. Jack Nadin, *The Chronology of British Coal Mining*, Skipton and Keighley, privately published, 2000. Figures are from the 1960 and 1980 editions of *The Guide to the Coalfields*, published by the *Colliery Guardian* magazine, London. David F. Wilson, *Dockers, the Impact of Industrial Change*, London: Pan, 1972, pp. 281 and 301. John Singleton, *Lancashire on the Scrapheap: The Cotton Industry 1945–1970*, Oxford: OUP, 1991. S. Chapman, 'Mergers and Takeovers in the Post-war Textile Industry', *Business History*, 30 (2) 1988. Lewis Johnman and Hugh Murphy, *British Shipbuilding and the State Since 1918. A Political Economy of Decline*, Exeter: EUP, 2002.
43 See Appendix 2 for numbers of clubs.
44 *1981 Census, Leeds MDC, Small Area Statistics*, London: HMSO, 1983. General Register Office, *Census 1951 County Report Yorkshire, West Riding*, London: HMSO, 1954.
45 *Rugby League Review*, July 1948.
46 Russell, *Football and the English*, p. 182. Brian Tabner, *Through The Turnstiles*, Harefield: Yore, 1992.
47 Yorkshire County Cricket Club, *Yearbooks*, 1954, 1968, 1978. I am grateful to Rob Light for bringing this information to my attention.
48 T. H. Evans Baillie, 'Rugby League Football' in James Rivers (ed.) *The Sports Book, 3*, London: Macdonald, 1949, p. 116. Harold Wagstaff's son Bob played for the Huddersfield rugby union club for many years.
49 RFL Council minutes, 8 July 1961. The impact of educational opportunity on rugby union was widely recognised and discussed by the RFU; see for example the discussion at the RFU annual general meeting of 1 July 1960.
50 David Storey interviewed in the *Independent* magazine, 8 April 1989. For discussion on the book and film see Richard Holt, 'Men and Rugby: David Storey's "This Sporting

Life"', *Northern Review*, 4 Winter 1996, and Alan Tomlinson, 'David Storey's and Lindsay Anderson's This Sporting Life: Reflections on the Aetheticization of the Sporting Body', *Diegesis: Journal of the Association for Research in Popular Fictions*, no. 4, Summer 1999.

51 Yorkshire Federation of RL Supporters' Clubs, Annual Conference minutes, 15 June 1963. *Rugby Leaguer*, 15 February 1963.
52 Raphael Samuel, *Island Stories: Unravelling Britain*, London: Verso, 1998, p. 165.
53 Arthur Hopcraft, 'Money for Brawn', *The Sunday Times Colour Magazine*, 3 May 1964, p. 11.
54 Minutes of a meeting of club representatives, 4 February 1960.
55 NRFL Management Committee, 6 February 1969.

7 'Chess with muscles': the rules of the game

1 For Canadian Football see Frank Consentino *Canadian Football: The Grey Cup Years*, Toronto: Musson, 1969, pp.13–18 and appendices. For American, see Michael Oriard, *Reading Football*, Chapel Hill: UNC, 1993, Ch. 1, and David M. Nelson, *Anatomy of Game*, Delaware: UDP, 1994.
2 Northern Union Council minutes, 12 November 1921.
3 RFL Annual Conference minutes, 24 June 1935. The Kearney story is in Clive Churchill, *They Called Me the Little Master*, Sydney: Percival, 1962, p. 145. Michael Oriard in his excellent *Reading Football* (p. 28) claims that exploiting the rules to the maximum is a distinctively American characteristic, a view which would no doubt surprise almost all rugby league scrum-halves and hookers of the past.
4 RFL annual general meeting minutes, 22–26 June 1928, Annual Conference minutes, 20 June 1938. For justification for the proposal, see Harry Sunderland, 'About that Throw-in Proposal', *Wigan Examiner*, 11 February 1939.
5 RFL Council minutes, 15 December 1947.
6 J. K. Sharp, *Report Overseas Tour* (sic), January 1949, p. 33.
7 See, for example, the transcript of the discussion on the contrasting styles of play at the RFL Council Meeting of 11 October 1948 in Sharp, *Report Overseas Tour*, pp. 6–10.
8 RFL annual general meeting minutes 17–21 June 1927, Special General Meeting minutes, 10 August 1927, RFL Council minutes 29 November 1933 and 23 June 1934.
9 RFL Press and Publicity Committee minutes, 28 October 1946. Other ideas included Hull and Huddersfield's proposal at the 1946 RFL annual general meeting that the tackled player throw the ball between his legs to the acting half-back, similar to the snap in American football.
10 Leake to Wilson, 4 and 9 June 1941 (RFL Archives). RFL Emergency Committee minutes, 15 July 1942.
11 *Yorkshire Post*, 9 January 1950.
12 Gus Risman, *Rugby Renegade*, p. 74.
13 International Board minutes, 28 October 1954.
14 RFL Council minutes, 25 June 1955.
15 RFL Council minutes, 25 June 1955.
16 RFL Council minutes, 23 June 1956.
17 RFL Council minutes, 7 May, 26 June and 8 October 1956.
18 Ray French, *My Kind of Rugby*, London: Faber, 1979, p. 110.
19 W. Fallowfield, *Memorandum to Council on 'Play-the-Ball' Law*, 5 November 1963.
20 NRFL Management Committee minutes, 21 December 1964. The competition attracted a total of 15,179 spectators.
21 See, for example, Harry Edgar's assessment of it in *Chocolate, Blue and Gold*, Wetherby: privately published, 1998, p. 96. For the rules of the tournament, see for example, the Doncaster versus Batley programme of 5 May 1965. Fallowfield's rare self-criticism is

in the International Board minutes, 25 July 1966. Costs are in NRFL Annual Report 1964–5.
22 NRFL Emergency General Meeting minutes, 7 April 1965.
23 David Watkins, *An Autobiography*, London: Cassell, 1980, p. 200.
24 Fallowfield letter to Robin Prescott, 17 March 1963 (RFL Archives).
25 RFL Council minutes, 22 November 1973.
26 Robert Armstrong, 'New laws put a strain on brain and brawn', *The Guardian*, 23 December 1992.
27 A Moortown RUFC selection card for Fallowfield, dated 2 January 1951, can be found in the RFL Archives. The RFU appear to have been unaware that he continued to play the game. For Airey, see *Rugby Football*, 12 January 1924. For Smallwood, see *Rugby League Magazine*, December 1967.
28 RFL Council minutes, 28 September 1966. Reverend Michael Murphy to John Wilson, 12 April 1940 (RFL Archives, WW2 Correspondence file). Former RFL president J. B. Cooke had expressed a similar sentiment as far back as 1923; see *Rugby League Review*, March 1948.
29 George Oldroyd speech at the January 1956 Yorkshire County Rugby League annual dinner, quoted in Irvin Saxton, *History of Rugby League 1955–56*, Purston: privately published, undated, p. 3. RFL Council minutes, 14 April 1964.
30 NRFL Management Committee, meeting to consider the current standard of play minutes, 3 March 1954.
31 See *Leigh Rugby Supporters' Club Handbook 1955–56*, p. 22.
32 Robert Fassolette, 'Hold Up', *Open Rugby*, no. 184, April 1996, pp. 36–7.
33 International Board minutes, 25 and 26 July 1966. For St George, see Larry Writer, *Never Before, Never Again*, Sydney: Macmillan, 1995.
34 RFL Council minutes, 28 September, 12 and 26 October, 1996.
35 *Rugby League Magazine*, February 1967.
36 For St George's response to the new rule, see Larry Writer, *Never Before, Never Again*, pp. 255–7. For teams at the other end of the scale, see Edgar, *Chocolate, Blue and Gold*, p. 101.
37 RFL Council minutes, 7 March 1972.

8 'The Kangaroo connection: Anglo-Australian rugby league

1 *Athletic News*, 18 June 1923.
2 See Robert Gate, *The Struggle for the Ashes*, Ripponden: privately published, 1986, pp. 48–9 and Ian Heads, *The Kangaroos*, Sydney: Ironbark, 1990, pp. 70–1. Parkin's belief that it was a try is in Eddie Waring, *The Great Ones*, London: Stanley Paul, 1969, p. 39.
3 Telegram from Harry Waller, 10 January 1930 (RFL Archives).
4 *Yorkshire Post*, 6 January 1930.
5 Quoted in Gate, *Struggle for the Ashes*, p. 20.
6 *Sydney Sun*, 26 June 1932.
7 Undated interview with Alf Ellaby, cassette tape (RFL Archives). Claude Corbett, *Sydney Sun*, 26 June 1932. Fallowfield quoted in Churchill, *Little Master*, p. 145. Ray Stehr, *Sydney Sun*, 7 May 1958.
8 Minutes of the Australian Rugby League Board of Control, Sydney, 21 July 1950 (copy in RFL Archives).
9 Quoted in the diary of Harold Bowman in M. Ullyatt and D. Bowman, *Harold Bowman on Tour Down Under*, Beverley: Hutton Press, 1992, p. 13.
10 RFL Council minutes, 18 November 1954.
11 Quoted in Bennett Manson, *Another Battle for Britain*, Altrincham: Sherratt & Son, 1958, p. 58.
12 See Andrew Moore, 'Opera of the proletariat: rugby league, the labour movement and working-class culture in New South Wales and Queensland', *Labour History*, 2000, p. 79.

For discussions on the ambiguities of the imperial link and 'colonial nationalism' see, among many, John Eddy and Derek Schreuder (eds) *The Rise of Colonial Nationalism*, Sydney: Allen & Unwin, 1988 and Michael Dunn, *Australia and the Empire*, Sydney: Fontana, 1984.

13 Quoted in Graham McInnes, *The Road to Gundagai*, 2nd edn. London: Hogarth, 1985, p. 72.

14 Vince Karalius, *Lucky 13*, London: Stanley Paul, 1964, p. 78. Churchill, *Little Master*, p. 40.

15 H. M. Moran, *Viewless Winds*, London: Davies, 1939, p. 69. See also Greg Ryan, '"A Lack of Esprit de Corps": The 1908 Wallabies and the legacy of the 1905 All Blacks', *Sporting Traditions*, 17 (1) November 2000.

16 RFL Special General Meeting minutes, 27 April 1927. RFL Annual Conference minutes, 24 June 1936. RFL Council minutes, 16 December 1936. RFL Tour sub-committee minutes, 28 July 1937. RFL Council minutes, 15 March 1948, 25 August 1949, 25 June 1955.

17 RFL Council minutes, 18 November 1954 and 8 July 1961.

18 The war cry came from the aboriginal people of Stradbroke Island, but had more to do with Edwardian notions of imperial identity than any link between rugby league and the Islanders.

19 Northern Rugby Football Union General Committee minutes, 9 November 1909.

20 Rugby Football League, Special General Meeting minutes, 12 July 1923.

21 Circular to clubs from John Wilson, 28 August 1931 (RFL Archives).

22 Northern Rugby Football League Council minutes, 23 January and 18 March 1946.

23 *Yorkshire Post*, 30 July 1946.

24 Eddie Waring, *England to Australia and New Zealand*, Leeds: privately published, 1947, p. 42.

25 RFL Council minutes, 7 August 1947.

26 Churchill, *Little Master*, pp. 9–11.

27 Letter from J. K. Sharp, secretary of Australian Board of Control, to RFL, 7 July 1950 (RFL Archives).

28 Rex Mossop with Larry Writer, *The Moose That Roared*, Sydney: Ironbark, 1991, p. 74.

29 Jeff Hill, 'Cricket and the Imperial Connection: Overseas Players in Lancashire in the Inter-War Years' in Bale and Maguire (eds), *The Global Sports Arena*, 1994, p. 56.

30 Mossop, *The Moose*, p. 83.

31 Adrian MacGregor, *Simply The Best: The 1990 Kangaroos*, St Lucia: UQP, 1991, p. 2.

32 Writer, *Never Before, Never Again*, pp. 36–7. Mossop, *The Moose*, p. 80.

33 See Moore, *The Mighty Bears*, pp. 290–8 and Ian Heads, *True Blue*, Sydney: Ironbark, 1992, pp. 298–9. British considerations in 1957 can be seen in the RFL Council minutes, 10 October 1957.

34 See Chadwick, *Claret & Gold*, p. 45. Tom McCabe, the 1908 Kangaroo tourist, played for Widnes before moving to Australia but his decision to emigrate was not rugby-related.

35 RFL Council minutes, 6 March 1963. Ironically. Hallas did not settle in Sydney and returned to England, although Jackson never returned to live in Britain.

36 RFL Council minutes, 23 December 1963.

37 Thomas Keneally, 'The Other Code', *Esquire*, November 1991

38 Quoted in Les Bettinson, *In the Lions' Den*, London: Kingswood 1991, p. 9.

39 For Giggs' league background, see *Western Mail*, 28 April 2003.

9 'Sporting apartheid': rugby union's war against rugby league

1 Rules as to Professionalism, taken from RFU annual general meeting minutes, 1914.

2 RFU Committee minutes, 24 September 1920.

3 Rugby Union International Board minutes, 14 March 1958.
4 Harding to Ward, 30 January 1956, PRO FO 371/122750.
5 RFU Committee minutes, 5 December 1949, 2 January and 25 June 1948, 6 October 1950. RFU Executive Committee minutes, 26 September 1968.
6 RFU Committee minutes, 28 May 1920, 28 September 1928, 26 April and 18 January 1935.
7 RFU Finance and Emergency Committee minutes, 29 September and 7 November 1933. RFU Committee minutes, 1 December 1933 and 14 September 1934. Mark Hoskins and Dave Fox, *Bristol Football Club (RFU) 1888–1945*, Stroud: Tempus, 2000, p. 91.
8 Baxter to Sir E. Henry Palmer, 15 February 1936 and reply of 21 February; Copy of RFU sub-committee 'Subject of Enquiry': all at PRO ED 12/527. RFU Committee minutes, 14 February and 20 March 1936, 18 March 1936.
9 RFU Committee minutes, 26 September 1958. RFU Executive Committee minutes, 7 October 1966.
10 RFU Committee minutes, 11 July 1947. Finance and Emergency Committee minutes, 18 September 1921.
11 RFU Committee minutes, 11 July 1947. RFU annual general meetings, 11 July 1947 and 27 June 1958.
12 Northern Counties Sub-Committee minutes, 27 February 1953, 14 December 1951, 27 February 1959, 6 October 1950, 16 March 1951. R. F. Oakes to W. Fallowfield, 26 February 1951, reply from Fallowfield, 27 February 1951 (copies in RFL Archives).
13 RFU Executive Committee minutes, 9 February 1962. Northern Counties sub-committee minutes, 23 November 1956.
14 Huddersfield RUFC membership application form, c. 1972, at PRO AT 25/234.
15 Pallant, *A Sporting Century 1863–1963*, p. 111. Bev Risman in *Open Rugby*, January 1986.
16 See for example the poster featured in Plate 2. Gus Risman recalls seeing this poster in a pub in Stroud in 1929, Risman, *Rugby Renegade*, p. 17.
17 Gareth Edwards, interviewed *Gone North – The Story of Welsh Players in Rugby League*, BBC Radio Wales, 2000.
18 Margaret Stacey, *Tradition and Change: A Study of Banbury*, Oxford: OUP, 1960. See also McKibbin, *Classes and Cultures*, passim. *Rugby Football Weekly*, 1 December 1928. Philip Trevor, *Rugby Union Football*, London: Cassell, 1922, p. 27.
19 *Yorkshire Telegraph and Star* (Sheffield), 12 January 1932.
20 Eric Dunning and Kenneth Sheard, *Barbarians, Gentlemen and Players*, New York: NYUP, 1979, p. 237.
21 McKibbin, *Classes and Cultures*, p. 100.
22 T. H. Evans Baillie, 'Rugby League Football' in Rivers (ed.), *The Sports Book 3*, p. 102.
23 English Schools Rugby Union Committee minutes, 12 July 1930.
24 Trevor, *Rugby Union Football*, pp. 14 and 22. *Rugby Football*, 1 December 1923, 2 February 1924.
25 *Rugger*, 26 September 1931. O. L Owen, 'Introduction' in Kenneth Pelmear (ed.) *Rugby Football: An Anthology*, London: Allen & Unwin, 1958, p. 10. C. J. B. Marriott, *The Rugby Game and How to Play It*, London: Bell, undated (c. 1922), p. 30. Baxter quoted by George Nepia in *I, George Nepia*, p. 112. Lewis Jones, *King of Rugger*, London: Stanley Paul, 1958, p. 66. *Evening Standard*, 18 February 1993.
26 David Hinchliffe, *Rugby's Class War*, London: LLP, 2000, p. 32. For a discussion of the portrayal of rugby league see Phil Melling, 'Definitions for the Definer, Not the Defined', *The Sports Historian*, no. 16, May 1996. Craven quoted in *The Times*, 23 December 1985.
27 Watcyn Thomas, *Rugger-Playing Man*, London: Pelham, 1977, p. 43.

28 *Cumberland News*, 31 July 1948. Thomas, *Rugby Playing Man*, p. 56. Graham Williams, *Glory Days*, Leeds: privately published, 1998, p. 136. *Rugby League Gazette*, April 1955.

29 Trevor Delaney, *The Roots of Rugby League*, Keighley: privately published, 1984, p. 87. Ray French, *My Kind of Rugby*, pp. 99–100.

30 Bill Fallowfield, 'These Professionals!' in the Wales versus England rugby league international programme, 6 December 1947. *Yorkshire Evening Post*, 7 January 1948. Letter from Maurice Blain to Fallowfield, 15 December 1947 (RFL Archives).

31 *Rugby League Review*, August 1948. *The Oval*, Christmas holiday edition 1946.

32 Edward Said, *Culture and Imperialism*, London: Vintage edition, 1993, p. xiii. On the Wollen painting, see my 'Myth and Reality in the 1895 Rugby Split', *The Sports Historian*, no. 16, May 1996 and Piers Morgan's 'Comment' in *The Sports Historian, 7* (1), May, 1997.

33 Clinton Sayer (Sports Council) to Robin Prescott, 1 May 1973, PRO AT 25/234.

34 For example, RFU Executive Committee minutes, 11 April 1980. RFU, Notes of a meeting to discuss the Rugby Union's attitude to amateur rugby league in the North of England, 2 Dec. 1983, Museum of Rugby, Twickenham.

35 RFL Council minutes , 5 December 1968. RFU Executive Committee minutes, 13 October 1967, 17 January and 21 November 1969. The full story of the campaign can be found in Hinchliffe, *Rugby's Class War*.

10 The working-man's game: class, gender and race

1 Figures from Andrew Adonis and Stephen Pollard, *A Class Act: The Myth of Britain's Classless Society*, Harmondsworth: Penguin, 1998, p. 8.

2 Tom Danby in 1950 (Castle Barnard School), Jim Bowden in 1954 (Giggleswick), David Stephenson in 1982 (Arnold), Martin Offiah in 1988 (Woolverstone Hall) and Barrie-Jon Mather in 1994 (Arnold).

3 Jackson and Marsden, *Education and the Working Class*, p. 6. For the occupational structure of the early leadership of the NU, see Collins, *Rugby's Great Split*, pp. 196–8.

4 Data taken from *Leeds RLFC Supporters' Club Handbook 1969–70*, Leeds, 1970, p. 12.

5 Details of crowd disturbances are taken from RFL Council minutes and NRFL Committee minutes. Referees' responses are from Yorkshire Society of Referees' Management Committee minutes, 2 March 1961 and 21 April 1966. For scarf stealing see RFL Council, 19 October 1967. Yorkshire Federation of RL Supporters' Clubs committee minutes, 10 November 1967. *Rugby League Magazine*, October 1967.

6 RFL Council minutes, 5 February and 11 March 1975. Featherstone Rovers RLFC Committee minutes, 7 January 1975.

7 Reported in *Rugby Leaguer*, 22 October 1969.

8 RFL Council minutes, 17 June 1966. NRFL Executive Committee minutes, 2 October 1974. RFL Council minutes, 5 October 1983. *Open Rugby*, November 1983.

9 French, *My Kind of Rugby*, p. 128.

10 Arthur Clues in Colin Welland, 'Hard. Honest. Beautiful', *Independent, 1* May 1999.

11 Ian Clayton and Michael Steele, *When Push Comes to Shove*, Pontefract: Yorkshire Arts Circus, 1993, p. 23.

12 Eric Hobsbawm, *The Jazz Scene*, revised edn, New York: Pantheon, 1993, p. 294.

13 Karalius, *Lucky 13*, p. 77. Clayton and Steele, *When Push Comes to Shove*, p. 77. Terry Clawson, *All the Wrong Moves*, Dewsbury, privately published, 2001, p. 63.

14 'Scrubber Dale Remembers', *Yorkshire versus Lancashire* match-day programme (at Hull KR), 25 September 1968.

15 Featherstone Rovers RLFC Committee minutes, 12 August 1970.

16 See, for example, Paul Hardisty, *Alan Hardisty, RL Maestro*, Castleford: privately published, 2000, p. 38, and Featherstone Rovers RLFC Committee minutes, 12 August 1970 and 24 July 1973.

17 Alex Murphy, *Saints Hit Double Top*, London: Stanley Paul 1967, p. 68.
18 On 'fiddling' at work, see Gerald Mars, *Cheats at Work. An Anthropology of Workplace Crime*, London: Unwin, 1983; Jackson, *Working-Class Community*, pp. 100–2, and Trevor Griffiths, *The Lancashire Working Classes c. 1880–1930*, Oxford: OUP, 2001, p. 46.
19 Rugby Football League, *Manual of Rugby League Coaching*, Leeds: RFL, 1948, p. 63. *The Oval*, 22 March 1947.
20 S. Mellor and W. J. Murphy, Players' attitudes to violence and foul play in amateur rugby league' in T. Reilly, A. Lees. K. Davids and W. J. Murphy (eds), *Science and Football*, London: RKP, 1987, pp. 583–8.
21 Walter Greenwood, *Love on The Dole*, London: Vintage, 1993 (originally published in 1933), p. 19. Paul Willis, *Learning to Labour: How Working-class Kids Get Working-class Jobs*, London: RKP, 1977, especially pp. 52–3. Joanna Bourke, *Working-Class Cultures in Britain 1890–1960: Gender, Class and Ethnicity*, London: Routledge, 1994, pp. 130–3.
22 Neil Hanson, *Blood, Mud and Glory*, London: Pelham, 1991, p. 88 for Edwards and p. 21 for slogan. Lockwood story in *Open Rugby*, May 1983.
23 Joe Gormley, *Battered Cherub*, London: Hamish Hamilton, 1972, p. 20. Gormley was a regular at Wigan's Central Park for decades.
24 *Coal*, August 1948.
25 *Coal*, May 1950 and June 1953. *Rugby League Review*, April 1948. Edgar, *Chocolate, Blue and Gold*, p. 19.
26 Quoted in Simon Kelner, *To Jerusalem and Back*, London: Macmillan, 1996, p. 161.
27 Dave Sampson, *Fast Lane to Shangri-La*, Skipton: Vertical Editions, 2001, p. 6.
28 *Coal*, January and February 1950.
29 *Coal*, March 1950.
30 RFL Council minutes, 24 August 1967.
31 Ian Roberts, *Finding Out*, Sydney: Macmillan, 1997.
32 *Yorkshire Post*, 20 October 1930. Risman, *Rugby Renegade*, p. 132. 'Report on Standard of Play. Presented to the NRFL Management Committee, 3 March 1954 (RFL Archives). NRFL Management Committee, 1 August 1973. Service, *Saints in their Glory*, pp. 124 and 132.
33 Terry Kelly and Dominic Gilroy, *Wakefield's Sporting Catholics*, Wakefield: privately published, 1999, p. 46. Bev Risman, *The Rugby League Football Book*, London: Stanley Paul, 1963, pp. 60–2.
34 Edgar, *Chocolate, Blue and Gold*, p. 118.
35 *Yorkshire Post*, 25 October 1917. Ian Clayton (ed.) *Running for Clocks and Dessert Spoons*, Pontefract: YAC, 1988, pp. 34–5. For women's soccer see Althea Melling, ' "Plucky Lasses", "Pea Soup" and Politics: The Role of Ladies Football during the 1921 Miners' Lock-Out in Wigan and Leigh', *International Journal of the History of Sport*, 16(1) March 1999. For the women's game in Australia and New Zealand, see Charles Little, ' "What a Freak Show they Made!" Women's Rugby League in 1920s Sydney', *Football Studies*, 4(2), October 2001, and *Rugby League Magazine*, October 1966.
36 *Yorkshire Post*, 6 November 1978. *Rugby Leaguer*, 24 January 1980. *B.A.R.L.A. Handbook* 1984–85, p. 123. *Huddersfield Examiner*, 7 November 1987.
37 See also Karl Spracklen, *'Playing the Ball': Constructing Community and Masculine Identity in Rugby: an Analysis of the Two Codes of League and Union and the People Involved*, Unpublished PhD thesis, Leeds Metropolitan University, 1996.
38 *Yorkshire Post*, 29 January 1912.
39 *Yorkshire Evening Post*, 26 January 1912. *Yorkshire Post*, 29 January 1912.
40 For the information relating to Broughton I am grateful to Graham Morris. Brodetsky's misgivings are in Todd M. Endelmann, *The Jews of Georgian England, 1714–1830: Tradition and Change in a Liberal Society*, Philadelphia: Jewish Publication Society, 1979, p. 176. For the information on Yiddish songs I am grateful to Cliff Spracklen. The St Helens comment is from Alex Service, *Saints in their Glory*, p. 112.

41 *Jewish Chronicle*, 15 March 1935.
42 For black boxers, see Peter Fryer, *Staying Power: The History of Black People in Britain*, London: Pluto, 1984.
43 On race in rugby league, see Tony Collins and Phil Melling (eds) *The Glory of their Times*, Skipton: Vertical Editions, 2004. For the racism towards Francis at North Sydney, see Moore, *The Mighty Bears,* pp. 214–26.
44 *Rugby League Gazette*, 4(12), 1957.
45 For black GIs and Walter White, see Graham Smith, *When John Bull Met Jim Crow: Black American Soldiers in WW2 Britain*, London: I.B. Tauris, 1987, pp. 123–9. Peter Read, *Charles Perkins. A Biography*, revised edn, Ringwood, Australia: Penguin, 2001, p. 61. Dennis, Henriques and Slaughter, *Coal is Our Life*, p. 30. Doug Laughton with Andrew Quirke, *A Dream Come True*, London, LLP, 2003, p. 78.
46 Cec Thompson, *Born On The Wrong Side*, London: Pentland Press, 1995, p. 27.
47 *John Player Rugby League Yearbook 1973–74*, London, 1973, p. 28.
48 J. W. Loy and J. W. McElvogue, 'Racial Segregation in American Sport', *International Review for the Sociology of Sport*, 5(25), 1970. J. A. Maguire, '"Race" and Position Assignment in English Soccer: A Preliminary Analysis of Ethnicity and Sport in Britain', *Sociology of Sport Journal*, 5(3), 1988. C. J. Hallinan, 'Aborigines and Positional Segregation in Australian Rugby League', *International Review for the Sociology of Sport*, 26(2), 1991.
49 J. Long, N. Tongue, K. Spracklen and B. Carrington, *What's The Difference? A Study of the Nature and Extent of Racism in Rugby League*, Leeds: Leeds Metropolitan University, 1995. For Australia, see Hallinan, pp. 74–5.
50 Barry Maranta, quoted in *Rugby League Express*, 28 April 1995.
51 See Thompson, *Born On The Wrong Side*, pp. 29 and 34.
52 Waring, *The Great Ones*, p. 95. See also Jack Winstanley, *The Billy Boston Story*, Wigan: privately published, 1963, pp. 74–5. RFL Council minutes, 1 February 1978.
53 J. Long *et al.*, *What's The Difference?*. RFL Council minutes, 1 February 1978.

II The other amateurs: beyond the heartlands

1 *Rugby Leaguer*, 11 August 1949.
2 *Sporting Chronicle*, 24 April 1947, 20 May 1947, 1 and 6 April 1948. RFL Council minutes, 7 August 1947. RFL Press and Publicity Committee minutes, 12 January and 19 April 1948. *Rugby League Gazette*, December 1949.
3 Lush and Farrar, *Tries in the Valleys*, p. 100.
4 *Sporting Chronicle*, 29 March 1949. RFL Council minutes, 28 April 1949. Welsh Liaison Committee minutes, 15 August and 15 December 1949.
5 For the Cardiff club and the Welsh league see Ch. 8 of Lush and Farrar, *Tries in the Valleys*.
6 RFL Council minutes, 27 June 1949, 28 June 1952, 26 June 1954 and 22 February 1968. RFL Report and Accounts 1952–53.
7 Jackson and Marsden, *Education and the Working Class*, p. 107.
8 RFL Council minutes, 8 July 1961, and 28 April and 22 October 1964. *John Player Rugby League Yearbook 1973–74*, London, 1974, p. 302.
9 *BARLA Yearbook 1979–80*, Huddersfield, 1980, p. 107. *Daily Telegraph*, 26 October 1990.
10 RFL Council minutes, 31 August 1967.
11 RFL Council minutes, 12 April and 9 December 1973, 29 May 1974.
12 *Yorkshire Evening Post*, 3 January 1976.
13 For comparative statistics, see the Sports Council, *A Digest of Sports Statistics for the UK*, London: Sports Council, 1986, p. 108.
14 Article 16 of the British Amateur Rugby League Association's *Constitution*, Huddersfield, 1973. For the IRFB's regulations of the same period, see the RFU's *Handbook 1974–75*, London, 1974, pp. 222–33.

15 Geoffrey Moorhouse, *A People's Game. The Official History of Rugby League 1895–1995*, London: Hodder, 1995, p. 328.
16 For the Fulham story, see Lush and Farrar, *Touch and Go*, and Harold Genders, *The Fulham Dream*, London: LLP, 2002.
17 Editor of *Rothman's Football Yearbook 1984–85* quoted in Russell, *Football and the English*, p. 206. Clay in Lush and Farrar, *Touch and Go*, p. 117.
18 Quoted in Paul Fitzpatrick, *Rugby League Review 1982–83*, London: Faber, 1983, p. 180.

12 From slump to Super League 1975–95

1   David Oxley, 'The Rugby League Business', *John Player Rugby League Yearbook 1975–76*, London 1975, p. 11.
2   Collins and Vamplew, *Mud, Sweat and Beers: A Cultural History of Sport and Alcohol*, p. 59.
3   NRFL Management Committee minutes, 9 March 1971.
4   NRFL Management Committee minutes, 18 June 1970.
5   RFL Council minutes, 9 March 1971.
6   *John Player Rugby League Yearbook 1974–75*, London, 1974. RFL Council minutes, 15 May 1974.
7   See, for example, RFL Council minutes, 4 December 1974, 2 September 1977 and 2 November 1977.
8   RFL Council minutes, 4 May and 25 July 1977, 5 October 1983.
9   *John Player Rugby League Yearbook 1973–74*, London, 1974, pp. 28 and 209. *John Player Rugby League Yearbook 1974–75*, p. 16.
10 Hardcastle, *The Thrum Hall Story*, p. 112.
11 *John Player Rugby League Yearbook 1973–74*, p. 209.
12 RFL annual general meeting, 1972. RFL Council minutes, 20 July 1975 and 25 April 1979. NRFL Management Committee minutes, 27 August 1970. RFL Council minutes, 6 October 1976.
13 RFL Council minutes, 24 July 1977.
14 All figures relating to players and coaches are taken from *Rothman's Rugby League Yearbook*, London, 1982–83 to 1994–95.
15 *Open Rugby*, October 1983.
16 *Daily Telegraph*, 3 November 1982.
17 Paul Fitzpatrick, *Rugby League Review 1982–83*, London: Faber, 1983, p. 180. RFL Management Committee minutes, 27 September 1984.
18 RFL Management Committee minutes, 12 June, 22 August and 18 September 1985. Trevor Delaney's masterful *The Grounds of Rugby League*, Keighley, 1991, from which the Kevin Harcombe story is taken, remains the definitive account of the impact on rugby league of the Bradford City disaster. The amount of loans is calculated from the minutes of the RFL Management Committee. Oxley's estimate is in Delaney, *The Grounds of Rugby League*, p. 16.
19 *Open Rugby*, October 1988.
20 Home Office, *The Hillsborough Stadium Disaster. Inquiry by the Rt Hon Lord Justice Taylor*, London: HMSO, 1990. See p. 88 for a list of grounds visited.
21 Adrian MacGregor, *King Wally*, St Lucia: UQP, 1987, pp. 146–57.
22 *Hull Daily Mail*, 25 June 1957. I am grateful to Margaret MacDonald for bringing this to my attention.
23 Bill Fallowfield, Notes on Retain and Transfer System [evidence for a Ministry of Labour tribunal, September 1951] undated (RFL Archives).
24 Dave Farrar and Peter Lush (eds), *From Fulham to Wembley: 20 Years of Rugby League in London*, London: LLP, 2001, pp. 124–6. *Financial Times*, 31 August 1985. RFL Council minutes, 21 and 26 November, 5 December 1984.

25 For more on the evolution of the contract system, see Margaret Groenveld, *Transferring Assets, Transferring Athletes: an Anthropological Analysis of Financial Categorisation and Commodification in English Rugby League*, unpublished DPhil thesis, University of Oxford, 2004.

26 *Open Rugby*, April 1991. Jeff Connor, *Rugby League Who's Who*, London: Guinness, 1991.

27 Lindsay quoted in *The Rugby League Yearbook 1993–94*, London, 1993, p. 123.

28 *Rothman's Rugby League Yearbook 1993–94*, London, 1993, p. 19. *Rothman's Rugby League Yearbook 1994–95*, London 1994, p. 18.

29 Simon Kelner, *To Jerusalem and Back*, London, 1996, p. 99.

30 RFL Council minutes, 26 January and 6 April 1983. Jack Robinson in *Open Rugby*, January 1986.

31 For a brief biography of Lindsay, see Kelner, *To Jerusalem and Back*, pp. 130–9.

32 See Featherstone Rovers RLFC, General Committee minutes, 10 January 1967 and 12 December 1974, held in West Yorkshire Archives, Wakefield.

33 See, for example, *Open Rugby*, January 1995, which predicted precisely the proposed club mergers for the British Super League.

34 The definitive jounalistic account of the Super League war so far produced is Mike Colman, *Super League: The Inside Story*, Sydney: Ironbark 1996. See pp. 38–9 especially for the pre-history of the struggle.

35 Colman, *Super League*, p. 69 and pp. 196–218. Accounts vary as to who was at the 4 April meeting. See also Kelner, *To Jerusalem and Back*, p. 103. For a chronology of events in Britain see *Rothman's Rugby League Yearbook 1995–96*, London, 1996, pp. 11–14.

36 *Open Rugby*, May 1995, p. 8.

13 A proletariat at play

1 Quoted in Ian Clayton, Ian Daley and Brian Lewis (eds), *Merging on the Ridiculous*, Pontefract: YAC, 1995, p. 14. *Independent*, 15 April 1995.

2 For a more detailed discussion of this idea see pp. 231–7 of Collins, *Rugby's Great Split*.

3 For Leigh and Wigan and miners, see *Wigan Examiner*, 2 and 9 October 1926, respectively. For St Helens, see *St Helens Reporter*, 15 October 1926 and Charles Forman, *Industrial Town: Self-Portrait of St Helens in the 1920s*, Newton Abbot: David & Charles, 1978, p. 254. For Sullivan, see *Daily Worker*, 17 September 1930.

4 *Daily Worker*, 17 September 1930. For Davies, see Phil Melling, 'Wales, Rugby League and the Spanish Civil War', *Our Game*, no. 2, Autumn 2000, and Hywel Francis, *Miners Against Fascism: Wales and the Spanish Civil War*, London: Lawrence and Wishart, 1984, p. 80. For Clynes, see *Open Rugby*, January 1989.

5 McKibbin, *Classes and Cultures*, p. 87.

6 J. B. Priestley, 'T'Match', in Pelmear (ed.), *Rugby Football. An Anthology*, p. 107. *Alex Fiddes Testimonial Brochure*, Huddersfield: privately published, 1946, p. 7.

7 *St Helens Newspaper & Advertiser*, 27 August 1926.

8 John Bentley with Neil Squires, *John Bentley, My Story*, London: Andre Deutsch, 1999, p. 229. Nigel Williams, *Bradford Northern*, p. 105. It is not only rugby league fans who do not want to see the England rugby union side win; for example, see Dave Hill, 'Game of Two Psyches', *Guardian*, 29 March 2003.

9 Match-day programme, 'The Rugby Football League v New Zealand', 4 October, 1947, p. 8.

10 For Formby, see Simon Louvish, 'That Lad Will Go Far' in the *Guardian*, 6 December 2002. Richard Hoggart, *A Local Habitation*, London, 1988, p. 54.

11 Firth quoted in Lush and Farrar, *Tries in the Valleys*, p. 109. Featherstone Rovers RLFC, committee minutes, 17 and 24 October 1967.

12   Tulson Tollett, who was born in Hastings but brought up in Australia, was selected for the 1997 British touring side to New Zealand.

13   Quoted in Clayton, Daley and Lewis (eds), *Merging on the Ridiculous*, p. 38.

14   See, for example, Joanna Bourke, *Working Class Cultures in Britain: 1890–1960: Gender, Class and Ethnicity*, London: Routledge, 1994, p. 157.

15   *Mail on Sunday*, 9 April 1995.

16   For the impact of Super League on rugby league, see Lisa O'Keeffe, *An Analysis of the Economic and Social Effects of Changing the Structure of Rugby League 1996–99*, unpublished PhD thesis, Sheffield Hallam University, 2000. Fassolette in *Midi-Olympique*, 12 January 2004.

17   *Guardian*, 10 May 2002. *The Spectator*, 5 April 2003. An examplar of post-world cup triumphalism can be found in the *Daily Telegraph* editorial of 24 November 2003.

18   Thomas Keneally, *A Family Madness*, London: Hodder & Stoughton (paperback edition), 1985, p. 31. For social mobility, see 'Social mobility declines despite education gains', *Financial Times*, 17 June 2002. For poverty, see 'Gap between rich and poor growing fast under Blair', *The Independent*, 2 August 2004.

Bibliography

Archive sources

Annual Reports and/or Financial Statements: Bradford Northern FC Ltd. British Playing Fields Society. Featherstone Rovers RLFC. Huddersfield Cricket and Athletic Club Ltd. Hull FC. Hull Kingston Rovers RLFC. Northern Rugby Football Union. Rugby Football League. St Helens RFC. Swinton RLFC. Wakefield Trinity RLFC.

Australian Rugby League Board of Control, Sydney: minutes 1950.

BBC Written Archives, Caversham.

Featherstone Rovers RLFC: Committee minutes. Ledgers 1922–24. West Yorkshire Archives, Wakefield.

Imperial War Museum, London.

Leeds Cricket, Football and Athletic Club Co., Ltd: *Training Rules and Players Instructions*, August 1938.

Liverpool Stanley RLFC: Committee minutes.

Mass-Observation Archive, University of Sussex.

Oldham FC: Committee minutes.

Public Record Office, London.

Rugby Football League, Leeds: Northern Rugby Football League Management Committee minutes. Northern Union All Black Tour sub-committee minutes. Northern Union General Committee minutes. Players' Registers. RFL Australian Tour sub-committee minutes. RFL Council minutes. RFL Cup Committee minutes. RFL Emergency Committee minutes. RFL Finance Committee minutes. RFL Press and Publicity committee minutes. RFL Welsh Liaison Committee minutes. Rugby League International Board minutes.

Rugby Football Union, Twickenham: English Schools Rugby Union Committee minutes. RFU Committee minutes. RFU Finance and Emergency Committee minutes. RFU Northern Counties sub-committee minutes. Rugby Union International Board minutes.

St Helens RFC: Committee minutes. Wages books, 1930–33.

Yorkshire Federation of Rugby League Supporters' Clubs, Leeds: minutes 1922–71.

Yorkshire Society of Referees (Northern Union), Leeds: minute books 1899–1978

Government and official reports

1981 Census, Leeds MDC, Small Area Statistics, HMSO, 1983.

Board of Trade Report on Strikes and Lock-Outs in 1913.

Culture, Media and Sport Committee, *Second Report, The Future of Professional Rugby*, HC99, HMSO, 1999.

General Register Office, *Census 1951 County Report Yorkshire*, West Riding, HMSO, 1954.
Home Office, *The Hillsborough Stadium Disaster. Inquiry by the Rt Hon Lord Justice Taylor*, HMSO, 1990.
Sports Council, *A Digest of Sports Statistics for the UK*, London, 1986.

Newspapers and periodicals

Athletic News
Barrow News
Boy's Own Paper
Coal
Code 13
Colliery Guardian
Cumberland News
Daily Chronicle
Daily Mail
Daily Mirror
Daily Telegraph
Daily Worker
Evening Standard
Financial Times
Huddersfield Examiner
Huddersfield Rugby News
Hull Daily Mail
Independent
Jewish Chronicle
Leigh Journal
Liverpool Echo
Mail on Sunday
Manchester Guardian
News Chronicle
Northern Union News
Oldham Evening Chronicle
Open Rugby
Pontefract and Castleford Express
Rochdale Observer
Rugby Football
Rugby Football Weekly
Rugby League Express
Rugby League Gazette
Rugby League Magazine
Rugby League Review
Rugby League Week (Sydney)
Rugby Leaguer
Rugger
Spectator
Sport in Industry
Sporting Chronicle
Sports Post (Leeds)
St Helens Newspaper & Advertiser
St Helens Reporter
Sunday Pictorial
Sydney Sun
The Boy's Realm
The Oval
The Referee (Sydney)
The Times
Western Mail
Wigan Examiner
Wigan Observer
Yorkshire Evening Post
Yorkshire Evening Press
Yorkshire Observer
Yorkshire Post
Yorkshire Telegraph and Star

Annuals, directories and yearbooks

British Amateur Rugby League Association, Official Handbooks
Eddie Waring Rugby League Annuals
John Player Rugby League Yearbooks
Kelly's Directory of the West Riding of Yorkshire, London, 1936.
Northern Rugby Football Union, *Official Guides*
Rothman's Football Yearbooks
Rothman's Rugby League Yearbooks
Rugby Football League, *Official Guides*
Windsor's Rugby League Annuals
Yorkshire County Cricket Club, *Yearbooks*, 1954, 1968, 1978.

Match-day programmes, brochures and supporters' handbooks

Alex Fiddes Testimonial Brochure, Huddersfield, 1946.
Ben Gronow Benefit Brochure, Huddersfield, 1924.
Bradford Northern versus Keighley, match-day programme, 25 December 1943.
Doncaster versus Batley, match-day programme, 5 May 1965.
Douglas Clark: Footballer and Wrestler, Huddersfield, 1925, p. 36.
G. F. *Hutchins Memorial Stand Brochure,* Oldham, 1949.
Huddersfield Cricket, Athletic and Football Club, *Rugby League Jubilee Cup Final Souvenir,* Huddersfield, 1935.
Leeds RLFC Supporters' Club Handbook 1969–70, Leeds, 1970.
Leigh Rugby Supporters' Club Handbook 1955–56.
The Rugby Football League versus New Zealand, match-day programme, 4 October, 1947.
Rugby League Challenge Cup Final, match-day programme, 1929.
Souvenir History of Swinton, Manchester, 1929.
The Scrum: the magazine programme of Broughton Rangers, match-day programme, 9 April 1938.
Wales versus England, match-day programme, 6 December 1947.
Warrington versus Villeneuve, match-day programme, 8 September 1934.
Wembleigh – The History of Leigh Rugby Club 1878–1971, Leigh, 1971.
Yorkshire versus Lancashire, match-day programme, 25 September 1968.

Books

Adonis, Andrew and Pollard, Stephen, *A Class Act: The Myth of Britain's Classless Society,* Harmondsworth: Penguin, 1998.
Alderson, Frederick, *View North: A Long Look at Northern England,* Newton Abbott: David & Charles, 1968.
Arnold, John, Spearritt, Peter and Walker, David (eds), *Out of Empire. The British Dominion of Australia,* Port Melbourne: Mandarin, 1993.
Ashley, Jack, *Acts of Defiance,* London: Reinhardt & Evans, 1992.
Back, Les and Ware, Vron, *Out of Whiteness,* Chicago: UCP, 2001.
Bailey, John, *Not Just on Christmas Day,* Upminster: privately published, 1999.
Bailey, Ron *Images of Sport: Featherstone Rovers R.L.F.C.,* Stroud: Tempus, 2001.
Baxendale, John and Pawling, Christopher, *Narrating the Thirties,* London: Palgrave, 1996.
Bennett, John (ed.), *Useful Toil: Autobiographies of Working People from the 1820s to the 1920s,* Harmondsworth: Penguin, 1974.
Bennett, John (ed.), *Destiny Obscure: Autobiographies of Childhood, Education and Family from the 1820s to the 1920s,* Harmondsworth: Penguin, 1982.
Bentley, John with Squires, Neil, *John Bentley, My Story,* London: Andre Deustch, 1999.
Bettinson, Les, *In the Lions' Den: Great Britain's Rugby League Revival,* London: Kingswood, 1991.
Bonnery, Louis, *Le Rugby à XIII, Le Plus Français Du Monde,* Limoux: privately published, 1996.
Booth, Alan, *The British Economy in the Twentieth Century,* London: Palgrave, 2001.
Bourke, Joanna, *Working-Class Cultures in Britain 1890–1960: Gender, Class and Ethnicity,* London: Routledge, 1994.
Bourke, Joanna, *Dismembering the Male: Men's Bodies, Britain and the Great War,* London: Reaktion, 1996.
Branson, Noreen, *Britain in the Nineteen Twenties,* London: Weidenfeld & Nicholson, 1975.

Branson, Noreen and Heinemann, Margot, *Britain in the Nineteen Thirties,* London: Weidenfield & Nicholson, 1971.

Briggs, Asa, *The History of Broadcasting in the UK. Vol. 4: Sound and Vision,* revised edn, Oxford: OUP, 1995.

Brown, Judith M. and Lewis, W. R. (eds), *The Oxford History of the British Empire, Vol. 4: The Twentieth Century,* Oxford: OUP, 1999.

Buckley, Ken, Dale, Barbara and Reynolds, Wayne, *Doc Evatt,* Melbourne: Longman, 1994.

Calder, Angus, *The People's War: Britain 1939–1945,* London: Harper, 1969.

Cannadine, David, *Class in Britain,* Yale: YUP, 1998.

Chadwick, Stanley, *Claret and Gold,* Huddersfield: privately published, 1946.

Churchill, Clive, *They Called Me the Little Master,* Sydney: Percival, 1962.

Clark, Peter, *British Clubs and Societies, 1580–1800,* Oxford: OUP, 2000.

Clawson, Terry, *All the Wrong Moves,* Dewsbury: privately published, 2001.

Clayton, Ian, *One Hundred Years of Featherstone Rugby,* Featherstone: privately published, 1985.

Clayton, Ian (ed.), *Running for Clocks and Dessert Spoons,* Pontefract: YAC, 1988.

Clayton, Ian and Steele, Michael, *When Push Comes to Shove,* Pontefract: Yorkshire Arts Circus, 1993.

Clayton, Ian, Daley, Ian and Lewis, Brian (eds), *Merging on the Ridiculous,* Pontefract: Yorkshire Arts Circus, 1995.

Collini, Stefan, *English Pasts,* Oxford: OUP, 1999.

Collins, Tony, *Rugby's Great Split,* London: Frank Cass, 1998.

Collins, Tony and Melling, Phil, (eds), *The Glory of Their Times: Crossing the Colour Line in Rugby League,* Skipton: Vertical Editions 2004.

Collins, Tony and Vamplew, Wray, *Mud, Sweat and Beers. A Cultural History of Sport and Alcohol,* Oxford: Berg, 2002.

Colls, Robert, *Identities of England,* Oxford: OUP, 2002.

Colls, Robert and Dodd, Phillip (eds) *Englishness, Politics and Culture 1880–1920,* London: Routledge, 1986.

Colman, Mike, *Super League: The Inside Story,* Sydney: Ironbark, 1996.

Connor, Jeff, *Rugby League Who's Who,* London: Guinness, 1991.

Consentino, Frank, *Canadian Football: The Grey Cup Years,* Toronto: Musson, 1969.

Courtenay, Tom, *Dear Tom. Letters From Home,* London: Doubleday, 2000.

Crabtree, Peter, *Fartown Supporters Golden Jubilee,* Huddersfield: privately published, 1971.

Crick, Bernard, *George Orwell, A Life,* Harmondsworth: Penguin edition, 1980.

Cronin, Mike and Mayall, David, (eds) *Sporting Nationalisms,* London: Frank Cass, 1998.

Dalby, Ken, *The Headingley Story,* 1890-1955, Leeds: privately published, 1955.

Daunton, Martin (ed.), *The Cambridge Urban History of Britain: Vol. 3, 1840–1950,* Cambridge: CUP, 2001.

Davie, Michael, *Anglo-Australian Attitudes,* London: Pimlico, 2000.

Davies, Andrew and Fielding, Stephen, *Workers' Worlds,* Manchester: MUP, 1992.

Davies, Norman, *The Isles: A History,* Oxford OUP, 1999.

DeGroot, Gerald, *Blighty: British Society in the Era of the Great War,* London: Longman, 1996.

Delaney, Trevor, *The Roots of Rugby League,* Keighley: privately published, 1984.

Delaney, Trevor, *Lawkholme Lane: 100 Years of Rugby,* Keighley: privately published, 1985.

Delaney, Trevor, *The Grounds of Rugby League,* Keighley: privately published, 1991.

Delaney, Trevor, *The International Grounds of Rugby League,* Keighley: privately published, 1995.

Dennis, Norman, Henriques, Fernando and Slaughter, Cliff, *Coal Is Our Life*, (2nd edn), London: Tavistock, 1969.

Dine, Phillip, *French Rugby Football: A Cultural History*, Oxford: Berg, 2001.

Dintenfass, M., *The Decline of Industrial Britain, 1870–1980*, London: Routledge, 1992.

Dunn, Andrew, *Australia and the Empire*, Sydney: Fontana, 1984.

Dunning, Eric and Sheard, Kenneth, *Barbarians, Gentlemen and Players*, New York: NYU, 1979.

Eddy, John and Schreuder, Derek, (eds) *The Rise of Colonial Nationalism*, Sydney: Allen & Unwin, 1988.

Edgar, Harry, *Chocolate, Blue and Gold*, Wetherby: privately published, 1998.

Farman, Christopher, *The General Strike, May 1926*, London: Panther, 1972.

Farrar, Dave and Lush, Peter, (eds), *From Fulham to Wembley: 20 Years of Rugby League in London*, London: LLP, 2001.

Farrar, Dave, Lush, Peter and O'Hare, Michael, *Touch and Go A History of Professional Rugby League in London*, London: LLP, 1995.

Fishwick, Nicholas, *English Football and Society 1910–50*, Manchester: MUP, 1989.

Fitzpatrick, Paul, *Rugby League Review 1982–83*, London: Faber, 1983.

Forman, Charles, *Industrial Town: Self-Portrait of St Helens in the 1920s*, Newton Abbot: David & Charles, 1978.

Francis, Hywel, *Miners Against Fascism: Wales and the Spanish Civil War,* London: Lawrence and Wishart, 1984.

French, Ray, *My Kind Of Rugby*, London: Faber, 1979.

Fryer, Peter, *Staying Power: The History of Black People in Britain,* London: Pluto, 1984.

Garbett, Len, *Castleford RLFC, A Sixty Year History*, Castleford: privately published, 1986.

Gardner, Mike, *Willie, the Life and Times of a Rugby League Legend*, Barrow: privately published, 1996.

Garvin, William, *Warrington RLFC Centenary*, Warrington: privately published, 1979.

Gate, Robert, *The Struggle for the Ashes*, Ripponden: privately published, 1986.

Gate, Robert, *Gone North, Vol.1*, Ripponden: privately published, 1986.

Gate, Robert, *Rugby League, An Illustrated History*, London: Arthur Barker, 1989.

Gate, Robert, *The Great Bev*, London: LLP, 2002.

Gate, Robert and Latham, Michael, *They Played for Wigan*, Aldington: privately published, 1991.

Genders, Harold, *The Fulham Dream*, London: LLP, 2002.

Gormley, Joe, *Battered Cherub*, London: Hamish Hamilton, 1972.

Greenwood, Walter, *There Was A Time*, Harmondsworth: Penguin, 1967.

Greenwood, Walter, *Love on The Dole*, London: Vintage, 1983 edition.

Griffiths, Trevor, *The Lancashire Working Classes c.1880–1930*, Oxford: OUP, 2001.

Hadfield, Dave, *Playing Away*, London: Kingswood, 1992.

Hall, Tony, *King Coal*, Harmondsworth: Penguin, 1981.

Hanson, Neil, *Blood, Mud and Glory*, London: Pelham, 1991.

Hardcastle, Andrew, *The Thrum Hall Story*, Halifax: privately published, 1986.

Hardcastle, Andrew, *Thrum Hall Greats,* Halifax: privately published, 1994.

Hardisty, Paul, *Alan Hardisty, RL Maestro*, Castleford: privately published, 2000.

Hargreaves, John, *Sport, Power and Culture*, London: Palgrave, 1986.

Heads, Ian, *True Blue*, Sydney: Ironbark, 1992.

Heads, Ian, *The Kangaroos*, Sydney: Ironbark, 1990.

Hey, Vic, *A Man's Game: Ten Years in English Rugby League*, Sydney: Market Printery 1950.

Hill, Jeff, *Sport, Leisure and Culture in Twentieth Century Britain*, London: Palgrave, 2003.

Hill, Jeff and Williams, Jack, (eds) *Sport and Identity in the North of England*, Keele: KUP, 1996.

Hinchliffe, David, *Rugby's Class War*, London: LLP, 2000.

Hobsbawm, Eric, *The Jazz Scene*, revised edn, New York: Pantheon, 1993.

Hobson, Dominic, *The National Wealth: Who Gets What in Britain*, London: Harper Collins, 1999.

Hoggart, Richard, *The Uses of Literacy*, London: Chatto, 1957.

Hoggart, Richard, *A Local Habitation*, London: Chatto, 1988.

Holt, Richard, *Sport and the British*, Oxford: OUP, 1989.

Holt, Richard (ed.), *Sport and the Working Class in Modern Britain*, Manchester: MUP, 1990.

Holt, Richard and Mason, Tony, *Sport in Britain 1945–2000*, Oxford: Macmillan, 2000.

Hoskins, Mark and Fox, Dave, *Bristol Football Club (RFU) 1888–1945*, Stroud: Tempus, 2000.

Huxley, John, *The Rugby League Challenge Cup*, London: Guinness, 1982.

Inglis, Simon, *League Football and the Men Who Made It*, London: Harper Collins, 1988.

Jackson, Brian, *Working-Class Community*, Harmondsworth: Penguin, 1968.

Jackson, Brian and Marsden, Dennis, *Education and the Working Class*, London: Routledge, 1962.

Jenkins, John, *A Rugby Compendium*, Wetherby: British Library, 1998.

Johnes, Martin, *Soccer and Society: South Wales, 1900–39*, Cardiff: UWP, 2002.

Johnman, Lewis and Murphy, Hugh, *British Shipbuilding and the State Since 1918. A Political Economy of Decline*, Exeter: EUP, 2002.

Jones, J. R., *The Encyclopaedia of Rugby Football*, London: Sportsman's Book Club, 1958.

Jones, Lewis, *King of Rugger*, London: Stanley Paul, 1958.

Jones, Stephen, *Workers at Play: A Social and Economic History of Leisure 1918–39*, Manchester: MUP, 1986.

Jones, Stephen, *Sport, Politics and the Working Class*, Manchester: MUP, 1992.

Joyce, Patrick, *Visions of the People*, Manchester: MUP, 1991.

Karalius, Vince, *Lucky 13*, London: Stanley Paul, 1964.

Kelly, Terry and Gilroy, Dominic, *Wakefield's Sporting Catholics*, Wakefield: privately published, 1999.

Kelner, Simon, *To Jerusalem and Back*, London: Macmillan, 1996.

Kilburn, J. M., *In Search of Rugby Football*, London: Arthur Barker, 1938.

King, John, *Grove Park in the Great War*, London: privately published, 1983.

Laughton, Doug with Quirke, Andrew, *A Dream Come True*, London: LLP, 2003.

Laybourne, Keith, *The General Strike Day By Day*, London: Sutton 1996.

Lester, Gary, *The Story of Australian Rugby League*, Sydney: Lester Townsend, 1988.

Lock, Ron and Quantrill, Peter, *Zulu Victory*, London: Greenhill, 2003.

Lofthouse, Geoffrey, *A Very Miner MP*, Pontefract: YAC, 1986.

Long, J., Tongue, N., Spracklen, K. and Carrington, B., *What's The Difference? A Study of the Nature and Extent of Racism in Rugby League*, Leeds: Leeds Metropolitan University, 1995.

Lush, Peter and Farrar, Dave (eds), *Tries in the Valleys: A History of Rugby League in Wales*, London: LLP, 1998.

Macdonald, Lyn, *Somme*, London: Michael Joseph, 1983.

MacGregor, Adrian, *King Wally*, St Lucia: UQP, 1987.

MacGregor, Adrian, *Simply The Best: The 1990 Kangaroos*, St Lucia: UQP, 1991.

McKibbin, Ross, *The Ideologies of Class*, Oxford: OUP, 1990.

McKibbin, Ross, *Classes and Cultures. England: 1918–1950*, Oxford: OUP, 1998.

Manson, B. *Another Battle for Britain*, Altrincham: Sherratt and Sons, 1958.

Marriott, C. J. B., *The Rugby Game and How to Play It*, London: Bell, undated (c. 1922).

Mars, Gerald, *Cheats at Work. An Anthropology of Workplace Crime*, London: Unwin, 1983.

Marwick, Arthur, *British Society Since 1945*, Harmondsworth: Penguin, 1982.

Mason, Tony, (ed.) *Sport in Britain, A Social History*, Cambridge: CUP, 1985.

Mason, Tony, *Sport in Britain*, London: Faber, 1988.

Melling, Phil, *Man of Amman*, Dyfedd: Gomer, 1993.

Milne, Seamus, *The Enemy Within*, London: Verso, 1994.

Mitchell and Butlers, *Fifty Years of Brewing 1879–1929,* Birmingham: M&B, 1929.

Mitchell, B. R., *British Historical Statistics,* London: HMSO, 1988.

Moore, Andrew, *The Mighty Bears*, Sydney: Macmillan, 1996.

Moorhouse, Geoffrey, *A People's Game. The Official History of Rugby League 1895–1995*, London: Hodder, 1995.

Moorhouse, Geoffrey, *At the George*, London: Hodder, 1989.

Moran, H. M. *Viewless Winds*, London: Davis, 1939.

Morgan, Kenneth O., *Wales 1880–1980*, Oxford: OUP, 1981.

Mosse, George, *Fallen Soldiers. Reshaping the Memory of the World Wars*, Oxford: OUP, 1990.

Mossop, Rex with Writer, Larry, *The Moose That Roared*, Sydney: Ironbark, 1991.

Munt, S. R. (ed.), *Cultural Studies and the Working Class*, London: CIPG, 2000.

Murphy, Alex, *Saints Hit Double Top*, London: Eden Books, 1967.

Nadin, Jack, *The Chronology of British Coal Mining,* no place of publication: privately published, 2000.

Nelson, Donald M., *Anatomy of Game*, Delaware: UDP, 1994.

Nepia, George, *I, George Nepia,* revised edn, London: LLP, 2002.

Nicholson, Geoffrey, *The Professionals*, London: Sportsman's Book Club, 1964.

O'Toole, Peter, *Loitering with Intent: The Apprentice*, London: Macmillan, 1996.

Oriard, Michael, *Reading Football*, Chapel Hill: UNC Press, 1993.

Oriard, Michael, *King Football*, Chapel Hill: UNC Press, 2001.

Orwell, George, *The Collected Essays, Journalism and Letters of George Orwell, Vol. 1, An Age Like This, 1920–1940,* Harmondsworth: Penguin edition, 1968.

Orwell, George, *The Road to Wigan Pier*, Harmondsworth: Penguin edition, 1972.

Pallant, Anne, *A Sporting Century 1863–1963*, Callington, Cornwall: privately published, 1997.

Paris, Michael, *Warrior Nation: Images of War in British Popular Culture, 1850–2000*, London: Reaktion 2000.

Pearce, Cyril, *Comrades in Conscience. The Story of an English Community's Opposition to the Great War*, London: Francis Boutle, 2001.

Pelmear, Kenneth (ed.), *Rugby Football: An Anthology*, London: Allen & Unwin, 1958.

Pettingale, Don and Nutter, Keith, *The History of Barrow RLFC*, Barrow: privately published, 1981.

Poulton, E. B., *The Life of Ronald Poulton*, London: Sidwick and Jackson, 1919.

Priestley, J. B., *English Journey*, London: Heinemann, 1935.

Purcell, Steve (ed.), *Wembley: Venue of Legends*, London: Wembley, 1998.

Read, Peter, *Charles Perkins. A Biography,* NSW: Penguin, 2001.

Risman, Bev (ed.), *The Rugby League Football Book No. 2*, London: Stanley Paul, 1963.

Risman, Gus, *Rugby Renegade*, London: Stanley Paul, 1958.

Robbins, Keith, *The British Isles, 1901–1951*, Oxford: OUP, 2002.

Roberts, Ian, *Finding Out*, Sydney: Macmillan, 1997.

Rose, Jonathan, *The Intellectual Life of the British Working Classes*, Yale: YUP, 2001.

Rose, Mary B. (ed.), *The Lancashire Cotton Industry: A History Since 1700*, Preston: Lancashire County Books, 1996.

Routh, G., *Occupation and Pay in Great Britain 1906–79*, London: Macmillan, 1980.

Rugby Football League, *Manual of Rugby League Coaching*, Leeds: RFL, 1948.

Russell, Dave, *Football and the English*, Preston: Carnegie, 1997.

Rylance, Mike, *The Forbidden Game: The Untold Story of French Rugby League*, Brighouse: League Publications, 1999.

Said, Edward, *Culture and Imperialism*, London: Vintage, 1993.

Said, Edward, *Orientalism*, revised edn, Harmondsworth: Penguin, 1995.

Sampson, Dave, *Fast Lane to Shangri-La*, Skipton: Vertical Editions, 2001.

Samuel, Raphael, *Island Stories: Unravelling Britain*, London: Verson 1998.

Saxton, Irvin, *History of Rugby League 1955–56*, Purston: privately published, undated.

Scargill, T., Fox, R. and Crabtree, K., *The Official History of Dewsbury RLFC*, Ossett: privately published, 1989.

Seebohm Rowntree, B., *Poverty and Progress. A Second Social Survey of York*, London: Longman, 1941.

Service, Alex, *Saints in their Glory*, St Helens: privately published, 1985.

Simkins, Peter, *Kitchener's Army*, Manchester: MUP, 1988.

Singleton, John, *Lancashire on the Scrapheap: The Cotton Industry 1945–1970*, Oxford: OUP, 1991.

Smalley, R.W., *Recollections of Rugby League*, Hull: privately published, 1999.

Smith, David and Williams, Gareth, *Fields of Praise*, Cardiff: UWP, 1980.

Smith, Graham, *When John Bull Met Jim Crow: Black American Soldiers in WW2 Britain*, London: I.B. Tauris, 1987.

Stacey, Margaret, *Tradition and Change: A Study of Banbury*, Oxford: OUP, 1960.

Stendhal, *Love*, Harmondsworth: Penguin, 1975.

Stevenson, John, *British Society 1914–45*, Harmondsworth: Penguin, 1984.

Stevenson, John and Cook, Chris, *Britain in the Depression: Society and Politics 1929–39*, 2nd edn, London: Longman, 1994.

Storey, David, *This Sporting Life*, Harmondsworth: Penguin, 1960.

Storey, David, *The Changing Room*, London: Metheun, 1972.

Tabner, Brian, *Through the Turnstiles*, Harefield: Yore, 1992.

Taylor, A. J. P., *Essays in English History*, Harmondsworth: Penguin, 1976.

Thompson, Cec, *Born On The Wrong Side*, London: Pentland Press, 1995.

Thornett, Ken with Easton, Tom, *Tackling Rugby*, Melbourne: Lansdowne, 1966.

Trevor, Phillip, *Rugby Union Football*, London: Bell, 1922.

Turner, Royce, *Coal Was Our Life*, Sheffield: Perpetuity Press, 2000.

Twydell, Dave, *Rejected F.C., Vol. 3*, Harefield: Yore, 1995.

Ullyatt, M. and Bowman, D., *Harold Bowman on Tour Down Under*, Beverley: Hutton Press, 1992.

Walton, John, *Lancashire: A Social History 1558–1939*, Manchester: MUP, 1987.

Walton, John, *Fish and Chips and the British Working Class. 1870–1940*, Manchester: MUP, 1994.

Walton, John and Walvin, James (eds) *Leisure in Britain 1780–1930*, Manchester: MUP, 1983.

Walvin, James, *The Peoples' Game. The History of Football Revisited*, Edinburgh: Mainstream, 1994.

Ward, Stuart, *Australia and the British Embrace*, Melbourne: Melbourne University Press, 2001.

Ward, Stuart (ed.), *British Culture and the End of Empire*, Manchester: MUP, 2001.

Waring, Eddie, *England to Australia and New Zealand,* Leeds: privately published, 1947.

Waring, Eddie, *The Great Ones,* London: Stanley Paul, 1969.

Watkins, David, *An Autobiography,* London: Cassell, 1980.

Weight, Richard, *Patriots. National Identity in Britain, 1940–2000,* London: Macmillan, 2002.

Whittingham, Richard (ed.), *The Fireside Book of Pro Football,* New York: Simon & Schuster, 1989.

Wild, Stephen, *The Lions of Swinton,* Manchester: privately published, 1999.

Williams, Gareth, *1905 and All That,* Dyfed: Gomer, 1991.

Williams, Graham, *Glory Days,* Leeds: privately published, 1998.

Williams, Nigel, *Bradford Northern, The History 1863–1989,* Bradford: privately published, 1989.

Williams, Raymond, *Culture and Society 1780–1950,* Harmondsworth: Penguin, 1958.

Williams, Raymond, *The Long Revolution,* Harmondsworth: Penguin, 1961.

Willis, Paul, *Learning to Labour: How Working-class Kids get Working-class Jobs,* London: RKP, 1977.

Wilson, David F., *Dockers, the Impact of Industrial Change,* London: Pan, 1972.

Winstanley, Jack, *The Billy Boston Story,* Wigan: privately published, 1963.

Winter, J. M., *The Experience of World War One,* Oxford, OUP 1988.

Writer, Larry, *Never Before, Never Again,* Sydney: Macmillan, 1995.

Articles and book chapters

Bird, P. J. W. N., 'The Demand for League Football', *Applied Economics,* 14, 1982.

Chapman, S., 'Mergers and Takeovers in the Post-war Textile Industry', *Business History,* 30 (2), 1988.

Collins, Tony, 'Myth and Reality in the 1895 Rugby Split', *The Sports Historian,* no. 16, May 1996.

Collins, Tony, 'Racial Minorities in a Marginalised Sport: Race, Discrimination and Integration in Rugby League Football', *Immigrants and Minorities,* 17(1), March 1998.

Collins, Tony, 'English Rugby Union and the First World War', *The Historical Journal,* 45(4), December 2002.

Cronin, Mike, 'Arthur Elvin and the Dogs of Wembley', *The Sports Historian,* 22 (1), May 2002.

Delaney, Trevor, 'Rugby League on Tyneside', *Code 13,* no. 4, August 1987.

Doyle, Barry, 'Return of the Super Cinema in the United Kingdom', *History Today,* February 1998.

Evans Baillie, T. H., 'Rugby League Football' in James Rivers (ed.), *The Sports Book, 3,* London: Macdonald, 1949.

Hallinan, C. J., 'Aborigines and Positional Segregation in Australian Rugby League', *International Review for the Sociology of Sport,* 26 (2), 1991.

Hill, Jeff, 'Cricket and the Imperial Connection: Overseas Players in Lancashire in the Inter-War Years' in John Bale and Joseph Maguire (eds), *The Global Sports Arena,* London: Frank Cass, 1994.

Hill, Jeff, 'Rites of Spring: Cup Finals and Community in the North of England' in Jeff Hill and Jack Williams (eds), *Sport and Identity in the North of England,* Keele: Keele University Press, 1996.

Hill, Jeff and Varrasi, Francesco, 'Creating Wembley: The Construction of a National Monument', *The Sports Historian,* 17(2), November 1997).

Holt, Richard, 'Men and Rugby in the North', *Northern Review,* 4, Winter 1996.

Hopcraft, Arthur, 'Money for Brawn', *The Sunday Times Colour Magazine*, 3 May 1964, p. 11.

Howkins, Alan and Saville, John, 'The Nineteen Thirties: A Revisionist History' in Miliband, R. and Saville, J. (eds), *The Socialist Register 1979*, London: Spokesman, 1979.

Jones, Stephen, 'The Economic Aspects of Association Football in England 1918–39, *British Journal of Sports History*, 1 (3), December 1984.

Keneally, Thomas, ' The Other Code' *Esquire*, November 1991.

Little, Charles, ' "What a Freak Show they Made!" Women's Rugby League in 1920s Sydney', *Football Studies*, 4 (2), October 2001.

Louvish, Simon, 'That Lad Will Go Far' in the *Guardian*, 6 December 2002.

Loy, J. W. and McElvogue, J. W., 'Racial Segregation in American Sport', *International Review for the Sociology of Sport*, 5 (25), 1970.

McCabe, Edmund, 'Rugby and the Great War' in *Stand To! The Journal of the Western Front Association*, no 52, April 1998.

Melling, Althea, ' "Plucky Lasses", "Pea Soup", and Politics: The Role of Ladies Football during the 1921 Miners' Lock-Out in Wigan and Leigh', *International Journal of the History of Sport*, 16 (1), March 1999.

Melling, Phil, 'Definitions for the Definer, Not the Defined', *The Sports Historian*, no. 16, May 1996.

Melling, Phil, 'Wales, Rugby League and the Spanish Civil War', *Our Game*, no. 2, Autumn 2000.

Metcalfe, Alan, 'Football in the Mining Communities of East Northumberland', *International Journal of the History of Sport*, 5 (3), December 1988.

Moore, Andrew, 'Opera of the Proletariat: Rugby League, the Labour Movement and Working-Class Culture in New South Wales and Queensland', *Labour History*, no. 79, November 2000.

Morgan, Piers, 'Comment on Tony Collins' "Myth and Reality in the 1895 Rugby Split" ', *The Sports Historian*, 17 (1), May 1997.

Osborne, John, 'To Keep the life of the Nation on the Old Lines: The *Athletic News* and the First World War', *Journal of Sport History*, 14 (2), Summer 1987.

Russell, Dave, 'Football and Society in the North West, 1919–39', *North West Labour History*, 24, 1999–2000.

Ryan, Greg, ' "A Lack of Esprit de Corps": The 1908 Wallabies and the Legacy of the 1905 All Blacks', *Sporting Traditions*, 17 (1), November 2000.

Sewell, E. H. D., 'The State of the Game', *Fortnightly Review*, 89, 1911.

Tomlinson, Alan, 'This Sporting Life: Reflections on the Aestheticisation of the Sporting Body', *Diegesis*, no. 4, Summer 1999.

Werbner, Pnina, 'Our Blood is Green: Cricket, Identity and Social Empowerment among British Pakistanis' in J. MacClancy (ed.), *Sport, Identity and Ethnicity*, Oxford: Berg 1996.

Williams, Gareth, 'The Road to Wigan Pier Revisited: the Migration of Welsh Rugby Talent Since 1918' in John Bale and Joseph Maguire (eds), *The Global Sports Arena*, London: Frank Cass, 1994.

Williams, Graham, 'How the West Was (Almost) Won!' *Open Rugby*, March and April 1983.

Williams, Jack, ' "Up and Under" Eddie Waring, Television and the Image of Rugby League', *The Sports Historian*, 22 (1), May 2002.

Winter, J. M., 'Upper Class Casualties' in *London Review of Books*, 5 March 1987.

Theses

Fassolette, Robert, *Histoire Politique du Conflit des Deux Rugby en France*, PhD thesis, INSEP, 1996.

Fuller, J. G. *Popular Culture and Troop Morale in the British and Dominion Forces 1914–1918*, PhD thesis, Cambridge University, 1988.

Greenhalgh, P., *The History of the Northern Rugby Football Union 1895–1915*, PhD thesis, University of Lancaster, 1992.

Groeneveld, Margaret, *Transferring Assets, Transferring Athletes: an Anthropological Analysis of Financial Categorisation and Commodification in English Rugby League*, DPhil thesis, University of Oxford, 2004.

O'Keeffe, Lisa, *An Analysis of the Economic and Social Effects of Changing the Structure of Rugby League 1996–99*, PhD thesis, Sheffield Hallam University, 2000.

Schleppi, John, *Rugby League in Wartime*, PhD thesis, University of Dayton, 1981.

Spracklen, Karl, '*Playing the Ball': Constructing Community and Masculine Identity in Rugby: an Analysis of the Two Codes of League and Union and the People Involved*, PhD thesis, Leeds Metropolitan University, 1996.

Audio-Visual sources

Lindsay Anderson (director), *This Sporting Life*, 1963, DVD, Carlton, 2000.

Stanley Holloway, *The Classic Monologues*, Audio CD, Avid, 2000.

Gone North – The Story of Welsh Players in Rugby League, BBC Radio Wales, 2000.

Index

Lightning Source UK Ltd.
Milton Keynes UK
UKOW020755031111

181410UK00003B/66/P